COST–
Technic...
work fo...
Novem...
Europe...
nationa...

The f...
suppor...
EUR 3(...
researc...
financi...

A "b...
from t...
countri...
is oper...
Europe...
manag...

As p...
tant ro...
comple...
"bridg...
the mo...
"Netw...
and M...
Service...
Scienc...
ment;...
Develop...ment, individuals, societies,...

more applied research and also addresses issues of pre-normative nature or of
societal importance.

Web: www.cost.esf.org

EUROPEAN
SCIENCE
FOUNDATION

Musical Gestures
Sound, Movement, and Meaning

Edited by

Rolf Inge Godøy
University of Oslo

and

Marc Leman
Ghent University

Routledge
Taylor & Francis Group

NEW YORK AND LONDON

Foreword

Textbooks that lay the systematic foundations of a research area are not made overnight. Whether they are good or bad, successful or not, they are always the final corollary of a long process of collecting huge amounts of data, experiments, papers, presentations, explanations and discussions—discarding most of it afterwards to distill the generalities and the varieties that describe, compose and enrich the domain itself. Both steps are impossible to manage without the deepest collaboration among institutions and, ultimately, the researchers themselves.

Musical Gestures: Sound, Movement, and Meaning is a result of the COST Action 287, called "ConGAS—Gesture Controlled Audio Systems." The origin of this Action can be traced back to the end of the 1990s, when another very successful COST Action (COST-G6—DAFx—Digital Audio Effects) contributed to the constitution of a strong and wide board of researchers from all over Europe dedicated to refine and adapt traditional digital signal processing techniques to Sound and Music Computing. While working on sound processing, it became evident that gesture and control constitute an essential part not only of music making, but also of sound formation, processing, and even listening. The times were ripe for another COST Action, which began in 2003 under the name COST287—ConGAS—Gesture Controlled Audio Systems. The scientific board grew in strength and size, and in the span of four years it did nothing less than charter the new domain, setting its boundaries and defining guidelines, methodologies and techniques for it. Roughly at the same time, S2S2 (which stands for Sound to Sense, Sense to Sound), another coordination action funded by the European Commission through its IST–FET program, produced a research roadmap for the next ten to fifteen years of Sound and Music Computing investigation. In this roadmap, musical gesture and sonic interaction constitute perhaps the research area facing the brightest future.

Musical Gestures: Sound, Movement, and Meaning is born out of this exceptionally rich context and at the same time it constitutes its most precious asset to date. And as it often happens, this book is both the endpoint of a long and complex history of multi-disciplinary collaborations masterfully conducted by its editors, and the starting point of some other unchartered territories. Thus, it is no coincidence that its publication takes place during yet another COST Action, IC0601 SID—Sonic Interaction Design—which will indeed exploit the COST287–ConGAS Action and this book to produce further discoveries and achievements.

Nicola Bernardini, coordinator of COST287

Editors' Preface

We believe that experiences of music are intimately linked with experiences of movements: Musicians make music with movements, and people very often make, or imagine, movements when listening to music. We would go so far as to claim that music is basically a combination of sound and movement, and that music means something to us because of this combination. We use the expression "musical gestures" to denote this meaningful combination of sound and movement, hence the title and subtitle of this book: *Musical Gestures: Sound, Movement, and Meaning*.

The relationship between sound and movement has been a recurrent topic in Western thought since antiquity, however, we have in the last decade seen a surge of interest in this topic. In our mediated world, we are bombarded with music as the combination of sound and movement everywhere, in musical performance, dance, music videos, television advertisements, computer games, animations, and movies, just to mention the most prominent occurrences. In parallel, we also see the development of new multi-modal interfaces for computers and digital instruments (actually a subcategory of computers), interfaces that try to make meaningful combinations of sound and movement. In addition, we have seen a growing interest in human perception and cognition as a multi-modal and embodied phenomenon. One of the main ideas in this development is that we experience and understand the world, including music, through body movement. When we hear (or see) something, we are able to make sense of it by relating it to our body movements, or some image in our minds of body movements. For music research, this embodied perspective is a significant change of paradigm, as it shifts the focus away from more abstract symbols of music notation towards the holistic experience of continuous sound and movement in relation to our bodies. This embodied paradigm is also one of the basic tenets of this book.

Musical gestures is an eminently interdisciplinary topic, drawing on ideas, theories, and methods from disciplines such as musicology, music perception, human movement science, cognitive psychology, and computer science. One of our ambitions with this book has been to present a coherent overview of this interdisciplinary topic. And likewise, it is our hope that this book should have a broad interdisciplinary appeal. We believe that this book would be of interest to musicians, musicologists, dancers, choreographers, theatre and film directors, movement researchers, psychologists, and computer scientists, or to anyone who may want to learn more about the relationship between sound and body movement. For this reason we have tried as best we can to make the presentations as accessible as possible for a broad audience.

The initiative for making this book came from the highly interdisciplinary research project COST287—ConGAS—Gesture Controlled Audio Systems. This project, running from 2003 to 2007, brought together musicians, musicologists, computer scientists, and psychologists with the aim of developing gesture controlled audio systems. In the course of this project, it became clear that there were very many and often divergent notions of what is meant by the term "gesture," and it also became clear that we needed to dive deeper into fundamental issues of sound and body movement. The idea of this book emerged from these discussions, namely to make an overview of various notions of gestures and to give an extensive presentation of the relationships between sound and movement in music.

Also, in the face of fast developing technologies for capturing, processing, and representing body movement, as well as for applying body movement data to the generation and processing of musical sound, we felt that the main focus of our book ought to be on basic issues of sound and movement in musical experience for two main reasons: First, with technological development it becomes clear that many challenges are actually more of a conceptual or perceptual–cognitive nature, or that technological advances are dependent on having a basis in human experience. Second, we believe that sound–movement interaction in music is a general topic with ramifications beyond any technological contexts, actually concerning the very basis of music as a phenomenon.

Needless to say, "musical gestures" is a very extensive topic, and there are certainly many issues that we have not been able to cover in this book. We look upon this book as a contribution to the beginning of a much more extensive exploration of music as an art of sound and movement in the years to come. With the manifestations of music as a multimedia art that we see all around us, we are confident that we have significant and exciting developments ahead of us. The proliferations of research projects, networks, workshops, and conferences, nationally and internationally, bears witness to this development.

In this connection, we thank the people of this international "musical gestures community" who have contributed to this book, in particular

N. Bernardini, the coordinator of the COST287 Action. Our sincere thanks to each and everyone of our authors for taking part in making this book, for their patience and willingness to adopt their contributions to the overall aims of this book. The authors wish to express their sincere thanks to the COST office, to Constance Ditzel, music editor at Routledge, and to Michael Berry and Eugene Montague for their editorial help, as well as several anonymous reviewers for useful comments.

Oslo, Ghent, June 2009
Rolf Inge Godøy and Marc Leman

Part I

Gestures in Music

Chapter 1

Why Study Musical Gestures?

Marc Leman and Rolf Inge Godøy

1 Introduction

People seem to be making gestures to music everywhere, swaying their bodies and waving their hands to the beat of the music while dancing, attending a concert, or walking down the street while listening to their MP3 players. Listeners often imitate the gestures of musicians by playing air guitar, for example, or mimicking the facial movements and body language of pop stars or conductors, and they often do so without any formal musical training. Why is it that so many listeners are able to spontaneously make gestures that seem to fit the music? Why do they make these gestures? Furthermore, how are these gestures related to the music, and how are these gestures related to the gestures of performers? Or in general, what are gestures? And how do gestures function in the contexts of music performance and listening?

Seeing how ubiquitous music-related gestures are, and seeing the enthusiasm and joy that people express through these gestures, we conceive of musical gestures as an expression of a profound engagement with music, and as an expression of a fundamental connection that exists between music and movement. In fact, we believe that musical experience is inseparable from the sensations of movement, and hence, that studying these gestures, what we call *musical gestures*, ought to be a high priority task in music research.

Studying musical gestures is not something new. Indeed, in previous studies, many scholars of music have pointed out that music is somehow related to gesture. However, in contrast with these earlier and often more philosophical studies, we believe that it is now a favorable moment in time to make more systematic studies of musical gestures. First and foremost, we now have at our disposal technologies that allow us to study musical gestures with great detail and precision. These technologies include various so-called motion capture technologies, which enable us to monitor gestures very precisely. From motion capture data we can extract a diverse set of features, so as to reveal various properties of gestures.

Thus, these technologies open up new views on the fleeting, ephemeral sensations of gestures. Second, and in parallel with this, we now see the emergence of a conceptual apparatus that is more attuned to the primordial role of gestures and movement in human perception and cognition in general. Under the label of "embodied cognition," we can now better understand the integration of gesture with perception and with thinking in general, including insights on how body movement is both a response to whatever we perceive and an active contribution to our perception of the world.

Given this context, we feel that the study of musical gestures, as well as the mental images of musical gestures, is indeed reshaping our conceptions of music and sound in general. The study of musical gestures appears as a core area of modern music research, with links to engineering, neuroscience, and both human and social sciences.

Yet the concept of musical gestures is not without its problems. *Gesture* is an often used word, and it has quite diverse connotations. We often encounter the term in various contexts such as linguistics, psychology, anthropology, aesthetics, musicology, and human–computer interaction. In these disciplines the term denotes various aspects of human movement, such as hand movements and movements of other body parts including the vocal apparatus (lips, tongue), but it also denotes semantic actions or deeds such as in "making a gesture of goodwill" by doing someone a favor. Therefore, in studying musical gestures, one of the first challenges will be that of trying to map out the various usages and meanings of this term, as well as of other related and often used terms that we may encounter in this context such as *movement, motion,* and *action.*

In fact, the diverse use of the word "gesture" can be seen as a testimony to the great importance that people attach to the idea of making some kind of recognizable action or movement. In most cases, the notion of gesture refers in some way to notions of action, which itself testifies, again, to the ubiquitous role of human movement and an embodied (rather than a disembodied "mentalesque") engagement with our environment. Although the many significations of the word "gesture "may appear to be problematic, they are, at the same time, advantages in that they provide us with a very broad and highly interdisciplinary basis for reflecting upon what meaningful music-based interactions are all about.

The multiple uses of the word "gesture" within different disciplines and contexts are also related to the many and often very various potential approaches to its systematic study. It is our hope that this book will familiarize the reader with a broad selection of theories and methods, ranging from the more introspective and/or philosophical approaches to the more empirical and/or experimental approaches, from the qualitative to the more quantitative, and from "hardcore" measurement to various historical, aesthetic and semiotic perspectives. In the rest of this introductory chapter, we shall give a brief sketch of the various concepts and aspects of musical gestures that are presented in the ensuing chapters of this book.

2 Gesture as Body Movement

A straightforward definition of gesture is that it is a movement of part of the body, for example a hand or the head, to express an idea or meaning. In the context of musical performance, gestures are movements made by performers to control the musical instrument when playing a melodic figure, to coordinate actions among musicians (conducting gestures), or to impress an audience (for example, moving the head during a solo performance). In the context of listening to music, gestures are movements that accompany or express the activity of listening, such as tapping along with the beat, swaying, or dancing. In many circumstances, gestures are learned movements, but sometimes they are made spontaneously as they go along with the articulation of the musical idea or meaning.

2.1 Primary and Secondary Focus

It should be admitted that the above definition has a primary focus on physical movement, whereas expression and meaning appear on a secondary plane. One could say that the primary focus is on *extension*, namely the human body and its movement in space, whereas the secondary focus is on *intention*, namely that which is imagined or anticipated. However, it is hard to separate the primary focus from the secondary focus. The reason is that not all movements can be considered to be genuine gestures. In order to call a movement a genuine gesture, it is required that this movement is in some way a carrier of expression and meaning. Clearly, this second focus introduces a subjective aspect as well as a context-dependent aspect. Indeed, for a particular observer, in a particular context, movements may be conceived as having expression and meaning, while for another observer, even in the same context (but likely also in a different context), the same movements may be conceived as having no particular expression or meaning. Due to this subjective and context-dependent aspect of gestures, many researchers prefer to focus on extension, rather than on intention. Clearly, it is indeed extension, and thus movement, that can be easily measured using video recordings and all sorts of kinetic and physiological sensors, whereas intention is something that exists inside the minds of people. The latter is often vague and subject to interpretation.

2.2 Gesture as Movement, in Musical Communication

By concentrating on the primary aspect of gesture, namely movement, it is tempting to consider the whole chain of musical communication as based on movement. Indeed, bodily movements control instruments that generate movements of air particles. These movements are in turn transmitted to the listener, and are taken over by the listener's auditory system, which, through a neuronal coupling with the listener's motor system, sets the listener's body in motion.

2.3 Body-Related Gestures and Sound-Related Gestures

This framework allows for an interesting distinction between body-related gestures and sound-related gestures, as can be seen in various chapters in this book. Body gestures can be described from different perspectives, such as the biomechanical constraints of the human body (Chapter 9), control movements like conducting movements (Chapter 11) or sound-producing movements (Chapter 3), as coalition signals (Chapter 7), or simply as body posture (Chapters 4, 10).

Sound-related gestures, on the other hand, can be understood as movements in sound, such as pitches going up, rhythms that have a galloping character and so on (Chapters 5, 6). Obviously these movements in sound are produced by movements of the human body (Chapter 8). Analysis of sound, in particular the movements in sound, can therefore be used as a starting point in identifying sound-related musical gestures. The whole approach entails that musical communication is fundamentally driven by movement. In particular, musical communication is steered by bodily motion, which is encoded by the player, transmitted through audio, and decoded by the listener.

2.4 Problems of Reducing Gesture to Movement

Although the notion of gesture as movement is very common in modern scientific approaches, its reduction to movement as such (also called motion) is not entirely satisfying because in many cases music-related movement as such cannot be studied without having additional knowledge of the underlying expression of meaning. Consider the movements of a listener in response to music. We can measure and extract features from these movements, but how can we be sure that such observed movements are the genuine expression of the listener's embodied perception of music? How can we be sure that the listener is not cheating us? We can only solve this problem by considering fully the second focus of the above definition; in other words, by checking its expression and meaning in relation to music. This secondary focus introduces a number of complexities that greatly interfere with the apparently simple approach to gesture as movement.

Indeed, if music draws upon the communication of motion or movement, what then is the meaning of these movements? Are listeners capable of decoding the expression or meaning of the performer? If yes, what is the nature of these meanings? Is there a proper account of the relationship between movement, expression and meaning?

If performers use body movement to produce music, then what types of movement do they produce? Are all movements equally effective in the production of sound? What about movements such as tapping along or shaking the head? Do these body movements have a communicative value, do they facilitate sound making, or are they just ancillary, intended for show? Is there an appropriate typology of movements that relates to gestures? Is there a way to observe their distinction?

If we assume that music communicates movement, where can we find movement in sound, or what does it mean that sounds contain movement? Obviously, when we look at sound representations, such as waveforms or their corresponding spectral representations, there is no clear indication of where a gesture has started or ended. Moreover, it is not clear how the movements of air particles, or the corresponding frequencies and amplitudes, can be interpreted in terms of human movement. Does an increase in amplitude imply a movement with more energy? Does an ascent in pitch mean that the movement goes up? In other words, it is not very straightforward how body gestures, both in performance and in listening, relate to sound gestures. Body movements are supposed to encode sound gestures, but once sound is produced it is hard to identify unambiguously the gesture that is contained in it. Is it possible to clarify the relationship between bodily gesture and sonic gesture? Is it possible to clarify the relationship between gestures made by musicians and gestures made by listeners?

Finally, if gestures express an idea or meaning, what kind of idea or meaning is it? Is the gesture an expression of a particular character, or does it point to a particular event? Is the perception of gesture a causal matter, in the sense that we hear particular sounds (such as footsteps, a baby crying) in terms of their cause? Or, are these gestures merely related to our own body movements? In the latter sense, gestures would express nothing besides our own actions. Can we then explain gesture in relation to causal and referential meanings, in particular as it relates to gesture in spoken language?

Clearly, these are complicated questions, and the list is far from exhaustive. Some of the questions are likely to turn up with every definition of gesture. What they reveal is that movement is an essential part of gesture, but that the notion of gesture is not identical to the notion of movement. Indeed, in the definition of "gesture" we need a subjective and context-dependent component, something that forces us to understand gesture as movement with respect to the perception–action system of both the producer and the observer of the movement.

3 Gesture as a Category of our Perception–Action System

The above list of problems suggests that apart from movement, the notion of gesture is linked with a number of other notions such as action (moving with a purpose), intentionality (goal-directed movement), agency (being moved), and embodiment (movement-based mental schemata). Therefore, it may be worth the effort to try another approach to defining gesture, namely one that is more focused on the way in which humans interact with their environment from the perspective of embodied cognition. In this approach, gesture can be defined as a pattern through which we structure our environment from the viewpoint of actions. Gesture conceived that way is thus a category, or structural feature, of our perception–action system. In this approach, gesture is both a mental and a corporeal phenomenon.

3.1 Body Schema and Body Image

A convenient way of understanding gestures as patterns of embodiment is in terms of body schema and body image. Body schemata are motor patterns that we have learned and that require little or no mental effort to carry out, such as grasping a glass of water. Once the action is initiated, we grasp the glass without being aware of all the muscles that have to be stretched or relaxed in order to reach and grasp. All of this is done by so-called motor programs, through which we interact with our environment. We have little access to these motor programs at any given moment. They appear to function automatically, without our awareness.

Trained musicians, for example, can play a particular melodic figure by heart. They do not have to think about how to move their fingers on the instrument and they do not have to think about how to play the melody. Instead, the melodic pattern is just something that appears to come out of the body. The melodic pattern is a motor program that deploys itself in time. The only thing musicians have to do is to focus on the gesture in advance, "out of time" so to speak, as a global mental pattern or goal, in order to set the body schema to work and get the gesture realized "in time" through the automated motor program, just like grasping a glass of water.

Body image, however, is about the representation or the awareness of our body in relation to the environment. This image can be a global non-verbal concept or a global gesture "out of time." It can equally be a global awareness of the gesture "in time." Indeed, while playing the melody, I can be aware of my body's interaction with music. As such, the concept of gesture, as a pattern through which we structure our environment from the viewpoint of actions, is related both to automated motor patterns that set our body into action "in time," and to bodily awareness of performance "in time" and "out of time."

In that sense, the definition of gesture as a functioning feature of our perception–action system implies much more than just movement. It implies that movements can be chunked into patterns and that these patterns can be conceptualized and held in our mind as single units. This chunking is carried out by the performer as well as by the listener. The definition implies that musical communication is not merely about movement, but about structured interactions. It implies gestures, gestural sequences, and gestural hierarchies as means for an efficient structuring of large amounts of information. Clearly, this structuring is not something that comes out of the blue. Instead, it is all about the embodiment of our perceived environment. We believe that this is an essential point that any study of music-related gesture should seriously consider.

3.2 Problems

However, the above definition of gesture as a category of our perception–action system is not without its own problems. For example, one might question whether all actions can be considered to be gestures. Very often, the notion of gesture is reserved for actions that have an expressive character. To reach a glass of water might be considered a gesture, but to reach that glass in a particular way, as a peasant (holding both hands around the glass) or as an aristocrat (with stretched pinky finger) is even more likely to be considered as a genuine example of a gesture because it refers to a cultural context and to a number of particular semantic meanings. In a similar way, playing a melody is based on a gesture, but playing this melody in a particular mood (happy, sad), or in the particular style of another musician (Charlie Parker, Sonny Rollins) is even more likely to be considered as an example of gesture. Playing music in this way involves gestures that point to cultural context. Moreover, it is often assumed that the listener knows the cultural context in order to make sense of the movement.

This viewpoint on gesture may bring us back to the aforementioned communication model. We can now say that what is encoded in, transmitted by, and decoded from music is movement, upon which we impose culturally related actions.

However, some researchers may argue that in a social context music often involves movement without semantic meanings. Just consider how people move and dance during live music performances. What they do is synchronize with the beat of the music, and move in resonance with the music. The interactions of performers and listeners mutually entrain their movements so that the whole system (considered as performers and listeners) starts vibrating. When one's movement is in time with the movements of others, this may lead to very intense experiences of unity or social bonding. In this sense, the meaning of music is not something external to the movement itself, but something that is tightly connected to it. These movements need not be experienced as having external meanings, or even as goal-directed actions. They just happen and, by themselves, are sufficient to yield these very intense experiences of connectedness and social bonding. Put as such, one may argue that the primary focus of musical gestures is movement, indeed, and not action or cultural reference. However, it is equally arguable that in the social context, many of the movements of performers and listener/dancers are perceived as gestures, because gestures, after all, may have their ultimate origin in social communication. Thus, again, we return to the idea that movement by itself is not sufficient to understand how music works.

4 The Study of Musical Gestures

The aforementioned viewpoints give a brief glimpse of the background and the reason why we need this book, and the reason why we need further study of the relationship between gestures and music.

It is our hope that the chapters in this book will be of relevance for this study. We address readers with different backgrounds and interests, such as musicians, dancers, choreographers, psychologists, computer scientists, engineers, neuroscientists; in short, anyone interested in this topic of musical gestures. For this reason, we have tried to make the style and language of this book as accessible as possible, and reduced the amount of technical terms and material in the hope that any interested reader should be able to get a decent grasp on this material.

We have tried to organize the material in this book so that it can be read from the beginning to the end. Thus, it begins with discussions of the term "gesture," including a number of examples and various historical perspectives, and then continues with studies of the various significations of musical gestures, and of the generation and perception of sound and gesture, before concluding with discussion of the practical applications of gestural control in musical contexts.

The book is organized in three parts. Part I, "Gestures in Music," introduces definitions, examples, and a history of gesture and music. It provides a presentation of basic terms and discussion of their various ramifications in music (Chapter 2), followed by an overview of gestures in various musical performance situations (Chapter 3), as well as an historical overview of gesture (Chapter 4). Part II, "Gestural Significations," provides a theoretical framework for the formation of signification in gesture and music. This part provides studies of the various possible elements of gesture in music (Chapter 5), their descriptions and significations (Chapter 6), and embodied reactions to musical sound (Chapter 7). Part III, "Gesture Generation and Control," concerns the processing and control of gesture and music. This includes studies of the features of sound in relation to sound-producing gestures (Chapter 8), the production and control of gestures (Chapter 9), methods for capturing and processing gestures (Chapter 10), and finally, gestures as means for control in music (Chapter 11).

Needless to say, musical gestures unfold in time, and therefore, in addition to the text of this book, we have also made a number of video examples available on the web. The reader is encouraged to visit the website and review the material there, see http://musicalgestures.uio.no.

In spite of the extent of the material presented in this book, we believe in all modesty that we are still only at the beginning of a more comprehensive and systematic understanding of musical gestures. It is our hope that, with this book, we can create an impetus for continued interest and effort in this topic, a topic that we firmly believe is at the very core of musical experience.

Chapter 2

Musical Gestures

Concepts and Methods in Research

Alexander Refsum Jensenius, Marcelo M. Wanderley, Rolf Inge Godøy, and Marc Leman

1 Introduction

In the last decade, cognitive science underwent a paradigm shift by bringing human movement into the focus of research. Concepts such as embodiment and enactive have been proposed as core concepts reflecting the role of the human body in complex processes such as action and perception, and the interaction of mind and physical environment (Varela et al. 1991; Noë 2004). In music research, body movement has often been related to the notion of gesture. The reason is that many musical activities (performance, conducting, dancing) involve body movements that evoke meanings, and therefore these movements are called gestures. However, there are many ways in which music-related body movements can be approached, measured, described and applied. For example, in Camurri et al. (2005), musical gestures are addressed from the viewpoint of their expressive character. Accordingly, there are many ways in which musical gestures can be meaningful. Given the different contexts in which gestures appear, and their close relationship to movement and meaning, one may be tempted to say that the notion of gesture is too broad, ill-defined, and perhaps too vague. Yet the use of this notion is very convenient in modern music research because it builds a bridge between movement and meaning. A closer look at the term "gesture" reveals its potential as a core notion that provides access to central issues in action/perception processes and in mind/environment interactions.

This chapter starts with a review of some current definitions of "gesture." The second part presents a conceptual framework for differentiating various *functional* aspects of gestures in music performance. The third part presents a brief overview of some methodological approaches that can be used in gesture research.

2 Musicians' and Dancers' Gestures

Musical gestures—that is, human body movement that goes along with sounding music—can be divided into two main categories: the gestures of those that produce the sounds (the musicians), and the gestures of those that perceive the sounds (the listeners or dancers). Obviously, the musicians also listen to musical sounds, but their role is nevertheless somewhat more specific in that they are involved in the creation of sounds, whereas listeners or dancers respond to these sounds. When dancers are connected to a computer system that produces music based on features of the dance movements, then dancers also can be considered musicians because they generate the sounds.

Obviously, musicians and dancers each have their own subcategories of musical gestures. For example, the gestures of musicians may be categorized as sound producing, communicative, ancillary or sound facilitating, and sound accompanying. There has been an increased interest in research on musicians' gestures in recent years, e.g. in Wanderley (2001; see also Chapter 3 in this volume). Conductors' gestures and gestures that are more or less purely communicative, are also included in this main category of musicians' gestures (see Chapter 11 in this volume). The gestures of dancers may be thought of as having sound-accompanying characteristics, since they often follow or contrast with the musical sound. Dance movements in relation to sound have been studied in e.g. (Hodgins 1992; Haga 2008) (see also Chapters 7 and 10 in this volume).

When speaking about the musical activity of musicians and dancers, it is tempting to call the involved embodiment "gestures" rather than "movements." The main reason for doing this is that the notion of gesture somehow blurs the distinction between movement and meaning. *Movement* denotes physical displacement of an object in space, whereas *meaning* denotes the mental activation of an experience. The notion of gesture somehow covers both aspects and therefore bypasses the Cartesian divide between matter and mind. In that sense, the notion of gesture provides a tool that allows a more straightforward crossing of the traditional boundary between the physical and the mental world. The crossing of this boundary is at the core of the entire embodiment paradigm and it forms the strength of the current extension from disembodied music cognition to embodied music cognition (Leman 2008a). In this context, *action* can be understood as coherent chunks of gestures, or delimited segments of human movement having an intentional aspect.

However, the term "gesture" has been used with so many significations that an overview of some different types of definitions is needed. This overview may help to clarify the terminology used in the rest of this chapter and the book as a whole.

3 Definitions of Gesture

Based on the work of Zhao (2001) and McNeill (2000), it is possible to define a general framework that considers gestures from the viewpoints of communication, control and metaphor. (1) *Communication* is involved when gestures work as vehicles of meaning in social interaction. This use of the term is common in linguistics, behavioral psychology, and social anthropology. (2) *Control* is involved when gestures work as elements of a system, such as in the control of computational and interactive systems. This is common in the fields of human–computer interaction (HCI), computer music, and similar areas. (3) *Metaphor* is involved when gestures work as concepts that project physical movement, sound, or other types of perception to cultural topics. This use of the term is common in cognitive science, psychology, musicology, and other fields. The following sections will present examples of definitions of gesture within each of these three main categories.

3.1 Gesture as Communication

In recent work on gesture, "gesture" is often used to denote bodily actions that are associated with speech, particularly hand movements and facial expressions. This definition of gesture as "visible action as utterance" (Kendon 2004) is most commonly used in linguistics, psychology and behavioral studies. In particular, Kendon (1972) used the term "body motion" and later, "gesticulation" (Kendon 1980), before finally settling on the word "gesture" (Kendon 1982). Through a series of observational studies of people's storytelling, McNeill (1992; 2005) showed how hand movements and facial expressions are not just random movements that accompany speech, but are actually an integral part of communication. McNeill (1992) provides a taxonomy of different gestural functions based on the five types of nonverbal behavior outlined earlier by Ekman and Friesen (1969): (1) *Iconics* represent a particular feature of an object, and can be described in terms of the shape and spatial extent of the gesture. Iconic gestures are often used to illustrate an action: for example, imitating a knocking movement with a hand while saying "knocking on the door." (2) *Metaphorics* are similar to iconics, but represent an abstract feature of an object. An example of a metaphoric gesture may be to say "something happened" while holding up the hands to refer to "something." (3) *Beats* occur together with spoken words to highlight discontinuities and stress specific words. Beats are typically carried out as in/out or up/down movements, and may be seen as emphasizing the most important words in a narrative. (4) *Deictics* indicates a point in space, for example pointing in a specific direction while saying "over there." (5) *Emblems* are stereotypical patterns with agreed meaning, such as the "goodbye" or "OK" sign.

McNeill's theory of gesture is built on the idea that gestures coexist with speech. This is not to say that they have to co-occur, but rather that gestures and speech are co-expressive, or co-articulatory. In this respect, McNeill adopts Damasio's saying that "language is inseparable from imagery" (McNeill 2000, 57), and argues that mental imagery is embodied in the gestures that co-occur with speech. To explain the relationships between gesture and speech, McNeill (1992) presented what he calls the "Kendon continuum," based on the typology of gestures suggested in (Kendon 1982): gesticulation, emblems, pantomime and sign language. As shown in Figure 2.1, this continuum covers two extremes: *gesticulation* is used to denote the types of gestures that only co-occur with speech, and *sign language* is used to denote the types of gestures that are linguistically self-contained.

Goldin-Meadow (2003) follows a similar line of thought but the difference is that she uses the term *gesture* to denote only hand movement and leaves out other types of body movement, including facial expression. She argues that gestures may not only support, but also contradict speech. For example, it may be possible to spot when people are lying because their facial expression and body movements contradict what they are saying. McNeill (2005) therefore suggests that studying *overt* gestures may reveal interesting aspects of our covert mental activity.

Clearly, these definitions focus on linguistic communicative aspects of gestures. As such, the term gesture does not refer to body movement or expression *per se*, but rather to the intended or perceived meaning of the movement or expression, often in accompaniment with verbal utterances. In that respect, Feyereisen and de Lannoy (1991) use a slightly wider definition when they say:

> To some extent, any movement or change in position of a body segment may be considered a gesture. Accordingly, the very notion of gesture refers to a great variety of phenomena. In an extended sense, the term gesture encompasses gestures that are used in various professions and that often involve tool use, e.g. a carpenter's hammering

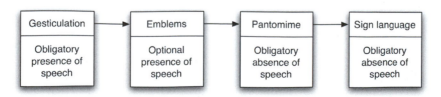

Figure 2.1 McNeill's (2005) *Kendon continuum* of gestures, and how they relate to speech.

or sawing gestures. In such a perspective, gestures are mainly actions before becoming means of communication (p. 3).

The latter definition implies that the term *gesture* might not be restricted to human—human communication, but could also be used for describing communication between humans and machines.

3.2 Gesture for Control

In the field of human–computer interaction (HCI), there is now a considerable amount of research on how to use various kinds of body movement as input to computers. In contrast to human–human communication, it is obvious that computers traditionally have had comparably limited sensing capabilities. For example, Kurtenbach and Hulteen (1990) state that "A gesture is a motion of the body that contains information. Waving goodbye is a gesture. Pressing a key on a keyboard is not a gesture because the motion of a finger on its way to hitting a key is neither observed nor significant. All that matters is which key was pressed" (p. 310). Pressing the key is highlighted as the meaning-bearing component, while the rest of the movement of the person is considered irrelevant. It is an example of a computer-centric approach to interaction design, in the sense that the constraints of the computer define the interaction.

However, a more recent trend in the HCI community is to focus on creating computer systems that can sense a broader range of human expressions. Here the challenge is to develop sensor and computer vision solutions, and corresponding computational algorithms, which understand the gestures (here used in the communication sense) in a continuous stream of movement. While humans have few problems separating a hand gesture (e.g. waving goodbye) from other types of movement (e.g. waving away a fly), this is much more problematic for computers. This is not only due to the remarkable capacity of *visual scene analysis* in humans, but is also due to the fact that we understand the intended meaning of the gesture based on its context and on our life-long experience of multimodal communication.

One approach to make computers understand the meaning of human gestures is to create means for extracting the expressiveness of body movement. Camurri et al. (2001) introduce the term *expressive gesture* to denote aspects of body movement that convey information about affect and emotion: "It seems likely that expressiveness in gestures is conveyed by a set of temporal/spatial characteristics that operate more or less independent from the denotative meanings (if any) of those gestures. In that sense, gestures can be conceived as the vehicles that carry these expressive characteristics and it is likely that expressiveness as such subsumes certain universal patterns and general rules (p. 1)."

Gesture is here used to denote what can be observed, namely body movement, and it implies that a set of expressive characteristics can be extracted from these movements (see more on this in Chapter 10 in this volume). As such, this definition is quite different from the afore-mentioned definitions found in linguistics where the term "gesture" often refers to the actual meaning of the movement, and where the movement as such is subordinate to this meaning.

A similar definition of gesture may be found in the computer music literature, albeit with reference to sound. For example, Cadoz (1988, 64) states that "If we call first of all, 'gesture' all physical behavior, besides vocal transmission, by which a human being informs or transforms his immediate environment, we may then say that there can be no music without gesture, for music is not exclusively vocal." Miranda and Wanderley (2006, 5) state that "gesture is used in a broad sense to mean any human action used to generate sounds. The term refers to actions such as grasping, manipulation, and non-contact movements, as well as to general voluntary body movements."

An important difference between the control definitions and the com-munication definitions presented in the previous section is that the former focus mainly on *manipulative gestures* (Quek et al. 2002, 172) and the latter on *empty-handed gestures*. Manipulative gestures thus denote gestures that are based on physical contact, or what may also be called ergotic, haptic, or instrumental contact. In contrast, empty-handed ges-tures have been called semaphoric, free, semiotic, or naked gestures (Miranda and Wanderley 2006).

3.3 Gesture as Metaphor

In the two previous sections the notion of gesture has referred to some kind of physical body movement, however, this section considers the use of gesture in a metaphorical sense. For example, Métois (1997, 16) states that "[B]oth [physical and auditory gestures] present the ability to communicate musical intentions at a higher level than an audio wave form. The similarity of their level of abstraction motivated the author to label them both as Musical Gestures." Interestingly, musical gesture is here used to denote the combined sensations of physical movement and sound. This is along the lines of how several musicologists have thought about musical gesture in recent decades. From a popular music research perspective, Middleton (1993), referring to Coker's (1972) discussion of affections and emotions that could be associated with gestures, writes (p. 177): "[H]ow we feel and how we understand musical sounds is organised through processual shapes which seem to be analogous to physical gestures." Middleton further argues that the idea of gestures in music should be founded on the concept of rhythm. This seems similar to

Todd's (1995, 1941) idea regarding the relationships between musical sound and body movement. Todd claims, without actually using the word "gesture," that musical movement is similar to, and imitates, movement in physical space.

A similar way of thinking about gesture as a mental entity that can be evoked from musical sound is suggested by Hatten (2004, 95), who argues that a musical gesture is "significant energetic shaping through time." His theory of musical gesture is based on what he calls gestural competency, which arises from physical (i.e. biological and cognitive) and social (i.e. cultural and multi-stylistic) experience. Hatten (2003) states, "Musical gesture is biologically and culturally grounded in communicative human movement. Gesture draws upon the close interaction (and intermodality) of a range of human perceptual and motor systems to synthesize the energetic shaping of motion through time into significant events with unique expressive force." Hatten is here making reference to the experience of musical gesture "within" music, either through the score or the musical sound, but he seems not to refer to the body movement or the generating actions that create the sound.

François Delalande (1988) defines musical gesture as the intersection of observable actions and mental images. He further argues that musical gestures may be studied at various levels, ranging from the purely functional to the purely symbolic, using the terms *effective*, *accompanying* and *figurative* gestures (Cadoz and Wanderley 2000, 77–78).[1] The term *effective gesture* denotes what we would call a sound-producing gesture, while the term *accompanying gesture* is used for the movement that supports the effective gesture in various ways. Delalande suggests the term *figurative gesture* to refer to a mental image that is not directly related to any physical movement, but which may be conveyed through sound.

A somewhat analogous definition to those of Delalande and Hatten is suggested in (Gritten and King 2006, *xx*) who state, "[A] gesture is a movement or change in state that becomes marked as significant by an agent. This is to say that for movement or sound to be(come) gesture, it must be taken intentionally by an interpreter, who may or may not be involved in the actual sound production of a performance, in such a manner as to donate it with the trappings of human significance." The definition implies that there is a flow of communication between the performer and the perceiver, and movement becomes a gesture only if it is understood as such by the perceiver. An interesting question then arises: Does an action have to be carried out consciously in order to be perceived as a gesture? In human communication, Kendon has argued that gestures have to be carried out consciously since they are intentional (Kendon 2004, 15). Hatten, on the other hand, argues that musical gestures may be performed unconsciously but still be valid as gestures if they are observed as significant by the perceiver (Hatten 2006). We would assume that there are also ambiguous cases where one person may perceive an action as intentional and another person may see it as unintentional.

3.4 Terminological Considerations

The definitions presented so far range from using gesture as more or less equivalent to body movement, to using gesture in a metaphorical sense to describe some emergent qualities in musical sound. There are also several other types of definitions that have not been discussed, such as the concepts of articulatory or phonological gesture sometimes encountered in linguistics (Liberman and Mattingly 1985). There are other research fields focused on body movements that seldom use the term gesture, such as kinesiology and biomechanics. A similar situation can be found in some of the music literature, where terms like motion/movement (Shaffer 1980; Gabrielsson 1985; Clarke 1993; Davidson 1993), expressive movement (Pierce and Pierce 1989; Davidson 1994) or corporeal articulations (Leman 2008a) have been used to denote various types of gestures.

Based on the above viewpoints, it seems straightforward to define musical gesture as an action pattern that produces music, is encoded in music, or is made in response to music. Qualifications can be added to the term musical gesture whenever needed to avoid misunderstandings. For example, one can speak about sound-producing gestures, sound-modifying gestures, sound-accompanying gestures, sonic gestures, playing gestures, and so on. The essential point is to have a terminological apparatus that is sufficiently specific for differentiating subtle aspects of gestures when dealing with music. The main advantage of using the term gesture is that it surpasses the Cartesian divide between physics and the mind. As mentioned above, we may think of movement as the changing of a physical position of a body part or an object, which can be objectively measured. The notion of gesture goes beyond this purely physical aspect in that it involves an action as a movement unit, or a chunk, which may be planned, goal-directed, and perceived as a holistic entity (Buxton 1986) (see Chapter 5 in this volume).

4 Concepts for Studying Musical Gestures

Musical gestures may be studied from different viewpoints, such as the subjective, objective and communicative viewpoint (see Chapter 6 in this volume), or the phenomenological, biomechanical and functionalist viewpoint (Ramstein 1991). The subjective phenomenological level focuses on the descriptive aspects of gestures, such as describing a gesture in terms of its *cinematic* (e.g. the speed), *spatial* (the amount of space), and *temporal* dimensions (e.g. frequency range). The objective or intrinsic level focuses on the conditions for gesture generation, such as various biomechanical and motor control constraints (see Chapter 9 in this volume). The communicative or functional level has a focus on the purpose of a movement or action in a certain context, e.g. whether it is sound-producing, sound-modifying, and so on. All three of these levels operate within a performance environment in which spatial aspects of musical gestures are constrained. Below, we first define the role of the performance environment. Then we go deeper into the communicative/functional level.

4.1 Spatial Aspects of Musical Gestures

The performance environment in which musical gestures are carried out can be conceived in terms of three concepts, namely *scene*, *position* and *space*, as illustrated in Figure 2.2. First, the performance scene may be thought of as a physical space that both the performer and the perceiver recognize as one in which a performance is carried out. This is evident as both performers and perceivers tend to change their attention when the performer enters the performance scene. In a typical concert situation the performance scene is clearly defined as a part of the stage, a location everyone's attention is naturally focused on due to the seating and general expectation of what is to come. But a performance scene may also refer to a social construct, and may thus be created anywhere. A typical example is how street musicians claim a part of the pavement as their performance scene, which people walking past will usually respect.

Concerning the performance positions, it is possible to define the home position of a performer to be the resting position in which the performer sits or stands before starting to act (Sacks and Schegloff 2002). In a musical context, and particularly in Western classical music, this can be understood as when a musician is standing or sitting at ease with the instrument before starting to perform. When in home position, the perceiver will usually know that the performance has not yet begun and will wait until the performer moves into start position before expecting any sound to be produced. Finally, the performance position is the one from which the performance action originates.

Reference can then be made to a set of *performance spaces*, or a personal space. Laban's (1963) term *kinesphere* denotes an imaginary box surrounding a person that defines the maximum movement possibilities from a certain point in space. Laban argues that the kinesphere is a mental construct that one is always aware of in the course of interacting with the environment and with others. Within the kinesphere, it is possible to further distinguish among different performance spaces or gesture spaces, i.e. imaginary bounding boxes for various types of musical gestures. For example, when playing the piano the performer has a well-defined sound-producing gesture space in the visual part of the keyboard, as indicated in Figure 2.3. This gesture space can usually be observed by both the

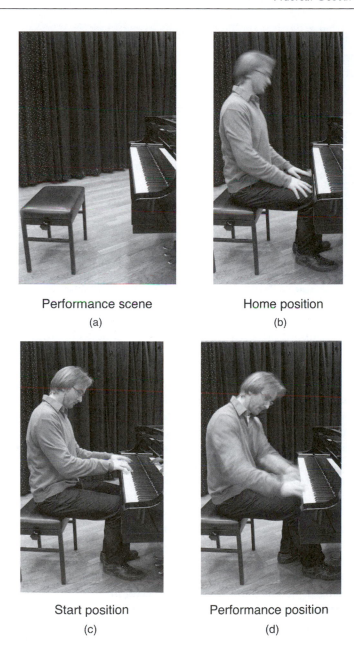

Performance scene
(a)

Home position
(b)

Start position
(c)

Performance position
(d)

Figure 2.2 The *performance scene* (a) is the imagined area in which performance can happen. The *home position* (b) is the position where the musician is sitting (or standing) at ease before starting to perform. The *start position* (c) is where the performance starts, and the *performance position* (d) is the position(s) of the musician during performance.

Ancillary,
sound-accompanying,
and communicative

Sound-producing

Sound-modifying

Figure 2.3 The *gesture space* can be seen as an imaginary box surrounding the space in which performance movements can be carried out. Here the gesture spaces for various musical movements are indicated.

performer and the perceiver, and makes it possible to identify where the sound-producing gestures are being carried out.

Figure 2.3 also indicates the performance spaces of other types of musical gestures. It is necessary to identify these spaces in order to have a clear understanding of where different types of gestures should be carried out in relation to an object (e.g. an instrument). This knowledge of performance spaces for various types of musical gestures is helpful for setting up expectations when perceiving a performance. This is why audiences may be surprised if a musician happens to perform outside of such conventional performance spaces, for example by playing with the fingers on the strings of the piano instead of on the piano keyboard.

Furthermore, a sound-producing gesture can be defined as an excitatory action, i.e. an action of setting some object (e.g. parts of an instrument) into motion by hitting, stroking, or bowing. Godøy (2008) has suggested that a sound-producing gesture can be seen as consisting of an *excitation* phase (where there is contact with, and energy transfer to, the instrument) combined with a preceding *prefix* (a movement trajectory to the point of contact) and a succeeding *suffix* (a movement trajectory away from the point of contact) as depicted in Figure 2.4. The prefix is the part of a sound-producing gesture quite simply because the effector (finger, hand, arm) has to move from an initial position to the contact position, but is also important for defining the quality of the excitation (see also Chapter 6 in this volume, Figure 6.5). The suffix is the return to equilibrium, or the initial position, after the excitation. Adapting Kendon's terminology, one could talk of a *gesture unit*, defined as a

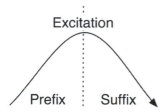

Figure 2.4 A sound-producing gesture may be seen as having an excitation phase surrounded by a prefix and suffix. These three are closely connected and are important for both its performance and its perception (Godøy 2008).

goal-directed movement excursion, which starts and ends in a home position (Kendon 2004, 111).

It should also be noted that gestures might be nested, in the sense that several actions that follow each other may be perceived as one coherent gesture. For example, playing a scale run on a piano may be seen as a series of separate actions if the focus is on the finger movements, but can also be perceived as one coherent gesture if the focus is on the movement of the hand or the upper body. Apparently, humans are able to perceive many concurrent actions simultaneously, and these concurrent action layers are often an integral part of the musical texture (see Chapter 5 in this volume).

4.2 Functional Aspects of Musical Gestures

To understand more about the functions of various musical gestures, it is easy to discern four functional categories of musical gestures, based on work by Gibet (1987), Cadoz (1988), Delalande (1988) and Wanderley and Depalle (2004); namely, *sound-producing* gestures, *communicative* gestures, *sound-facilitating* gestures, and *sound-accompanying* gestures (see also Chapter 3 in this volume).

- Sound-producing gestures are those that effectively produce sound. They can be further subdivided into gestures of *excitation* and *modification*. Sound-producing gestures are called instrumental gestures in (Cadoz 1988), and effective gestures in (Delalande 1988).
- Communicative gestures are intended mainly for communication. As will be discussed later in this chapter such movements can be subdivided into *performer–performer* or *performer–perceiver* types of communication. Communicative gestures are called semiotic gestures in (Cadoz and Wanderley 2000). Several of these can also be considered gestures in the way Kendon (2004) and McNeill (1992) use the term.

- Sound-facilitating gestures support the sound-producing gestures in various ways. As will be discussed and exemplified in a later section, such gestures can be subdivided into *support*, *phrasing*, and *entrained* gestures. Sound-facilitating gestures are called accompanying gestures in (Delalande 1988), non-obvious performer gestures in (Wanderley 1999), and ancillary gestures in (Wanderley and Depalle 2004).
- Sound-accompanying gestures are not involved in the sound production itself, but follow the music. They can be *sound-tracing*, i.e. following the contour of sonic elements (Godøy et al. 2006a), or they can *mimic* the sound-producing gestures (Godøy et al. 2006b).

Figure 2.5 shows an illustration of different types of musical gestures involved in piano performance. Note that the different categories are not meant to be mutually exclusive, as several gestures have multiple functions. For example, hitting a final chord followed by a theatrical lift can be seen as having sound-producing and sound-facilitating as well as communicative functions. This functional multiplicity is illustrated in the dimension spaces in Figure 2.6. Dimension spaces are commonly used to analyze interactive systems (Graham et al. 2000), and have also been used to analyze the functionality of digital musical instruments (Birnbaum et al. 2005). Here they are used to visualize how the gestures of a musician and a dancer cover different functions.

Based on the typology presented by Cadoz (1988), the sound-producing gestures can be further divided into excitation and modification gestures Excitation gestures may be subdivided into impulsive, sustained, and iterative actions, each kind having distinct energy profiles. Excitation gestures are either direct or indirect, depending on whether or not there is an object between the sound-producing element of the instrument and the

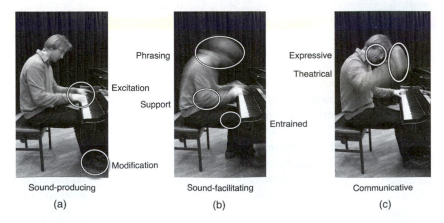

Figure 2.5 Examples of where different types of musical gestures (sound-producing, sound-facilitating and communicative) may be found in piano performance.

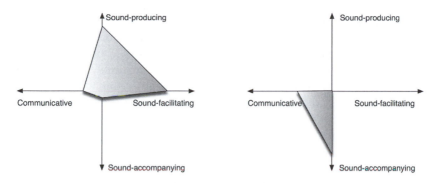

Figure 2.6 Dimension spaces illustrating how the gestures of a musician (left) and a dancer (right) may be seen as having different functions. Here the musician's movements have a high level of sound-producing and sound-facilitating function, while the dancer's movements have a high level of sound-accompanying and some communicative function.

object carrying out the excitation. For example, the actions of playing the harp or congas are direct since fingers and hands are directly in control of the resonating objects (strings and drum membrane). But there are also many indirect instrumental actions that involve one or more objects in the interaction, for example the bow in string instruments, the key mechanism on the piano, or sticks for drums.

Modification gestures do not actually produce sounds themselves, but they modify the quality of the sound. Cadoz (1988) suggests further subdivision of these gestures into (1) parametric gestures that continuously change a parameter, such as bow pressure in violin playing, and (2) structural gestures that modify or change the structure of the object, such as placing a mute on a trumpet.

Most musical instruments are played with both excitation and modification gestures (Kvifte 1989). These two gestural functions may to a certain extent be separable, as on stringed instruments where the two hands play different roles: the left hand is mainly modifying the sound (choosing the pitch) while the right hand is carrying out the excitation, yet there are features of the bowing movement such as speed, pressure, acceleration, and tilt, that can be used to modify the sound (see Chapter 8 in this volume).

It is important to keep in mind that a gestural typology, like all other typologies, is not intended to create an absolute classification system, but rather to point out some of the different functions of gestures. Furthermore, all performance movements can be considered a type of communication, but we find it useful to have a separate category for movements that are primarily intended to be communicative. These may be performer–performer and performer–perceiver types of communication, and range from communication in a linguistic sense (emblems), to a more abstract form of communication.

The term *sound-facilitating gesture* is used to cover different types of musical gestures that are not directly involved in sound production, but still play an important part in shaping the resultant sound. For example, hitting a piano key involves not only the active finger, but also the hand, arm, and upper body. Such movements are support movements of the sound-producing actions. In fact, it is the preparatory movements of this complex multi-joint system that determine the trajectory and velocity of the finger before and after it hits the key. Thus, such support movements play an important role in supporting the sound-producing actions, and they may even have audible components, as shown by Wanderley (1999) in a study of clarinet performance. Here the performer's ancillary movements were seen in the movement of the clarinet bell, and this clarinet movement was shown to have an audible component due to the changing sound diffusion pattern of the instrument.

A different type of sound-facilitating gesture is the so-called phrasing gesture, since it is closely connected to musical phrasing. Wanderley (2002) has shown that the ancillary movements of clarinetists are an integral part of the instrumentalists' performance and are stable and reproducible even after long periods of time. Many of these repeatable movement patterns seem to be closely connected to the phrases in the music being performed, and are often related to movement of the clarinet bell (Campbell et al. 2005; Quek et al. 2006). However, it should be noted that these movements might also have a communicative function in enhancing the perceivers' experience of the phrasing of the sound.

The multi-functionality of a gesture is well illustrated in so-called entrained gestures, like tapping a foot, nodding the head or moving the whole upper body in synchrony with the music. These gestures may help the musician to keep track of the tempo, and serve as a signal to other performers, dancers, or the perceiver. Although such gestures vary considerably between performers and performance styles, they may be thought of as important for the timing in a performance. It is important to notice that entrained gestures can be a generator of rhythm and timing, in the same way as the rhythm and timing in music can be a generator of movements (Clarke 1999). In the clarinet experiments by Wanderley et al. (2005), the performers continued to move, albeit less, when asked to play "immobilized." The function of ancillary gestures is to meet the performer's needs, and these gestures could be separated from gestures that are intended mainly for communication with the other performers and the audience. As such, ancillary gestures are usually not carried out with a specific intention other than being the basis for, or the result of, the sound-producing gestures.

Examples of support and phrasing gestures can be observed in a study[2] of a clarinetist performing the beginning of the Allegro appassionato from the Clarinet Sonata Op. 120, No. 1 in F minor by Brahms (1894). Figure 2.7 shows a snapshot from the video, and Figure 2.8 shows a motiongram (see (Jensenius 2006 for details) of the vertical movements of the clarinetist over time. The motiongram facilitates studying the vertical movement of the clarinet bell, and the movement of the center of gravity of the performer. Note how the motiongram visualizes the rhythmic sway and weight changes of the clarinetist, which seem to correspond to the breathing patterns and musical phrasings as discussed by Wanderley et al. (2005).

The sound-facilitating gestures can be distinguished from sound-accompanying gestures. These are neither part of, nor ancillary to, the sound-production, but rather intended to follow features in the sound. Dancing to music is perhaps the most common type of sound-accompanying movement, a topic that was explored in an observation study of how dancers' movements followed qualities in the music (Casciato et al. 2005; Jensenius 2007; Haga 2008). However, sound-accompanying gestures may also involve entrainment. The Brazilian samba provides an interesting example (Naveda and Leman 2008a; in press), with strong evidence that dancing imposes a corporeal metrical grid onto musical structures that are inherently ambiguous (see Chapter 7 in this volume, Figure 7.7). Thus, it is through sound-accompanying gestures, or dancing, that structure is given to the music. This complies with other recent findings that motion may influence perception (Phillips-Silver and Trainor 2008).

Another type of sound-accompanying movement is what could be called sound-tracing, meaning tracing by hand in the air, or on a surface,

Figure 2.7 Mark Bradley performing the beginning of the *Allegro appassionato* from Clarinet Sonata Op. 120, No. 1 in F minor by Brahms at the Input Devices and Music Interaction Laboratory, McGill University.

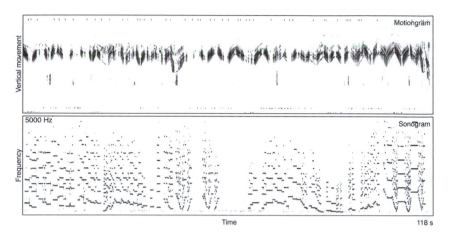

Figure 2.8 Motiongram (top) and sonogram (bottom) made from a video recording of clarinet performance (as shown in Figure 2.7). The thin dotted line in the top part of the motiongram represents the changing light from an infrared motion capture camera that was also active during recording. The thin dotted line at the bottom of the display is the rhythmic tapping of the clarinetist's toes. The few vertical lines below the movement of the clarinet, shows where the clarinetist shifted his weight during performance.

some prominent feature or features of sound. This was studied in (Godøy et al. 2006a; Leman et al. 2009), where people were asked to trace sounds with a digital pen on a graphical tablet, and with a telescopic stick. Yet another example of a sound-accompanying gesture is air instrument performance, meaning imitating sound-producing gestures in the air. This is something which has received increased interest with the annual air guitar world championship, and been studied in (Godøy et al. 2006b) (see also Chapters 5, 6, and 7 in this volume).

5 Methods for Studying Musical Gestures

Musical gestures are characterized by a multi-functional nature through which multiple meanings are generated. Consequently, the study of musical gesture requires an interdisciplinary approach, with contributions from a diverse set of disciplines including physics of musical instruments and acoustics, biomechanics and human motor control, auditory and visual perception, musical performance and dance, music theory, music technology, robotics and HCI, aesthetics, and various social sciences including the study of emotions. Given the nature of musical gestures, progress will be obtained by combining different scientific methodologies, most particularly, the methodologies from the natural sciences and the human sciences (Leman 2008b). Indeed, it is a major challenge to combine overt, observable, and measurable information with more subjective, descriptive, or even effable sensations. Being an eminently interdisciplinary enterprise, and in particular an enterprise that combines traditionally purportedly conflicting approaches in the human sciences epitomized in "qualitative" versus "quantitative," it is instructive to have a brief look at some of the main perspectives in the study of musical gestures.

First, consider observation and/or introspection. The challenge is in bridging the gap between what we can spontaneously see or sense of musical gestures, be that in performance, in various sound-related movement, or in just listening, and that which we can somehow document in motion and sound data. The long-term goal would be that of discerning and giving explicit representations of as many features of musical gestures as possible, and in our work towards such a goal, there will probably be a need for alternation between observation and introspection.

Second, consider qualitative and/or quantitative methods. There seems to be converging evidence that we are quite good at perceiving movement qualities such as fast, slow, agitated, calm, tense, and relaxed, in both musical gestures and in sound. One important challenge here will then be that of substantiating or documenting the basis in movement and sound for these sensations. This means to move from initial qualitative sensations to more quantitative representations by mapping out as many as possible pertinent features of movement and sound. This presents us with many methodological and technological issues of motion capture, processing, and representation of motion and sound data.

Third, consider motion capture. This is about trying to find out as much as possible of the motion in musical gestures. The technologies for this include video-based computer vision techniques, infrared, electromagnetic, ultrasound, mechanical and inertial motion capture systems, and many other techniques. Such technologies can to varying degrees of precision and accuracy send out streams of data indicating the position and/or relative motion of various points on the body. This will in most cases result in large data sets, presenting important challenges of processing and representation in order to be useful for further analyses.

Fourth, consider processing and representation. Most kinds of motion capture data need to be filtered and transformed in order to be useful. Also, the way this data is displayed presents substantial challenges, such as how to visualize the simultaneous movements at different speeds of different points on the body in different dimensions. Synchronizing and comparing such motion capture data with other related data (e.g. MIDI) and media (e.g. audio and video) is yet another challenge, to say nothing of trying to find some criteria for judging similarities and differences between variant types of movements and sounds.

Next consider simulations and/or animations. Trying to simulate the kinematics and dynamics of various musical gestures may be very instructive for understanding how these gestures work. This approach implies work that is more in line with the so-called *analysis-by-synthesis* strategy practiced for several decades in the domain of digital sound synthesis. This means synthesizing incrementally different variants in order to discover what are the perceptually most salient features. Examples of such analysis and synthesis strategies are presented in (Bouënard, Gibet and Wanderley 2008a; b; Naveda and Leman 2008b) (see also Chapter 9 in this volume).

Finally, consider annotation and interpretation. Apart from the increasingly sophisticated methods and technologies for motion capture, "naked eye" observations of musical gestures will always be needed, similar to "naked ear" observations of gesture-related cues in the musical sound. Various schemes for making annotations have already been developed, but there is clearly a need to continue this work in parallel with various motion capture technologies. This also goes for the largely unexplored field of social identities in musical gestures, such as studying how different cultures or cultural subgroups have developed specific features of musical gestures and how they seem to work in various social contexts.

Needless to say, the study of musical gestures is a vast area comprising several different insights and skills.

6 Conclusion

Up until now, there has been no single unequivocal definition of gesture, although most authors seem to agree that gestures involve both body movement and meaning. Gestures connect well with recent approaches in embodied music cognition, and they can be considered vehicles of human musical communication. However, this approach to the notion of gesture remains vague to some extent. In many instances of the use of the notion of gesture it will therefore be necessary to differentiate in more detail. This chapter shows that it is indeed possible to develop a proper conceptual apparatus for differentiating various functions that may be attached to musical gestures. Also it was briefly mentioned that sound-accompanying gestures can be observed in the movements of perceivers (e.g. dancers). In all of this, it is important to remember the multi-functionality of gestures: that one single gesture may have multiple functions and significations, and in most (if not all) cases, these different functions and/or significations are but different facets of our rich musical experiences. Lastly, we should keep in mind that musical gestures also have multiple significations ranging from the more physical to the more metaphorical, hence we also should welcome a multiplicity of approaches to the study of musical gestures.

Notes

1   Cadoz and Wanderley (2000) translated the French term *geste accompagnateur* used by (Delalande 1988) to the English term *accompanist gesture*. We are using the term *accompanying*, so as not to confuse such movements with those of an accompanist.
2   Workshop on Motion Capture for Music Performance at McGill University in October 2006, http://www.idmil.org/mocap/mocap.html

References

Birnbaum, D., Fiebrink, R., Malloch, J., and Wanderley, M. M. (2005). Towards a dimension space for musical artifacts. In *Proceedings of the International Conference on New Interfaces for Musical Expression (NIME '05)*. Vancouver, BC, Canada, 192–195.

Bouënard, A., Gibet, S., and Wanderley, M. M. (2008a). Enhancing the visualization of percussion gestures by virtual character animation. In *Proceedings of the International Conference on New Interfaces for Musical Expression (NIME '08)*. Genova, Italy, 38–43.

Bouënard, A., Wanderley, M. M., and Gibet, S. (2008b). Analysis of percussion grip for physically based character animation. In *Proceedings of the 5th International Conference on Enactive Interfaces (ENACTIVE '08)*. Pisa, Italy, 22–27.

Buxton, W. (1986). Chunking and phrasing and the design of human-computer dialogues. In H.-J. Kugler (ed.), *Information Processing 86, Proceedings of the IFIP 10th World Computer Congress*. Dublin, Ireland, 475–480.

Cadoz, C. (1988). Instrumental gesture and musical composition. In *Proceedings of the 1998 International Computer Music Conference*. The Hague, The Netherlands, 60–73.

Cadoz, C. and Wanderley, M. M. (2000). Gesture – Music. In M. M. Wanderley and M. Battier (eds.), *Trends in Gestural Control of Music [CD-ROM]*. Paris, France: IRCAM, 71–93.

Campbell, L., Chagnon, M.-J., and Wanderley, M. M. (2005). On the use of Laban-Bartenieff techniques to describe ancillary gestures of clarinetists. Research report. IDMIL, McGill University.

Camurri, A., De Poli, G., Leman, M., and Volpe, G. (2001). A multi-layered conceptual framework for expressive gesture applications. In *Proceedings of the International MOSART Workshop, November 2001*. Barcelona, Spain.

Camurri, A., Volpe, G., De Poli, G., and Leman, M. (2005). Communicating expressiveness and affect in multimodal interactive systems. *IEEE Multimedia*, 12(1), 43–53.

Casciato, C., Jensenius, A. R. and Wanderley, M. M. (2005). Studying free dance movement to music. In *Proceedings of ESCOM 2005 Performance Matters! Conference*. Porto, Portugal.

Clarke, E. (1993). Generativity, mimesis and the human body in music performance. *Contemporary Music Review*, 9(1), 207–219.

Clarke, E. (1999). Rhythm and timing in music. In D. Deutsch (ed.), *The Psychology of Music*. San Diego: Academic Press, 473–500.

Coker, W. (1972). *Music and Meaning: A Theoretical Introduction to Musical Aesthetics*. New York: Free Press.

Davidson, J. (1993). Visual perception and performance manner in the movements of solo musicians. *Psychology of Music*, 21(2), 103–113.

Davidson, J. (1994). Expressive movements in musical performance. In *Proceedings of the Third International Conference on Music Cognition (ESCOM)*. Liège, Belgium, 327–329.

Delalande, F. (1988). La gestique de Gould: élements pour une sémiologie du geste musical. In G. Guertin (ed.), *Glenn Gould Pluriel*. Québec: Louise Courteau, 85–111.

Ekman, P. and Friesen, W. V. (1969). The repertoire of nonverbal behavior: categories, origins, usage, and coding. *Semiotica*, 1, 49–98.

Feyereisen, P. and de Lannoy, J.-D. (1991). *Gestures and Speech: Psychological Investigations*. Cambridge: Cambridge University Press.

Gabrielsson, A. (1985). Interplay between analysis and synthesis in the studies of music performance and music experience. *Music Perception*, 3(1), 59–86.

Gibet, S. (1987). *Codage, Représentation et Traitement du Geste Instrumental: Application à la Synthèse de Sons Musicaux par Simulation de Mécanismes Instrumentaux*. PhD thesis, Institut National Polytechnique de Grenoble.

Godøy, R. I. (2008). Reflections on chunking in music. In A. Schneider (ed.), *Systematic and Comparative Musicology: Concepts, Methods, Findings*. Frankfurt am Main, Germany: Peter Lang, 117–132.

Godøy, R. I., Haga, E., and Jensenius, A. R. (2006a). Exploring music-related gestures by sound-tracing: a preliminary study. In K. Ng (ed.), *Proceedings of the COST287-ConGAS 2nd International Symposium on Gesture Interfaces for Multimedia Systems*. Leeds, UK, 27–33.

Godøy, R. I., Haga, E., and Jensenius, A. R. (2006b). Playing "air instruments": mimicry of sound-producing gestures by novices and experts. In S. Gibet, N. Courty, and J.-F. Kamp (eds.), *Gesture in Human-Computer Interaction and Simulation*, LNAI 3881. Berlin, Heidelberg, Germany: Springer, 256–267.

Graham, T. C. N., Watts, L. A., Calvary, G., Coutaz, J., Dubois, E., and Nigay, L. (2000). A dimension space for the design of interactive systems within their physical environments. In *Proceedings of the Conference on Designing Interactive Systems (DIS '00)*. New York, 406–416.

Gritten, A. and King, E., (eds.) (2006). *Music and Gesture*. Aldershot, UK: Ashgate.

Haga, E. (2008). *Correspondences Between Music and Body Movement*. PhD thesis, University of Oslo.

Hatten, R. S. (2003). Musical gesture: Theory and interpretation. course notes, Indiana University. http://www.indiana.edu<deanfac/blfal03/mus/mus_t561_9824.html (accessed 1 June 2007).

Hatten, R. S. (2004). *Interpreting Musical Gestures, Topics, and Tropes: Mozart, Beethoven, Schubert*. Bloomington, IN: Indiana University Press.

Hatten, R. S. (2006). A theory of musical gesture and its application to Beethoven and Schubert. In A. Gritten and E. King (eds.), *Music and Gesture*. Aldershot, UK : Ashgate, 1–23.

Hodgins, P. (1992). *Relationships Between Score and Choreography in Twentieth*

Century Dance: Music, Movement and Metaphor. Lewiston, NY: Edwin Mellen Press.

Jensenius, A. R. (2006). Using motiongrams in the study of musical gestures. In *Proceedings of the 2006 International Computer Music Conference.* New Orleans, LA, 499–502.

Jensenius, A. R. (2007). *Action–Sound: Developing Methods and Tools to Study Music-Related Body Movement.* PhD thesis, University of Oslo.

Kendon, A. (1972). Some relationships between body motion and speech. In A. Siegman and E. Pope (eds.), *Studies in Dyadic Communication.* New York: Pergamon Press, 177–210.

Kendon, A. (1980). Gesticulation and speech: two aspects of the process of utterance. In M. Key (ed.), *The Relationship Between Verbal and Nonverbal Communication.* The Hague, The Netherlands: Mouton Publishers, 207–227.

Kendon, A. (1982). The study of gesture: some remarks on its history. *Recherches Sémiotiques/Semiotic Inquiry,* 2, 45–62.

Kendon, A. (2004). *Gesture: Visible Action as Utterance.* Cambridge: Cambridge University Press.

Kurtenbach, G. and Hulteen, E. A. (1990). The art of human-computer interface design. In B. Laurel (ed.), *Gestures in Human-Computer Communication.* Reading, PA: Addison Wesley, 309–317.

Kvifte, T. (1989). *Instruments and the Electronic Age. Towards a Terminology for a Unified Description of Playing Techniques.* Oslo, Norway: Solum Forlag.

Laban, R. v. (1963). *Modern Educational Dance.* London: Macdonald and Evans Ltd.

Leman, M. (2008a). *Embodied Music Cognition and Mediation Technology.* Cambridge, MA: MIT Press.

Leman, M. (2008b). Systematic musicology at the crossroads of modern music research. In A. Schneider (ed.), *Systematic and Comparative Musicology: Concepts, Methods, Findings.* Frankfurt am Main, Germany: Peter Lang, 89–115.

Leman, M., Desmet, F., Styns, F., Van Noorden, L., and Moelants, D. (2009). Sharing musical expression through embodied listening: a case study based on Chinese guqin music. *Music Perception,* 26(3), 263–278.

Liberman, A. M. and Mattingly, I. G. (1985). The motor theory of speech perception revised. *Cognition,* 21(1), 1–36.

McNeill, D. (1992). *Hand and Mind: What Gestures Reveal About Thought.* Chicago, IL: University of Chicago Press.

McNeill, D. (ed.) (2000). *Language and Gesture.* Cambridge: Cambridge University Press.

McNeill, D. (2005). *Gesture and Thought.* Chicago, IL: University of Chicago Press.

Métois, E. (1997). *Musical Sound Information: Musical Gestures and Embedding Synthesis.* PhD thesis, Massachusetts Institute of Technology.

Middleton, R. (1993). Popular music analysis and musicology: bridging the gap. *Popular Music,* 12(2), 177–190.

Miranda, E. R. and Wanderley, M. M. (2006). *New Digital Musical Instruments: Control and Interaction Beyond the Keyboard.* Middleton, WI: A-R Editions, Inc.

Naveda, L. and Leman, M. (2008a). Representation of samba dance gestures, using a multi-modal analysis approach. In *Proceedings of the 5th International Conference on Enactive Interfaces (ENACTIVE '08)*. Pisa, Italy, 68–74.

Naveda, L. and Leman, M. (2008b). Sonification of samba dance using periodic pattern analysis. In A. Barbosa (ed.), *Proceedings of the 4th International Conference on Digital Arts (ARTECH '08)*. Porto, Portugal, 16–26.

Naveda, L. and Leman, M. (in press). A cross-modal heuristic for periodic pattern analysis of samba music and dance. *Journal of New Music Research*.

Noë, A. (2004). *Action in Perception*. Cambridge, MA: MIT Press.

Phillips-Silver, J. and Trainor, L. J. (2008). Vestibular influence on auditory metrical interpretation. *Brain and Cognition*, 67(1), 94–102.

Pierce, A. and Pierce, R. (1989). *Expressive Movement: Posture and Action in Daily Life, Sports, and the Performing Arts*. Cambridge, MA: Perseus Publishing.

Quek, F., McNeill, D., Bryll, R., Duncan, S., Ma, X.-F., Kirbas, C., McCullough, K., and Ansari, R. (2002). Multimodal human discourse: gesture and speech. *ACM Transactions on Computer-Human Interaction (TOCHI)*, 9(3), 171–193.

Quek, O., Verfaille, V., and Wanderley, M. M. (2006). Sonification of musician's ancillary gesutres. In *Proceedings of the 12th International Conference on Auditory Display*, London, UK, 194–197.

Ramstein, C. (1991). *Analyse, Représentation et Traitement du Geste Instrumental*. PhD thesis, Institut National Polytechnique de Grenoble, France.

Sacks, H. and Schegloff, E. (2002). Home position. *Gesture*, 2(2), 133–146.

Shaffer, L. H. (1980). Analyzing piano performance: a study of concert pianists. In G. Stelmach and P. Vroon (eds.), *Tutorial in Motor Behaviour*. Amsterdam: North-Holland, 443–456.

Todd, N. P. M. (1995). The kinematics of musical expression. *The Journal of the Acoustical Society of America*, 97(3), 1940–1949.

Varela, F. J., Rosch, E., and Thompson, E. (1992). *The Embodied Mind: Cognitive Science and Human Experience*. Cambridge, MA: MIT Press.

Wanderley, M. M. (1999). Non-obvious performer gestures in instrumental music. In A. Braffort, R. Gherbi, S. Gibet, J. Richardson, and D. Teil (eds.), *Gesture-Based Communication in Human-Computer Interaction. International Gesture Workshop*, LNAI 1739. Berlin, Heidelberg, Germany: Springer, 37–48.

Wanderley, M. M. (2001). *Performer-Instrument Interaction: Applications to Gestural Control of Sound Synthesis*. PhD thesis, Université Pierre et Marie Curie, Paris VI.

Wanderley, M. M. (2002). Quantitative analysis of non-obvious performer gestures. In I. Wachsmuth and T. Sowa (eds.), *Gesture and Sign Language in Human-Computer Interaction: International Gesture Workshop*, LNAI 2298. Berlin, Heidelberg: Springer, 241–253.

Wanderley, M. M. and Depalle, P. (2004). Gestural control of sound synthesis. *Proceedings of the IEEE*, 92(4), 632–644.

Wanderley, M. M., Vines, B. W., Middleton, N., McKay, C., and Hatch, W. (2005). The musical significance of clarinetists' ancillary gestures: an exploration of the field. *Journal of New Music Research*, 34(1), 97–113.

Zhao, L. (2001). *Synthesis and Acquisition of Laban Movement Analysis Qualitative Parameters for Communicative Gestures*. PhD thesis, CIS, University of Pennsylvania, Philadelphia, PA.

Chapter 3

Gestures in Performance

Sofia Dahl, Frédéric Bevilacqua, Roberto Bresin, Martin Clayton, Laura Leante, Isabella Poggi, and Nicolas Rasamimanana

1 Introduction

On occasion, one can observe a whole orchestra section moving and playing in unison. In such an instance, all violinists play the melody using the same type of bowing movements and lean forward in unison at a given time during a specific passage in the music. Thus, not only do the musicians use very similar movements to produce the same notes but they sometimes also coordinate bodily sways or other movements with the other players. The musical gesture seems to manifest itself in both sound and movement. Whether we are watching as audience, or participating and interacting in the actual performance itself, we receive a considerable amount of gestural information. The aim of this chapter is to give examples of gestures that may be observed during performance, and to consider the kind of information they might convey, either to other performers or to the audience.

As suggested in Chapter 2 in this volume, the gestures appearing in musical performance can be classified according to their function:

- sound-producing gestures (responsible for the sounding note);
- communicative gestures (intended for communication with others);
- sound-facilitating gestures (facilitating performance although not producing sound);
- sound-accompanying gestures (made in response to the sound).

However, some gestures would fit equally well into several of these categories. For instance, gestures primarily intended for note production can also convey important cues for observers and co-performers. In fact, sound-producing, sound-facilitating and communicative gestures are partially overlapping, and the functions of gestures may be difficult to distinguish and/or separate. Does the swaying motion of a player help the player to express a particular intention through sound or through body language? Or, does the player sway in response to what he/she is hearing?

These and similar questions will be discussed in this chapter, taking the aforementioned classification of performance-related gestures as our point of departure.

2 Sound-Producing Gestures

The primary goal of most of the movements that musicians make is to *produce* or *modify* sound. Such sound-producing gestures typically involve the hands and arms. For many types of instruments these are also the movements that are most readily noticed by an observer.

2.1 Factors Determining Movement Strategies

When watching experts perform, difficult tasks frequently appear to be easy. The sound-producing gestures we see as observers are part of the movement strategies that musicians have acquired over many years. Although the gestures may aim toward the same goal—for example the striking of middle C on the piano at a specific instant in time—the characteristics of movements typically vary a great deal among performers. Movement patterns tend to be replicated with little variability by a single player, whereas different players typically use different movement strategies to achieve the same goal. These inter-individual differences make comparisons of gestures between performers somewhat difficult.

There are several reasons why movement strategies differ between players. First, there are almost an infinite number of possible combinations of muscle contractions and joint rotations that could result in the same movement. The "degrees of freedom problem" (see Chapter 9 in this volume) states that the many possibilities of movement execution make the optimal solution for a particular end result very hard to find.

The degrees of freedom problem may have special implications for musicians, whose movements are evaluated on the basis of the resulting sound. In music, the optimization of motor performance is done using the auditory system. In general, the player is not aiming to perfect a characteristic of movement, but the sound resulting from it. Moreover, since the combination possibilities are so numerous, it is likely that many different movement strategies can result in the same sound event. For a player, it remains to select the optimal strategy to fulfil the goal of playing a particular sequence within the given constraints. These constraints vary with playing conditions (e.g. overall tempo and dynamic level) and, naturally, with the instrument played. Some instruments clearly allow more range in different sound-producing gestures than others. For instance, a DJ can use a variety of hand positions to achieve a particular scratch technique (Hansen 2002), whereas in cello playing the bow has to be maintained horizontal and perpendicular to the strings (Winold et al.

1994). In percussion playing, where both the positions and the feedback from instrument tend to vary a great deal, a flexible movement strategy could be considered a prerequisite in order to adapt to different playing conditions.

In practice, it is not only a question of producing the desired note on time. An optimal strategy is also economical in the sense that it allows the player to minimize effort and avoid fatigue. Such an optimal strategy will differ with performer, but certain general criteria for control movements that are better than others can be outlined. Larger joints and muscles are capable of controlling fine movements, but are more suitable for large ones. It is better to use the arm rather than the finger for slow pacing movements with large amplitudes, whereas fast movements of small amplitudes are best suited for the fingers (Rosenbaum et al. 1991). Another principle that may govern optimal movement strategies is to avoid extreme joint angles. When a joint is close to its extreme, the muscles and tendons will be close to the limit of how stretched or compressed they can be, leaving little room for adjustments. In a study of classical guitar playing, the principle of keeping the joints in the middle of their range was important for the players (Heijink and Meulenbroek 2002). Ortmann argued that "a coordinated movement is a movement which permits the joints involved to act as near to their mid-range of action as possible" (Ortmann 1929).

The differences in physiology between players also may contribute to what movement strategy is to be used. Due to biomechanical constraints, a solution that is optimal for one player may not be so for another. That is, while one person has a wide range of movement in her joints, another may have a smaller range, but longer limbs. The optimal movement pattern, i.e. a movement that maximizes the desired outcomes (e.g. timing, attack, various timbral features, see also Chapter 8 in this volume) and minimizes the undesired (strain, fatigue), will of necessity differ between these performers. Ortmann recognized a difference in arm weight of 233 percent among his piano students (excluding children), and concluded that the same gesture results in very dissimilar tonal intensities due to the variation in arm size and shape (Ortmann 1929).

Another example of how differences in sound-producing gestures in piano playing are influenced by physiological differences is that a larger hand size allows for playing chords with a wider pitch range. For instance, jazz pianist Art Tatum was well known for being able to play 13th chords thanks to his large hands. Similarly, long arms can allow a player to quickly reach keys far away relative to the torso position. The anatomical constraints of the hand also play an important role in musical passages where legato playing is required. In legato playing, the key corresponding to the first of two legato notes is released after the next key is being pressed. This results in the acoustical overlapping of the two corresponding tones (Repp 1997; Bresin and Battel 2000). The use of an optimal fingering combined with consideration of the biomechanics of the hand can help pianists to obtain the best compromise in difficult musical passages (Parncutt et al.1997; Wagner 1988).

The sound-producing gestures used in performance are affected by tempo. Typically, a playing gesture may consist of several separate elements at slow tempi. With increasing tempo these elements tend to be combined and interwoven, resulting in a new, more "overarching," gesture. The change of movement strategies with overall tempo has been reported for, for example, piano (Ortmann 1929; Kay et al. 2003), cello (Winold et al. 1994), and drums (Waadeland 2006).

2.2 Playing Techniques/styles

In the following, we will look more closely at some examples of movement strategies and sound-producing gestures for different instruments. We will see examples of gestures used not only in the production of the actual sound event (see also Chapter 8 in this volume), but also in preparation for it.

A general characteristic of the playing strategies of any instrument that requires transitions of the hands or arms is to prepare for the upcoming note event as soon as possible. For instance, a violin player typically starts moving fingers in advance for the next note to be played when this is possible (Baader et al. 2005; Wiesendanger et al. 2006). By maximizing the time between the release of one note and the onset of another, the player is able to free precious time that can be used for adjusting expressive features such as attack characteristics and timbre. It also makes more combinations of tempo and dynamic level playable, thus helping the player to expand the "working area" of his/her instrument. Ortmann argued that for moderate speeds, a gesture that covers a large distance can also help the player control the dynamics more precisely than would be possible with a smaller sound-producing gesture (Ortmann 1929).

Drumming Gestures

Playing drums and percussion involves playing not one single instrument, but many. The instruments vary in size, placement, force needed for excitation, and kinesthetic feedback to the player, who has to adapt accordingly. Range and types of movements can vary considerably with the kinds of percussion that are to be played in one particular setting.

Percussion instruments generally produce sounds with impulse-like characteristics, a shared property that distinguishes them from most other instruments (such as woodwind or strings). Normally, onset times and durations are short and the player's direct contact with the instrument is limited to a few milliseconds. Because of the short contact times, the player has little control over the tone once it is initiated. This implies that whatever resulting striking force and dampening effect the percussionist wants to induce needs to be integrated into the entire striking gesture. That is, the movement trajectory of the striking gesture will be directly linked to the sound level, duration, and timbre of the stroke.

Although a lot of percussion is played with the hands, it is more common to use a striking tool of some kind. Striking with a mallet, stick, or hammer allows the player to excite the instrument more vigorously (through a higher striking velocity) than would be possible using only the hand. By changing the shape, hardness, and weight of the tool it is also possible to alter the timbre of the instrument played (something otherwise difficult for many percussion instruments). Typically, a percussionist or drummer will grip the drumstick or mallet so that it is free to rotate around a fulcrum point, most commonly between the thumb and index finger. In this way, the stick is free to rotate in the vertical plane, but the player can use the other fingers to stabilize or "lock" it if needed.

The sound-producing gestures in percussion playing include preparatory movements where the player ensures that the stick and hand are placed in the right position before the onset of each downstroke (Dahl 2004; 2006; Famularo 1999; Moeller 1956). Three examples of such movement strategies in preparation for a single stroke can be seen in Figure 3.1. Typically, the upward lift starts from the arm and the wrist, with the hand and the stick following. The middle stroke in Figure 3.1 shows clearly how the stick is lifted with the tip pointing down, and then flicked back before the actual downstroke. The leading of the wrist also makes it possible to start the preparation for a stroke even before the previous stroke is played. Such a strategy allows the player to reach a long distance in a short time span, useful both to cover large setups and to change between strokes of different dynamic levels (Dahl 2004; Famularo 1999).

Strokes at higher dynamic levels tend to be initiated from a greater height. By having a longer "runway" for stronger strokes, the player can play loudly at low physiological cost. The gestures become more smooth and efficient with practice. Professional players of drums and percussion tend to display flexible, whip-like gestures when playing, whereas students and beginners show less control over the drumstick (Trappe et al. 1998; in press). However, skilled players also experience problems when playing at extreme tempi and dynamic levels. To reach a desired high initial position becomes increasingly demanding when tempo increases and thus the combination very fast/very loud is difficult to achieve (Dahl 2006).

The stiffness of the drumstick or mallet does not only allow the player to excite the instrument with more force than possible with bare hands. The stiffness also allows the player to utilize the rebound from the

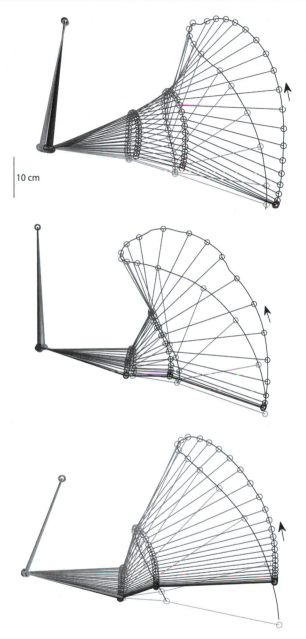

Figure 3.1 Examples of preparatory movements for single drum strokes. The stick figures display the position of three players' shoulder, elbow, wrist, finger knuckle, and drumstick each twenty-fifth millisecond. The arrows indicate the direction of movement at the initial part of the stroke. As can be seen, the movement strategies used by the players show both similarities and differences.

surface by letting the stick move "on its own." In this way, a single striking gesture of the hand can result in several hits, as, for example, Waadeland has shown for swing patterns (2006). Particularly in snare drum playing, the rebound of the stick can help the player perform more than one stroke per gesture, something that makes rolls and other complicated two-hand patterns possible to play. In studies of the closed roll, Miura (2005) reported that the players utilized "clusters" of strokes of three or more. The players controlled the onset of the initial stroke in each cluster, but the number of strokes for each cluster could vary from three to six.

The sound-producing gesture is closely linked to the sounds played, but its execution also affects our auditory *perception*. Schutz and Lipscomb (2007) have shown that subjects rate marimba notes as having longer duration if the striking gesture is longer. That is, even though the note duration in itself is not affected by how high up from the bar the mallet is lifted after a stroke, our perception of the tone length changes.

Gestures in Piano Playing

A standard grand piano has an extension of eight octaves, the keyboard having 88 keys placed over a length of 1.5 meters. When playing, pianists use both hands for the keyboard but also control the sound using three pedals: the *soft* or *una corda* pedal (also noted as 1C in scores), the *sustaining* or *damper* pedal, and the *sostenuto* pedal. Similar to percussionists, pianists experience short contact times and limited access to timbre and note duration. The combined control of sound level and articulation (legato/staccato, i.e. whether a note is overlapping with, or separated from the following) is what results in the "touch quality," one of the main characteristics of the playing style of a pianist. By controlling the key-motion, the pianist can control the final striking velocity of the hammer and, to a certain extent, the noise in finger-key touch, the vibration of the hammer shank, and the noise in the piano mechanism (Askenfelt et al. 1998; Goebl et al. 2004).

According to classical piano tradition a player can achieve a correct and effective posture by:

- Being seated in the frontal half of the piano bench so that the upper body can tilt towards the keyboard, facilitating weight distribution on the keyboard;
- Relaxing shoulders and arms;
- Keeping the elbows at a 90-degree angle when the hand is on the keyboard in order not to load the shoulders.

In jazz playing elbow position is traditionally higher compared to classical piano playing. This implies that jazz pianists by default use higher force on the keys compared to classical players, and therefore have a tendency to perform with louder sound.

In contrast with musical instruments such as the flute, there are a large number of possible fingering choices in piano performance (Parncutt et al. 1997). The player has to choose the optimal fingering based on the musical context and on the anatomy of the hands. To control a piano key not only are the fingers used, but also most of the upper limb, including the wrist, arm and shoulder (Ortmann 1929). The forearms in particular are used for transitions to keys placed further away from the torso. To manage transitions between adjacent keys, the player from time to time needs to reach under or over fingers of the same hand, a movement that typically involves a rotation of the wrist. Examples of such movements are ascending and descending in arpeggios and scales. The preparation for the transition starts at different times, depending on the context. Engel et al. (1997) showed anticipatory behavior for a "thumb-under movement" starting as early as 500 milliseconds, or several note events, before the actual note was to be played.

Ortmann (1929) performed detailed studies of different sound-producing gestures in piano playing. Using light bulbs fastened to players' hands he photographically recorded and analyzed different playing gestures. Figure 3.2 gives an example of hand movements during the playing of the first four measures of a Chopin *etude*. In the figure, the hand displays a continuous rotational and translational movement and the smaller

Figure 3.2 Piano gesture from Ortmann (1929, 290) showing hand movements during the playing of the first four measures of the Chopin *Etude in F Major*, Op. 25, No. 3. The letters in the figure denote the position in the score: *n, m* correspond to the second beat in the first and second measures; *o*, the last beat of measure three; and *p*, the last beat before measure four.

finger movements (not seen in the figure) are superimposed on this continuous, circling movement. Expert performers tend to focus on high-level aspects of the music performance, which may lead to more repeatability in movement strategies than less experienced players (Sforza et al. 2003).

Any additional force on the key after the onset of the note can be considered wasted work since it does not add to the sound level. Expert performers tend to reduce such unnecessary force on the keys (Jabusch 2006). However, this economical approach is not preferred during expressive playing. Pianists that play *con espressione* (with musical expression) display higher after-onset force acting on the keys, despite the fact that this does not add to the sound production. Experienced players also apply such "uneconomical" force to the keys during expressive playing (Tidemann et al. 2000). Interestingly enough, on the clavichord it is possible to produce a vibrato effect on the sounding note by varying the finger pressure on the key (Mulder 1981; Thwaites and Fletcher 1981). A similar control possibility, called aftertouch, has been implemented in modern synthesizers, allowing 127 different pressure values, which can be determined by the after-onset force (Välimäki et al. 2003).

Synchronization between key pressing and pedal pressing is required in order to achieve a clean sound. The usual technique is to press the soft pedal a few milliseconds before pressing the keys, and the sustaining and sostenuto pedals a few milliseconds after, corresponding to the notes being affected. Repp (1996; 1997) found that sustaining pedal timing has "a complex pattern that is sensitive to local and global tempo changes in varying degrees, yet exhibits consistency across repeated performances by the same pianist" (Repp 1996). He also found differences in pedal timing between pianists: for some pianists a constant ratio was found between Inter-Onset-Intervals (IOI) and pedaling timing, while for other pianists he found an absolute invariance of IOIs (Repp 1996; 1997). Playing with the sustaining pedal pressed requires a more controlled touch in the sense that any small error, such as pressing the wrong key, is amplified by all the strings vibrating in sympathy.

The above examples of drumming and piano gestures concern movements aimed to produce sounds at discrete points in time, such as a key press or a drum stroke. Although these gestures clearly aim toward a specific event, the hands generally display continuous, smooth movements that reach over several events (cf. Figure 3.2). This is typical for *serial movements*, i.e. "a series of individual movements tied together in time to make some 'whole'" (Schmidt and Lee 2005). For instruments that allow a continuous control of the sound parameters, segmentation of the sound-producing gestures is even less clear-cut. That is, the preparatory and the actual sound-producing movements overlap and are difficult to separate.

Bowing Gestures

Above we have dealt with gestures for instruments where precise control over timbre and duration is relatively limited. In contrast, skillful string players can, after several years of training, acquire the ability to control fine sound characteristics in detail. To achieve this, the player must master both intonation (i.e. position of the finger on the un-fretted grip board) and bowing; that is, the art of combining many parameters including bow velocity, bow pressure on strings, and the tilt of the bow. The complexity of the interaction between player and instrument is exemplified in the multitude of possible ways to play each note (see e.g. Young and Deshmane 2007). To be able to utilize the full range of notes of the instrument, the player has to perform whole-hand translations along the neck with one arm. Meanwhile, the non-bowing arm and shoulder are lifted and rotated in order to reach the correct string to be played. Consequently, most of the upper body is involved in playing. The dynamics of the bow itself can be regarded as the focal point of all the movements involved in the right shoulder, arm, wrist and hand. Figure 3.3 exemplifies this, showing the range of the vertical movement of the arm and bow during normal upbow and downbow strokes.

Winold et al. (1994) studied the recruitment of the elbow, wrist, and bow for specific bowing gestures during cello playing. This study compared excerpts by Brahms and Schubert that shared similar bowing patterns but were performed at different nominal tempi. They found more

Figure 3.3 Basic upbow and downbow strokes in violin playing. The curve and arrows indicate the direction and magnitude of the bow displacement.

special issue of *Organised Sound*, Myatt 2002). The mapping from gesture to sound can be fairly straightforward so that, for example, a fast
movement has a direct correspondence in the attack time or loudness of
the sound. However, with electronically generated sounds it is also possible to make incongruent, "unrealistic" links between gesture and
sound. Delle Monache et al. explored such incongruent mappings
between gesture and sound in a "dinner setting" ("Gamelunch," Delle
Monache et al. 2007). At a set table, sensors attached to bowls, glasses,
and cutlery were used to control sounds not typically associated with the
normal function of the objects (e.g. liquid sounds when interacting with
knife and fork).

Gestures can also be mapped to control higher aspects and structural
elements of the performance. For instance, it is possible to capture and
analyze a user's gestures and use them for controlling the emotional
expression of a given piece, much as a conductor would (Friberg 2006).
The gestures can be restricted to hand and arm movements, with the user
standing in front of a webcam, but full body gestures with the user walking, running, and jumping in a larger space are also possible. For instance,
Castellano et al. (2007) used a person's motion in a space to control tempo
and mapped how the body was contracted/expanded into sound level.

The gestural control of electronic instruments encompasses a wide range
of approaches and types of works, e.g. modifying acoustic instruments for
mixed acoustic/electronic music, public interactive installations, and performances where a dancer interacts with a sound environment. For these
types of performances and interactions the boundaries between, for
instance, control and communicative gestures tend to get blurred. In
the case of digital interactive performances, such as when a dancer is
controlling the sounds produced, there is very little distinction between
sound-producing gestures, gestures made, or accompanying movements.
To give enough freedom to the performers, the design of the interaction
between sound and gesture is generally not as deterministic as in performances of acoustic music. The performers, while still controlling
some aspects of sounds, can simultaneously adapt their movements in
response to the sound.

3 Communicative Gestures

Some gestures that musicians make are solely for the purpose of visual
communication. Other communicative gestures interact and overlap with
the sound-producing gestures. Davidson and Correia (2002) suggested
four aspects that influence the movements used in musical performances:
1) communication with co-performers, 2) individual interpretations of
the narrative or expressive/emotional elements of the music, 3) the performers' own experiences and behaviors, and 4) the aim to interact with

and entertain an audience. Although these aspects can differ, in a way they all relate to a performer's expression.

3.1 Communicating with Co-Performers

Gesture and non-verbal communication clearly play a role in the management of performance: manual gestures, nods, and winks are all important, as are musicians' postures and attitudes. For instance, by turning towards a co-performer and looking at her face, a musician opens up the possibility of eye contact.

Some gestures carry a specific meaning, such as the "thumbs up" or the sign for "ok" (the thumb and index finger touching to form a circle). Such "emblems" (Ekman and Friesen 1969) have to be performed in a specific way to retain their meaning. For instance, moving the thumb and the ring finger together to make a circle does not result in a sign understood as "ok." During playing, instrumental musicians generally have little opportunity to produce the right emblems, their hands being occupied with the production of the actual sound events. Nevertheless, players communicate with nods, smiles, and eyebrow flashes (Williamon and Davidson 2002). Players can also indicate direction using the head or other parts of the body not conventionally used for pointing. Such gestures tend to relate to the immediate (current) context and consequently they are commonly used to regulate the performance. Examples would be taking turns in improvisation or signaling a return to a certain passage in the music. Similarly, conductors have a number of these gestures to communicate to the players who needs to do what.

Clayton (2007b) argues that the topic of inter-performer communication should be opened for a discussion of inter-participant communication, acknowledging that people not regarded as performers can also play a role in the regulation or management of a performance, often through gestural means. This is certainly the case in Indian *raga* performance, particularly in intimate settings where performers and listeners are able to communicate easily through gesture and occasional verbal utterance. Similarly, Eldson (2006) proposes that pianist Keith Jarrett has a ritualized relationship with his audience and views his concerts as a creative collaboration.

On the basis of an analysis of one *raga* performance, Clayton (2007b) summarizes the role of the different musicians and the front rows of the audience in this process. In the case of performers he describes the different roles of the *tabla* and harmonium accompanists. The former actively engages both co-performers and listeners through gesture and gaze; the latter focuses predominantly on the singer she must follow. Clayton also distinguishes two distinct audience roles, which he describes as *response* and *participation*. In the former case listeners respond to a particularly impressive piece of singing, and can be observed to first prepare for such a response—exchanging glances with co-listeners and accompanists—and then respond physically and verbally after the event. In the second, listeners show their involvement in the music by physically demonstrating their participation in the long temporal structures of the music, joining the musicians in a gestural marking of the focal point of the meter (beat one, or *sam*). Gesture, therefore, provides evidence of different kinds of attentional behavior. Indian music moreover has well-established conventions for the gestural description of metrical structure: movements are not simply beat-markers, but have a more developed semiotic function in that different kind of hand movements can indicate particular points in a specified meter (see e.g. Clayton 2000, 61–62; Rowell 1992, 193–196).

3.2 Interpretation of a Musical Piece and Expressions of Emotional Intention

The communication of expressive intention through gesture to observers has been demonstrated in several studies. Davidson (Clarke and Davidson 1998; Davidson 1993; 1994; 1995), primarily used video recordings of musicians, utilizing point-light technique, where lights or reflective markers fastened onto a person are filmed in a darkened room, producing a clear impression of human movement (Johansson 1973). The violinists and pianists in Davidson's studies were instructed to play with three different expressive intentions: deadpan, projected, and exaggerated—instructions that were assumed to be used commonly in music teaching. The performances were then rated by observers on a scale of expressiveness that ranged from inexpressive to highly expressive. Davidson (1993) concluded that subjects were about equally successful in identifying the expressive intent regardless of whether they were allowed to only listen, only watch, or both watch and listen. Musically naïve subjects even performed better when only watching, compared to the other conditions (Davidson 1993). Similar results were also reported by Shinosako and Ohgushi (1996), thus implying that many listeners at a concert may grasp the expressiveness of the performance mainly from the artist's gestures rather than from the musical content.

Dahl and Friberg (2004; 2007) found that specific emotional intentions could be communicated to observers using movements only. In their study, players of marimba, soprano saxophone and bassoon performed the same musical excerpts to express sadness, anger, fear, and happiness. Observers rated the four intended emotions from video clips without sound and were able to identify sad, angry, and happy performances. However, the fearful performances were not successfully communicated in their study.

Reducing the visual information available affects the expressive communication between performer and observer. The effect depends on which parts of the performer are visible. In the study by Dahl and Friberg (2004; 2007), the marimba player was shown in full or partly occluded. The reduced visual information had an effect but mainly for the communication of sadness and anger. Specifically, observation of the performer's head proved to be important to identifying the sad performances. While the head movements do not appear to be connected to the sound-producing gestures, the head still displayed the same general movement characteristics as the whole body image for the sad intention: slow, small, smooth, and regular movements. Slow and smooth movements were associated with sad performances for all three recorded musicians. Anger was primarily associated with jerky movements; happy with large and somewhat fast movements; and fear with small and somewhat jerky movements. However, since the communication of fear failed, its characterization is questionable (Dahl and Friberg 2004; 2007).

Using movement tracking, Davidson (1994) measured the expressive movements used by a pianist and found that there were only small differences in the extent of hand movements between performance conditions. By comparison, the range of the head movements in both vertical and horizontal directions differed significantly between the different performances. Differences were particularly evident between deadpan and projected performances.

In dance, where the arms generally are free to move without being constrained by sound-producing gestures, the position of the arms is used to express and detect different emotional intentions. Camurri et al. (2003) found that dance performances of joy were characterized by fluent gestures with few movement pauses and with the limbs outstretched. Fear, in contrast, had a high contraction index, i.e. the limbs were often close to the center of gravity.

In interpreting a piece, the gestures of musicians tend to convey information about the musical structure. For example, in one study pianists have been observed to use gestures like elbow circles, wrist pulsations, and head tilts which occur on main beats in a bar, whereas hand lifts seemed to be used to highlight the end of phrases (King 2006). Davidson reports how the torso of one pianist displayed a "small wiggling movement" during a phrase, and how the musical section was ended by nodding with head and torso during the final chords (Davidson 2006). However, these observations are not enough to determine whether the gestures really have a causal relationship to the musical structure. That is, if they should be interpreted as the player's expression of, and not reaction to, the musical structure. For although Davidson has also shown that swaying movements, in the direction towards and away from the keyboard, appear frequently, their relation to the musical structure is not always clear (e.g. Davidson 2007; Clarke and Davidson 1998).

Woodwind Gestures

The sound-producing gestures of wind instrumentalists are not as large and readily observed as those used by, for instance, pianists or string players. In general, the fingers do not leave the keys and the main preparation for the onset of a note can be found in the breathing and embouchure. This does not mean that wind players display fewer gestures. The fact that wind instrumentalists are "attached" to their instrument via the mouth piece or reed makes the instrument somewhat of an extension of the player's own body. If the player raises the head or the arms the instrument must follow, amplifying the visual gesture and making it easier to see.

Gestures are frequently displayed among wind instrumentalists and have been shown to be an important part of performance (see e.g. Wanderley et al. 2005). Studying video recordings of five clarinettists performing the same solo piece, Wanderley and co-workers have reported a number of gestures (Wanderley et al. 2005), such as performing circular movements with the clarinet bell, raising or lowering the instrument, moving the head or shoulders up and down, bending at the waist or at the knees, stepping or shifting weight from one foot to the other, curling the back, and flapping the arms.

Different performers utilized the different types of movement to different extents, although moving the head or the clarinet bell up and down was frequently observed in all performers (Wanderley 2002; Wanderley et al. 2005). Each clarinettist also displayed these movements very consistently between different repetitions of the same piece, also with several months between measurements (Wanderley 2002). When the same piece was performed in different manners, "standard" or "expressive," the same type of movement features appeared with only a difference in magnitude. Also when instructed to try to play without unnecessary movements ("immobilized"), the performers tended to display similar vertical movement of the clarinet bell, only to a much lesser extent (Wanderley 2002).

3.3 Entertaining an Audience

As already noted, visual gestures play an important role in stage performance. To establish a relationship with an audience the performer will use gestures with multiple functions. Not only do the communicative gestures help an entertainer to deliver a musical narrative, but they also tell the audience something about his or her own personality. Davidson (2006) notes how certain self-referencing movements during a performance by Robbie Williams give the audience access to information about his own inner states. Examples of such "adaptive" behaviors, indicating comfort or discomfort, can be self-reassuring movements like stroking or touching ones own face with the hand, rubbing the ear lobe, or adjusting one's clothes. At the same time, the performer also acts out as the "stage persona", the star the audience is there to see, displaying "cliché" poses such as raising an arm and pointing to the sky, full body dance-like spins, and upward scooping hand gestures to encourage audience participation (Davidson 2006).

Using available video footage of the progressive rock band Genesis's performances, Leante (2007) has investigated the gestures used by singer Peter Gabriel on stage. Drawing on categories defined by McNeill (1992), Rimé and Schiaratura (1991), and Clayton (2005), and on the definition of gesture proposed by Kendon (2004), Leante investigated how the singer used gestures (alongside his costumes) to enrich the song "The Musical Box" with meanings that anticipate or highlight the content of the lyrics. For example, a single pantomimic gesture (the hands moving as though "grabbing" something) was associated with four different verbs ("wanting", "feeling", "knowing", and "touching"). Leante argues that the grabbing movement conveys a stronger sense of physicality, or tactility than is expressed in the text, and adds to the pathos of the already disturbing erotic implications of the story. Moreover, it acts as a preemptive strategy, as it anticipates the emergence of the explicit tactile element in the lyrics: once this is introduced in the text, the overall iconicity of the performance relies more on the introduction of deictic and beat marker gestures. The analysis of Gabriel's gesturality and its developments sheds light on the meaning attributed to this song, in the way it was thought up during the Genesis tours and, most of all, it allows one to understand how the performer structured the representation of the story narrated in the lyrics (Leante 2007).

4 Sound-Facilitating Gestures

Some gestures appear to be neither communicative, nor directly involved in the production of sound. Nevertheless, these gestures may have a sound-facilitating function in the sense that they aid the production or modification of sound. The unique contribution of such sound-facilitating gestures may be hard to isolate as they are overlapping with, and bridging between, the sound-producing and communicative gestures.

4.1 Co-Expressiveness Between Movement and Sound Gestures

In work on gestures in speech, McNeill has suggested that the origin of a gesture can be one and the same as the spoken word (e.g. McNeill 1992;

2005). That is, rather than being subordinate to speech, the movement is *co-expressive*. McNeill argues that because the two—movement and speech—are synchronized, "the mind is doing the same thing in two ways, not two separate things" (McNeill 2005). There are many examples from music performance that seem to indicate a similar relationship between movement and sound gesture.

One example of how auditory imagery and movement are intimately connected in musical performance is how jazz improvisers often vocalize while playing solos on their instrument. Indeed, jazz pianist Keith Jarrett has commented that he imagines hearing the voice, not the piano, when playing (Eldson 2006). Studying Keith Jarrett's gestures during improvisation, Eldson notes how the body movements seem to be melodies acted out physically, for example through head shakes and twitches or by bowing the head over the keyboard (Eldson 2006).

Several researchers have investigated head and facial movements in relation to music performance (e.g. Caterina et al. 2004; Bonfiglioli et al. 2006; Thompson and Russo 2006; 2007). In her observations of a pianist, Poggi (2006) found that head, face, gaze, and trunk movements are not only used for communicating to the audience or to the orchestra, but also for expressing the pianist's cognitive and emotional states. In addition, it also seems that these movements accompany the sound-producing gestures of the hands and, possibly, even help them. In other words, Poggi argues that a pianist can use body movements to support herself when playing a melody, to stress the harmonic structure and the timbre, and to help control the sound level. Poggi accounts for this by suggesting that an analogy holds between movements of the hands and movements of head, face, gaze and trunk (Poggi 2006).

According to Poggi, movements used to facilitate melody tend to exploit a spatial analogy with regard to the sound-producing gestures. That is, the direction and amplitude of the trunk, head, and face movements are analogous to the movements of the hands. Gestures made with the intention of aiding rhythm tend to have a rhythmical structure analogous to that of the sound-producing gestures. Similarly, the gestures facilitating harmony and emphasizing the musical structure show an analogy with the visual image of harmony relations; gestures facilitating maintenance of tempo use the same tempo of the hands; and in order to facilitate timbre, the tension of body movements is analogous to that of hands. Body gestures and facial expressions are also used to help the pianist control the sound level (see Figure 3.5). Summarizing, Poggi states that a pianist can employ different body movements to facilitate the performance of a particularly difficult part in the score or to emphasize and communicate it to the listeners (see Table 3.1).

In a project on Indian Classical music, Leante (in press) observed how *kinetic anaphones*, i.e. sonic rendition of paramusical experiences

Figure 3.5 Pianist Marcella Crudeli frowns when playing at a forte dynamic level. Possibly the gesture is helping the player to communicate a state of severity and strength.

(Tagg 2004) participate in processes of gestural interconversion. Such anaphones are implicated—albeit at different levels—in a single process of embodiment involved in the construction of meaning in music performance. In one specific example, several musicians associated distinct images to a *rag*, with particular reference to an ascending interval

Table 3.1 Observed movements used by a pianist during a performance, possibly used to help expressing the musical structure and the playing of technically demanding parts (see Poggi 2006)

Aim	Player's Body Movement	Meaning
Help Melody	Wave trunk and shoulders	Help arpeggio
	Moves trunk to left backward	Help play low keys
	Circular movement	Help hands go and back
	External eyebrows raised	Help high notes
	Internal eyebrows raised	Help grace notes
	Squeezes and then opens eyes	Help grace notes
Help Rhythm	Shakes head rhythmically every two 4-note groups	Help rhythm
	Shakes head at each stroke	Help rhythm
	Raises eyebrows rhythmically	Help rhythm
	Lowers and then raises eyebrows once	Help count during the point
Help Harmony – Musical structure	Lowers eyebrows	Help repeat a passage a major third lower
	Raises eyes	Help end of musical phrase
Help Tempo	Shakes head very fast	Help Tempo
Help Timbre	Raises external eyebrows	Help Timbre
	Smart and cunning smile	Help Timbre
Help Sound Level	Moves trunk to up left	Help playing with a soft touch
	Shakes head at each stroke	Help Forte
	Frowns	Help Forte
	Raises whole eyebrows	Help playing with a soft touch

that is characteristic of that *rag*. The performance of this interval, though, was in most cases accompanied by a similar gesture (see also Clayton 2005). One can argue that this gesture conveys something that is embedded in the *rag* at a deeper level than the meanings and the specific images attributed to it by the individual musicians. The different images described by the musicians, therefore, can be understood if considered in the light of this common gesture and the qualities that are embodied through it.

Clayton, Leante, and collaborators (Fatone et al. in press) have noticed how North Indian singers produce sound-facilitating gestures in order to obtain a specific sound quality and to organize the punctuation of musical phrases. Singer Sudokshina Chatterjee, for example, explained her habit of singing with her arm reaching out and up and with her hand open and the palm facing up. Sudokshina's explanation of this gesture refers to her own experience and the teaching her guru gave her. By drawing a parallel between "open/closed hand" and "open/closed sound," the singer highlights the co-expressiveness between gesture and sound: "Ustad Bade

Ghulam Ali Khan Sahab used to say you have an open sound if you have a open hand. My teacher also says [that] you should open you[r] hand. Then you will have an open sound" (Sudokshina Chatterjee—interview, April 20, 2004, Fatone et al. in press).

Another example from Indian music arose during a conversation with *khyal* singer Veena Sahasrabuddhe, who showed how she employs pantomimic gestures in order to stress certain moments of the performance. She explained in an interview how she uses the image of "tying a knot" when singing a specific embellishment called *khatka*, in which a degree of the scale is introduced by a quick ornament. The singer was observed, on another occasion, using this very gesture repeatedly in the context of a teaching session, in order to demonstrate *khatka* embellishments to her students (see Figure 3.6).

The gradual alteration of movements depending on, preceding, or following movement elements is called *coarticulation*. The phenomenon is well known in speech, where the sound of a phoneme is altered depending on what phoneme is to follow. Intuitively one might assume that such alterations are the result of the motor system looking for "shortcuts" between one action and the following, with no communicative purpose. However, studies indicate that one reason for coarticulation may be partly to enhance the certain communicative features of the sound or gesture. In an example from finger spelling, Jerde et al. (2006) found coarticulation to be a communicative strategy to enhance intelligibility. As shown in the examples from piano and bowing earlier in this chapter, it is quite possible, that coarticulation is also present in instrumental performances.

4.2 Movements Stabilizing and Supporting Performance

Some movements seem to have more of a stabilizing role than actually a controlling or communicative one. Examples would be body sway and different kinds of rhythmic tapping or rocking motions. The role of these kinds of movements has not been much studied in music performance but work in other areas gives some indication that these types of movements may, in fact, influence performance. For instance, Stoffregen et al. (2000) showed that reading was facilitated by body sway.

In a study of body posture during trumpet playing, Bejjani and Halpern (1989) found that the players bent the knees more when playing sustained high F than they did when playing a low C. The authors speculated that the changes in posture might be related to the respiratory process. As higher notes require higher expiratory air pressures, the abdominal muscles are recruited to greater extent, slightly displacing the center of gravity. Thus, the knee-flexion could be part of a postural adjustment, involving more of the body for the higher tones.

Figure 3.6 Veena Sahasrabuddhe using gestures to illustrate the tying of a knot when singing *khatka*, here showing different stages left to right, top to bottom.

It is not difficult to see breathing being intimately connected to tone production for singers or wind instrumentalists. However, for other instrumentalists gestures may also be influenced by breathing patterns. King (2006) discusses how respiratory patterns can be associated with certain gestures. For instance, inhalation can be associated with forward body sway during piano playing, or with an upstroke for the violin (as Szende and Nemessuri found in the performance of Bach *minuets*; see King 2006). Eldson (2006) also notes how Keith Jarrett seems to "consciously regulate his breath" to fit the phrases during playing.

Other examples of supporting gestures are batons, i.e. gestures that "beat out the tempo of mental locomotion" (Ekman 1999; Ekman and Friesen 1969), or "temporal highlighting" (McNeill 2005). Such gestures, used to keep synchronization with a beat can be hand-pacing movements, foot tapping, rocking motions, "bouncing," etc. Eldson reports how Keith Jarrett, while playing a groove, frequently stands up, rocks from heel to toe and regularly stamps with his left foot (Eldson 2006).

5 Sound-Accompanying Gestures

Certain gestures are performed in response to sound and may, in some cases, modify the production of subsequent phrases or notes. Examples of such modification can be found in improvisation, e.g. jam sessions among musicians and improvised head bobbing (or banging) to accompanying music.

When discussing gestures made in response to sound, dance naturally comes to mind. However, not all dancing is done in the context of music or sounds, and not all gestures made in response to sounds are dance. Dance is an art form of its own with a wide range of gestures and means for expression—far too many to be considered in this chapter. Instead, we will look more closely at phenomena that we can assume occur whenever dance is made in response to music; namely the conscious or unconscious synchronization and interaction between co-participants in a performance: entrainment.

Entrainment

The concept of entrainment describes the way in which different rhythmic systems interact with each other, and has been applied to the study of attention (Large and Jones 1999; Large 2000; Drake et al. 2000; Barnes and Jones 2000), and via Large and Kolen's (1994) model, into London's recent theory of musical meter (2004). Clayton (2007a) has proposed that a human tendency to spontaneously entrain physical movement may lead to the spontaneous emergence of musical meter. The temporal highlighting or batons, described in section 4.2, can well be considered as evidence for entrainment.

Synchronizing with music simply by tapping a foot or waving a hand may appear to have little to do with musical gesture. However, on this low movement level the musical structure also influences our behavior. Recent results highlight the difference between synchronizing with music and with metronomic (isochronous) tempo. In studies of tapping, Repp (2006) has shown that participants altered the durations between taps according to the metrical structure of the music. The metrical markings occurred when listeners tapped to music presented without expressive timing variations, but not for metronomic patterns without melody. Imagining the music while tapping to a metronome also resulted in markings of the metrical structure of the piece.

Visible movements are not necessary for entrainment to occur. Performers can refrain from moving while being attuned to an external pulse. However, the fact that visible movements so frequently occur with entrainment may indicate that these movements somehow makes the synchronization with external events easier and less attention demanding, thereby freeing cognitive resources for other tasks.

Clayton (2007a) used video-based observational analysis and circular statistics (Clayton et al. 2005) in a case study of Indian *rag* performance. The study concerned beat marking gestures and the playing of the *tanpura*, a drone-producing lute which is supposed to be played in a regular rhythm that is unrelated to any other rhythmic structure in the music. Clayton's study demonstrates that not only can the entrainment between two musicians marking the "same" beat be quantified—i.e. the strength of coupling and the mean phase angle between the two time series can be determined—it can also be shown that in some, though not all, cases, different *tanpura* players entrain to each other and/or to the beat being marked gesturally.

Musicologists tend to assume that in musical performance different participants intend simply to be "in time" with each other, i.e. synchronized and in-phase. However, various factors complicate the true picture, as follows. (1) Even if musicians intend to play exactly in time, their actual behavior will certainly involve a continual mutual adjustment in order to maintain their mutual entrainment. (2) Even if musicians believe they are playing exactly in time, in practice playing fractionally ahead of or behind another player often feels better: the terms *swing* and *groove* refer, at least in part, to these timing relationships. (3) There are many instances of musical behavior in which musicians do not intend to play in time with each other. One is the *tanpura* playing example cited above. Another example described in the literature is the Afro-Brazilian *Congado* ritual, in which different groups (comprising drummers, percussionists and dancers) intend to play together with each other, but resist entrainment to other groups who are co-present in the same space (see Lucas 2002). This intention is linked to social and spiritual factors, and ethnographic research is essential in order to understand participants' intentions, just as statistical analysis is necessary in order to establish the extent to which these intentions are achieved in practice. Observation of gesture, as well as analysis of sound recordings, can be an important source of information regarding both conscious and unconscious entrainment processes.

6 Conclusion

In this chapter we have seen examples of the different roles that gestures have during music performance. Gestures function on many levels, both directly and indirectly controlling the sound and communicating with audience and co-performers.

A musical performance does not have to be seen in order to be understood. We are fully capable of appreciating music played from recordings. However, being able to see the movements of a performer obviously contributes a great deal of information that, in turn, adds to the experience. This may explain why we as listeners also are eager to get seats that allow us to see the performance. The visual gestures give us a richer experience and establish a sense of community in which we as audience participate more fully.

From a sound controlling point of view, one might ask whether there are specific benefits for musicians who use more movements than the "bare necessities," i.e. other than purely sound-producing gestures. Let us once again consider our starting example with the string section, all possessing the same basic skill and ability. What does it mean when a single player stands out by *not* moving? Does the absence of some of the gestures for this player make the playing different in any way? In other words, will this player perform with more ease or difficulty compared to the others?

There are different views as to whether or not gestures ought to be part of music performance. For instance, some schools of piano technique recommend very contained movements of trunk and head, sometimes even preventing facial and bodily expression of emotions. These schools theorize that the more you keep your emotions inside the body, the better you finally express them through the music (Caterina et al. 2004). In contrast, other technical schools instead encourage bodily gestures and expression during performance. The argument here is that musical execution and expression should not be wasted, and also that gestures can help the performer to obtain a better sound. There are also pianists who choose a third way, which calls for finding a balance between the two. In general, the choice of whether or not to use gestures beyond those that are sound-producing is a personal choice of the pianist, developed during years of practice and experience.

Indian singers present a different example, also covering a wide range, from extroverted performers who use exaggerated hand gestures as a prominent part of their performance, to others (particularly women) who consciously attenuate their gestures. The latter case can be linked, in general, to the past association of women performers with the courtesan's salon: modern-day female singers may restrict their movement in order to project a "respectable" image. This highlights the role of gender ideologies in influencing gestural styles.

The usefulness of co-expressive gestures may also differ between instrument groups. As noted earlier, players of piano and percussion have short contact times with the instrument and very limited control over the tone once it is initiated. It seems reasonable to assume that players of these instruments would be aided by learning larger gestures, which can be controlled in more detail. In contrast, wind and string players have continuous control over the tone and even minute changes in a sound-producing gesture will affect the sound in some way, which may not be desired. For instance, moving the clarinet during playing will have consequences as to how much of the sound is reflected from surrounding surfaces or reaches a microphone (e.g. Wanderley et al. 2005).

The gestures used in performance have different, frequently overlapping, functions. Some of the gestures musicians use are intimately connected to the sound production, whereas many others appear to function as sound-facilitating, communicative, or combinations of all these. For example, body sway or bending at the knees can be movements used to express the inner state of the musician, to communicate the musical structure, or postural adjustments made to facilitate the actual production of notes.

Most research studies tend to focus on one aspect of gesture at a time, e.g. analyzing communicative gestures during performance. However, with an increasing understanding of the importance of specific gestures to individual aspects such as the control, manipulation or communication of sound, it becomes more important to study how gestures interact. To fully disentangle the use of gestures and their role in music performance, sound-producing, facilitating, and communicative gestures would have to be studied in combination. Studies looking at more aspects are still not common, because the number of players, instruments, score parts, and performance instructions for such systematic investigations quickly exceeds what is feasible for individual researchers to handle. One way of approaching this problem would be to build databases where data can be used by different researchers studying different questions. A database of performances by many players of different instruments and with different musical excerpts and expressive intentions would open up the possibilities for studying gestures in preparation for specific, musically important, events—that is, to study sound-facilitating and communicative gestures in combination with those used for sound production for the same piece. Increased knowledge about how different gestures interact and their relative importance would also be beneficial for the performers themselves.

7 Acknowledgments

The authors are indebted to Kjetil Falkenberg Hansen for contributing with Figure 3.4, and to Jane Davidson for valuable input.

References

Askenfelt, A., Galembo, A., and Cuddy, L. L. (1998). On the acoustics and psychology of piano touch and tone. *Journal of the Acoustical Society of America*, 103(5), 2873–2873.

Baader, A. P., Kazennikov, O., and Wiesendanger, M. (2005). Coordination of bowing and fingering in violin playing. *Cognitive Brain Research*, 23(2–3), 436–443.

Barnes, R. and Jones, M. R. (2000). Expectancy, attention and time. *Cognitive Psychology*, 41(3), 254–311.

Bejjani, F. J. and Halpern, N. (1989). Postural kinematics of trumpet playing. *Journal of Biomechanics*, 22(5), 439–446.

Bonfiglioli, L., Caterina, R., Incassa, I., and Baroni, M. (2006). Facial expression and piano performance. In M. Baroni, A. R. Addessi, R. Caterina, and M. Costa (eds.), *Proceedings of the 9th International Conference on Music Perception and Cognition (ICMPC9)*. Bologna, Italy, 1355–1360.

Bresin, R. and Battel, G. U. (2000). Articulation strategies in expressive piano performance. Analysis of legato, staccato, and repeated notes in performances of the andante movement of Mozart's sonata in G major (K.V. 545). *Journal of New Music Research*, 29(3), 211–224.

Camurri, A., Lagerlöf, I., and Volpe, G. (2003). Recognizing emotion from dance movements: comparison of spectator recognition and automated techniques. *International Journal of Human–Computer Studies*, 59(1–2), 213–225.

Castellano, G., Bresin, R., Camurri, A., and Volpe, G. (2007). Expressive control of music and visual media by full-body movement. In *Proceedings of the 7th International Conference on New Interfaces for Musical Expression (NIME'07)*. New York, NY, 390–391.

Caterina, R., Bonfiglioli, L., Baroni, M., and Addessi, A. (2004). Mimic expression and piano performance. In S.D. Lipscomb, R., Ashley, R. O., Gjerdingen, and P. Webster (eds.), *Proceedings of the 8th International Conference on Music Perception and Cognition* [CD ROM].

Clarke, E. F. and Davidson, J. W. (1998). The body in performance. In W. Thomas (ed.), *Composition–Performance–Reception*. Aldershot: Ashgate, 74–92.

Clayton, M. R. L. (2000). *Time in Indian Music: Rhythm Metre and Form in Indian Rag Performance*. Oxford: Oxford University Press.

Clayton, M. R. L. (2005). Communication in Indian raga performance. In D. Miell, R. MacDonald, and D. Hargreaves (eds.), *Musical Communication*. Oxford: Oxford University Press, 361–381.

Clayton, M. R. L. (2007a). Observing entrainment in Indian music performance: video-based observational analysis of Indien musicians' tanpura playing and beat marking. *Musica Scientiae*, 11(1), 27–59.

Clayton, M. R. L. (2007b). Time, gesture and attention in a *khyal* performance. *Asian Music*, 38(2), 71–96.

Clayton, M. R. L., Sager, R., and Will, U. (2005). In time with the music: the concept of entrainment and its significance for ethnomusicology. *European Meetings in Ethnomusicology, 11 (ESEM CounterPoint 1)*, 3–75.

Dahl, S. (2004). Playing the accent—comparing striking velocity and timing in an ostinato rhythm performed by four drummers. *Acta Acustica united with Acustica*, 90(4), 762–776.

Dahl, S. (2006). Movements and analysis of drumming. In E. Altenmüller, M. Wiesendanger, and J. Kesselring, (eds.), *Music, Motor Control and the Brain*. New York: Oxford University Press, 125–138.

Dahl, S. and Friberg, A. (2004). Expressiveness of musician's body movements in performances on marimba. In A. Camurri and G. Volpe (eds.), *Gesture-based Communication in Human–Computer Interaction*, LNAI 2915. Berlin, Heidelberg: Springer, 479–486.

Dahl, S. and Friberg, A. (2007). Visual perception of expressiveness in musicians' body movements. *Music Perception*, 24(5), 433–454.

Davidson, J. W. (1993). Visual perception and performance manner in the movements of solo musicians. *Psychology of Music*, 21(2), 103–113.

Davidson, J. W. (1994). What type of information is conveyed in the body movements of solo musician performers? *Journal of Human Movement Studies*, 6, 279–301.

Davidson, J. W. (1995). What does the visual information contained in music performances offer the observer? Some preliminary thoughts. In R. Steinberg (ed.), *Music and the Mind Machine: Psychophysiology and Psychopathology of the Sense of Music*. Berlin, Heidelberg: Springer, 105–114.

Davidson, J. W. (2006). "She's the one:" Multiple functions of body movement in a stage performance by Robbie Williams. In A. Gritten and E. King (eds.), *Music and Gesture*. Aldershot: Ashgate, 207–224.

Davidson, J. W. (2007). Qualitative insights into the use of expressive body movement in piano performance. *Psychology of Music*, 35(3), 381–401.

Davidson, J. W. and Correia, J. S. (2002). Body movement. In R. Parncutt and G. E. McPherson (eds.), *The Science and Psychology of Music Performance. Creative Strategies for Teaching and Learning*. Oxford: Oxford University Press, 237–250.

Delle Monache, S., Polotti, P., and Papetti, S. (2007). Gamelunch: a physic-based sonic dining table. In *Proceedings of the* 2007 *International Computer Music Conference (ICMC'07)*. Copenhagen, Denmark, 41–44.

Drake, C., Jones, M. R., and Baruch, C. (2000). The development of rhythmic attending in auditory sequences: attunement, referent period, focal attending. *Cognition*, 77(3), 251–288.

Ekman, P. (1999). Emotional and conversational nonverbal signals. In L. S. Messing and R. Campbell (eds.), *Gesture, Speech, and Sign*. Oxford: Oxford University Press, 45–56.

Ekman, P. and Friesen, W. V. (1969). The repertoire of nonverbal behavior: categories, origins, usage, and coding. *Semiotica*, 1, 49–98.

Eldson, P. (2006). Listening in the gaze: the body in Keith Jarrett's solo piano improvisations. In A. Gritten and E. King (eds.), *Music and Gesture*. Aldershot: Ashgate, 192–206.

Engel, K. C., Flanders, M., and Soechting, J. F. (1997). Anticipatory and sequential motor control in piano playing. *Experimental Brain Research*, 113(2), 189–199.

Famularo, D. (1999). *It's Your Move. Motions and Emotions.* Warner Bros. Publications.

Fatone, G., Clayton, M. R. L., Leante, L., and Rahaim, M. (in press). Imagery, melody, and gesture in cross-cultural experience. In A. Gritten and E. King (eds.), *New Perspectives on Music and Gesture.* Aldershot: Ashgate.

Friberg, A. (2006). pDM: an expressive sequencer with real-time control of the KTH music performance rules. *Computer Music Journal*, 30(1), 37–48.

Galamian, Y. (1999). *Principles of violin playing and teaching.* Ann Arbor, MI: Shar Products (3rd ed.).

Goebl, W., Bresin, R., and Galembo, A. (2004). Once again: the perception of piano touch and tone. Can touch audibly change piano sound independently of intensity? In *Proceedings of the International Symposium on Musical Acoustics—ISMA'04* (CD-ROM). Nara, Japan: The Acoustical Society of Japan, 332–335.

Hansen, K. F. (2002). The basics of scratching. *Journal of New Music Research*, 31(4), 357–365.

Hansen, K. F. and Bresin, R. (2003). Analysis of a genuine scratch performance. In A. Camurri and G. Volpe (eds.), *Gesture-Based Communication in Human–Computer Interaction*, LNAI 2915. Berlin, Heidelberg: Springer, 519–528.

Heijink, H. and Meulenbroek, R. G. J. (2002). On the complexity of classical guitar playing: functional adaptations to task constraints. *Journal of Motor Behavior*, 34 (4), 339–351.

Jabusch, H.-C. (2006). Movement analysis in pianists. In E. Altenmüller, M. Wiesendanger, and J. Kesselring (eds.), *Music, Motor Control and the Brain.* New York: Oxford University Press, 91–108.

Jerde, T. E., Santello, M., Flanders, M., and Soechting, J. F. (2006). Hand movements and musical performance. In E. Altenmüller, M. Wiesendanger, and J. Kesselring, (eds.), *Music, Motor Control and the Brain.* New York: Oxford University Press, 79–90.

Johansson, G. (1973). Visual perception of biological motion and a model for its analysis. *Perception and Psychophysics*, 14, 201–211.

Kay, B. A., Turvey, M. T., and Meijer, O. G. (2003). An early oscillator model: studies on the biodynamics of the piano strike (Bernstein and Popova, 1930). *Motor Control*, 7, 1–45.

Kendon, A. (2004). *Gesture. Visible Action as Utterance.* Cambridge: Cambridge University Press.

King, E. (2006). Supporting gestures: breathing in piano performance. In A. Gritten and E. King (eds.), *Music and Gesture.* Aldershot: Ashgate, 142–164.

Large, E. W. (2000). On synchronizing movements to music. *Human Movement Science*, 19, 527–566.

Large, E. W. and Jones, M. R. (1999). The dynamics of attending: how people track time-varying events. *Psychological Review*, 106(1), 119–159.

Large, E. W. and Kolen, J. F. (1994). Resonance and the perception of musical meter. *Connection Science: Journal of Neural Computing, Artificial Intelligence and Cognitive Research*, 6 (2–3), 177–208.

Leante, L. (2007). Multimedia aspects of progressive rock shows: analysis of the performance of "The Musical Box." In G. Borio and S. Facci (eds.), *Proceedings of the International Conference "Composition and Experimentation in British Rock 1966–1976," Philomusica on-line*—http://www.unipv.it/britishrock1966–1976/index.htm.

Leante, L. (in press). The lotus and the king: imagery, gesture and meaning in Hindustani Rag. *Ethnomusicology Forum.*

London, J. (2004). *Hearing in Time: Psychological Aspects of Musical Meter.* Oxford: Oxford University Press.

Lucas, G. (2002). Musical rituals of Afro-Brazilian religious groups within the ceremonies of Congado. *Yearbook for Traditional Music*, 34, 115–127.

McNeill, D. (1992). *Hand and Mind: What Gestures Reveal About Thought.* Chicago: University of Chicago Press.

McNeill, D. (2005). *Gesture and Thought.* Chicago, IL: University of Chicago Press.

Miura, M. (2005). Inter-player variability of a roll performance on a snare-drum performance. In *Proc. of Forum Acusticum* 2005, (August), Budapest, Hungary, 563–568.

Moeller, S. A. (1956). *The Moeller Book.* Ludwig Music Publishing.

Mulder, G. W. (1981). Tuning and temperament of the clavichord: or what effect does the vibrato and *bebung* have on affective tuning of this percussive stringed instrument? *Journal of the Acoustical Society of America*, 69(S1), S88–S88.

Myatt, T. (2002). Editorial. *Organised Sound*, 7(2), 85–96.

Ortmann, O. (1929, reprinted 1962). *The Physiological Mechanics of Piano Technique.* New York: E. P. Dutton.

Parncutt, R., Sloboda, J., Clarke, E., Raekallio, M., and Desain, P. (1997). An ergonomic model of keyboard fingering for melodic fragments. *Music Perception*, 14(4), 341–382.

Poggi, I. (2006). Body and mind in the pianist's performance. In M. Baroni, A. R. Addessi, R. Caterina, and M. Costa (eds.), *Proceedings of the 9th International Conference on Music Perception and Cognition (ICMPC9).* Bologna, Italy, 1044–1051.

Rasamimanana, N. H., Fléty, E., and Bevilacqua, F. (2006). Gesture analysis of violin bow strokes. In S. Gibet, N. Courty, and J.-F. Kamp (eds.), *Gesture in Human–Computer Interaction and Simulation*, LNAI 3881. Berlin, Heidelberg: Springer, 145–155.

Repp, B. (1996). Pedal timing and tempo in expressive piano performance: a preliminary investigation. *Psychology of Music*, 24 (2), 199–221.

Repp, B. (1997). The effect of tempo on pedal timing in piano performance. *Psychological Research*, 60 (3), 164–172.

Repp, B. (2006). Musical synchronization. In E. Altenmüller, M. Wiesendanger, and J. Kesselring, (eds.), *Music, Motor Control and the Brain.* New York: Oxford University Press, 55–768.

Rimé, B. and Schiaratura, L. (1991). Gesture and speech. In R. S. Feldman and B. Rimé (eds.), *Fundamentals of Nonverbal Behavior.* Cambridge: Cambridge University Press, 239–281.

Rosenbaum, D. A., Slotta, J. D., Vaughan, J., and Plamondon, R. (1991). Optimal movement selection. *Psychological Science*, 2 (2), 86–91.

Rowell, L. (1992). *Music and Musical Thought in Early India*. Chicago: Chicago University Press.

Schmidt, R. A. and Lee, T. D. (2005). *Motor Control and Learning: a Behavioral Emphasis*. Champaign, IL: Human Kinetics.

Schutz, M. and Lipscomb, S. (2007). Hearing gestures, seeing music: vision influences perceived tone duration. *Perception*, 36(6), 888–897.

Sforza, C., Macri, C., Turci, M., Grassi, G., and Ferrario, V. F. (2003). Neuromuscular patterns of finger movements during piano playing. Definition of an experimental protocol. *Journal of Anatomical Embryology*, 108(4), 211–222.

Shinosako, H. and Ohgushi, K. (1996). Interaction between auditory and visual processing in impressional evaluation of piano performance. In *Proceedings of the Third Joint Acoustical Society of America and the Acoustical Society of Japan*, 357–361.

Stoffregen, T. A., Pagulayan, R. J., Bardy, B. G., and Hettinger, L. J. (2000). Modulating postural control to facilitate visual performance. *Human Movement Science*, 19(2), 203–220.

Tagg, P. (2004). *Gestural interconversion and connotative precision*. (www.tagg.org, accessed November, 2006).

Thompson, W. F. and Russo, F. A. (2006). Facial expressions of pitch structure. In M. Baroni, A. R. Addessi, R. Caterina, and M. Costa (eds.), *Proceedings of the 9th International Conference on Music Perception and Cognition (ICMPC9)*. Bologna, Italy, 1141–1143.

Thompson, W. F. and Russo, F. A. (2007). Facing the music. *Psychological Science*, 18(9), 756–757.

Thwaites, S. and Fletcher, N. H. (1981). Some notes on the clavichord. *Journal of the Acoustical Society of America*, 69(5), 1476–1483.

Tidemann, J., Drescher, D., and Altenmüller, E. (2000). Ausdruck beim Klavierspiel: Eine Untersuchung zur Tastendruckdynamik. *Musikphysiologie und Musikermedizin*, 7(1), 13–21.

Trappe, W., Katzenberger, U., and Altenmüller, E. (in press). Expertise-related difference in cyclic motion patterns in drummers: a kinematic analysis. *Medical Problems of Performing Artists*.

Trappe, W., Parlitz, D., Katzenberger, U., and Altenmüller, E. (1998). 3-D measurement of cyclic motion patterns in drummers with different skill. In *Procceedings of the Fifth International Symposium on the 3-D Analysis of Human Movement*. Chattanooga, Tennessee, USA, 97–99.

Välimäki, V., Laurson, M., and Erkut, C. (2003). Commuted waveguide synthesis of the clavichord. *Computer Music Journal*, 27(1), 71–82.

Waadeland, C. H. (2006). The influence of tempo on movement and timing in rhythm performance. In M. Baroni, A. R. Addessi, R. Caterina, and M. Costa (eds.), *Proceedings of the 9th International Conference on Music Perception and Cognition (ICMPC9)*. Bologna, Italy, 29.

Wagner, C. (1988). The pianist's hand: anthropometry and biomechanics. *Ergonomics*, 31(1), 97–131.

Wanderley, M. M. (2002). Quantitative analysis of non-obvious performer gestures. In I. Wachsmuth and T. Sowa (eds.), *Gesture and Sign Language in Human-Computer Interaction: International Gesture Workshop*, LNAI 2298. Berlin, Heidelberg: Springer, 241–253.

Wanderley, M. M., Vines, B. W., Middleton, N., McKay, C., and Hatch, W. (2005). The musical significance of clarinetists' ancillary gestures: an exploration of the field. *Journal of New Music Research*, 34(1), 97–113.

Wiesendanger, M., Baader, A., and Kazennikov, O. (2006). Fingering and bowing in violinists: a motor control approach. In E. Altenmüller, M. Wiesendanger, and J. Kesselring, (eds.), *Music, Motor Control and the Brain*. New York: Oxford University Press, 109–123.

Williamon, A. and Davidson, J. W. (2002). Exploring co-performer communication. *Musicae Scientiae*, 6(1), 53–72.

Winold, H., Thelen, E., and Ulrich, B. D. (1994). Coordination and control in the bow arm movements of highly skilled cellists. *Ecological Psychology*, 6(1), 1–31.

Young, D. and Deshmane, A. (2007). Bowstroke database: a web-accessible archive of violin bowing data. In proceedings of *International Conference on New Interfaces for Musical Expression (NIME'07)*. New York, USA.

Chapter 4

Music and Gestures

A Historical Introduction and Survey of Earlier Research

Albrecht Schneider

1 Introduction

In a theoretical paper comparing the semiotics of language to those of music, the linguist Manfred Bierwisch (1979) discusses a number of similarities and some specific differences between the two. According to Bierwisch, music in general bears a "gestural form" (*gestische Form*), whereas language basically exhibits a logical form. And while it is essential for a writer using a language to be able to "say" (*sagen*) something, it is essential for a composer or musician to be able, by means of music, to "show" or "demonstrate" (*zeigen*) something. Condensing Bierwisch's detailed considerations into a table, the relations between language and music could be shown thus:

domain	origin/background in organism	mode of expression	paradigm	function
language	cognitive structures and processes	logical form	proposition	denotation
music	emotive, affective and motivational situations and processes	gestural form	gesture	demonstration

Bierwisch, apparently influenced by Wittgenstein,[1] by no means argues that language and music are mutually exclusive. Language, for example, often conveys emotional states; music, on the other hand, also includes cognitive processes. The idea, rather, is to distinguish both spheres in respect to characteristic features. A proposition, in this sense, is more or less abstract and, as a logical structure, neither directly linked to physiological processes, nor dependent on the dimension of time. A gesture, by contrast, is a temporal structure that, in most cases, comprises a sequence of parts, and that typically communicates emotional states (which in turn have their origins in physiological processes). For a number of reasons

(Bierwisch 1979, 52–56), music seems to be that part of human communication which best expresses emotional experiences through gestural form. It is this aspect that indicates that music, based on gestural behaviour and gestural forms, might be phylogenetically much older than language (see below). Though music in general may be addressed as a gestural form of expression, the types of gestures are manifold; in addition, the degree to which musical structures can be understood as gestures seems to vary according to practice in different genres of music and dance as well as with respect to cultural and historical context. It should be clear that the concept of gesture is by no means confined to European traditions yet figures prominently in, for example, music and dance of South, East, and Southeast Asia (see e.g. Matsumoto 1983).

In this chapter, I will first (1.1) outline the semantic field of the term "gesture" and related terms such as *geste* and gesticulation. Then, some basic features of gestures as both patterns of bodily motion and expressive musical formations will be discussed (1.2). In the following section (1.3), which has a focus on the Baroque era, a sketch of the historical background of concepts such as mimesis, musical rhetoric, and musical affect will be provided. Section 2 is devoted to empirical research on music and motion. Three concepts that, for factual, methodological, and historical reasons seem to be of particular interest, will be discussed in some detail. In the conclusion, earlier research ideas are linked to more recent ones.

1.1 Semantic Field of the Term "gesture"

The English word "gesture" is derived from the Latin *gestus*, which means posture or pose, and indicates certain types of expressive behaviour, in particular of the hands (in order to communicate certain feelings). In Latin *gestus* also means attitude. The Latin verb "gestio" denotes happy or cheerful behaviour including jumping around and rejoicing. A second meaning of the verb is wishing, desiring, or craving for something. In French, *le geste* means posture and facial expression, yet relates also to "step" (as performed in walking, or in dances) as well as to action in general. The aspect of action is inherent in expressions such as the French *gesticulation* (Spanish *gesticulación*, English *gesticulation*), meaning to make expressive movements with one's hands and arms. Further, this aspect of action is alluded to in medieval historical genres known as *gesta* (the Latin word for "deeds," e.g. *Gesta Romanorum*), or *geste* in France. Most famous are the *Chanson de geste*, a collection of epics (of the 12th and 13th centuries) which apparently were performed by professional singers (*jongleurs, histriones*). Johannes de Grocheo (Jean de Grouchy) who lived in Paris in around 1300, mentions the *cantus gestualis* as a vocal genre of the *musica vulgaris* in his treatise *De musica* (Stockmann 1985). In this context "gestualis" may refer to the bodily gestures and facial expressions of the performers who were reciting parts of the Chanson de geste, and who may have tried to illuminate or illustrate the content of the epic stories by means of gestures. In Spanish, the term for medieval epics is *cantar de gesta*. Around 1500, in German sources the expression *Gesten machen* (making gestures) is used to denote the action of comedians performing in public (Frobenius 2005).

In 1511, a German humanistic scholar, Johannes Cochlaeus (Johannes Dobeneck; cf. Krones 2003), writing on the various tasks of music, distinguishes four types of persons involved with music (*genera musicorum*), the third of which is actors (*histriones, mimi*). He says that it is the task of the actors to move their bodies in imitation of their voice (*ad vocis imitationem gestibus corporis commovent*). The term "gesture" is found in many works, particularly in the Baroque era, that give a systematic account of gestures accompanying speech or being part of certain dances (see Legler and Kubik 2003). In German treatises on music theory, compositional and performance practice of the time, gesture typically is translated as *Geberde* (*Gebärde*) as in, for example, Mattheson (1739). Though *Geberden-Kunst* first of all denotes dance, the term *Geberde* has a wider meaning that, in most cases, relates to certain aspects of mimetic as well as emotive behaviour.

1.2 Characteristics of (Bodily and Musical) Gestures

The concept of gesture comprises at least two different aspects or components with respect to motion, one being connected with actions of the body, the other with motional patterns of expression in a more metaphorical way.

(1) In general, gestures are considered to consist of movements of the body, or of some of its parts, whereby actions based on motor behaviour are performed with the aim of expressing something. Gestures, therefore, in many instances can either supplement and reinforce verbal or musical communication, or can even constitute a separate communicative code as is the case with sign language (French: *langage des gestes*; German: *Gebärdensprache*) used to communicate verbal information by deaf persons.

An art completely based on gestures as a means to communicate meanings is, of course, pantomime. This art is by no means confined to western culture. Indeed, certain types of animal communication such as the dances of ants and other insects (bees) as well as those of certain birds can be considered bodily movements aimed at transmitting information among the members of a group.

With respect to gestures meant to supplement or enhance verbal or musical meaning, one may point to the hand movements made by a speaker (e.g. a politician addressing the public) whereby he or she tries to illustrate and emphasise the meaning of his or her sentences. In this respect, gestural information as conveyed by hands, mimics, etc. may strengthen verbal information and may also add to the plausibility of statements as perceived by an audience. Similarly, many conductors not only control musical parameters by bodily movements but also try to shape the overall dynamic and sound balance of a work as it is performed. Typically, the right hand beats time while the left is used to indicate dynamic levels and contours (e.g. crescendo–decrescendo, tension–relaxation), agogic nuances, etc. The gestures conductors make, however, are not confined to their two hands: they often include their arms, head, and even the upper part of the body down to the waist. In watching a maestro on stage, it sometimes appears as if (s)he is struggling physically to master the immense structural and dynamic complexity of a particular work as well as to keep the orchestra synchronised (especially when conducting intricate metric and rhythmic textures, such as found in Stravinsky, or in Milhaud's *La création du monde*). Of course, there may be also a bit of showmanship in conducting. Claude Debussy in one of his (somewhat sardonic) reviews characterised the American bandleader John Philip Sousa as someone "who performs circular movements while conducting, thoroughly mixing an imaginary salad with both hands, wiping invisible dust, and catching a butterfly which has flown out of a bass tuba" (Debussy 1971).

In fact, the gestural behaviour of conductors includes: (a) actions that relate directly to the musical structure as well as to its reproduction by musicians in a performance, (b) actions that relate to the music and the performance in a more mediated way, and (c) actions that relate to the music in a more or less symbolic way. Among (a), one would typically reckon the movements a conductor performs with his right hand (with or without a baton), and probably the movements of the left hand insofar as these regulate dynamics and agogics. Among (b), the swaying of both arms or even the upper part of the body to indicate the overall dynamic "flow" of a given piece of music. Among (c), the well-known gesture of a conductor throwing back his head from to time to time to indicate reso-luteness, or even an "heroic" stance, fitting the "heroic" gestus of the music (as, allegedly, in Beethoven's Fifth Symphony). To be sure, a con-ductor with his gestural actions also strives to realise the expression marks as prescribed by a composer for the execution of a certain movement; these marks can relate to several parameters such as tempo, dynamics, and mode of execution (e.g. *Allegro agitato ed appassionato assai*, Berlioz, *Symphonie fantastique*, first movement; *Stürmisch bewegt, mit größter Vehemenz*, Mahler, Fifth Symphony, second movement; *Presto in motu perpetuo*, Barber, Concerto for Violin and Orchestra, third movement).

With respect to musicians, one may also distinguish two kinds of actions: those directly connected to actual playing technique and sound production, and the gestural behaviour that accompanies those actions (e.g. breathing, movements of the chest; cf. Cadoz and Wanderley 2000). Again, a third type of gesture is symbolic rather than functional. For example, the movements a violinist performs with his arm while bowing relate to the actual phrasing of the notes, and in part illustrate sound production and expressive playing technique. In this case, gestures are of functional relevance. A trumpet player in a jazz band may move his instrument up and down along with the pitch bends and glides he produces while operating the valves of the instruments (watch, for example, performances of Louis Armstrong as documented on film). In this way, his gestural movements may have an "iconic" quality though the particular movements may not have functional relevance (the same notes and pitch effects might be produced by a player not moving his trumpet up or down).

In many instances, the border between sound-producing actions, sound-accompanying actions, and symbolic behaviour is not clearly marked. For example, rock guitarists playing their "axe" (a solid body electric guitar) on stage often pose in typical ways that have been interpreted as demonstrations of power, resoluteness, and masculinity (or even virility). These interpretations may be the case, however, one also has to take into account ergonomic aspects: to execute styles such as speed metal on a solid body electric guitar necessitates that the instrument is in a certain position relative to the player's body, and that both arms and hands can be moved with little effort (low muscular tension). Thus, there are certain postures and motion trajectories better suited to fast and precise playing than others. In live performances of rock bands, one can observe that the bodily movements of musicians often correspond quite closely to the sequences of sounds they produce. Of course, there are symbolic gestures as well since, after several decades of rock music, musicians, and in particular the "guitar heros" found in many hard rock and metal groups, have developed a routine of stereotyped movements to supplement the repertoire of standard sound patterns found in so many solo parts. Such stereotypical routines, including gestures that are often seen as expressing power, freedom, and perhaps also machismo, are apparently expected by the audience as a genuine ingredient of a good live rock show.[2]

(2) Though the notion of gesture in general implies a movement of a body in space and time, it is the aspect of expressiveness as connected to motion which has led to the view that music itself is gestural, and that gestures are intrinsic to music. Given the qualification that gestures require a movement of a body in space and time, one can substitute musical notes, realised as sounds, for this "body." In this case, the gestural quality of music might rest in sequences of notes that are ordered so as to form coherent, identifiable phrases with an expressive character. Such gestures are, of course, found in many works of music. As an example, we might point to the opening phrase of *Syrinx* by Claude Debussy, written

for flute solo in 1913. Figure 4.1a shows the musical notation of this phrase, ending on a fermata. Figure 4.1b is a sonagram of the same phrase as actually played by a flutist.[3] Though western staff notation comprises the axes of pitch (vertical, approximately logarithmic), and time (horizontal, linear), the sonagram illustrates the actual sound pattern of this phrase in a linear pitch/time-space so that both the melodic motion and the expressive nuances of the performance (vibrato) become evident.

An analysis of *Syrinx* shows that Debussy organised the thirty-five measures of the piece into gesture-like phrases that a flautist will work out in an actual performance. Thus, the musical and dynamic structure will in turn support the perceptual analysis in which listeners engage. According to Thomas Fay (1974), a musical gesture is a musically and perceptually meaningful unit that is the result of a listener's segmentation process. A musical gesture thereby may exhibit properties known from Gestalt theory (e.g. completeness, distinctiveness, conciseness) yet the aspect of "movement," and of temporal–dynamic organisation is often of special importance. Gesture in music accordingly has been described as "a holistic concept, synthesising what theorists would analyse separately as melody, harmony, rhythm and meter, tempo and rubato, articulation, dynamics, and phrasing into an indivisible whole" (Hatten 2001). Gesture further has been regarded as "a movement that can express something" and as "an expressive movement that embodies a special meaning" (Iazzetta 2000). In general, gestures in music can be viewed as patterns of elements grouped in such a way as to appear to the listener as being highly integrated into coherent and meaningful wholes, which make up expressive units or building blocks. With respect to their coherent pitch and

Figure 4.1 Opening of C. Debussy's *Syrinx*, (a) score excerpt and (b) sonagram of the same excerpt.

temporal organisation, such units could be labelled Gestalten as well. This term, however, refers primarily to structural properties, whereas "gesture" implies an attempt to communicate or to express something. Structural properties are the means that make such expression possible. For example, a fanfare (typically an arpeggio of ascending intervals making up a chord in a major key) is heard as a sequence of sounds that have a distinct tonal and temporal organisation. However, such a sound sequence will be perceived by many listeners as a "musical gesture," that is, as a characteristic pattern that may have an extra-musical meaning. In fact, such sound patterns can have some indexical or symbolic meaning (e.g. a fanfare in many countries announces the arrival of a sovereign or other authority, or serves as a signal in a military context).

In a broader sense, musical and other artistic expressions that are regarded as gestures often seem to communicate a certain attitude or point of view including protest and provocation, as has been the case with many works of modern art and music. It was in this respect that Theodor W. Adorno (1978, 47–53) spoke of the *Schockgesten* contained in the works of Schoenberg (e.g. the monodrama *Erwartung*) and Webern. Expressive power (and also political awareness), also motivated Kurt Weill when he called for a particular *gestische Musik* in 1927 (which he attempted to write when cooperating with Berthold Brecht). To give but two examples of how musical gestures were composed by Schoenberg, we may point, first, to the opening measures (1–3) of his *A Survivor from Warsaw* (op. 46, 1949):

Figure 4.2 The opening measures (1–3) of Schoenberg's *A Survivor from Warsaw* (op. 46).

This beginning, with its upward and downward motional pattern signalling that something of significance or consequence is to follow, is a good case for what Rowell (1999, 381), in a typology of emblematic openings in music, regards as the "plosive" category of what he calls "tactical beginnings" (as distinguished from "strategic beginnings"). Compositions in this category open with a dramatic, often hyperbolic motif or gesture (like Beethoven's Fifth Symphony). The gesture opening *A Survivor from Warsaw* can be regarded as indexical in terms of semiotics; later in the same work, we find gestures of an almost iconic character. One example occurs when, as the poor victims are forced to count themselves, the tempo increases (measures 72–80) rapidly (from a ♩ = 60 to ♩ = 160), and because of the triplets governing both the narrator's declamation and the orchestral accompaniment, a galloping rhythm is established. Both musical elements, taken together with the narrator's text, have been shaped by Schoenberg so as to depict a scene of horror as it actually occurred.

Gestural behaviour is a mode of non-verbal communication, and apparently is found in higher animals as well as in humans. Both have developed a rather broad repertoire of gestures based on movements of the head, hands, arms, legs, or the body as a whole, facial expressions, eye movements, etc. It is of interest to note that there are significant convergences in the way members of various ethnic and cultural groups express certain emotions by means of facial expressions (Ekman et al. 1969; 1972). Though there are inter-individual and even intercultural similarities in gestural behaviour, there are also individual elements, or uncommon usage of otherwise well-known elements (by analogy to language use, in a group of speakers, an individual "speech event" or *parole* occurs within the framework of a common speech).

Since animals and human beings alike use gestural behaviour to express themselves, it constitutes a communicative code that is understood by the members of a species group. We thus have reason to assume that gestural behaviour is quite old in terms of evolution, and that it probably developed well before verbal communication based on articulated speech. So perhaps did elementary forms of musical behaviour that included the use of acoustic signals (Tembrock 1978).

It has been argued that gestural behaviour is mimetic in that it often imitates certain actions. Such imitation need not be fully realistic: it can be done by hints. This is the case, for example, in a ballet performed on stage, or in pantomime performances. Mimesis taken as a behaviour that includes imitation can be also regarded as a most useful method to learn certain things, e.g. to play an instrument. The concept of mimesis, however, is not confined to imitation: it also points to aesthetic behaviour that aims at subjective expression of experiences, thoughts, and emotions.

1.3 Outline of Historical Background

The idea that music is suited to excite emotional states, and to influence the well-being, behaviour, and conduct of listeners, was discussed by Plato and Aristotle. Both refer to a principle of mimesis (μίμησις), which, to be sure, in Latin texts has very often been translated as *imitatio*. Mimesis, however, should not be reduced to "imitation" since its prevalent meaning, at least in Greek aesthetics and music theory, is that of an artistic expression or representation through which observers and listeners perceive psychic processes and emotional states by means of music (based on melody, mode, rhythm) and gestures. Aristotle (*Politics* 1340a) argues that in listening to certain rhythms and melodies, their specific mimesis leads to enthusiasm and affection. Of course, mimesis can include aspects of imitation insofar as, in a drama performed on stage, the behaviour of certain heroes may be imitated to illuminate their character and personality. Aristotle (*Poetics* 1447a–1449b), however, provides a quite systematic account of: (1) the *means* to realise mimesis (e.g. colour, form [schema], voice, words, ordered sequences of tones, rhythm as ordered movement, gestures inherent in movements), (2) the *objects* of mimesis (first of all, human characters), and (3) the different *kinds* (τρόπος) of mimesis (for a detailed discussion, see Karbusicky 1986, 178–209).

Aristotle further discussed the nature of affects (πάθος) which, as a (mechanical) arousal of the soul, is brought about by some force (δύναμις). Thus, there is a clear relationship of cause and effect, a view that was still held by Descartes (1649) who offered a physiological explanation for the occurrence of affects (passions). In perception, the relation of stimulus and response (as studied in psychophysics) is regarded as one of cause and effect. In principle, this view was also held by Aristotle and his followers (e.g. Klaudios Ptolemaios) in respect to affects. Consequently, certain melodic movements, played in a certain mode (e.g. Dorian, Phrygian) were believed to give rise to psychic movements in a group of listeners in a more or less uniform way. That is, specific music was thought to trigger specific affects, while subjective differences in perceiving such music were either neglected or believed to be small compared to the emotional power the musical stimuli exerted on listeners.

The point of view sketched here relates types of music to temperaments and affects, thereby offering a rational basis for a causal understanding of the emotions and affects elicited by music. Clearly, this view was still valid in the Baroque era where we find some basic concepts that relate music to, on the one hand, speech, texts and the explication of their meaning, and, on the other, affects as well as perceptual and emotional issues, (cf. Dammann 1967, chapters 2 and 4, and Braun 1994 for a detailed account). These concepts are of prime importance for an

understanding of the music of the late Renaissance and most of the
Baroque era, much of which was conceived in gestural categories.
In brief, of the developments found in music theory, compositional
theory and practice as well as in aesthetic and other writings from about
1500–1550 on, the following three seem of particular relevance for
gestural concepts of music.

(1) The so-called *musikalische Figurenlehre*, which connects music
to rhetorics, developed principally in humanistic, Protestant circles of
Germany between, roughly, 1600 and 1730. In the same way that a
speech is well-formed, accords to a syntax, and is based on rules of
rhetoric so as to incorporate a number of set phrases and ornaments
(*ornamenta*) known to members of a cultural group, music should also be
well-formed by obeying the rules of a syntax, and by containing *figurae
musicae*, which can demonstrate the content of a (biblical or other) text
through musical *ornamenta*. This implies that formulaic musical elements
(*clausulae, figurae*) are used in a way suited to establish a correspondence
between the words of a text (as sung, or referred to in instrumental
pieces) and the music itself. The idea was that music should not only
illustrate the text (as it often does in indexical or even iconic relation), but
also contribute to the understanding of the semantic meaning of a given
text (for an example, see the analysis of music by Heinrich Schütz
provided by Eggebrecht 1979, 106–139).

The *Figurenlehre* (which led to more than a hundred music-rhetoric
figures described and elaborated in the literature of the time, see Braun
1994) and the *musica poetica* in general resulted in a repertoire of musical
set phrases, often with distinct patterns of rhythm and pitch, which were
used quite frequently. Such figures can be aptly considered musical gestures. The music of J.S. Bach continued this tradition, which can be traced
in his sacred and his secular works (e.g. *Matthäuspassion*, St. Matthew's
Passion, BWV 244; cf. Platen 1997, and for a semiotic analysis also
HaCohen 1999). Moreover, the gestural quality is not confined to those
figurae but is also evoked by musical textures in instrumental pieces composed of two or more voices that appear to sustain a kind of well-formed,
logical and coherent "conversation" because of the tonal and motional
interaction of the voices. Johann Mattheson, the well-known music
theorist and composer, not only elaborated on instrumental music conceived as "a tone language or sound speech" (. . . *eine Ton-Sprache
oder Klang-Rede*; Mattheson 1739, cap. X, §63), he also composed a
set of fugues and related works which he published under the title that
translates literally as *The Well-Sounding Finger-Speech* (*Die wohlklin-
gende Finger-Sprache*, Hamburg 1735—the second edition of 1749 is
entitled *Les doits parlans*). With his fingers "speaking" in musical phrases
that constitute movements in the tonal pitch/time-space (cf. Cogan and
Escot 1976), and that relate and "answer" to each other," Mattheson

demonstrates the conversational character of fugues and similar musical forms.[4] The technique of treating two or more interlocking voices in the form of a "dialogue" is found in many of J.S. Bach's works.[5] The gestural character of many subjects and countersubjects invented by Bach (as well as by his predecessors and contemporaries) reflects a problem peculiar to music. As has often been discussed, music can be compared to (natural) languages in respect to grammatical and syntactic categories fairly well. Music differs most, though, from (natural) languages with respect to semantics as music normally is lacking a lexicon of words that denote a certain meaning. Musical semantics, therefore, has to be connected with grammar and syntax as was the case in the Baroque, an era that, moreover, saw attempts at establishing at least the core of a vocabulary (consisting of *musicae figurae* and other formulaic elements).

Composers, theorists and educated listeners of the time were familiar with *figurae* as well as with rhetoric. They knew how to combine and group such *figurae* to elucidate the meaning of a (often biblical) text and also to express certain affects. Further, the notion of a *syntax* adapted from rhetoric played a major role in music theory. Since music rhetoric was considered a science to be studied, and composition a craft and an art based thereon (cf. Dammann 1967, chapters 2 and 3), one had to learn how to build well-formed "phrases" and "musical sentences" according to rules. Treatises on music theory often included aspects of poetics, grammar and syntax as applied to music, along with chapters on scales and modes, consonance and dissonance of intervals, mathematical issues, etc. Thus, music was treated as an art based on (mostly syntactic) rules that made it logical and speech-like, but also capable of communicating affects.

(2) Apart from the *Figurenlehre* the development of monody in Italy brought about another approach that closely connects music to language and speech. In this approach, the gestural quality of music is achieved mainly by means of declamation (cf. Fecker 1989, section II.4).

In the monodic tradition (based on voice accompanied with chords) known from operas such as Claudio Monteverdi's *L'Orfeo*, the *stile espressivo* and, more so, the *stile rappresentativo* capture the audience because the singer expresses a poetic text in a highly affective declamation; thus, the singer's delivery comes close to that of an actor on stage who attempts to emphasize the meaning of the sentences he speaks by means of bodily gestures as well as mime. This is what Emilio de'Cavalieri states in the preface to his *Rappresentazione di Anima e di Corpo* of 1600 (Krones 2003, 30). The singer in the monodic opera commands a whole range of musico-dramatic gestures. In particular Monteverdi is said to have developed dramatic and gestural elements (e.g. *stile concitato*), which enabled him and other composers to create musical dialogues, and to shape music as a *Klang-Rede* (a speech composed of musically organized sounds; Harnoncourt 1985). The term

Klang-Rede later on was extended to instrumental music (Mattheson 1739, see above).

(3) The affective element most evident in the monodic (Italian) tradition, and also discernible in German Baroque music, had theoretical foundations in physiological (rather: psychophysical) considerations as worked out by Descartes (1649/50), and also by Athanasius Kircher in his comprehensive work *Musurgia universalis* (1650). This latter book, written by a Jesuit who was a former professor of science, is a treatise on music theory (in the true sense of the word; that is, including mathematics, acoustics, philosophy, psychology). Kircher gives a lucid account of the relations of music and affects. He deals with the effects music has on listeners as well as with other issues making up the *musica pathetica* (Lib. VII, pars III), and he uses mechanistic explanations to demonstrate how musical motion can arouse psychic motion (*motus*), in human beings. The conviction that specific musical means (e.g. patterns of sounds which, for their motional and affective content, can be called "gestures") lead to specific affects (*passiones*) in some causal relationship, is at the core of the theory of affects (French: *théorie des passions*, German: *Affektenlehre*) that was of prime importance to musical composition, performance practice, and music aesthetics, in the 17th and 18th centuries (Dammann 1967; Zoltai 1970). In particular, it was held that music is suited to express, in a basically unambiguous way, certain affects (such as joy, sadness, grief, anger) by means of melodic and harmonic structures, rhythm, meter and tempo. Moreover, it was believed that music could resonate with listeners on psychic and motor-mimetic levels to such an extent as to drive them into catharsis, into ecstasy, or into any other state of strong mental and physical arousal.

In Sections (1)–(3) above, some major factors influential for the development of gestural styles of western music have been summarised. In the 17th and early 18th century, the view that music can be regarded as speech-like (in that both make use of sequences of articulated sounds, and can be used to express affects),[6] was widely accepted. It is not necessary, at this point, to discuss whether or not music can be a "language" capable of carrying and communicating semantic meanings without reference to a text. In effect, certain styles of music in the Baroque era worked as a kind of a sign language where the repertoire of signs valid for a certain cultural group was known to theorists, composers, and educated listeners alike so that the meaning of signs was comprehensible (at least within certain limits). In respect to Frege's classical distinction between *Sinn* (sense) and *Bedeutung* (meaning, Frege 1892), musical *figurae* and other formulaic elements have both a sense defined by syntactic categories and rules, and also a semantic meaning constituted by convention as well as by obedience to aesthetic principles. As has been pointed out by Kurt Huber (1953, chapters 5 and 6), the gestural quality of Gestalt-like musical (and other) formations depends on a declarative structure that brings their expressive content to full effect (see e.g. Figure 4.2). This quality needed to be inherent in the textures of a musical work as it was composed. It was emphasised, in historical performance practice, by means of artistic execution, both by musicians and by the singers who acted on stage. Opera, being closest to theatrical art, combined the musical and the bodily component of gesture in complex ways as evidenced by, for example, the detailed information available concerning the positions, movements as well as the gestural behaviour prescribed for singers/actors when performing operas by Handel in London (Eisenschmidt 1940/41; 1987, chapter 2).

The gestural element always has been a constituent of opera. Fürst (1932, 28ff.), in a chapter on musical gestures, distinguishes between what he (in accordance with Cahn-Speyer 1927) calls *Zweckbewegungen* and *Ausdrucksbewegungen*. Whereas *Zweckbewegungen* (purposeful movements) relate closely to the story of the opera as it unfolds, *Ausdrucksbewegungen* (expressive movements) do not relate directly to the action going on on stage yet express some emotional or affective process. The gestural element becomes particularly evident with respect to the music of Wagner's operas, and the actual performance practice he had in mind (as to the *Ring der Nibelungen*, see Hapke 1927, Janz 2006, chapter 3). Actors, being already characterised by musical gestures, namely their respective *Leitmotivs* (for a semiotic interpretation including gestural aspects, see HaCohen and Wagner 1997), were expected to emphasise their roles even further by means of gestural behaviour. As documents from early performances show, such efforts could have quite awkward results.

Aside from opera and other genres that include singers as actors, gestural elements occur also in instrumental music (see above). From about 1600 on, we observe the development of musical idioms in Europe that were grounded in tonality (a process which seems to have started in Italy around 1600). In addition, rules of musical grammar and syntax were formulated in order to regulate musical compositions that were inspired by rhetorics and poetics. This led to the development of a concept of music as a well-formed *Tonsprache* (language of tones) that, because of its usage of Gestalten and gestures, conformed also to rules of perception (Albersheim 1980). As shown in many works composed around 1800, standardised patterns of melody, harmony, temporal, and formal organisation occur in large numbers besides individual traits.[7] Typical (or even archetypical, see Karbusicky 1986) elements and patterns form a kind of "vocabulary," in certain musical styles. Musicians and listeners knew these elements and, in addition, knew a number of established patterns in which elements have been grouped according to rules or common usage. Also, elements and patterns can have indexical or symbolic meaning. For example, the so-called *lamento*-bass figures (sequences of descending seconds) introduced by Monteverdi is indicative of weeping and lamenting, and melodic motives (of descending minor seconds) known as "sighs" (*Seufzer-Motiv*) are found in large number in works by composers of the 18th century (most of all, in the so-called Mannheim School). In this regard, musical gestures did have semantic connotations. This type of "sigh" is still found, in its characteristic structure, in Schoenberg's op. 46 (*A Survivor from Warsaw*, e.g. measures 44–46).

Standardized patterns may appear as musical gestures to listeners when they can be identified against a background or context as specific formations based on tonal and temporal features. In addition, such gestures typically include some dynamic and motional shape, and they should express something. For example, a concise theme defined by intervals, contour, and rhythmic and melodic accents may express a certain motion in tonal space, and can be apprehended as a kind of musical "statement." Such statements occur, for example, in the contrasting themes of sonatas or, perhaps even more clearly, in call-and-response-type musical situations where one singer or musician starts with a gesture that is answered by another. A good case in point is bands with two lead guitarists exchanging gestures as statements, and responding to each other. For a simple yet illustrative example, listen to the solos of Joe Walsh and Don Felder of the Eagles in a live rendition of their "Hotel California" (Eagles Live, Elektra/Asylum Records 1980).

To sum up part 1, I have argued that the notion of "gesture" implies certain types of behaviour including bodily movements, facial expressions, and other elements. This behaviour is used for non-verbal communication, or to emphasize and reinforce communication based on a natural language, some special type of language (e.g. whistle language), or music. Musicians make use of gestures while actually producing music in the course of improvisation, or when reproducing works composed by others in a live performance. Composers organise musical *Gestalten* in order to evoke impressions of motional–dynamic gestures, or even to openly imitate such gestures through melodic movement, rhythmical patterns, etc. Listeners may indeed be moved by music in response to its dynamic–temporal organization and sound structure, which causes a kind of bodily resonance. Also, the emotional and affective expressiveness of a certain piece of music as heard can move listeners both in terms of a physiological as well as a psychic reaction (cf. Meidner 1985; Davies 1994, 229ff.).

Obviously, what unites the composer, the performer, and the listener is their biological status as members of the species *homo sapiens*. As they share the same anatomical and neurophysiological brain organisation, they can be expected to activate identical brain functions relevant to sensation, perception, and motor behaviour. In this regard, a particular area of the brain known as the supplementary motor area (cf. Libet

2004/2005, chapter 2) is of special interest since, on the one hand, its stimulation can bring about bodily movements as well as vocalisations, and, on the other, it is believed to be a neural substrate that is active in both perception and action. This has led to the hypothesis that, as a rule, perception involves some kind of action, or motor behaviour in general (including imagined actions). In psychology, there are long-standing views that relate image formation to bodily movements, and vice versa; that is, images are said to be accompanied by (typically, small) movements of the hands or fingers, and kinaesthetic sensations are regarded as giving rise to imaginations (cf. Sartre 1940). More recently, it has been hypothesised that perceiving an object implies imagined actions of how to use it; similarly, there have been theories that relate perception of music to imagined or real actions (cf. Godøy 2001; Godøy et al. 2006; Reybrouck 2001).

The important point, in the context of this chapter, is that there is a mutual correspondence between perception and action for which the supplementary motor area might provide the neural substrate. Since each individual should experience this correspondence, certain actions based on motor behaviour should lead to, or go along with, certain perceptions (and vice versa). This hypothesis (which can be tested as such) might help to explain the fundamentals of the experience of "movement" in music. The pulse we feel in a given piece of music, the melodic, harmonic and dynamic processes that we believe express motion and correspond to bodily movements (e.g. waving of the arms as in conducting, swaying of the upper part of the body), the rhythmic patterns we hear when listening to a drum fill or drum solo, are perceived in that we imagine relevant, music-related actions. These actions can be ours or those of another person. For example, I may imagine myself conducting an orchestra while listening to a recording of a work rich in harmonic and dynamic structure such as Ralph Vaughan Williams's *Fantasia on a theme by Thomas Tallis* (1906), or may imagine the complex interaction of the motions of hands and feet while listening to the drumming of Elvin Jones as he accompanied John Coltrane on *Transition* (1965).

When listening to a piece of music, we can also imagine its composer performing music-related movements such as conducting, or playing an instrument. For example, listening to Bela Bartók performing his own piano works (which include many passages in tempo rubato indicating the influences of Hungarian folk music) leads to images of the motions of his hands and fingers while performing. The idea guiding our experience of music as imagined action is that the musical gestures we perceive represent, at least to some extent, the gestural movements a composer actually made or had in mind when composing music. In respect to classical music, we might further assume that his or her (real or imagined) gestural movements were put to paper in a score, and are preserved more or less adequately in notation from which they have to be translated into music as organised sound, by skilled performers sympathetic to the intentions of a composer.

Given these conditions, either the score or a performance based on it should suffice as a basis for an analysis directed towards determining not only musical gestures, but also the bodily movements a composer performed or imagined, and the motional patterns, the pulse and the accents he felt when composing a particular work. Indeed, this assumption has served as the point of departure for some research, which has continued to attempt to prove this idea through empirical investigations.

2 Theoretical and Experimental Contributions to Research on Music and Motion

Though musical gestures played a significant part in European musical styles and genres long before 1900, research into motion and aspects of dynamics in music was accelerated over the course of the 20th century. There are several developments that seem to have been important in this acceleration. First, the course of Western art music styles up to 1900 should be taken into account. By about 1900, listeners attending performances of symphonic works such as those written by Schumann, Berlioz, Bruckner and Brahms experienced music that comprised intricate patterns of melodic and harmonic motion, rhythmic complexity, rich instrumentation, and a variety of dynamic levels. The differences between such music and, for example, the motets of Dufay and Josquin, or the cantatas by Bach and Telemann, are evident. These differences are manifest not only in musical textures, but also in motional patterns for which the Latin word *ductus*, meaning stream, duct, or trace (also pipes, mains) has been used. This word indicates that such patterns are perceived as types of trajectories based on melodic, harmonic and dynamic processes as arranged by a composer in a particular work of music. Such trajectories will apply not only to works in total but also to musical gestures, that is, to ordered sequences of tones that, as sounds, constitute a motion in a three-dimensional space comprising the dimensions of pitch, time, and dynamics (for the concept of a musical space, see Cogan and Escot 1976, chapter 1).

In the 20th century, a number of studies have appeared that address the issue of motional patterns, melodic, harmonic, and dynamic trajectories, etc. These studies assume that the overall *ductus* of music is not only different for different periods of western music history but is also specific to individual composers. Composers are therefore said to have a different "pulse" (so that the "Mozart pulse" should be distinguishable from the "Beethoven pulse").

A second development to be mentioned included on the one hand a fresh interest in the human body as a means of artistic expression and, on the other, a realization of the relevance of dance and gymnastics for education. In this respect, one may point to the so-called "free dancing" practiced and taught by Isadora and Elisabeth Duncan (Duncan 1903). Another approach was that of Emile Jacques-Dalcroze (1907, 1921) who recommended rhythmic exercises and gymnastics as means of education and artistic expression, an approach that had (and still has, see Seitz 2005) a huge impact. Among his students in Germany was Rudolf Bode who, with a group of co-workers, propagated a concept of *Ausdrucks-gymnastik* (expressive gymnastics), which included a special type of music. Bode composed a large number of musical pieces to accompany performance of his gymnastics. He and his group had their own journal: "Rhythmus. Zeitschrift für rhythmische Gymnastik und Erziehung" (founded in 1922; by 1962, thirty-five volumes had appeared). Another prominent dance pedagogue who contributed to the development of *Ausdruckstanz* based on rhythmic patterns, and who worked also as a choreographer, was Rudolf von Laban (1948).

A third development certainly was the scientific study of non-Western music and European folk music that commenced around 1870. Field reports from Africa, Asia and the Americas suggested that dance and the motor behaviour of singers and musicians played a very important role in many music cultures. In particular African musical genres and styles offered a broad spectrum of motional aspects, whether in dance, in handling instruments, or in groups of people singing together (moving their bodies, clapping their hands, etc.). In addition, the expressive use of the voice was investigated. For example, the comparative musicologist in Hamburg, Wilhelm Heinitz published a detailed study on the temporal and dynamic ("energetic") qualities of singing based on a large number of field recordings and some experimental work (Heinitz 1930).

In the next sections (2.1–2.3), some of the central approaches taken in studies of the relations between music and motion and with respect to *ductus* and pulse will be discussed. Besides theoretical considerations, many studies also contain empirical data based on measurements or experimental work involving subjects (musicians, listeners).

2.1 The Concept of Sympathetic Movements (Mitbewegungen)

The ability of music to communicate a pulse as well as to induce perceptions and images of motion is well known. A range of pulse phenomena based on a strict meter against which various rhythmic patterns are played, will be found, perhaps most of all, in contemporary dance music. However, motional patterns may also be perceived or imagined when we attend to the proverbial "flow" of a melody, the step-by-step climbing or falling of a melodic line (*Sekundgang*), or the swaying movement of harmony in a sequence of chords, etc.

It was from the experiences of actual music in highly developed forms such as the symphonies of Bruckner and Brahms that music psychologists and aestheticians first came to analyze and describe musical works, and the melodic and harmonic processes included therein, in terms of dynamics. In particular Ernst Kurth, in his *Musikpsychologie* (1930) understood music in terms of forces, matter, and space where musical processes are equivalent to streams of energy, and thus suited to evoke images of movement, which may occur as a *Tonbahn* (tonal trajectory). After an actual musical performance is completed, or a recording has come to an end, such trajectories are often retained in one's memory as geometrical shapes.

In a somewhat similar approach, Hans Mersmann, in his seminal paper "Versuch einer Phänomenologie der Musik" (1922/23), tried to outline trajectories of tonal forces that account for a certain kinetic "drive" which he and others believed to be inherent in many, if not all works of music. In a generalized way, musical styles in toto may thus be characterized by specific dynamic trajectories. In a historical perspective, this would be a means to compare different styles of music, thereby finding convergent or contrasting types of movement and tonal dynamics.

If music can be regarded as the unfolding of dynamic forces in time and space, it is only natural to conclude that such forces affect the listener. He or she may be inclined not only to perceive the motion inherent in musical processes, but also to imagine movements of his or her own body, or of arms and hands, in concordance with the motion perceived in the music. Such movements as a person feels to fit with certain music might resemble, for example, those a conductor makes when at work with an orchestra, or they could be similar to those known from ballet dancers. The next step, then, is simply to carry out such motions along with the flow and pulse of the music.

This is indeed what many subjects do, at least in private. Such exercises can be regarded as specific motor behaviour induced by music. If we move along with some piece of music as we hear it, and in concordance with its metrical beat or pulse created by patterns of elements which imply some regular segmentation along the time axis, the phrase structure and the distribution of accents may become sensible in an intuitive way. Hence, motor behaviour such as "armchair conducting" may be useful to complement the mental act of listening, and indeed may add a new dimension to a person's experience of music.

Since different works may induce different patterns of motions, as well as communicating different beat and pulse structures, it has long been hypothesized that certain structures may be peculiar to certain composers. The idea has been that indeed there is something like a "Bach pulse," a "Mozart pulse," or a "Beethoven pulse" inherent in the musical works of these composers and that there are similar specific pulses, in works of other masters as well. The most widely accepted method of discovering such specific pulses has been that of sympathetic or accompanying movements (German: *Mitbewegungen, Begleitbewegungen*). From available sources it seems that a Bavarian customs inspector named Josef Rutz (who died in 1895, in Munich; see Sievers 1924, 28; Becking 1928, 61–62) was the first to point to what he believed was a unique correlation between on the one hand three typical body postures supported by optimal muscular tension, and, on the other, three types of songs and poetry to be recited. Moreover, Rutz claimed that these three (basically ahistoric) types would go along with three distinct vocal qualities (*Stimmtypen*), three mental dispositions or temperaments (*Gemütstypen*), and three stylistic types (*Stiltypen*).

Since Josef Rutz never published his ideas, they are known only from writings of his son, Ottmar (born 1881; he became a lawyer) who tried to popularize as well as to amend them (Rutz 1908; 1911a; 1911b). The ideas of Rutz were in part adopted by the then well-known philologist of Germanic languages, Eduard Sievers, who held that poems (and also songs) have a specific structure whereby ideas and psychic layers are embedded in the words. To convey such ideas, each poem calls for a certain declamation based on a specific sound quality of the voice maintained through the recital of a single poem, and on adjustments of the sound quality in concordance with the lines and words of each poem. Sievers (1924, 8) labelled the basic sound quality that is constant for each individual poem or song, *Einstellung* (disposition), and the variable part of the sound, *Bewegung* (motion, movement). He further said that the specific psychic motion inherent in a poem or song, as well as in an appropriate recital thereof, can be projected so that a curve expresses the type of motion felt by a person reading a poem or reciting it. Apparently, Sievers understood those types of motion, and the curves corresponding to them, as gestures since he explicitly labels the point where a curve starts a *Gestenpunkt* (gestural point as point of departure of the respective motion; see Sievers 1924, 7).

Without going into further detail, it should suffice to add that Sievers distinguished what he calls *Generalkurven* (general or basic curves characteristic of an individual subject, e.g. composer, poet or writer) from *Spezialkurven* (specific curves unique to certain works). Sievers attributes the discovery of the general curves to Gustav Becking, a musicologist with whom he had cooperated in 1919 on a study of metrical structures in music (see Becking 1928, 16–17). Becking (who was born in 1894 and killed in 1945 in Prague where he had worked as a professor of

musicology since 1930—see Kramolisch 1975) was quite critical of the
concepts of Sievers (see Becking 1923/24). He condensed his extensive
research on meter and rhythm into a monograph *Der musikalische
Rhythmus als Erkenntnisquelle: Musical Rhythm as a Source of Insight*
(into musical styles as well as into *Weltanschauungen* underlying works
of art, 1928). In this book, Becking argues that, in order to understand
the type of motion inherent in an original work of music, one should let
oneself *be conducted* by this work rather than trying to conduct the music
according to one's own preferences (Becking 1928, 19). In this context
Becking introduces the concept of *Mitbewegungen,* that is, sympathetic
movements induced by a piece of music. Sympathetic movements can be
translated into *Begleitfiguren* (figures similar to such produced by conductors) which always start with a downward stroke to mark the *Voll-
schwere eines jeden Taktes* (roughly translated: the downbeat), followed
by whatever upward movement of the baton, another downbeat, and
so on. From the analyses of many works composed between roughly
1580 and 1900, Becking generalized his findings into a number of curves
which fall into three basic categories: (1) pointed–round, (2) round–
round, and (3) pointed–pointed. In the first category, we find Händel,
Haydn, Mozart, and Schubert, in the second, Schütz, Telemann,
Beethoven, and Schumann, in the third, Johann Sebastian Bach,
Mendelssohn, and Wagner.

Becking's interpretation of such curves in respect to music history and
the history of ideas and philosophical issues is beyond the scope of this
brief overview. We may summarize that the "Becking curves" (as they
were labelled first by Sievers 1924) can be considered to express essential
patterns of motion inherent in a large number of individual works
through a small number of *Schlagfiguren* or *Begleitfiguren* (see Figure 4.3
which reproduces the table of *Schlagfiguren* [conducting curves] contained in Becking 1928). Even if these curves may fit to certain works, or
at least to parts and movements of such works, it seems questionable that
the variety of works created by one composer as well as this composer's
personal "pulse" can be adequately represented by a single curve. Obviously, it is this reductionism that makes it difficult to accept Becking's
scheme.

2.2 Essentic Forms and Sentics (Manfred Clynes)

As is widely known, Becking's approach has been revived, at least in
principle, by Manfred Clynes who maintains that for each composer he
has studied there is a distinct motor pulse form that is not dependent on
the individual execution of a work by various artists, and that is similar
"for various pieces by the same composer" (Clynes 1995, 272).

More than twemty years ago, Clynes put forward another hypothesis

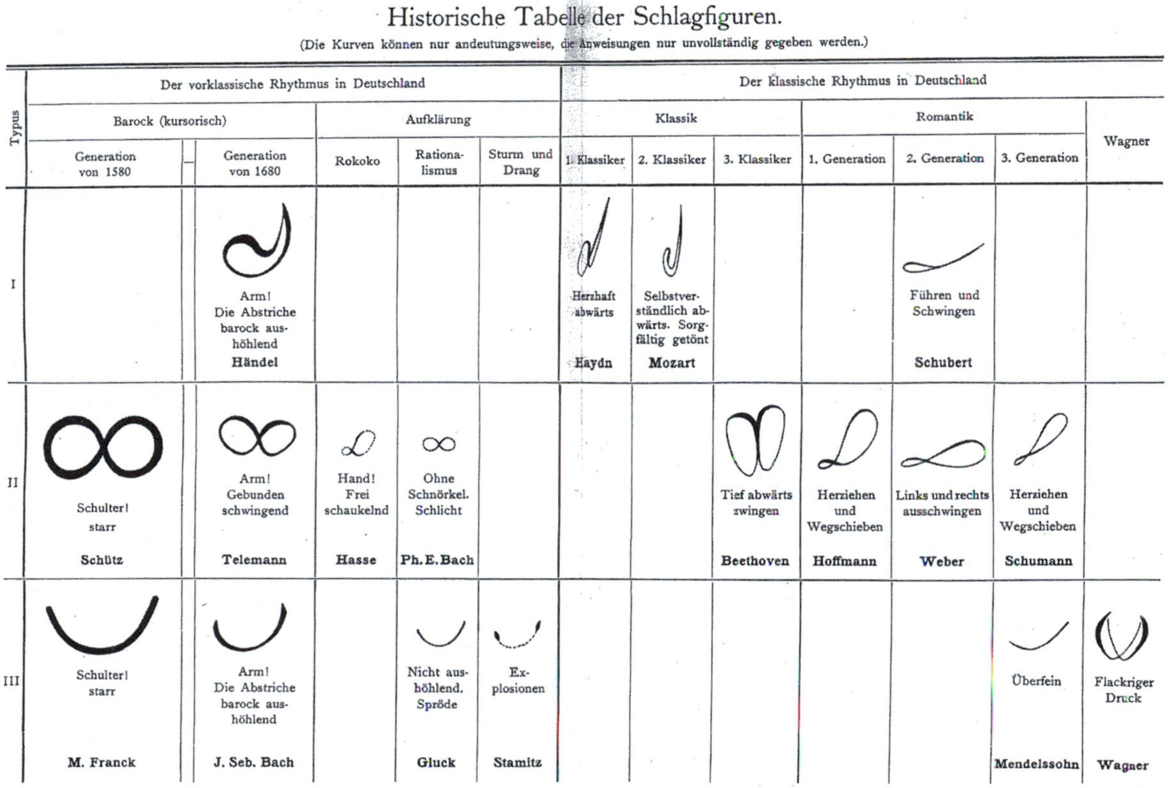

Historische Tabelle der Schlagfiguren.

(Die Kurven können nur andeutungsweise, die Anweisungen nur unvollständig gegeben werden.)

Typus	Der vorklassische Rhythmus in Deutschland					Der klassische Rhythmus in Deutschland						
	Barock (kursorisch)		Aufklärung			Klassik			Romantik			Wagner
	Generation von 1580	Generation von 1680	Rokoko	Rationalismus	Sturm und Drang	1. Klassiker	2. Klassiker	3. Klassiker	1. Generation	2. Generation	3. Generation	
I		Arm! Die Abstriche barock aushöhlend **Händel**				Herzhaft abwärts **Haydn**	Selbstverständlich abwärts. Sorgfältig getönt **Mozart**			Führen und Schwingen **Schubert**		
II	Schulter! starr **Schütz**	Arm! Gebunden schwingend **Telemann**	Hand! Frei schaukelnd **Hasse**	Ohne Schnörkel. Schlicht **Ph. E. Bach**				Tief abwärts zwingen **Beethoven**	Herziehen und Wegschieben **Hoffmann**	Links und rechts ausschwingen **Weber**	Herziehen und Wegschieben **Schumann**	
III	Schulter! starr **M. Franck**	Arm! Die Abstriche barock aushöhlend **J. Seb. Bach**		Nicht aushöhlend. Spröde **Gluck**	Explosionen **Stamitz**						Überfein **Mendelssohn**	Flackriger Druck **Wagner**

Figure 4.3 Table of *Historische Schlagfiguren* from Becking (1928).

according to which there is a range of "dynamic expressive forms for specific emotions" (Clynes 1983, 84). In respect to music, he further argued that there are "dynamic expressive sound forms for specific emotions" (Clynes and Nettheim 1982, 51). According to Clynes, an *essentic* sound form is one that "appears to act directly to communicate its quality," that is, one where no symbolic transformation is needed to understand its meaning. In some respect, *essentic forms* might be regarded as gestures in that they are dynamic wholes that express a certain emotional (or "sentic") state. Such essentic forms were developed by Clynes in relation to emotions such as anger, hate, love, grief, joy, and others. He then tested whether subjects might be able to identify the sentic state (or emotion) contained in each essentic form.

Technically, an essentic form is derived from transformations of the transient pressure generated by a finger touching a sensor on a touch-sensitive device called, in this case, a sentograph. The device apparently is suited to transform both the vertical pressure force and the angle at which the pressure force acts on a plane, into some analogue output (presumably, a DC voltage where the amplitude is proportional to the pressure). This output is converted and stored on a data tape recorder.

In order to transform touch pressure patterns (the essentic forms) into a sound signal, only the vertical pressure component was used. Without going into detail (see Clynes and Nettheim 1982, 61ff.), the vertical pressure component could apparently be used to generate an envelope, which was fed into a VCO (voltage-controlled oscillator), and a VCA (voltage-controlled amplifier), respectively. Together, the two generated a signal that underwent changes in frequency according to the envelope, and that also had an amplitude envelope. The latter was made to always start from zero (0 volts), and to end in zero amplitude. The result was a simple sinusoidal wave, which was modulated in frequency and amplitude. Since it was fairly easy to segment a continuous frequency trajectory into discrete steps, this process could yield a melody, which could then communicate the same sentic state (emotion) as did the original touch pressure curve.

Clynes, following Becking's original hypothesis, claimed that for particular composers there is a specific pulse. This pulse might be found by thinking of some music of, for example, Beethoven, while expressing its pulse by "conducting" on a sentograph with finger pressure alone (see Clynes 1983, 92ff.). Such experiments, in which world-famous artists (e.g. Pablo Casals, Rudolf Serkin) took part, yielded essentic forms that should represent the inner pulse peculiar to Mozart, Beethoven, or Haydn. The inner pulse is, to be sure, not identical with meter—nevertheless it implies some repetition at a rate of, approximately, 50–80 beats per minute (which implies a duration per pulse from ca. 0.7–1.2 seconds). These experiments led Clynes to formulate "pulse matrices" for Mozart,

Beethoven, and Schubert where relative amplitude sizes and duration deviations per pulse (consisting, typically, of four notes or tones, respectively) have been stated. If one plays actual pieces of music with such patterns, specific temporal and dynamical microstructures result that of course have an effect on the expressiveness of the music. If a piece is played with the correct pulse (that is, works of Mozart with the "Mozart pulse"), the rating for musical appropriateness should be high whereas it should be low for works played with the wrong pulse.

The claims Clynes made with respect to "inner pulses" peculiar to certain composers have been tested, in controlled experiments, by Bruno Repp (1989; 1990) who found that, for most of his subjects, there is a specific pulse that fits each singular piece rather than one pulse that fits various pieces of an individual composer. Repp's experiments therefore cast some doubt on the validity of the idea of a composer's pulse.

Clynes (1995), on the grounds of his own extensive experimental data obtained from 135 subjects, among them ten famous artists (including Sir Yehudi Menuhin and Paul Badura-Skoda), came to a different conclusion. He argued that "the scores for the 'wrong' performances decreased progresssively as the musical proficiency [of the subjects] increased." He took this as a sign that "on the whole the wrong pulse tends to be less appropriate (more unpleasant) for those who presumably understand the music best" (1995, 300).

This conclusion suggests that professional musicians and conductors should be much more sensitive to subtle differences in the microstructure of performed music than music students on a graduate level, not to speak of amateurs. Clynes had hypothesized that, during the 18th and 19th centuries, "good composers discovered, largely unaware, how to embody their own intimate pulse into music" (1995, 280). The task of professional musicians hence should be to somehow sense or feel this pulse, which, for reasons of authenticity, should then also be faithfully reproduced in performance practice. If this goal is achieved, we could expect the timing and amplitude microstructure of various artists to be similar, if not almost identical. Comparison of a sample of interpretations of a piece played by various artists indeed may reveal certain convergent features (e.g. the parabolic function for timing as revealed for renditions of Schumann's *Träumerei* by Repp 1992). However, close inspection of many interpretations often also shows significant differences in respect to phrasing and the temporal and dynamic shaping of individual notes. We may illustrate this by means of a brief excerpt from Chopin's *Ballade* in A flat major (op. 47, no. 3) which was used by Clynes (1983, 114–116 and sound example I:3 on a phonogram record attached to the publication) to demonstrate the particularities of Chopin. Clynes's own interpretation of the opening melodic phrase (upper voice, see Figure 4.4) as derived from "essentic forms" is shown in Figure 4.5 (upper oscillogram);

Figure 4.4 Score of the opening measures of F. Chopin's *Ballad No. 3* (op. 47).

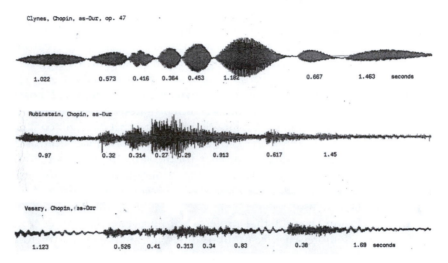

Figure 4.5 Oscillograms representing renditions of F. Chopin's *Ballad No. 3*, bars 1 and 2, performed by M. Clynes (top), A. Rubinstein (middle), and T. Vásáry (bottom). Numbers indicate durations of tones in seconds.

the oscillogram of the respective bars taken from a recording of Artur Rubinstein which Clynes himself had used for comparison, is in the middle of Figure 4.5. At the bottom of Figure 4.5, the oscillogram of the same bars played by Tamás Vásáry (Deutsche Grammophon 2535 284) is shown. Comparisons of the temporal envelopes of each rendition demonstrate that there are marked differences in dynamics. The same holds true with respect to durations of single notes (measured from the oscillograms by the present author; absolute values are given in Figure 4.5). One could extend such measurements to cover several recordings of one piece in total, and then conduct detailed statistical analysis on the data to calculate variance as well as the correlation between various interpretations. Of course, the variance must be within certain limits since all pianists start from the same score.

It should be noted that, besides Becking's intuitive approach to composer's pulses, which was adopted and elaborated later by Clynes and by his co-worker, Nigel Nettheim (Clynes and Nettheim 1982; Nettheim 1999), there was other research directed to motion, pulse, and timing as well as to expressive factors in Germany before World War II. A considerable part of such research was conducted at the Laboratory of Phonetics of the University of Hamburg, which included a small department of Comparative Musicology, where Wilhelm Heinitz (1883–1963), a musician and musicologist with a PhD in phonetics and a *Habilitation* in Comparative Musicology, was based. He was first employed to transcribe speech and music from phonographic recordings that anthropologists and linguists had brought home from field trips to many parts of the world. The material he had at hand included field recordings of languages and regional dialects from all over Europe as well as samples of tone languages from Africa.

Heinitz analyzed samples of European folk music and non-western musics with respect to its temporal-dynamic and "energetic" aspects. He pointed to the biological foundations of music and argued that "music as expressive motion segmented in an organic-rhythmic way cannot be separated from acts of motor behaviour" (1930, 24). By "segmentation in an organic-rhythmic way," Heinitz (1930, 18–19) understood, for example, the lengths of the phrases that singers settle upon in relation to breathing. Since Heinitz considered the production of (most of all, vocal) music to be closely dependent on motor behaviour and physiological parameters, he conducted experiments in which he investigated, among other problems, breathing (including the movements of the body) in relation to various sound stimuli (Heinitz 1929). Already, in the 1920s, he began investigating expressiveness in music on an empirical basis. He measured, for example, the relative amount of rubato in the renditions of "Am stillen Herd" from Wagner's *Meistersinger* by seven opera singers (Heinitz 1927). In this study, he also suggested a method of how to assign "energetic weights" to each note in such a song. Heinitz (1930; 1938) proposed a holistic approach to (comparative, or general) musicology that should ultimately lead to a "biology of music" (*Musikbiologie*), a view shared by some of his contemporaries such as the well-known Austrian musicologist Robert Lach (1924). Heinitz (1938, 45) labelled his approach to music analysis (which had a focus on motional and gestural aspects) *Kinetologie*. In his view, musical expression should be investigated in respect to the "macro- and microdynamic process of movements and motional streams which in total contribute to a musical formation." Though he did a fair amount of experimental work, his concept of a "physiological resonance" (a special version of the Sievers–Becking theory of sympathetic movements) included subjective evaluation and was intuitive in many ways.

2.3 Truslit on Bodily Motion and Musical Motion

Perhaps the most interesting publication on gestural and motional aspects of music before World War II was written by Alexander Truslit (whose family background apparently was in the Baltic countries). Truslit (1938, chapter II) held that motion is the most elementary stratum of music, and that all music originates from motion since the sense of motion is the most basic and common to all human beings. Anatomically and physiologically, our sense of motion is embodied in the vestibular organ (*vestibulum labyrinthi*) of the inner ear. In fact, we share this organ with many animals; in terms of evolution, it is very old since it is found already in fish (*pisces*) from where, in respect to anatomy as well as function, a line can be drawn connecting fishes and "higher animals" (*vertebratae*), up to the mammals to which our species *homo sapiens* belongs (cf. Romer 1962–1966, chapter 15). This organ regulates the motions our body undergoes, and in particular changes in position; it is thus important for kinesthesia.

According to Truslit (chapter II.5), motion can be translated into sound, and sound phenomena such as music can "trigger" sensations of motion in our ear. There are essential patterns of motion that occur in music, and that Truslit (chapter III) largely found embedded in melodic lines; these, to be sure, have to be viewed in respect to rhythm and harmony. Since motion that occurs in time and space can be described by trajectories, melodic movement can be also so described. The information contained in actual sound patterns of music performed live or played back from recordings, is enough to induce sensations of motion or movement, in listeners. These can follow the dynamic movements of the music by bodily movements which, in Truslit's demonstrations documented by graphs, photos, and sound examples, involve the upper part of the body plus both arms stretched out in parallel (cf. Truslit 1938). The trajectories of the movements he discusses are based on three basic forms (*offen, geschlossen, gewunden*, that is, open, closed, and winding). Truslit's kinematic interpretation of excerpts from sound recordings of actual performances yields quite complex curves that represent the dynamic motion of the music (including agogic subtleties) as perceived by a listener.

Truslit claimed that the same psychophysical parameters that are fundamentally relevant for any performer of music are also relevant for the listener. He believed (chapter IV.1) that the performer acts by some "inner motion" whereby the vestibulum, together with the central nervous system, regulates the interplay of muscles relevant for producing sounds (either by playing an instrument, or by singing). The sound pattern that results is said to have a *Dynamo–Agogik* (temporal–dynamic organization) identical to that of the muscles used for sound production.

From the perspective of the listener, the sound pattern he perceives according to Truslit (1938, 170) brings about a stimulation of the basilar membrane as well as of the vestibulum, which again has the same *Dynamo–Agogik*. Finally, this stimulation gives rise to a sensation of the musical sound that goes along with an experience of (inner) motion as well as with an interplay of the relevant muscles following the same *Dynamo–Agogik*.

Truslit thereby derived what he called a complete and coherent picture. His concept based on motion, human anatomy and physiology in general, and on *Dynamo–Agogik* in particular, succeeded in connecting the performer who generates musically articulate sound to the listener, who perceives such articulate sound sequences. These sequences induce an experience in the listener, which should be almost identical to that of the performer at the very moment he or she generates musical sounds.

Though Truslit was well aware of the relevant literature on musical motion, gestures and "pulse" (he mentions, among others, Rutz, Sievers, and Becking), he cannot be said to have been an expert on matters of anatomy or physiology. His hypothesis that the vestibular organ is of importance for sensations of motion, and acts as a mediator that somehow regulates muscular tensions relevant for the production and perception of music, would have needed more evidence than was available at the time. Consequently, Truslit's book did not provide a detailed explanation of how perceptual phenomena relating to musical motion are grounded in our perceptual system (comprising peripheral sense organs, neural pathways, and central stages of processing, memory, etc.). However, his book offers many stimulating ideas based on musical experience and insight, which should be taken into account in further experimental and theoretical studies.

It is interesting to note that there has been a focus on the *vestibulum labyrinthi* in some recent publications on music and motion (see Todd 1999). It has been noted elsewhere that Neil Todd "is in some ways the intellectual heir of Truslit" (Shove and Repp 1995, 75) not only for his focus on the vestibular organ but also for other aspects of his work on sensorimotor control. Of course, his approach differs from Truslit's work in that Todd employs experimental methodology as well as computational modelling.

3 Conclusion

The motional and gestural qualities of music have been known since antiquity, and have been developed in various musical styles and genres. Musical gestures can be defined as sequences of tones ordered in pitch as well as in respect to rhythm and meter; in many cases, both a clear melodic contour and a rhythmic and melodic accent structure can be detected. Gestures thereby gain a distinct "shape" as well as an articulation as a "phrase" (which is what makes them *Gestalt*-like as well as similar to phrase structures found in speech). As dynamic musical formations, they should have some expressive power as well. Musical gestures can have indexical or symbolic meaning.

The study of motion with respect to music started from an intuitive point of view involving music analysis, phenomenology, and hermeneutic interpretation. After 1920, experimental methods and empirical data based on observation and measurement were taken into account. Recently, scientific and computational methods have been included into research work on music, motion and gestures (see, e.g. Todd 1999; Friberg et al. 2000; Camurri et al. 2000; Godøy et al. 2006). It is of interest to note that the old "energetic" paradigm of "tonal forces" giving rise to motion in music (Mersmann 1922/23; Kurth 1930) also continues to be influential, and has found a new formulation (Larson 2004).

Notes

1   The difference between speaking (*sprechen, sagen, reden*) and showing or demonstrating (*zeigen*) plays a significant role in several of Wittgenstein's writings, in particular, the *Tractatus logico-philosophicus*, the *Philosophische Untersuchungen*, and the *Bemerkungen über die Philosophie der Psychologie* (contained in Wittgenstein 1984, Volume 1 and Volume 7)

2   A good case in point was Pete Townshend, guitarist in *The Who*, who was known for smashing guitars and amps on many occasions (as documented in, for example, the movies *Monterey Pop* [1967] and *The Kids are Alright* [1978]). His destructive habit apparently suited the expectations of an often riotous "mod" audience. Similar observations pertaining to gestural behaviour of musicians as well as actual violence originating from both the musicians and the crowd watching them could be made with respect to the European punk scene of the late 1970s.

3   Roger Bourdin (Philips 802 770 LY).

4   A fine rendition of *Les doits parlans* is given by Gerd Zacher (organ) available on CD (Aeolus 2001).

5   Good examples can be found in *Das Wohltemperierte Clavier* (BWV 846–893). The rhetorical character of certain organ works, among them the Toccata and Fugue in d-minor (BWV 538), has often been emphasised. Further, keyboard works such as the Prelude, Fugue, and Allegro in E flat major (BVW 998), presumably written to be performed on the *Lautenclavier* (lute–harpsichord), should be mentioned. A rendition that elaborates the gestural composition in particular of the Allegro is that of Motoko Nabeshima (EMS 1991/Koch Discovery Intern. DICD 920283).

6   The Latin phrase is *affectus exprimere*; the verb exprimere means to express, to speak out clearly, to imitate (or simulate), yet can also have the meaning of to press and to force.

7   It was this circumstance that led Hugo Riemann to condense such characteristic features into his *Musikalische Syntaxis. Grundriß einer harmonischen Satzbildungslehre*. Leipzig: Breitkopf & Härtel 1877. A syntax, of course, presupposes that there are typical ways of forming meaningful sentences.

References

Adorno, Th. W. (1978). *Philosophie der Neuen Musik*. (Originally published in 1949). Frankfurt/Main: Suhrkamp.

Albersheim, G. (1980). *Die Tonsprache*. Tutzing: H. Schneider.

Becking, G. (1923/24). Über ein dänisches Schul-Liederbuch, über Mitbewegungen und Gehaltsanalyse. *Zeitschrift für Musikwissenschaft* 6, 100–119. Reprinted in W. Kramolisch (ed.) (1975), *Gustav Becking zum Gedächtnis*. Tutzing: H. Schneider, 191–210.

Becking, G. (1928). *Der Musikalische Rhythmus als Erkenntnisquelle*. Augsburg: B. Filser (reprint, Stuttgart: Ichthys, 1958).

Bierwisch, M. (1979). Musik und Sprache. Überlegungen zu ihrer Struktur und Funktionsweise. In *Jahrbuch Peters* 1978. Leipzig: Edition Peters, 9–102.

Braun, W. (1994). *Deutsche Musiktheorie des 15. bis 17. Jahrhunderts*. T. II: *Von Calvisius bis Mattheson*. Darmstadt: Wissenschaftliche Buchgesellschaft.

Cadoz, C. and Wanderley, M. M. (2000). Gesture – Music. In M. M. Wanderley and M. Battier (eds.), *Trends in Gestural Control of Music [CD ROM]*. Paris: IRCAM, 71–93.

Cahn-Speyer, R. (1927). Ueber Gebärde und Musik in der Oper. *Melos*, 5, 8–9.

Camurri, A., Paolo C., Ricchetti, M., and Volpe, G. (2000). Expressiveness and physicality in interaction. *Journal of New Music Research*, 29(3), 187–198.

Clynes, M. (1983). Expressive microstructures in music, linked to living qualities. In J. Sundberg (ed.), *Studies in Music Performance*. Stockholm: Royal Swedish Academy of Music, Publication No. 39, 76–186.

Clynes, M. (1995). Microstructural musical linguistics: composer's pulses are liked most by the best musicians. *Cognition*, 55(3), 269–310.

Clynes, M. and Nettheim, N. (1982). The living quality of music. Neurobiologic patterns of communicating feeling. In M. Clynes (ed.), *Music, Mind, and Brain*. New York/London: Plenum Press, 47–82.

Clynes, M. and Walker, J. (1982). Neurobiologic functions of rhythm, time and pulse in music. In M. Clynes (ed.), *Music, Mind, and Brain*. New York/London: Plenum Press, 171–216.

Cogan, R. and Escot, P. (1976). *Sonic Design: The Nature of Sound and Music*. Englewood Cliffs, NJ: Prentice-Hall.

Dammann, R. (1967). *Der Musikbegriff im Deutschen Barock*. Köln: A. Volk.

Davies, S. (1994). *Musical Meaning and Expression*. Ithaca, London: Cornell University Press.

Debussy, C. (1971). *Monsieur Croche et Autres Ecrits*. Paris: Gallimard.

Descartes, R. (1649). *Passiones animae*. (*Les passions de l'âme*, Amsterdam and Paris). In Ch. Adam and P. Tannery (eds.), *Oeuvres des Descartes*, T. XI, Paris: Cerf 1911.

Duncan, I. (1903). *Der Tanz der Zukunft: eine Vorlesung* (German translation of *The Dance of the Future*). Leipzig: Diederichs.

Eggebrecht, H.-H. (1979). *Sinn und Gehalt. Aufsätze zur Musikalischen Analyse*. Wilhelmshaven: Heinrichshofen.

Eisenschmidt, J. (1940/41). *Die Szenische Darstellung der Opern Georg Friedrich Händels auf der Londoner Bühne seiner Zeit*. Wolfenbüttel: Möseler (repr. Laaber: Laaber-Verlag 1987).

Ekman, P., Sorensen, R., and Friesen, W. V. (1969). Pan-cultural elements in facial displays of emotion. *Science,* 164(4), 86–88.

Ekman, P., Friesen, W. V., and Ellsworth, P. (1972). *Emotion in the Human Face: Guidelines for Research and an Integration of Findings.* New York, Oxford: Pergamon Press.

Fay, T. (1974). Context analysis of musical gestures. *Journal of Music Theory,* 18(1), 124–151.

Fecker. A. (1989). *Sprache und Musik. Bd 2: Systematik der Vokalmusik.* Hamburg: K.D. Wagner.

Frege, G. (1892). Über Sinn und Bedeutung. *Zeitschrift für Philosophie und philosophische Kritik,* 100, 25–50.

Friberg, A., Sundberg, J., and Frydén, L. (2000). Music from motion: sound level envelopes of tones expressing human locomotion. *Journal of New Music Research,* 29(3), 199–210.

Frobenius, W. (2005). Gestische Musik. *Handwörterbuch der Musikalischen Terminologie.* 40. Auslieferung. Stuttgart: Franz Steiner.

Fürst, L. (1932). *Der Musikalische Ausdruck der Körperbewegung in der Opernmusik.* Miesbach: W.Fr. Mayr.

Godøy, R. I. (2001). Imagined action, excitation, and resonance. In R. I. Godøy and H. Jørgensen (eds.), *Musical Imagery.* Lisse, Holland: Swets and Zeitlinger, 237–250.

Godøy, R. I., Haga, E., and Jensenius, A. R. (2006). Playing "air instruments:" mimicry of sound-producing gestures by novices and experts. In S. Gibet, N. Courty, and J.-F. Kamp (eds.), *Gesture in Human-Computer Interaction and Simulation,* LNAI 3881. Berlin, Heidelberg: Springer, 256–267.

HaCohen, R. (1999). Fictional planes and their interplay: the alchemy of forms and emotions in Bach's St. Matthew Passion. In I. Zannos (ed.), *Music and Signs. Semiotic and Cognitive Studies in Music.* Bratislava: ASCO, 416–434.

HaCohen, R. and Wagner, N. (1997). The communicative force of Wagner's Leitmotifs: complementary relations between their connotations and denotations. *Music Perception,* 14(4), 445–475.

Hapke, W. (1927). *Die musikalische Darstellung der Gebärde in Richard Wagners Ring des Nibelungen.* Borna-Leipzig: Noske.

Harnoncourt, N. (1985). *Musik als Klangrede.* München/Kassel: dtv/Bärenreiter.

Hatten, R. S. (2001). *Musical gesture.* Course description. http://chass.utoronto.ca/epc/srb/cyber/hatout.html

Heinitz, W. (1927). Musikalische Ausdrucksstudien an Phonogrammen. *Zeitschrift für Musikwissenschaft,* 9, 568–575.

Heinitz, W. (1929). Das Studium musikalischen Ausdrucks an Atembewegungskurven. *Zeitschrift für Laryngologie,* 17, 487–493.

Heinitz, W. (1930). *Strukturprobleme in Primitiver Musik.* Hamburg: Friederichsen, De Gruyter and Co.

Heinitz, W. (1938). Musikwissenschaft und Völkerkunde. *Mitteilungsblatt der Gesellschaft für Völkerkunde,* 8, 43–54.

Huber, K. (1953). *Ästhetik.* Ettal: Buch-Kunstverlag Ettal.

Iazetta, F. (2000). Meaning in musical gesture. In M. M. Wanderley and M. Battier (eds.), *Trends in Gestural Control of Music.* Paris: IRCAM, 71–87.

Jacques-Dalcroze, E. (1907). *Der Rhythmus als Erziehungsmittel für das Leben und die Kunst: Sechs Vorträge*. Basel: Helbing and Lichtenhahn.

Jacques-Dalcroze, E. (1921). *Rhythmus, Musik und Erziehung*. (translation from the French by Julius Schwabe). Basel: Schwabe.

Janz, T. (2006). *Klangdramaturgie. Studien zur theatralen Orchesterkomposition in Wagners Ring des Nibelungen*. Würzburg: Königshausen and Neumann.

Karbusicky, V. (1986). *Grundriß der Musikalischen Semantik*. Darmstadt: Wissenschaftliche Buchgesellschaft.

Kircher, A. (1650). *Musurgia universalis sive ars magna consoni et dissoni in X libros digesta*. Romae 1650 (German transl. by A. Hirsch, Schwäbisch-Hall 1662).

Kramolisch, W. (ed.) (1975). *Gustav Becking zum Gedächtnis: Eine Auswahl seiner Schriften und Beiträge seiner Schüler*. Tutzing: H. Schneider.

Krones, H. (2003). Oratores, Poet[a]e, Mimi and Musici. Affekt, Gestik und Rhetorik in der Musik. In B. Siegmund (ed.). *Gestik und Affekt in der Musik des 17. Jahrhunderts*. Stiftung Kloster Michaelstein, 19–41.

Kurth, E. (1930). *Musikpsychologie*. Bern: Krompholz (2nd ed. 1947).

Laban, R. v. (1948). *Modern Educational Dance*. London: Macdonald and Evans (2nd ed. 1963).

Lach, R. (1924). *Die Vergleichende Musikwissenschaft, ihre Methoden und Probleme*. Wien: Hölder-Pichler-Tempsky.

Larson, S. (2004). Musical forces and melodic expectations: comparing computer models and experimental results. *Music Perception, 21*(4), 457–498.

Legler, M. and Kubik, R. (2003). Prinzipien und Quellen der barocken Gestik. In B. Siegmund (ed.). *Gestik und Affekt in der Musik des 17. Jahrhunderts*. Stiftung Kloster Michaelstein, 43–64.

Libet, B. (2004). *Mind Time: The Temporal Factor in Consciousness*. Cambridge, MA: Harvard University Press (German translation Frankfurt/Main: Suhrkamp 2005).

Matsumoto, C. (1983). Movement and symbol: a comparative analysis of *Chhau* dance styles. In F. Koizumi et al. (eds.). *Dance and music in South Asian drama. Chhau, Mahākālī pyākhan and Yakshagāna. Report of Asian Traditional Performing Arts 1981*. Tokyo: Academia Music Ltd., 144–156.

Mattheson, J. (1739). *Der vollkommene Capellmeister*. Hamburg: Herold (new edition Kassel: Bärenreiter 1999).

Meidner, O. M. (1985). Motion and E-motion in music. *British Journal of Aesthetics, 25*(4), 349–356.

Mersmann, H. (1922/23). Versuch einer Phänomenologie der Musik. *Zeitschrift für Musikwissenschaft, 5*, 226–269.

Nettheim, N. (1999). A Schubert fingerprint related to the theory of metre, tempo and the Becking curve. *Systematische Musikwissenschaft/Systematic Musicology, 6*(4), 363–413.

Platen, E. (1997). *Johann Sebastian Bach. Die Matthäus-Passion*. 2nd ed. Kassel: Bärenreiter.

Repp, B. (1989). Expressive microstructure in music: a preliminary perceptual assessment of four composers. *Music Perception, 6*(3), 243–274.

Repp, B. (1990). Further perceptual evaluations of pulse microstructure in computer performances of classical piano music. *Music Perception, 8*(1), 1–33.

Repp, B. (1992). A constraint on the expressive timing of a melodic gesture: evidence from performance and aesthetic judgment. *Music Perception,* 10(2), 221–242.

Reybrouck, M. (2001). Musical imagery between sensory processing and ideomotor simulation. In R. I. Godøy and H. Jørgensen (eds.), *Musical Imagery.* Lisse, Holland: Swets and Zeitlinger, 117–135.

Romer, A. S. (1962). *The Vertebrate Body.* 3rd ed. Philadelphia: W. Saunders (German transl. *Vergleichende Anatomie der Wirbeltiere.* 2nd ed. Hamburg. P. Parey 1966).

Rowell, L. (1999). Emblematic openings in music. In I. Zannos (ed.), *Music and Signs. Semiotic and Cognitive Studies in Music.* Bratislava: ASCO, 379–390.

Rutz, O. (1908). *Neue Entdeckungen von der Menschlichen Stimme.* München: Beck.

Rutz, O. (1911a). *Musik, Wort und Körper als Gemütsausdruck.* Leipzig: Breitkopf and Härtel.

Rutz, O. (1911b). *Sprache, Gesang und Körperhaltung: Handbuch der Typenlehre Rutz.* München: Beck.

Sartre, J.-P. (1940). *L'Imaginaire. Psychologie Phénoménologique de l'Imagination.* Paris: Gallimard.

Seitz, J. (2005). Dalcroze, the body, movement and musicality. *Psychology of music,* 33(4), 419–435.

Shove, P. and Repp. B. (1995). Musical motion and performance: theoretical and empirical perspectives. In J. Rink (ed.), *The Practice of Performance: Studies in Musical Interpretation.* Cambridge: Cambridge University Press, 55–83.

Sievers, E. (1924). *Ziele und Wege der Schallanalyse. Zwei Vorträge.* Heidelberg: C. Winter.

Stockmann, D. (1985). Musica vulgaris im französischen Hochmittelalter: Johannes de Grocheio in neuer Sicht. *Musikethnologische Sammelbände 7,* Graz: Akademische Druck- und Verlagsanstalt, 163–180.

Tembrock, G. (1978). Bioakustik, Musik und Sprache. *Sitzungsberichte der Akademie der Wissenschaften der DDR; Mathematik – Naturwissenschaften – Technik,* Jg. 1978, Nr. 1/N. Berlin: Akademie-Verlag.

Todd, N. P. M. (1999). Motion in music: a neurobiological perspective. *Music Perception,* 17(1), 115–126.

Truslit, A. (1938). *Gestaltung und Bewegung in der Musik. Ein Tönendes Buch vom Musikalischen Vortrag und seinem Bewegungserlebten Gestalten und Hören.* Berlin-Lichterfelde: Fr. Vieweg.

Wittgenstein, L. (1984). *Werkausgabe.* Vol. 1–8. Frankfurt am Main: Suhrkamp.

Zoltai, D. (1970). *Ethos und Affekt. Geschichte der Philosophischen Musikästhetik von den Anfängen bis zu Hegel.* Budapest, Berlin: Akademie-Verlag.

Part II

Gestural Significations

Chapter 5

Gestural Affordances of Musical Sound

Rolf Inge Godøy

I Introduction

Musical sound has great power to make us move, or to create sensations of movement in our minds. This is obvious from ubiquitous situations of people dancing, marching, gesticulating, nodding their heads, or tapping their feet to music, or of people giving verbal accounts of imagining moving to music. Yet, we may see great variations in the movements that people actually make to any single piece of music. People may perceive some salient features of musical sound similarly: for example, people may all move in synchrony with the pulse of a dance tune, yet at the same time individually make hand movements that reveal a focus on different features in the music, such as the melodic line of the singer or of the lead guitar, or the drum patterns. Adopting the notion of *affordance* from ecological psychology (Gibson 1979), meaning that people, dependent on their individual background, expertise, particular situation or mood at any moment, may focus on different features in any single phenomenon of the world, I shall in this chapter present some ideas on *gestural affordances of musical sound*.

In this book, we can see considerable effort dedicated to studying music-related gestures, but we can also see that we still have a long way to go toward developing better theories and methods here. This of course also applies to the topic of gestural affordances of musical sound, but specifically, I believe the main challenge here is to acquire a conceptual apparatus for observing sound–gesture relationships. This means having some kind of preconception of what we are looking for, including both a typology of sound-related gestures and an overview of gesture-pertinent features of musical sound, before making choices regarding the setup of observation studies, experiments, choosing motion capture technologies, and so on. This is so because we may see people making seemingly divergent gestures to the same musical excerpts, but if we reflect upon the different concurrent features of the observed gestures (e.g. speed, amplitude, direction), and the different concurrent features in the musical sound (e.g. tempo, intensity, contours), we may see that there are similarities in some respects after all, in spite of the apparent divergences. To provide the rudiments of such a conceptual apparatus for gestural affordances of musical sound, I shall in the following first present some reflections on listening and on embodied cognition (sections 2 and 3), followed by an overview of sound-related gestures and of sound features (sections 4 and 5) and some examples of gestural rendering of musical sound, i.e. examples of how people make gestures to musical sound (section 6), before discussing gestural affordance in view of the perception–action cycle in music (section 7).

2 Listening

As an example of gestural affordances of musical sound, consider the famous barber scene from Charlie Chaplin's *The Great Dictator*. At the beginning of this scene, we see a radio and hear a voice from the radio announcing: "This is the Happy Hour Program. Make your work a pleasure, move with the rhythm of the music. Our next selection: Brahms Hungarian Dance Number 5." With the music started, we see the barber (Charlie Chaplin) mixing shaving cream and applying it to the face of a client in preparation for a shave. All of the subsequent gestures of the scene are made to the music, such as the fast back-and-forth hand movements of applying the shaving cream to the client's face accompanied by a corresponding flurry of notes in the music, and the subsequent single rapid downward stroke of the whole arm to shake off the remaining shaving cream accompanied by one single accented tutti chord, and a little later, more protracted upward gestures with the razor accompanied by protracted crescendo sounds (see Figure 5.1). Created by this great master of gestural art, the entire barber scene shows how the music has very rich gestural affordance, i.e. among other things, it can afford an entire shaving session, and at the same time, it shows how gestures shape our perception of the music, i.e. the stream musical sound is chunked by the shaving actions.

Studying gestural affordances of musical sound confronts us with some fundamental issues of music perception. How it is that listeners seem to be able to spontaneously render often complex musical sounds into body movements regardless of their level of musical training? How is it that listeners are able to spontaneously parse continuous streams of musical sound into gesture chunks? Studying gestural affordances of musical sound is thus about how listeners extract movement-inducing cues from streams of musical sound. But it is also the other way around, i.e. about how listeners use images of sound-related movement in making sense of what they hear. Thus, there is a two-way process here where sound induces images of movement, and conversely, where previously learned

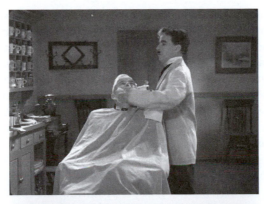

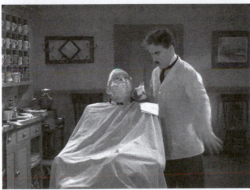

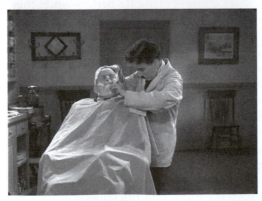

Figure 5.1 Top: The barber (Charlie Chaplin) applying shaving cream with small rapid back and forth hand movements similar to the rapid short up and down bow strokes in the music. Middle: The barber shaking off the shaving cream from his hand with one rapid whole arm movement similar to the rapid long down-bow movement at the accented tutti chord. Bottom: The barber making protracted upward shaving gestures with the razor similar to sustained crescendo sounds (probably up-bow, i.e. from tip to frog movements in the strings in the crescendos). Reprinted with permission from Association Chaplin, Paris.

images of sound-related movement are projected onto sound, actually manifesting an instance of what has been called the *perception–action cycle* in the cognitive sciences (Neisser 1976). The constant shift between perceiving and acting, or between listening and making (or only imagining) gestures, means that music perception is *embodied* in the sense that it is closely linked with bodily experience (Leman 2008), and that music perception is *multimodal* in the sense that we perceive music with the help of both visual/kinematic images and effort/dynamics sensations, in addition to the "pure" sound (Godøy 2003).

The idea of gestural affordances of musical sound initially rests on the assumption that musical sound is a transducer of *source-information*, meaning both the actions that go into producing the sound, e.g. hitting, stroking, blowing, bowing (Godøy et al. 2006a), and the material properties of the sound source, e.g. plates, strings, tubes, membranes (Gaver 1993; Rocchesso and Fontana 2003). This capacity for source-recognition can be summarized as *ecological knowledge* in listening, meaning knowledge acquired through massive experience of sound-sources in general and musical performances in particular. From various instances of so-called "air instrument" performance, it seems that listeners are even able to actively mimic sound-producing gestures, i.e. to reproduce the geometry of movement trajectories, as well as the dynamics, i.e. the speed, acceleration, force, effort, quite well (Godøy et al. 2006a). This acquired knowledge of sound-producing gestures apparently also extends to various so-called *ancillary gestures* (see Chapter 2 in this book). Ancillary gestures facilitate performance: they assist in avoiding fatigue, or shaping expressive or articulatory features in the music. This acquired knowledge also applies to *communicative gestures*, which are gestures used to communicate with other performers in an ensemble, or that have more theatrical functions for the benefit of the audience, as is evident for instance in various air guitar championships.[1]

This massive ecological knowledge of sound production means that listeners will have a repertoire of sound-producing gestures so that in situations where there are no visible musicians (such as listening to music through loudspeakers or earphones), the listeners may mentally recreate the choreography of sound-producing gestures. The re-creation will vary among listeners and will depend on their intentional focus at any given time. This capacity for imagining the sound-producing gestures will of course depend upon the expertise of the listener, as is the case in the seemingly involuntary mental simulations of sound-producing gestures of professional musicians (Haueisen and Knösche 2001), however the capacity for such mental simulations may also be quickly learned by novices (Bangert and Altenmüller 2003).

We understand this ecological knowledge in listening as generalizable across different contexts and different instances. For instance, hitting a drum with a mallet is in the same category as hitting a key on a piano, as both actions belong to the category of *impulsive* sound-producing gestures, a category quite distinct from *sustained* or *iterative* sound-producing gestures (see section 4 below). This is also what enables us to see similarities between sound-producing gestures and other types of gestures, as was the case in the Chaplin barber scene where the rapid back-and-forth movements of applying shaving cream are similar to rapid back-and-forth movements of the bow in playing notes, hence an example of *iterative* gestures, or the fast full-arm movement of shaking off the shaving cream is similar to the rapid, whole bow down-stroke of an accented chord, hence an example of *impulsive* gestures, or the protracted upwards movement of the razor is similar to the upward bow movement of the sustained crescendo sounds, hence an example of *sustained* gestures. The point here is that several instances of similar types of gestures with similar sensations of effort may be generalized into more generic types, or schemata. These schemata may in turn be used in the perception of a novel musical sound, i.e. be projected onto "new," even synthetic, previously unheard sounds, as long as the dynamic envelope or shape of the sounds are similar (Godøy 2006). The same holds for listening to highly complex musical sound such as that of large ensembles or orchestras: we are apparently able to perceive the gist of what we hear (Harding, Cooke, and König 2007) and to translate such complex sonic textures into more simple gestures (Haga 2008).

There is now evidence that auditory-motor couplings may have a privileged role in behavior (Thaut 2005), and that some auditory-motor couplings are even "hard-wired" (Kohler et al. 2002), all in all suggesting that our capacity for spontaneous and robust associations of sound and movement extends from very basic neurophysiological predispositions to more learning-based associations, making sound-movement relationships solid but also variable. Learned schemas may in turn become solid to the point of becoming independent of what is actually going on in the music, compensating for what is missing in rhythmical patterns (Large 2000) or subjectively interpreting the rhythm of sounds from a holistic perception of sound fragments (rather than from the acoustic amplitude peaks) in what are called *p-centers* (for "perceptual centers," see McAnally 2002), or even projecting elements onto the sound that are actually non-existent in the sound, such as various metrical patterns onto a series of unaccented pulses (Fraisse 1982). This means that in listening, we see a whole range of relationships between sound and assumed sound-producing gestures, ranging from the immediate and synchronous (and probably hard-wired) coupling of sound-event to action-event, to the more interpretative and holistic coupling of sound-event to action-event, and even to the projection of non-existent action-events into sound-events.

3 Embodied Cognition

The idea of gestural schemas emerging on the basis of a combination of various hard-wired audio-motor coupling and learned sound–movement associations can be seen as an instance of what is now often called *embodied cognition*. Common to different variants of this concept is the idea that our perception of the world, and our mental activity in general such as reasoning, imagining, planning, etc., is a process of incessant mental simulation of various body movements, both those made by other people and those made by ourselves, as well as both those we can see and those we can only assume.

Elements of embodied cognition can be found in phenomenological philosophy, in particular in the work of Merleau-Ponty (Gallese 2003), however, a more specific version was suggested several decades ago in linguistics by the so-called *motor theory of perception*, meaning that perception in language makes use of mental images of the articulatory movements involved in language production (Liberman and Mattingly 1985). For several decades, this theory was considered quite controversial, however with the advent of brain imaging techniques there now seems to be solid evidence in support of the idea of motor involvement in language perception (Fadiga et al. 2002), as well as in most other perceptual-cognitive activities for that matter (Galantucci et al. 2006). In general, it could be said that mental simulation of action is integral to all mental activity (Gallese and Metzinger 2003), even to what is usually considered rather abstract forms of reasoning (Gallese and Lakoff 2005). Interestingly, ideas of embodied cognition have evolved in parallel within the domain of so-called *cognitive linguistics* during the last couple of decades, leading to the idea of body-based cognitive schemata and categories emerging from massive experience of being and acting in the world (Johnson 1987; Lakoff 1987), something which now converges with ideas from neuroscience (Gallese and Lakoff 2005).

One important element of embodied cognition is our inclination to spontaneously (and largely involuntarily) mentally imitate the movements that we see other people making, as well as the movements that we assume other people are making in cases where we cannot actually see their movements. Imitative behavior as an essential element in human learning and understanding was suggested several decades ago (Meltzoff and Moore 1977), but advances in neuroscience have demonstrated a neurophysiological basis for such imitative behavior in what has been called *mirror neurons* in the brain (Keysers et al. 2003). This hard-wired inclination for imitation can be considered advantageous from an evolutionary point of view because it enables us to predict behavior and therefore respond quickly (Wilson and Knoblich 2005), as well as to understand the intentions of others, hence facilitating social interaction

(Gallese and Goldman 1998). In other words: "to perceive an action is equivalent to internally simulating it," and "this enables the observer to use her/his own resources to penetrate the world of the other by means of an implicit, automatic, and unconscious process of motor simulation" (Gallese and Metzinger 2003, 383).

This element of imitation is important in our context because it may explain why listeners are so readily induced to move to musical sound by spontaneously imitating both the elements of the sound-producing gestures and the various other gestures that they have experienced as associated with the music. With training, there seems to be hardly any limit as to what listeners may spontaneously imitate of what they hear, as is evident from all so-called oral musical cultures, i.e. non-notated music, where transmission and sharing is based on imitation. Interestingly, the capacity for vocal imitation extends to very many different kinds of sounds, as is evident in *scat singing* in jazz and even more so in *beatboxing* in hip hop, which features vocal imitation of all kinds of percussion instruments.

This last point attests to another important feature of embodied cognition and imitative behavior in that there is a considerable amount of flexibility in both the effectors used (e.g. vocal apparatus used for imitating instrumental sounds), by what has been called *motor equivalence* (Kelso et al. 1998), and in the flexibility of the imitation itself as long as certain key features are retained, i.e. that there is what could be called *goal-directed imitation* or GOADI (Wohlschläger et al. 2003). However, the *hands* seem to have a privileged role in music-related gestures, something that also seems to be a more general cognitive phenomenon in that hand movements are closely linked with reasoning and expression (Rizzolatti and Arbib 1998; Goldin-Meadow 2003). In several cases of music-related gestures we see what could be termed a translation from one instrumental or vocal medium to bi-manual movement, e.g. from quite complex musical textures to simplified bi-manual movements as a kind of "piano reduction." The essential point is that this is an active rendering of musical sound, and that it is done from a volitional, "I do," first-person, egocentric perspective, regardless the complexity of the sound source (see section 6 below on gestural rendering).

Western musical culture has been able to create highly complex organizations of musical sound with large-scale forms and large ensembles, thanks to the development of notation. But this has happened at the price of splitting music into a "score" part and a "performance" part, where the score part is essentially a set of symbols for discrete actions, e.g. tones to be played at certain points in time and with certain durations and with approximate intensity on prescribed instruments, and sometimes with the addition of various metaphorical labels for intended expressivity. Further details of how the tones are to be played have been left to the performers to decide as best they can with their (often unarticulated) knowledge of performance traditions within different stylistic idioms. In cultivating notation, we could claim that Western musical thinking often tends to ignore the fact that any sonic event is actually included in a sound-producing gesture, a gesture that starts before, and often ends after, the sonic event of any single tone or group of tones. In other words, Western musical thought has not been well equipped for thinking the gestural-contextual inclusion of tone-events in music, hence also not well equipped for handling issues such as grouping of tone-events and expressivity in music. An embodied perspective on music could turn this around and rather claim that the gestures are primordial to the individual tones, meaning that all tones are *a priori* included in gesture trajectories, something that I have previously termed a *motormimetic* element in the perception and cognition of musical sound (Godøy 2003). The consequence of such a motormimetic perspective on music is to think of music as a multimodal combination of gestures and sound, and to always look for gestural schemas in musical sound.

4 Sound-Related Gestures

Because musical sound may have very rich gestural affordances, it could be useful to have some kind of conceptual apparatus for distinguishing various types of gestures (see Chapters 2 and 3 in this book for more extensive discussions of gesture types). In view of gestural affordances of musical sound, let us briefly recapitulate that we have:

- *Sound-producing gestures*, meaning body movements necessary for producing sound. These include both excitatory movements such as hitting, stroking, blowing, and bowing, and modulatory movements such as vibrato movements and mute movements, but we should also include here various so-called *ancillary* and/or *sound-facilitating* gestures that serve to avoid fatigue and discomfort (e.g. making circular whole arm movements in addition to the finger movements when playing piano in order to minimize strain), as well as those that serve articulation (e.g. various large amplitude or jerky movements) and expressivity (e.g. various larger-scale, phrase-level movements in addition to the local, note-by-note movements).
- *Sound-accompanying gestures*, meaning all kinds of body movements that may be made to music but which are strictly speaking not necessary to produce the sound, such as dancing, marching, gesticulating, nodding the head, and so on. Usually, but not always, we have some kind of synchrony between events in the music and the sound-accompanying body movements. In view of gestural affordances, it is important to note that an excerpt of musical sound may offer different features and different time-scales to synchronize with, i.e.

may often have events at different concurrent textural layers in the music such as the foreground (melody) and the background (accompaniment) or in any other layer of more complex textures, as well as the different time-scales of beat level, measure level, and phrase or period level. As is the topic of this chapter, musical sound may obviously afford very many sound-accompanying gestures, i.e. there may be very many alternative choreographies to the one and same musical excerpt, yet there are in most cases particularly salient events and features in the musical sound that the choreographies will tend to mirror and synchronize with.

In view of gestural affordances of musical sound, the distinction between sound-producing and sound-accompanying gestures may of course be unclear in many cases: performers may make gestures that produce sound, e.g. hitting keys on a piano, yet exaggerate the up-beat preparatory trajectory for this key-hitting in order to communicate a cue to fellow musicians, and simultaneously also use this as a theatrical gesture for the benefit of the audience. This means that in terms of gestural affordance, music-related gestures should again be considered *multi-functional* (cf. the discussion of this in Chapter 2), and that this multi-functionality may be efficiently evoked in the minds of the listeners who are familiar with performance situations assumed to be at the source of the music that is heard.

We can furthermore regard music-related gestures, both sound-producing and sound-accompanying, as usually belonging to one of the following three main categories that we are already acquainted with from Chaplin's barber scene:

- *Iterative*, meaning rapid repetition of small movements such as to fuse these into a single gesture, e.g. as in the stroking of a washboard where the stick bounces back from the surface, or in the rapid bouncing movements of a drum roll, or the rapid shaking movement of a string instrument tremolo, as in Chaplin's rapid shaking movements when applying the shaving cream to the client's face.
- *Impulsive*, meaning discontinuous effort such as in hitting, kicking, rapid stroking or bowing, such as in the rapid accented tutti chord synchronous with Chaplin's rapid whole-arm gesture for shaking off the shaving cream from his hand.
- *Sustained*, meaning continuous effort such as in continuous bowing or blowing, and as in the sustained crescendo sounds accompanying Chaplin's protracted razor movements.

These different gesture categories are quite distinct in terms of bio-mechanics and probably also in terms of motor control, and also quite distinct in their auditive effects: An impulsive sound typically starts with an impact and has a decaying envelope, whereas a sustained sound generally has a more protracted and curved envelope and may contain various modulations (fast "ripples" or slower fluctuations) during its course as well. Also, these different sound-producing gestures may be combined in musical textures, be that as juxtaposed strata, e.g. a flurry of iterative sounds on the background of sustained sounds, or as singular composite sounds, e.g. in an impulsive sound "coloring" the attack of a sustained sound. Actually, orchestration is very much a matter of combining different types of sound-producing gestures, in particular this combining of sustained background sounds with rapid impulsive or iterative foreground sounds. This is found almost everywhere in orchestration, e.g. in a Mozart symphony, in a combination of sustained tones and rapidly moving foreground tones; in a rather "wet," Mantovani-style arrangement with heavy use of sustained violin tones fanning out as a kind of explicitly composed reverberation; or in a Lutoslawski-style orchestral texture with *fortissimo* percussive coloring of the attack of *pianissimo* sustained sounds. The point is that orchestration affords an intrinsic choreography of sound-producing gestures, a choreography that in turn may be appreciated by listeners as rich gestural affordances of the orchestral sound.

These categories of sound-producing gestures also seem to follow various principles of grouping, or what is called "phase-transition" in dynamical theory (Haken et al. 1985) in the sense that with changes in speed and/or amplitude, gestures may fuse into super-ordinate gestures, or conversely, gestures may split into sub-gestures. There are limits as to how fast individual impulsive sounds may be played before fusing into a group of iterative sounds, and conversely, there are limits to how slow a group of iterative sounds can be played before splitting into individual impulsive or sustained sounds. Perceived effects of grouping in music are often also related to the principle of *coarticulation*, meaning a fusion of micro-gestures into more super-ordinate gestures, where there is a contextual smearing of individual sounds and gestures so that they are no longer perceived as individual events (Godøy 2008a). This is for instance the case with various ornaments and other textural figures, and the effects of fusion, as well as of fission, i.e. of transition from melody to ornament and *vice versa*, can from our gestural perspective be understood on the background of biomechanical and motor control constraints and phase transitions.

In general, it seems we have good reason to speak of ecologically founded "energy schemata" at work in the perception and cognition of musical sound, and that these energy schemata are at work in most gesture sensations evoked by musical sound. These sensations can range from experiences of strong, energetic entrainment (see Chapters 2, 3, and

7 in this book) to experiences of deep relaxation and/or of being carried, in the case of extremely protracted and slowly changing sounds (Aksnes and Ruud 2008), sounds that may be associated with ethereal, religious sensations as suggested by Laban (1980). However, it should also be mentioned that our sensations of movement sometimes may be due to vestibular input (i.e. the motion sensor in the inner ear), because of head movements induced by either our own movement or by being moved by someone else or by some other force, e.g. being in a boat (Phillips-Silver and Trainor 2008). In our context of music-related gestures, we shall however focus on the sensations of effector movement, i.e. the visual, proprioceptive (feedback from the muscles), and tactile (touch) sensations of movement from our fingers, hands, arms, and shoulders. This may of course also entrain torso and head movements.

5 Sound Features

One major problem in Western musical thought is the lack of a very good conceptual apparatus for dealing with holistically experienced musical sound, meaning not score-based "analysis," but auditive features of real musical excerpts. In such excerpts, several concurrent features such as pitch, loudness, and timbre interact. There are several challenges for music theory and music cognition here, but for now, it could be useful to try to make a sketch of a conceptual apparatus for detecting and classifying perceptually salient and gesture-affording features of musical sound.

To conceptualize most (if not all) features of musical sound in relation to their gestural affordance, we can think of these features as *trajectory shapes in time and space*. The term "space" is here used not only in the usual sense of three-dimensional Euclidian space for body movement, but also in a metaphorical sense to denote different feature dimensions. Such is the case with the use of pitch-space as a conceptual scheme for ordering differences in pitch, but also as something that may be mapped onto the "real" space of the keyboard with the keys arranged on a horizontal plane, left to right, from the lowest to the highest. In other words, we may encounter a mixed usage of the notion of "space" here, and a lucid discussion of the relationship between the more directly physical sense of "space" and the more metaphorical (and thus also culturally variable) use of the term, can be found in (Eitan and Granot 2006). Such metaphorical use of spatial concepts can be applied to several other features of musical sound such as intensity (*crescendo, decrescendo*) and tempo (*accelerando, ritardando*), texture (spread, focused, thick, thin), and so on, or to more general and composite sensations such as increase or decrease of tension. One of the interesting conclusions in (Eitan and Granot 2006) is that there seems to be an interdependence of features, or what they call "spill over" effects, e.g. that a crescendo could also be perceived as an accelerando by some listeners even when there was in fact no increase in tempo. Although the point of departure for (Eitan and Granot 2006) was what could be called note-based Western musical idioms, it is interesting to see how the resultant feature-interdependence is challenging for mainstream Western musical thinking.

A radical departure from Western notation-based thinking, and a turn towards auditive perceptual features, was presented in the 1960s by Pierre Schaeffer and his research group (Schaeffer 1966). Schaeffer's point of departure was to encourage the listener to disregard the source and everyday significations of any sound fragment, of what is called the *sonic object*, and to focus on the various perceived features of the sonic object such as its overall dynamic shape (or envelope), its spectral shape, its intensity evolution, its spectral evolution, its pitch contour (if applicable), its slow fluctuations in intensity, in spectral content, in pitch, its faster fluctuations in intensity, in spectral content, in pitch, etc. (see Chapter 8 in this book for a brief discussion of these and other basic acoustic terms). In short, Schaeffer proposed a top-down feature-differentiation scheme, starting out with the most superordinate features of the sonic object (which typically would be quite short, roughly in the 0.5 to 5-second range), such as its overall dynamic shape. He would then successively differentiate more and more features, sub-features, sub-sub-features, and so on. Nevertheless, the point of departure would always be the seemingly simple question of "what do we hear now?" The strategy involved thinking of all of these features as *shapes*, shapes that reflect basic action categories such as sustained, impulsive, iterative, flat, curved, steep, etc. (Godøy 2006). In terms of the aforementioned ecological approaches to listening, we could say that Schaeffer's approach is a shift of focus towards more generalized schemata for sound categorizations, and that Schaeffer's method of feature differentiation is applicable to all kinds of music, Western or non-Western, electroacoustic or acoustic, notated or non-notated. The guiding principle of always thinking in terms of feature dimensions and shapes should be understood as a universal method, as a universal geometric mode of reasoning (Thom 1983), similar to what has been called *image schemata* in cognitive linguistics (Johnson 1987; Lakoff 1987). This mode of reasoning can also be used for ordering spontaneously perceived features of musical sound into some kind of conceptual apparatus (Godøy 1997).

As for features of musical sound in relation to gestural affordance, the principle is quite simply that of regarding any feature of musical sound as a shape that may be gesturally rendered, such as the following:

- *Onsets*, i.e. the beginnings of tones or other sonic events, either as singular gestures, or fused into groups by phase-transition or coarticulation when many onsets occur in rapid succession.

- *Pulses*, i.e. sonic events in succession, both regular and more irregular, that induce us to move.
- *Cyclical patterns*, i.e. groupings of sonic events, such as in meter where we make recurrent gestures, and continue to do so even when the details of the sounding patterns change.
- *Accents and articulations*, usually with very clear gestural requirements of energetic and/or jerky kinds of motions.
- *Dynamic contours*, both of sustained sounds and of repeated sounds, affording increased (for *crescendo*) or decreased (for *decrescendo*) amplitude of gestures.
- *Pitch contours*, requiring motions on the instruments.
- *Tessitura contours*, also requiring shifts in the position and spread on the instrument.
- *Timbral contours*, requiring various changes of effector shape, of mute position, of bow position, etc.
- *Modulations*, implying fast back and forth motion of some effector as in *vibrato* or *tremolo* or slower motion as in various textural patterns.
- *Ornaments* and/or various kinds of *textural patterns,* such as trills, mordents, turns, double turns, various arpeggiations, etc. and all types of more elaborate textural patterns as found in Western music for example in the Baroque, Classical, or Romantic area, or in other kinds of music; in sum note-event patterns that require a gesture chunk in performance.

In short, we can say that *anything that moves* in the soundscape of music could potentially afford gestural responses by the listeners, but the responses would of course vary according to what expertise they have, i.e. what they know of sound-producing actions related to the sound they hear. This also goes for the more stationary or even static features of musical sound that may have gestural affordance for listeners such as the shape of the effector (shape of hand, spread of fingers on the keyboard, shape of the vocal apparatus, and so on) in relation to the shape of the sound (the feature of a chord or the formantic shape of a vocal sound). Also the position of the effectors (the position of the hands on the keyboard, the bow on the string, etc.) may be related to sound gestures, and even the tonus or muscular tension required for certain performances may be correlated to sound features.

Lastly, as we have seen in our own observation studies (see next section), listeners may invent new and non-obvious gestures to the music, i.e. gestures based on quite selective listening to the music, and sometimes even seemingly quite independent of the motion sensations of the music, hence effectively adding new "contrapuntal voices" to the music. In such cases, we may speak of more global correspondences between music and gestures based on the overall sensations of effort and motion, and not on any specific sound shape.

6 Gestural Rendering of Musical Sound

Eager to find out more about which sound features listeners with different levels of expertise focus on, we have carried out some studies of listeners' spontaneous gestures to different kinds of musical excerpts, of what we call *gestural rendering of musical sound* (Godøy 2008b). A basic idea in these studies was to ask listeners to make spontaneous gestures to various musical excerpts; hence, to ask them to make a gestural rendering of what they just heard. Another basic idea was to design the tasks so that there were some constraints that would help us to see more clearly various sound-gesture relationships. We would go from rather well-defined tasks and musical material, such as asking listeners to make gestures as if they were playing an instrument when listening to excerpts that were quite clear with regard to the underlying sound-producing gestures, to more open tasks where listeners were asked to make spontaneous gestures to a series of musical excerpts ranging from what we thought would be rather unambiguous in gestural affordance, to musical excerpts that were more complex and rich in gestural affordances. It should be noted as a point of method that we consistently used excerpts of real music, as we found the idea of using artificially created sound examples for the sake of control problematic in view of the ecological validity of our studies.

In Godøy et al. (2006a) listeners with very different levels of expertise were asked to play air-piano to various musical excerpts. The gestural affordance was quite well defined, and all subjects said they clearly understood that they were to make gestures as if they were playing piano, however some of the subjects complained that they felt awkward making gestures in empty air, i.e. not feeling the impact on the surface of the keys. In evaluating the video recordings of these air-piano performances we defined a baseline of minimum necessary movements to produce the sound, i.e. the necessary finger, hand, arm, and sometimes also shoulder and torso movements, and evaluated all the air-piano performances in comparison with this baseline. We found that in general there were clear correspondences between the gestures made by the listeners and the movements required by the music in terms of onsets and pitch-space, i.e. the horizontal movement along the imaginary keyboard, but not unexpectedly, the experts had more details than the novices in their gestural renderings of the music. In other words, that an onset of a sound requires a gesture, and that changes in pitch requires horizontal movement seem to be solid gestural affordances of musical sound that all listeners, regardless of musical training, would spontaneously focus on.

In Godøy et al. (2006b) and Haga (2008) listeners with different levels of expertise were asked to draw on a digital tablet the shape of gestures they felt corresponded to sounds in a series of excerpts, i.e. to do what we called *sound-tracing*. The musical excerpts were chosen so as to have different numbers of salient features ranging from one (basically just various pitch contours) to several (more composite textures and also timbral changes). Not surprisingly, we found that there were more similarities between the gesture shapes for singular feature excerpts than for multiple feature excerpts. In particular, we got divergent results for pitch-steady sounds with timbral changes, with some listeners drawing just a straight line and some listeners drawing various curved lines, and some listeners expressed frustrations with having to render two-dimensionally (that is, on the digital tablet) what they experienced as multi-dimensional (see Figure 5.2 for an example of this sound-tracing).

In another series of observation studies (Haga 2008), we asked listeners, this time mostly professional dancers, to make spontaneous gestures (with fingers, hands, arms, head, torso, but feet fixed to the floor) to a set of musical excerpts, what we called *free movements*. Also in these studies, musical excerpts were carefully chosen in view of what we considered to be various salient features and/or feature sets, and again there was a reasonable degree of consensus in the overall character of the gestures, but increasing variation in detail when the music became more complex or less clearly periodic. In particular, the professional dancers had a tendency to make their own "complement" to the music when periodicity was weak, as if to "fill in" passages of sustained, non-pulsed sounds, perhaps using various movement elements from previous training and/or performances. In sessions where excerpts were repeated several times,

Figure 5.2 Synoptic presentation of sound-tracings of the entire *composite object* from Schaeffer's *Solfège de l'Objet Sonore* (Schaeffer 1998, CD3, track 3). The tracings are arranged according to the decreasing levels of musical training of the subjects starting from top left corner going to the right and downwards in the rows.

these professional dancers seemed to remember what they had done previously, making new embellishments in their gestures as if they were actively exploring new movement possibilities.

Musical sound may be very complex and densely packed with events, yet all participants in our various observation studies seemed to be able to make some kind of rendering, in some cases with much detail, but in other cases with quite coarse, approximate or sketchy kinds of gestures to complex music. For this reason, we may talk about *variable resolution* in listeners' gestural renderings of musical sound, meaning that the gestures may vary between being quite detailed and very approximate in their correspondence with the musical sound. Actually, musical sound is itself often intrinsically "multi-resolution" in the sense that it consists of juxta-positions of events at different time-scales: when a pianist plays a rapid ascending passage on the piano, this passage contains the fast com-ponents of the individual tones in rapid succession, yet at the same time contains the slower components of the movements of the hand and arm (or even the shoulder and torso) in order to position the fingers for the right keys. With such concurrent high-frequency components of the indi-vidual tones, and low-frequency components of the overall contour of the ascending passage, we may understand the variable acuity in the gestural rendering of musical sound as a matter of focus on different time-scales in musical sound.

When listeners "zoom out" of the musical sound and make low-resolution, coarse gestural renderings of musical sound, we have some conceptual challenges of how to deal with approximate, low-acuity, sketch-like information. Present motion capture technology can provide us with spatially and temporally quite accurate data of human move-ments, but it seems that we need to develop better methods of comparing and evaluating approximate resemblances between the trajectories of dif-ferent gestures. Also, we may have sound–gesture correspondences where the main point is actually not so much the kinematics (the gesture trajec-tory shapes that we see) as it is the dynamics of movement (the sensation of effort that we feel through our embodied capacity for mental simula-tion of the actions of others) (Gallese and Metzinger 2003). For this reason, it may sometimes make sense to focus on sensations of effort when we observe various gestural renderings of musical sound. Obvi-ously, kinematics and dynamics cannot be separated in the sense that when observing human motion, we are bound to simultaneously have some sensation of effort, and conversely, when considering effort, we also do this in relation to kinematics. Yet what seems to survive even the most severe reduction in acuity (cf. the novice's gestural rendering in air-playing) is the sensation of effort: agitated music with many tone onsets invariably resulted in agitated, very active gestural renderings, and calm music with protracted sounds invariably resulted in calm and protracted gestures, whereas the kinematics, or the geometry of the gesture trajectories, could vary among participants.

In the study of air-piano playing, the strongest correspondence was found in what we called *overall activity correspondence*, meaning density of gestures in relation to density of onsets in the music, regardless of the position in relative pitch space and regardless of the rhythmic onset precision, and in what we called *coarse onset correspondence*, meaning synchrony at downbeat or event level, "event" here denoting salient points in cases of non-periodic music. Another fairly good correspondence was found in what we called *dynamics correspondence*, meaning amplitude and speed of hands/arms/body gestures in relation to loudness, and to a certain extent also to finer details of articulation (Godøy et al. 2006a). Similarly, in the free-dance studies, there seemed to be a fairly strong correspondence across both different excerpts and different dancers, as well as across different variant renderings, of activity level in the musical sound and the gestures (Haga 2008). For instance we saw seemingly rather divergent gesture trajectories in the rendering of the opening of the Lento movement from Ligeti's *Ten Pieces for Wind Quintet*, an excerpt dominated by protracted and slowly changing sound; however, all dancers made slow and extended movements to this excerpt. This means that we had a divergence in geometry, i.e. differences in action trajectories, yet a convergence in effort, i.e. similar slow, protracted movements.

7 The Perception–Action Cycle and Music-Related Gestures

It seems clear that listeners with different levels of expertise in music and movement are able to spontaneously make gestures that correspond to some feature, or features, of the musical sound. We may understand this in terms of the perception–action cycle, where we incessantly relate what we hear to some image of the assumed sound-producing action behind what we hear, or to some other gestures that we assume correspond with the music.

This perception–action cycle is not only a matter of spontaneous response to what we hear, but is actually also a way of familiarizing ourselves with the sounds: we progressively enhance our capacity for discrimination and our detailed knowledge of the various features of the sounds. This progressive learning and discrimination by repeated sound–gesture simulations is one of the basic tenets of the motor theory of perception, but it could also be seen in a wider context as a way to explore sound with our hands (or other effectors), as a kind of "hermeneutic circle" of progressively becoming closer to the sounds by attaching them to our gestures. This kind of "manual cognition" of musical sound attests to the primordial role of *hand movements* that several researchers now seem to attach to gestures, i.e. suggesting that the role of gestures goes far beyond that of underlining verbal communication (Rizzolatti and Arbib 1998; Goldin-Meadow 2003), and is actually an essential tool for thinking, whereas the geometry and effort of hand gestures enhance conceptual structures of what we think.

There is now a considerable amount of research that supports the idea of perception–action interaction in all human activity (see e.g. Gallese and Metzinger 2003), however what seems to have received less attention is the temporal aspect in this: given a continuous stream of sound, we somehow have to decide "what is what" in this continuous stream; that is, we have to segment the stream of sound into chunks in order to decide what are the sonic events and what are the gestures that correspond to these sonic events. This means that in the perception–action cycle, we have to insert points where we make decisions about chunking related to the basic gesture-units, i.e. to iterative, impulsive, or sustained, and various other grouping principles such as coarticulation. When listening to unfamiliar music, we obviously will do this chunking and gesture assignment in retrospect, except in cases where the type of music is very predictable, whereas in familiar music, we may also do this prospectively: we may think ahead in terms of gesture chunks before we actually hear the sound. But in all cases, we will tend to associate continuous sound with action-units, and hence, we will always find an element of discontinuity in the perception–action cycle.

The relationship between continuity and discontinuity in perception, action, and thinking has intrigued researchers in the past. First of all, the idea that perception and cognition in general proceeds in a discontinuous manner by a series of "now-points," was suggested by phenomenological philosophy more than a century ago, with the argument that if we were submerged in a continuous stream of impressions, the world would only appear to us as an amorphous mass of indistinct sensations (Husserl 1991). Interestingly, similar ideas of discontinuity in perception and cognition based on various neurocognitive findings have been suggested more recently (e.g. Pöppel 1997; Varela 1999). In the domain of human movement, similar issues of discontinuity versus continuity have also been debated for more than a century, since Woodworth's suggestion that there is an "initial impulse" in motor control (Woodworth 1899). That is, it has been debated to what extent human movement is continuously controlled or proceeds more by preprogrammed action units; however, there seems to be a consensus now that there is both preprogramming and continuous adjustment (Elliott et al. 2001). Another important element is that of goal-directed actions in general (Gallese and Metzinger 2003) and in imitation in particular as mentioned above (Wohlschläger et al. 2003), meaning that simulation and imitation of behavior seems primarily concerned with arriving at certain goals, i.e. at certain positions in time and space, whereas the continuous trajectories to and from these goals are subordinate to these goals.

In studying music-related gestures it would be a good idea then to try to detect what we could call *goal-points* in the perception–action cycle (Godøy 2008a). The idea with goal-points is that they are goal-postures in the form of the position and shape of the effectors (the hands in the case of gestures, but could also be the vocal apparatus in the case of vocal imitation) at certain important moments in the flow of musical sound, such as at downbeats or at various other accented events or at melodic, textural or timbral peaks. For instance, the accented tutti chord in the Chaplin example (where Chaplin shakes off the shaving cream with a rapid, whole-arm gesture) would be such a goal-point because it is accented and marks the endpoint of the phrase.

This element of goal-points, i.e. goal postures at certain points in time, is a general phenomenon of motor behavior, and similar schemes of goal-postures with intervening motion can be observed in various other tasks such as writing, speaking, manipulating tools, etc. This phenomenon is sometimes also referred to as *keyframes* and *interframes* (Rosenbaum et al. 2007), terms borrowed from animation where it was a well-established procedure to draw the most important scenes and postures first, i.e. the keyframes, and then draw the continuous interpolation between these keyframes, i.e. the interframes.

Most importantly, goal-points have the attractive feature of giving us intrinsic and "natural" criteria for chunking continuous streams of sound and gestures into meaningful units: goal-points are based on combined biomechanical, motor control, and perceptual constraints. In terms of size, we are here talking about sound and gesture chunks typically in the range of 0.5 to 5 seconds (as was the case for Schaeffer's sonic object; see section 5 above). These durations are generally accepted as the optimal size of chunks that can be retained in short-term memory (Snyder 2000), but where the duration first of all is determined by the principle of the goal-points and the movements between the goal-points. In terms of ordinary musical contexts, these sound and gesture units can be regarded as "meso-level" units in the sense that on a smaller time-scale, at what we could call the "micro-level," we have more or less continuous sound or movement, and on a larger time-scale than the meso-level, we could speak of a "macro-level" where meso-level gesture units may be concatenated into larger-scale gestural scripts.

Such an understanding of sound-gesture chunks centered on goal-points could perhaps also shed light on our evident ability to have prospective (as well as retrospective) images of musical sound, i.e. as performers or improvisers we are able, "in a split second" to overview what we have just played, what we are playing now, and what we will be playing in the near future. In the terminology of Husserl, this would mean having the cumulative effects of *retention, primary impressions*, and *protentions* (images of past, present, and future) present in our minds all at once or "in a now" (Husserl 1991) by way of such goal-points. Goal-points may thus serve as compressed images of more extended action-trajectories, similar to what are called "thumbnails" in audio and video data retrieval, enabling us to think of longer passages of musical sound as gestural scripts with concatenations of several such goal-points.

8 Conclusion

We are only in the beginning of more systematic studies of gestural affordances of musical sound, and needless to say, there are very many theoretical and methodological challenges here. As for future research, we clearly need better means for motion capture, in particular less obtrusive technologies that can accurately capture listeners' spontaneous music-related gestures in non-laboratory settings, as well as better means for processing and representing or displaying such motion capture data. But also on the sound side, we need to work for better conceptual and practical means for extracting gesture-affording features of musical sound. On a more fundamental level, we need to have a better understanding of auditory-motor coupling in our minds, and of the inseparable issue of chunking of continuous sound and gestures into meaningful units.

However, the growing evidence for the existence of imitative behavior (both overt and covert) and of incessant mental simulation of action in perception and cognition, are significant advances, and point towards a general model of a perception–action cycle at work in the experience of music. This perception–action cycle is an indication of listeners' strong and embodied involvement with music, and also an opportunity for us to explore how gestures help us to listen, or how the experience of musical sound is enhanced by concurrent experiences of gestures, as well as possibilities for mediating between technology, sound, and mind.

More systematic knowledge of gestural affordances of musical sound could have significant impacts not only on our general understanding of music as a phenomenon, but also within fields such as music history, music analysis, orchestration and composition. Understanding musical works as rich, multidimensional gestural scripts in interaction with sound would be a welcome change of orientation within these areas, and gestural affordances of musical sound could be regarded as the basis for descriptions of musical style as well as emotive and aesthetic sensations in music.

Note

1   See http://www.airguitarworldchampionships.com/home.html

References

Aksnes, H. and Ruud, E. (2008). Body-based schemata in receptive music therapy. *Musicae Scientiae*, 12(1), 49–74.

Bangert, M. and Altenmüller, E. O. (2003). Mapping perception to action in piano practice: a longitudinal DC-EEG study. *BMC Neuroscience*, 4(26).

Eitan, Z. and Granot, R. Y. (2006). How music moves: musical parameters and listeners' images of motion. *Music Perception,* 23(3), 221–247.

Elliott, D., Helsen, W., and Chua, R. (2001). A century later: Woodworth's (1899) two-component model of goal-directed aiming. *Psychological Bulletin,* 127(3), 342–357.

Fadiga, L., Craighero, L., Buccino, G., and Rizzolatti, G. (2002). Speech listening specifically modulates the excitability of tongue muscles: a TMS study. *European Journal of Neuroscience,* 15(2), 399–402.

Fraisse, P. (1982). Rhythm and tempo. In D. Deutsch (ed.), *The Psychology of Music.* (First edition). New York: Academic Press, 149–180.

Galantucci, B., Fowler, C. A., and Turvey, M. T. (2006). The motor theory of speech perception reviewed. *Psychonomic Bulletin and Review,* 13(3), 361–377.

Gallese, V. (2003). The roots of empathy: the shared manifold hypothesis and the neural basis of intersubjectivity. *Psychopathology,* 36(4), 171–180.

Gallese, V. and Goldman, A. (1998). Mirror neurons and the simulation theory of mind-reading. *Trends in Cognitive Science*, 2(12), 493–501.

Gallese, V. and Lakoff, G. (2005). The brain's concepts: the role of the sensory-motor system in conceptual knowledge. *Cognitive Neuropsychology,* 22(3/4), 455–479.

Gallese, V. and Metzinger, T. (2003). Motor ontology: the representational reality of goals, actions and selves. *Philosophical Psychology,* 16(3), 365–338.

Gaver, W. W. (1993). How do we hear in the world? An ecological approach to auditory event perception. *Ecological Psychology,* 5(4), 285–313.

Gibson, J. J. (1979). *The Ecological Approach to Visual Perception.* Hillsdale, NJ: Lawrence Erlbaum Associates.

Godøy, R. I. (1997). *Formalization and Epistemology.* Oslo: Scandinavian University Press.

Godøy, R. I. (2003). Motor-mimetic music cognition. *Leonardo,* 36(4), 317–319.

Godøy, R. I. (2006). Gestural–sonorous objects: embodied extensions of Schaeffer's conceptual apparatus. *Organised Sound,* 11(2), 149–157.

Godøy, R. I. (2008a). Reflections on chunking in music. In A. Schneider (ed.), *Systematic and Comparative Musicology: Concepts, Methods, Findings.* Frankfurt am Main: Peter Lang, 117–132.

Godøy, R. I. (2008b). Geometry and effort in gestural renderings of musical sound. In M. S. Dias, S. Gibet, M. M. Wanderley, and R. Bastos (eds.), *Advances in Gesture-Based Human–Computer Interaction and Simulation,* LNCS 5085. Berlin, Heidelberg: Springer, 205–215.

Godøy, R. I., Haga, E. and Jensenius, A. R. (2006a). Playing "air instruments:" mimicry of sound-producing gestures by novices and experts. In S. Gibet, N. Courty, and J.-F. Kamp (eds.), *Gesture in Human-Computer Interaction and Simulation,* LNAI 3881. Berlin, Heidelberg: Springer, 256–267.

Godøy, R. I., Haga, E. and Jensenius, A. R. (2006b). Exploring music-related gestures by sound-tracing: a preliminary study. In K. Ng (ed), *Proceedings of the COST287-ConGAS 2nd International Symposium on Gesture Interfaces for Multimedia Systems.* Leeds, UK, 27–33.

Goldin-Meadow, S. (2003). *Hearing Gesture: How Our Hands Help Us Think.* Cambridge, MA: The Belknap Press.

Haga, E. (2008). *Correspondences between Music and Body Movement.* PhD thesis. Oslo: University of Oslo.

Haken, H., Kelso, J.A.S., and Bunz, H. (1985). A theoretical model of phase transitions in human hand movements. *Biological Cybernetics,* 51(5), 347–356.

Harding, S., Cooke, M., and König, P. (2007). Auditory gist perception: an alternative to attentional selection of auditory streams? In L. Paletta and E. Rome (eds.), *Attention in Cognitive Systems,* LNAI 4840. Berlin, Heidelberg: Springer, 399–416.

Haueisen, J. and Knösche, T. R. (2001). Involuntary motor activity in pianists evoked by music perception. *Journal of Cognitive Neuroscience,* 13(6), 786–792.

Husserl, E. (1991). *On the Phenomenology of the Consciousness of Internal Time, 1893 -1917.* (English translation by John Barnett Brough.) Dordrecht, Boston, London: Kluwer Academic Publishers.

Johnson, M. (1987). *The Body in the Mind.* Chicago: University of Chicago Press.

Kelso, J.A.S., Fuchs, A., Lancaster, R., Holroyd, T., Cheyne, D., and Weinberg, H. (1998). Dynamic cortical activity in the human brain reveals motor equivalence. *Nature,* 392(23), 814–818.

Keysers, C., Kohler, E., Umiltá, M. A., Nanetti, L., Fogassi, L., and Gallese, V. (2003). Audiovisual mirror neurons and action recognition. *Experimental Brain Research,* 153(4), 628–636.

Kohler, E., Keysers, C., Umiltà, M. A., Fogassi, L., Gallese, V., and Rizzolatti, G. (2002). Hearing sounds, understanding actions: action representation in mirror neurons. *Science,* 297, 846–848.

Laban, R. v. (1980). *The Mastery of Movement* (fourth edition by Lisa Ullmann). Plymouth: Northcote House Publishers.

Lakoff. G. (1987). *Women, Fire and Dangerous Things. What Categories Reveal about the Mind.* Chicago: University of Chicago Press.

Large, E. W. (2000). On synchronizing movement to music. *Human Movement Science,* 19(4), 527–566.

Leman, M. (2008). *Embodied Music Cognition and Mediation Technology.* Cambridge, MA: MIT Press.

Liberman, A. M. and Mattingly, I. G. (1985). The motor theory of speech perception revised. *Cognition,* 21(1), 1–36.

McAnally, K. I. (2002). Timing of finger tapping to frequency modulated acoustic stimuli. *Acta Psychologica,* 109(3), 331–338.

Meltzoff, A. N. and Moore, M. K. (1977). Imitation of facial and manual gestures by human neonates. *Science,* 198(4312), 75–78.

Neisser, U. (1976). *Cognition and Reality.* San Francisco: W.H. Freeman.

Phillips-Silver, J. and Trainor, L. J. (2008). Vestibular influence on auditory metrical interpretation. *Brain and Cognition,* 67(1), 94–102.

Pöppel, E. (1997). A Hierarchical model of time perception. *Trends in Cognitive Science*, 1(2), 56–61.

Rizzolatti, G. and Arbib, M. A. (1998). Language within our grasp. *Trends in Neuroscience*, 21(5), 188–194.

Rocchesso, D. and Fontana, F. (eds.) (2003). *The Sounding Object*. Firenze: Edizioni di Mondo Estremo.

Rosenbaum, D., Cohen, R. G., Jax, S. A., Weiss, D. J., and van der Wel, R. (2007). The problem of serial order in behavior: Lashley's legacy. *Human Movement Science*, 26(4), 525–554.

Schaeffer, P. (1966). *Traité des Objets Musicaux*. Paris: Éditions du Seuil.

Schaeffer, P. (1998). *Solfège de l'Objet Sonore*. (first published in 1967, with sound examples by G. Reibel, and B. Ferreyra). Paris: INA/GRM.

Snyder, B. (2000). *Music and Memory: An Introduction*. Cambridge, MA: MIT Press.

Thaut, M. (2005). *Rhythm, Music, and the Brain: Scientific Foundations and Clinical Applications*. New York: Routledge.

Thom, R. (1983). *Paraboles et Catastrophes*. Paris: Flammarion.

Varela, F. (1999). The specious present: the neurophenomenology of time consciousness. In J. Petitot, F. J. Varela, B. Pachoud, and J. M. Roy (eds.), *Naturalizing Phenomenology*. Stanford, CA: Stanford University Press, 266–314.

Wilson, M. and Knoblich, G. (2005). The case for motor involvement in perceiving conspecifics. *Psychological Bulletin*, 131(3), 460–473.

Wohlschläger, A., Gattis, M. and Bekkering, H. (2003). Action generation and action perception in imitation: an instance of the ideomotor principle. *Philosophical Transactions of the Royal Society London B*, 358, 501–515.

Woodworth, R. S. (1899). The accuracy of voluntary movement. *Psychological Review*, 3, 1–119.

Chapter 6

Music, Gesture, and the Formation of Embodied Meaning

Marc Leman

1 Introduction

In previous work, scholars of music have identified gesture as a core component of musical meaning formation (Pratt 1931/1968; Truslit 1938; Coker 1972; Broeckx 1981; Hatten 1994; Cumming 2000). Broeckx (1981) holds that, through gesture, music can be experienced as the action of a dynamic organism similar to a human organism. Such an experience allows for the construction of meaningful relationships with the structural properties of music (pitch, rhythm, articulation, timbre) as well as with its cultural/historical contexts. For example, an aria in Mozart's *Don Giovanni* can be experienced as being extremely gallant, with the musical properties of a dance (a *Menuet*) that can be linked to prototypes of aristocratic behaviour, and, perhaps, to Mozart's implied criticism of aristocratic privileges (Allanbrook 1983). In this case, the formation of meaning is both direct and indirect. It is direct at the moment when the music is corporeally experienced (or should we say: felt) as a gallant gesture. It is indirect, and mediated by thinking, when this experience is understood as an expression of prototypical aristocratic behaviour, or of social class relationships in general. The gesture thereby appears as a vehicle for the construction of music-related meanings: first in our experience and next through our understanding and connection with structural features and cultural topics.

In talking about gesture, the musicological literature often provides an understanding of gesture and the formation of meaning in terms of a written account of connected events, or narrative. Even when lower levels of meaning formation are taken into account, as a ground for bodily engagement and corporeal signification, as in (Lipps 1903; Merleau-Ponty 1945), the account is still narrative rather than empirical or instrumental. This narrative approach is often valid and necessary, as it provides core philosophical insight into the relationship between gesture and subjective experience. However, it lacks a concrete empirical understanding of gesture as a causal physical and biological phenomenon that is connected with experience. This empirical understanding is needed in view of recent developments that aim at extending and exploiting novel frontiers of artistic expression and social communication, using new media and electronic technologies. Therefore, the narrative approach should be complemented with an empirical approach in such a way that both approaches can reinforce each other. But how can this be achieved?

In my book on *Embodied Music Cognition and Mediation Technology* (Leman 2008), I suggest that the narrative and empirical viewpoints may be integrated through a particular approach to the concept of embodiment. The human body is thereby understood as a mediator between the musical mind and the physical environment, and gestures can be conceived as the way in which this mediator deploys itself in space and time. What is important in this framework is the idea that music is performed and perceived through gestures whose deployment can be directly felt and understood through the body, without the need for verbal descriptions. Seen as such, the approach of embodied music cognition aims to offer a framework in which subjective experiences and physical/biological mechanisms are connected as tightly as possible. This approach is also related to theories that focus on human action, such as activity and enactive theory (Nardi 1996; Kaptelinin and Nardi 2006; Varela et al. 1991). Its historical roots can be found in the work of Apostel, Merleau-Ponty, Piaget, Vygotsky and others.

In this chapter, I will explore the framework of embodied music cognition further as a means for the study of gesture and the formation of musical meaning. In the first part, I will introduce a layered framework for meaning formation, based on a developed understanding of the connection between corporeal and cerebral activity. In the second part, I will show how gesture may be studied by combining three different perspectives: a third-person perspective, which is based on the measurement of body parts and sonic forms, a first-person perspective, which is based on self-observation and interpretation of experiences and, finally, a second-person perspective, which is based on how gestures function as social cues. The latter perspective is of particular interest because it entails the view that gestures can be understood as social signals for meaningful music-driven interactions with music and with other subjects. I argue that the study of musical gesture can be grounded in an empirical methodology that combines these three different perspectives.

2 A Layered Approach to Musical Meaning Formation

The above example of Mozart's menuet has already shown that meaning formation involves different levels of information processing. The formation of musical meaning can initially start from sensations and perceptions of qualia, and then evolve into phenomenal representations, conscious awareness and finally, hermeneutic interpretations and linguistic descriptions. Although a description of the details of these different levels goes far beyond the scope of the present chapter, it is instructive to introduce here a more general phenomenologically-based approach, which is based on that of Broeckx (1981).

The first step in the course of meaning formation may be seen in terms of processes that account for the transformation of sonic features into the presence of sensory qualities and motor action-related features. These transformations can be termed either synaesthetic or kinaesthetic. During synaesthetic transformation, physical properties of musical sound, such as frequency, duration, spectral density, and loudness, are first perceived as auditory categories, (such as pitch, duration, timbre and volume). Via a multi-sensory integration, they become related to impressions of space, visual and tactile nature, such as extension, density, weight, smoothness, roughness, hardness, softness, liquidness, and ephemerality. During kinaesthetic transformation, it is the dynamics of physical properties (frequency, amplitude, and so on) through time that generate in our perception segregated streams and objects that lead, via integrated processing, to impressions of movement, gesture, tension, and release of tension.

An account of how these synaesthetic and kinaesthetic processes are actually realized by the causality of our biological system goes far beyond the scope of the present chapter. Phenomenology limits itself to the more global context in which these processes function. From that perspective, we can immediately proceed to a further level of transformation, called the cenaesthetic transformation.[1] This transformation starts from the synaesthetic and kinaesthetic level and links these with conceptualization and cognition. However, the cenaesthetic transformation is assumed to have both an embodied and a conceptualized aspect, which makes it an interesting case. The embodied aspect refers to the sensing of the body in relation to the music. This can be understood as a kind of mindfulness that is a phenomenal awareness of bodily presence in response to music (see Varela et al. 1991). In contrast, the conceptualized aspect refers to a reflexive cognizing in which the listener represents this mindfulness in terms of verbal description. Thus, the latter allows the synaesthetic experience to be described in terms of multi-modal attributes, and the kinaesthetic experience to be described in terms of verbs and adjectives that relate to movement and gesture. Again, an account of the underlying causality of this transformation goes far beyond the scope of the present account.

It suffices here to say that the cenesthetic transformation can be seen as a precondition for a fully symbolized type of meaning formation, which Broeckx calls the analogical process, but which other authors have called the semiotic (Tarasti 2003; Monelle 2000) or the hermeneutic process (Hatten 2003). It is the level at which felt properties or descriptions thereof are linked with cultural symbols and topics. It is the level at which we say that a *menuet* by Mozart expresses the aristocratic class, or at which we say that the pounding rhythms in Stravinsky's *Rite of Spring* express the anxiousness of mankind to accommodate to nature. In saying this, we project musical structures that appeal to gestural movement onto cultural topics that we have learned to categorize. In addition, we could project descriptions of synaesthetic and kinaesthetic experience onto cultural categories, or focus on emotions. Hermeneutics lends itself very well to these projections.

Clearly, the model of the formation of musical meaning described above is narrative, which means that it is a conceptual construction about how corporeal and cerebral accounts of gesture may be linked, rather than a causal, functional, or operational, model of gesture. However, this approach can and, I will argue, should be extended to include an empirical approach in order to clarify its concepts and to make the model as concrete as possible. For example, in order to access the synaesthetic and kinaesthetic experiences from an empirical point of view, we can record body movement and study the relationship between musical properties, felt experiences of motion, and recorded kinematic and kinetic features. In a similar way, we can measure skin conductance and muscle tension, and study the relationship between recorded body data, musical properties, and the experience of stress. Although these measurements transcend the narrative account, it is still possible to link them with narrative descriptions of experiences, so that a broad range of meaning formation can be covered.

3 Considering Gestures as Fully Embodied

In light of the above, gestures can be understood as close to body movements and close to meaning. Several types of music-related physical movement may be distinguished, ranging from mere passive resonance (response to loud sound), to synchronization (tapping with the beat), to attuning (singing along with the melody, harmony, or tonality), to empathy (behaving as if feelings engendered by the music are shared), and to entrainment (mutual adaptation of subjects' behaviour while involved with music). Similarly, several types of music-related meaning may be distinguished, for example: in respect to expressive emotional engagement, in respect to intended actions, in respect to social interaction, as metaphor, and so on. The list is not exhaustive, as there are many different ways in which physical movement may relate to meaning. However, what is important is the role of physical movement as a property of the mediation between mind and physical environment. From that perspective, gestures appear as the patterns that deploy or articulate this mediation. It is even tempting to say that gestures *express* this mediation. Therefore, it can be said that gestures are neither purely physical, nor purely mental but are embodied by nature. They form part of a mediation process, and therefore exceed the classical Cartesian division between mind and matter.

Figure 6.1 clarifies how gesture and meaning formation may be accessed in a simple scientific context. On the left hand side, the figure shows a viol player in action. In playing, a musical goal is turned into bio-mechanical energy, which is then transformed into sonic energy. Through feedback loops, the viol player will be able to handle the viol as an extended body part so that he can focus on the goals of the sound-performing gestures rather than having to focus on the execution of the sound-performing gestures on the mediator.

To the right hand side, the figure shows a listener in action. The listener perceives the sonic energy and expresses her engagement with music through arm movements, which can be recorded via a telescopic stick, which is an adapted joystick mediator. The movements of the listener are music-driven and can be called corporeal coarticulations of the perceived music. We assume that these corporeal articulations may give rise to a feeling of agency: of being moved, or activated, by the music. Meaning formation may start from the moment that the listener is able to engage with music in terms of physical movement that appears to have this character of agency.

Next to the player, we see an observer. His task is to study gestures in view of physical movement and meaning formation. To understand this,

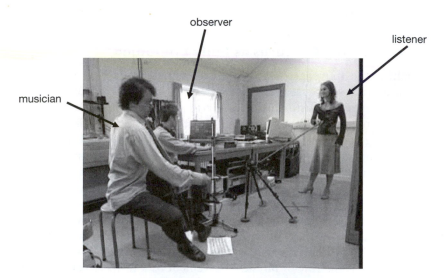

Figure 6.1 Music communication model, with musician, listener, and observer.

the observer looks at three forms of activity: (1) physical activity, related to the generation and transmission of energy along different communication channels (audio, haptic, visual . . .), which allows objective measurement of gestures; (2) bodily activity, related to the mediation between the mental and physical levels at which gesture occur; and (3) mental activity, related to the way in which music is experienced as gesture. In this view, the gestures appear as physical movement in relation to music, involving both kinematic (such as the displacement, velocity or acceleration of different joints) and kinetic (such as force or power) aspects. He is interested in discovering how this entire context can be meaningful, and how gestures express this meaning formation.

The model illustrated above is thus based on the interplay of both mental and physical aspects, with the human body acting as mediator. Depending on the viewpoint, gesture can be studied as mere body movement (starting with kinematics and kinetics), or as an expression of human intentionality and an experience that is implied by this body movement (starting with agency).

So far, the framework shown above for the formation of musical meaning and its link with embodiment provides a general phenomenology, which, in view of the development of applications in the cultural and creative sector, should be expanded to an empirical methodology. Gesture can then be approached from three different perspectives: namely, the first-person, second-person and third-person perspectives. Based on the results of a few case studies, performed at the IPEM laboratory of the Department of Musicology at Ghent University, I will argue that gesture can best be studied by combining these three viewpoints.

4 The Third-Person Perspective on Gesture

The so-called third-person perspective on gesture focuses on the objective, and in principle repeatable, measurement of moving objects. The observation can be done by any person, even a machine, or a combination of human and machine, provided that it follows a pre-established procedure in a proper way. The adjective "third-person" implies the perspective of a person who observes certain activities, whether or not the actors are aware of the person's presence. This third-person perspective can be measured in respect of all objects that have an extension, including vibrations and moving air particles in the case of sound (measured through audio-recording), movement of body parts (measured through kinetic sensors, and video-recording), brain activity (measured through brain scans), and physiological body changes such as sweat, heart rate, breath rate, skin conduction, hormones and so on (measured through biological or physiological sensors). So far, these methods have been used in studies that aim to quantify different aspects of music performances and expressive gestural control (Friberg and Sundberg 1999; Friberg et al. 2000; Wanderley and Battier 2000; Camurri, Volpe et al. 2005; Vines et al. 2003).

In addition to developing monitoring tools, studies have identified several cues. For example, by using kinetic sensors, many authors believe that movement velocity (Figure 6.2) is a highly relevant cue for expressive movement in response to music (see also Gibet et al. 2004; Knoblich and Flach 2003; Camurri, Mazzarino et al. 2004a; 2004b). A typical movement velocity pattern is shown in Figure 6.2a. This specific pattern resulted from a setup that was similar to the setup of Figure 6.1 but, instead of a viol player, the subject was a *guqin* player (see Figure 6.3). Markers were attached to her head and joints (shoulders, elbow, wrist, fingers), and her movements were recorded with an infrared camera. Listeners had to move using a stick (as in Figure 6.1) while listening to the recorded music via a headset. In contrast to the didactical setup of Figure 6.1, in this experiment player and listener were not able to see each other.

The full line in Figure 6.2a shows the movement velocity of the listener's arm, while the dashed line shows the movement velocity of the player's head. At first sight, the original patterns show little correspondence. However, by allowing for small local time shifts, similar to anticipation and delay in movement, we immediately derive patterns that are much more similar to each other (Figure 6.2b). In comparing these kinematic data, small disparities in timing can be justified by the fact that delayed or anticipated movements may still be considered to be "in time," and therefore meaningful in terms of a connection between these movements, called "muscular bonding" (McNeill 1995).

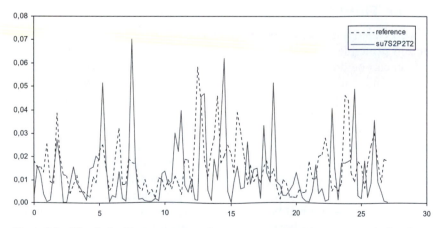

Figure 6.2a The dashed line represents the movement velocity pattern of the head of a *guqin* player. The full line represents the movement velocity pattern of the listener (using the stick as shown in Figure 6.1).

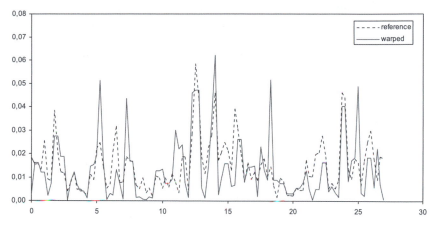

Figure 6.2b The dashed line again represents the movement velocity pattern of the head of a *guqin* player. However, the full line now represents the warped movement velocity pattern of the listener.

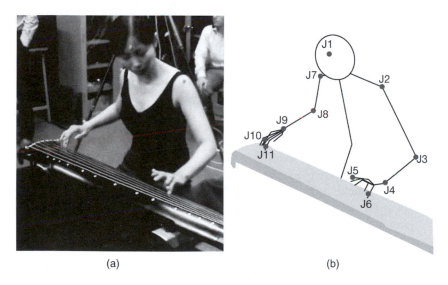

(a)   (b)

Figure 6.3 Infrared recording of eleven joints of the player results in a stick figure of which the trajectories of eleven joints can be followed over time.

Leman et al. (2009) compared the arm movements of thirty listeners with the movements of a *guqin* player. The study showed that, although the listeners could not see each other, their movements showed correlations. In considering the similarities between the movements of listeners and those of the player (also deprived of seeing each other), it emerged that the movements of listeners' arms correlated best with the movements of the player's shoulders (again, neither player nor listeners could see each other). The study suggests that body movement expresses inter-subjective features that are relevant to the communicative properties of music (see the second-person perspective below).

To sum up, the third-person perspective is based on techniques of objective measurement, feature extraction, and pattern matching. Given a careful experimental setup, characteristics of body movement can be studied in view of their mediating role as carriers of meaningful information, which we then consider to be gesture. However, to reveal properties of body movement as gesture, a more detailed level of analysis may be needed.

5 The First-Person Perspective on Gesture

The first-person perspective on gesture shows what a gesture means for the subject that makes it. In what follows, I make a difference between an action-oriented approach and an experience-based approach.

5.1 An Action-Based Approach to Gesture

In this approach, gesture is studied from the viewpoint of a subject's own action-oriented ontology: that is, the set of things that exist for the subject as agent. For example, if playing a note on the trumpet exists in my action-oriented ontology, then it means that I am able to mentally represent this action as a gestalt, I can imagine this action as it is deployed over time, and that I probably have the capacity to execute this action (even if I in fact have not played the instrument for several years). If you are not a trumpet player, but a guitarist, then you may have a global representation of this trumpet playing action, but you will not be able to deploy the action in your imagination, nor will you have the skills to execute the action at the same level of detail that I can. In this case, the trumpet note-playing action is not part of your action-oriented ontology, because it is not part of your embodied imagination (body image) or your actual skills (body schema).

From this action-based viewpoint, a gesture can be considered as a hierarchically structured action pattern to which we can have mental access. For example, I can mentally deconstruct the playing of a melodic pattern into smaller actions at the level of playing individual notes, and I can further deconstruct these actions into even smaller ones, such as breathing and lip pressure actions. However, this deconstruction comes to an end when I am no longer able to access my underlying muscle movement, or my low-level sensorimotor system (the body schema) that executes this action for me. This part of the body schema is impenetrable because it is not accessible as a representational category of my action. The muscle movement is automatically achieved, so to speak, as if my mental functions are protected from an unlimited access to the peripheral parts of my motor system. In a similar way, my mind cannot penetrate its own neuronal activity (see Metzinger 2003). As a consequence of that limitation, cognitive deconstruction ultimately leads to the idea that gestures can be segmented into elementary gestures that cannot be further cognitively penetrated. Let us look at a concrete example to see if this idea can be worked out.

In a study on *guqin* playing, Li and Leman (2007) analyzed the gestural characteristics of sliding-tones in Chinese *guqin* music. The method of analysis was a manual segmentation of the different sliding-pitch gestures of each tone of an audio recording of *guqin* music. This segmentation was based on the intuitive awareness of the player's sound-generating gestures, which underlaid the sonic gestures. By drawing on a player's action-oriented ontology, it was thus possible to understand complicated sliding-pitch gestures as concatenations of elementary sound-generating gestures.

Using a bootstrap methodology, where segmentation rules were based on sound-generation gestures, and where sound-generation gestures were in turn considered from the viewpoint of segmentation rules, it was possible to identify a set of elementary patterns, and a set of rules for the syntactic concatenation of these patterns. Table 6.1 shows the alphabet of these elementary patterns, which contains four basic sliding-tone forms: namely, flat, linear oblique, accelerated and decelerated. Each of these can have an upward or downward direction. Given the tight connection between sound and control gesture in *guqin* music, these sonic patterns can also be considered the most elementary patterns from the viewpoint of sound-generation gestures.

Figure 6.4 gives an example of how this works in practice. The dotted line shows the pitch change of a recorded *guqin* tone. The horizontal axis represents time, while the vertical axis represents pitch (expressed in cent values). Such patterns are typically obtained by plucking the string with a finger of the right hand and shortening and lengthening the string with one single finger of the left hand. The resulting gestural form can be understood as a concatenation of the following elementary gestures:

1. The head part of the gesture (HD) has a V-like shape, consisting of two sub-gestures having an s-like shape. Typically, the s-like shaped gesture consists of three elementary gestures, namely, a + l + d. This is most clearly expressed in the upward (U) direction.
2. The head part is followed by a so-called self-contained component (SC) consisting of a flat shape (F-like). This flat part stresses a pitch that is about one tone (200 cents) higher than the rest of the tone.
3. The next part is a melodic movement (MM) towards the lower pitch.

Table 6.1 Alphabet of pitch contour shapes with the specification of the curvature and the direction

Curvature:		Direction:
f: flat	(no perceptible pitch change)	U: upward
l: linear oblique	(pitch-slide in uniform velocity)	(change from lower to higher pitch)
a: accelerated	(accelerated pitch-slide, smooth curve or in 2 fixed velocities: $lv_1+lv_2\ lv_2>lv_1$)	D: downward
d: decelerated	(decelerated pitch-slide, smooth curve or in 2 fixed velocities: $lv_2+lv_1\ lv_2>lv_1$)	(change from higher to lower pitch)

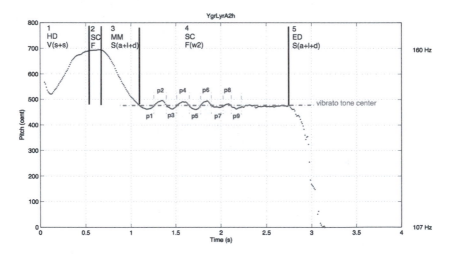

Figure 6.4 Example of a sliding-tone, annotated according to the typology of elementary *guqin* sliding-tone gestures (Li and Leman 2007).

This melodic movement is characterised by an S-like gesture which is typically composed of a + l + d (in D-direction)

4. The fourth part is again a self-contained unit that is characterized by a vibrato pattern on a flat tone. Hence the notation F(w2), where the "w" points to a concatenation of V-like shapes.

5. The end of the tone (ED) is again an S-like gesture, composed of (a + l + d) in D-direction.

The sequential concatenation of the elementary gestures is constrained in two ways, first, by the biomechanics of body movement, and second, by cultural tradition. Certain combinations of elementary gestures are just impossible to realize from a biomechanical point of view, while other combinations of elementary gestures are never used. For example, the combination aU + lU + aD is impossible to make because of the all-too-sudden changes in the pattern lU + aD. Other combinations like a + l + d + a + l + d in U-direction or D-direction are possible but never appear. Clearly, the repertoire of concatenated gestures is determined by cultural factors, which, in case of the *guqin*, is highly constrained by narrative and mimetic meanings. Further study is needed to figure out the exact relationship between the musical patterns and these narrative meanings.

Although the concept of gesture applies to both sonic and control gestures, there is still an important distinction between them. For example, there are basic sonic gestures that cannot be produced and understood without taking into consideration a larger underlying control gesture. Due to inertia, a straight upward glissando in pitch from A to B (see the l-shape in the alphabet of Table 6.1) cannot be produced as an elementary move of the finger starting from the position that corresponds with pitch A and ending at the position that corresponds with pitch B. Instead, this straight glissando should be produced by a *gestural momentum*, in which the glissando is produced in the final part of the movement, starting at the moment where the finger touches the string. Figure 6.5 gives a concrete example of this relationship between control gesture and sonic gesture. The upper curve shows the displacement of the finger. From the viewpoint of the player, the symbol "up" equals a movement towards the left (shortening the string), while "down" equals movement towards the right. The lower curve shows the velocity of the same movement. The lower part of the figure shows the corresponding sound pattern. Clearly, the straight glissando pattern (shown in the sonogram below) corresponds with the final quarter part of the control movement. The entire control gesture thus prepares for the glissando by producing a momentum. At the point where this momentum is at its maximum, the finger strikes the string, so that the straight glissando can be produced. The example shows that elementary gestures often cannot be understood without taking into account larger sound-generating gesture units. By extension, one could say that gestures may subsume whole body postures. In summary, the example shows that control gesture and sound gesture are not identical, even in an instrument where the control gesture has a very direct relationship with the sound.

Interestingly, the alphabet of elementary *guqin* gestures shown above, which has been determined by using a combination of a third person and first person perspective, can now be used in a concrete application: that is, in connection with a physical model of the strings of a *guqin* instrument. In this case, the gesture alphabet allows a description of how the (computational) string can be controlled in order to synthesize tone-slidings for *guqin* sounds in such a way that they sound similar to real *guqin* sounds. Figure 6.6 shows how the elementary gestures from Table 6.1 can be concatenated into larger culturally relevant *guqin* gestures that define

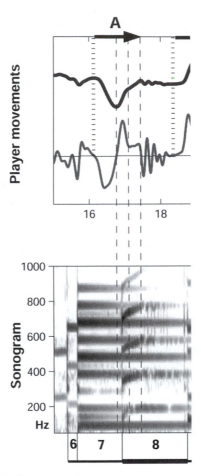

Figure 6.5 A straight glissando (consisting of the elementary pattern I + d in upward direction) is shown in the sonogram at the bottom part of the figure. On top, one sees two curves. The upper curve shows the displacement (upward indicates a movement of the finger towards the left, downward indicates a movement of the finger towards the right) and the lower curve shows the movement velocity. The movement was recorded with an infrared camera (see Figure 6.3).

the pitch modulation patterns for the string synthesis. The notes that need to be played according to these cultural gestures are written in Western music notation. The gestures are drawn in boxes on top of the score. Note that some tones are played on open strings: these tones cannot be modulated.

This application illustrates what we gain by using methods that combine both the first-person and the third-person approaches: namely, the control of very complex systems in a way that is close to the way in which we effectuate our own actions in the physical environment.

It is interesting to note that the action-based approach to elementary gestures is rather common in music teaching. For example, in learning to play a musical instrument, the instructor has to teach the pupil how to move fingers in the most economical and musically relevant way, using techniques of conscious access to lower-level gestures. Typically, when the elementary gestures are mastered, they no longer require the full attention of the pupil because they then form part of the body schema. At that time, the elementary gestures have become, so to speak, habits that make up the musical body schema, so that the pupil's attention can be freed to concentrate on the gestural characteristics that appear at higher, more abstract, atemporal levels. However, it is likely that access to the constituent elementary "in time" gestures remains possible once it has been acquired.

5.2 The Experience-Based Approach to Gesture

Apart from the action-based approach, where the focus is on the cognizable elementary units of one's own gestures, there is another and perhaps more traditional interpretation of the first person perspective. In this interpretation, the focus is on gesture in relation to the subject's personal experience or sensitivity. Obviously, there are several ways to proceed here, and the choice depends on the type of personal experience to be addressed. Accordingly, the methods may range from in-depth interviews (asking questions of the subject), to semantic differentials (assessing the properties of experience through the use of a defined set of adjectives and so-called Likert scales), and from protocol analysis (analyzing how the subject reports about interaction with music), to the use of metaphors and hermeneutic methods.

With respect to the effect of gesture on experience, there are three types of personal experience that deserve some particular attention: namely, the experience of *flow*, the experience of *presence*, and the experience of *cause–effect*.

The experience of flow (Csikszentmihalyi 1990) can be characterized as an experience in which the subject's skills are fully preoccupied with a task. For example, in playing music, you are likely to be in flow when you are fully occupied with music playing rather than with the instrument on which you play, the environment, or yourself. To obtain flow, there should be a balance between skills and challenges, as the task may become boring if challenges are too small, or frustrating if they are too great, in relation to the skills of the subject. Flow has been measured using narrative descriptions, retroactive evaluations, and survey methods based on a so-called experience sampling, where subjects evaluate their activity over a longer period of time (e.g. using a survey instrument

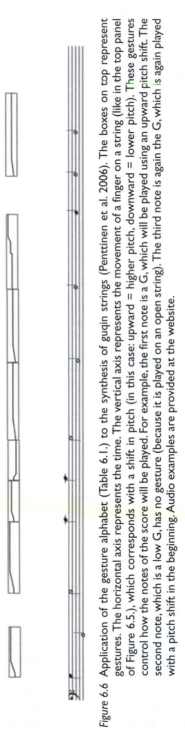

Figure 6.6 Application of the gesture alphabet (Table 6.1.) to the synthesis of guqin strings (Penttinen et al. 2006). The boxes on top represent gestures. The horizontal axis represents the time. The vertical axis represents the movement of a finger on a string (like in the top panel of Figure 6.5.), which corresponds with a shift in pitch (in this case: upward = higher pitch, downward = lower pitch). These gestures control how the notes of the score will be played. For example, the first note is a G, which will be played using an upward pitch shift. The second note, which is a low G, has no gesture (because it is played on an open string). The third note is again the G, which is again played with a pitch shift in the beginning. Audio examples are provided at the website.

that indicates the time at which the evaluation should take place). The measurement would then typically focus on the features of flow, such as attention focus, experienced quality of performance, type of control, intrinsic interest, experienced challenge, required skills, enjoyment, mood and motivation, and so on. These measurements can be complemented with physiological measurements as well. Studies about flow in music focus mostly on education, although the flow experience has also been explored in connection with new technologies (e.g. Pachet 2003; 2004; Addessi and Pachet 2005). Although the relationship between flow experience and gesture requires further study, it seems likely that the expressiveness of the gestural trace may provide an indication of flow. In addition, in both playing music and listening, gestures may be helpful in bringing about an experience of flow. In short, the measurement of flow may be one way to access the personal experience of gestures.

The experience of presence is different from the experience of flow, although neither experience necessarily excludes the other. While flow is more about a state of attention, presence can be defined as the illusion of non-mediation (Lombard and Ditton 1997). This illusion may occur when your musical instrument is no longer considered as an obtrusive object but as an instrument that gives you a way of expressing yourself in music. Presence is a typical effect of embodied interaction with technology, and it occurs when the technological mediator is integrated with the natural mediator (which is the human body) in such a way that the mind can operate in the environment to which the mediator provides access (Leman 2007). Thus, a musical instrument provides access to the musical environment, and the human body playing the musical instrument can be considered the mediator between mind and environment. Without the instrument, music production would not be possible and the mind would not be able to access music. If gesture is defined as the pattern that deploys the mediation in space and time, and presence is defined as the (first-person subjective) illusion of non-mediation (although mediation *is* involved from a third-person perspective), then it is tempting to define gesture as the deployment of body movement that expresses the subject's illusion of non-mediation. In other words, the body movement through which a gesture is deployed, includes something that goes beyond this deployment: namely, the mental focus on the environment to which this mediation provides access. It is indeed through gestures that we can perceive other persons' intended engagement with music. This is an aspect of gesture that plays a fundamental role in communication, which is a topic addressed in the next section.

The perception of a cause–effect relationship, in the domain of music perception and gesture, can be considered an experience of the cause of a sound from a gestural perspective, rather than a conceptual understanding of the causality relationship as such. Let me illustrate this by means of the example of footsteps. When I perceive footsteps in the corridor, I do not hear these footsteps in terms of their acoustic properties. Rather, I hear the sound of moving feet, and perhaps even the character of the person, that causes these acoustic properties. In other words, I do not hear the proximal cues, which are the acoustic properties that can be measured by ear (from a third person perspective), but I do hear the distal cues, which are the cues that cause these sounds. The perception of cause–effect is an experience (and not an understanding) because the inferences on which it relies—the perception of proximal cues and their subsequent processing towards the cause—are entirely subconscious and very rapid processes. Moreover, if we do not hear these distal cues, then most of the time we are not aware of the sound's proximal cues either. Many everyday sounds are thus experienced in terms of the agent, the actor, or even the gesture, that causes them. In discussions of new technologies for music making, electronic music instruments have some-times been criticised for not being able to engender this cause–effect relationship.

In short, flow, presence, and cause–effect experiences point to a first person perspective on the formation of musical meaning, in which music and gestures have an experienced aspect. By focusing on the contexts in which flow, presence, and cause–effect experience occur, interesting information can be obtained about the personal involvement of a subject. Empirical methods (such as questionnaires and other reporting strategies) provide information that gives access to the subject's personal experi-ences. Although these methods do not allow other persons to access these experiences directly, they may provide valuable information for building applications that are relevant in the cultural and creative sector.

The action-based and experience-based approaches thus provide valid contributions to the way in which the subject can approach gesture and its relation to the formation of meaning from her personal perspective.

6 The Second-Person Perspective on Gesture

In the second-person perspective, gesture is more explicitly addressed in terms of other people's engagement with music, or what I call *music-driven social interactions*. This advances another viewpoint on gesture, which is rather different from those in the first person and third person perspectives. In this viewpoint, gesture appears as a mediator for music-driven social interaction or as the vehicle through which a "me-to-you" relationship is established in space and time, through musical engagement. Thus, gesture is seen as the expression of a communicative act, rather than an expression of "my own" personal experience. This perspective on the understanding of bodily expression can be traced back in the literature at least as far as Charles Darwin's book on expression (Darwin 1872).

The core mechanism for understanding social interactive gestures can be understood in terms of embodiment. More particularly, it is the mirroring through which "my" perception of "your" movement is grasped in terms of the (overt or covert) deployment of "my own" body movement in the environment, so that "your" movement is corporeally understood as an action. This mirroring may ultimately account for the fact that we perceive the (sonic) moving forms of music as gestures, and therefore, that we engage with music as if music was another social being (Broeckx 1981; Leman 2008).

There is some evidence that this mirror system is grounded in brain regions where the perception of action and the execution of action partly overlap (for a recent review, see Agnew et al. 2007). Due to this overlap, the perception of your action is mirrored in my simulated re-enactment of that action, and vice versa. As such, we no longer see each other's body movements as movements, but as actions. The movements become the carriers of meaning that we enact on the basis of our own action-oriented ontology. In that sense, the mirror system forms the neuronal basis for understanding social interactive gestures (Gallese 2005). More particularly, it offers a neuronal explanation of how subjects can understand each other's intentions without having to rely on building a mental representation, or needing to construct a theory of what goes on in the mind of another person (Gallese and Goldman 1998; Iacoboni et al. 2005).

Through the capacity, or should we say bias, for re-enactment, movements are perceived as actions with an intention, provided that they have biological plausibility (Kilner et al. 2003). This is one of the strongest arguments against the reduction of gestures to mere movement: namely, because "my" perception of "your" movement touches my action-oriented ontology. In embodied listening (shown in Figure 6.1), the listener expresses an engagement with sonic moving forms (and also in this didactical setup the visually observed movements of the player) through corporeal articulations. These articulations often involve anticipations because the listener's movements are based on her re-enactment of the perceived movement, which involves intentionality (goal-directedness) in the sense of a prediction (at micro-level) of the position of these movements in the future.

In Leman (2008), a distinction is made between two types of intentionality, called corporeal intentionality and cerebral (or mental) intentionality. These two types of intentionality illustrate two ways in which gestures can be understood by human subjects. The corporeal intentionality of the *Menuet* gesture in Mozart is achieved by a simulated re-enactment of the *Menuet* gesture "in time," and it is likely that this involves micro-anticipations. In addition, and in line with Broeckx's notion of cenaesthesia, this corporeal intentional activity may also lead to a cerebral intentional activity, which is the mental, atemporal, representation of the *Menuet* gesture as gestalt, and, possibly, its subsequent projection onto cultural or social topics. In between these two levels, it may be possible to distinguish more levels of awareness that focus on different aspects of the deployment of gestures (see Chapter 5). However, while musical and cultural studies have focused on a cerebral understanding of social interactive gestures (see for example Elias 1937/2000; Bremmer and Roodenburg 1992), new observation technologies make it possible to go deeper into the temporal and spatial deployment of gestures, in order to reveal how body movements function in social interactions (e.g. Grammer et al. 1998). Music is such a complex phenomenon that it allows these different degrees of intentional engagement.

6.1 The Subjective Experience of Social Interactive Gestures

Before going deeper into a case study that focuses on the temporal deployment of social interactive gestures, it is interesting to consider the subjective experience of social interactive gestures. One of the major effects of gesture on the experience of social interaction is social bonding. In social psychology, for example, gesture has been studied in the context of courtship, non-verbal communication, and interpersonal orientations. According to Bargh and Chartrand (1999), most of a person's everyday life is determined by automatic and non-conscious processes. Such processes often rely on non-conscious imitation or mimicry behaviour expressed in movement synchrony, behaviour matching, as effectuated in speech patterns, facial expressions, emotions, moods, postures, gestures, mannerisms, and idiosyncratic movements (Lakin et al. 2003; Niedenthal et al. 2005). Within a social group setting, a subject is more likely to get along harmoniously with others in the group if it behaves similarly to them, and the reverse is true if it is "out of sync" and behaves differently. According to Bargh and Chartrand (1999) all of these effects tend to keep us in touch with the realities of our world in a way that transcends the limits of our capabilities for conscious self-regulation. Studies in social psychology show an interesting relationship between non-conscious imitation on the one hand, and feelings of affection on the other (Lakin et al. 2003). Mimicking the behaviours of others actually increases feelings of affection between interactive partners. It leads to feelings of closeness and fondness, and makes social bonding easier and more harmonious. These studies show that the body is in fact closely tied to the processing of social and emotional information and that, via the body, important and socially relevant information can be accessed by the mind, such as information about stereotypes and traits, attitude change and mood congruence (Niedenthal et al. 2005). The role of music-driven gestures in social bonding is well known in musicology as well. McNeill (1995) observed that, throughout history, moving and singing together have made collective tasks far more efficient, playing a profound role in creating and sustaining human communities. The underlying mechanism of "muscular bonding," that is, a corporeal connectedness, can, in view of the above discussion about the embodiment mechanism, now be understood in terms of a mirror system, re-enactment, synchronization and anticipation (see also Clayton 2007; Keller 2008).

Apart from social bonding there is another important effect of music interaction, namely, the capacity to have empathy with music, or art in general. Empathy is the ability to share another's feelings and emotions as if they were your own. For example, Lipps (1903) argued that the understanding of an expressive movement (or *Ausdrucksbewegung*) in music is based on empathy (*inneren Mitmachen, Einfühlung*), which he conceived as founded upon the use of motor muscles that are involved when genuine emotions are felt. Through such embodiment, we have access to the intended emotional meaning of the music (for the neurological foundations for this idea see Sebanz et al. 2006; Jackson and Decety 2004; Decety and Jackson 2004; Berthoz and Jorland 2004). Moving the body along to music may involve different degrees of empathic relationship, from physical synchrony, to emotional involvement. In this perspective, moving along to music can be seen as an act of social training and music thereby functions as a virtual agent with whom the listener's expressive behaviour is harmonized (Broeckx 1981).

6.2 The Temporal Deployment of Social Interactive Gestures

The temporal deployment of social interactive gestures can be studied using sensing technologies. These provide a very powerful (third-person) empirical approach, especially when used in the framework of a (first-person) perspective where interaction is related to experiences of flow, presence, social bonding, and empathy. In a study by De Bruyn et al. (2009), four participants had to move a remote *Wii* controller in response to music. In the individual condition, the participants could not see each other while in the social condition, the participants could see each other. Desmet et al. (2009) introduced the notion of coherence as a way to study this effect of music on social interaction. The first step in this study is the compensation for micro-anticipations and micro-delays that are typical in body movement responses to music. In a similar approach to that illustrated in Figure 6.2, this is accounted for by allowing small local-time shifts in the movement patterns of the participants. The second step is then based on a correlation analysis of the movements, which results in a graphical representation of the movement coherence among participants (Figure 6.7). The participants are represented by dots, while the lines and their distances represent the signification and the strength of

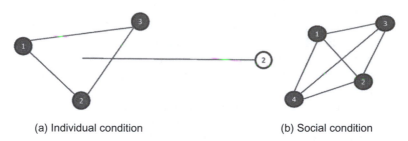

(a) Individual condition   (b) Social condition

Figure 6.7 Example of a graphical representation of the coherence in social interaction among a group of four participants in response to one musical piece. (a) individual condition, where participants could not see each other, (b) social condition, where participants could see each other (Desmet et al. 2009).

the coherence. Interestingly, in the individual condition, the movement of subject 2 is not coherent with the movements of the other subjects, while in the social condition, the movement of subject 2 is in tune with the movements of the other participants. Moreover, the coherence is weaker in the individual condition than in the social condition.

This finding suggests that the mere observation of the movements of other persons (in the social condition) interferes with one's execution of a similar action, which interference in this case leads to a better coherence of the group movements. Biological motion in particular, seems to play a key role in the formation of social coupling, and this can be explained by making a reference to the mirror system (Puce and Perrett 2003; Iacoboni et al. 2005). Typically, in musical tasks, subjects find the social condition much more pleasant than the individual condition, which suggest a positive effect on social bonding (De Bruyn et al. 2009).

However, Figure 6.8 shows that the type of music has an important effect on coherence among participants. Interestingly, the social condition has a larger effect when coherence in the individual condition is weak than when the coherence is already strong. For example, for songs S3 and S5, the coherence is 0.1 in the individual condition and 0.2 in the social condition. In contrast, for song 4, the coherence is about 0.5 in the individual condition and about 0.55 in the social condition. The finding of this study suggests that the effect of the social condition on coherence may be limited for music that has a clear beat to which the subjects may attune. In other words, when the musical beat is more ambiguous, then subjects seem to rely more on the movements of other subjects. However, further studies are needed to refine this observation and to clarify the relationship between coherence, subjective background and social bonding (Clayton 2007; Keller 2008). Moreover, the role of gesture in social interaction should be further explored by considering particular choreographies and movement imitations in dance (see also Chapter 7 in this volume).

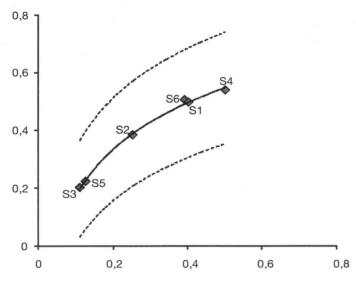

Figure 6.8 Social (vertical) versus individual (horizontal) coherence (dashed lines represent 95 percent confidence interval) (Desmet et al. 2009).

7 Music is Gesture

We are now at a point where we should consider the question to what extent music *is* gesture. There are at least two ways to look at this.

A first approach is based on the idea that gesture is a corporeal co-articulation of our musical perception. Co-articulation here means that body movements go together with musical perception. Hence, it is through the corporeal imitation of sonic moving forms in music that it becomes possible to experience music as the action of a dynamic organism similar to a human organism. Consequently, we can say that music contains gesture, or that music is gesture, when it appears as an action of a dynamic organism similar to a human organism (Broeckx 1981). Moreover, if aspects of the temporal deployment of sonic moving forms can be imitated by or simulated through the human body, then there are serious grounds for considering the formation of meaning at the level of embodiment. At this level, music can set a mirroring process into action, which in itself is sufficient to term this a formation of meaning.

A second approach, perhaps more traditional, is based on the idea that gesture in music is referential. A self-referential semantics can easily emerge when musical gestures have structural features in common with other musical gestures, giving rise to what Coker (1972) calls intramusical or congeneric meanings. Examples of this type of gestural semantics are abundant in music. For example, Beethoven often bases his compositions on the ongoing variation and development of short motives (motives that are often easy to imitate as body gestures). This practice creates a self-referential context in which musical gestures that are similar to others within the same piece can be recognized as such. As another example, in Berio's *Sinfonia*, musical gestures from Mahler, Ravel and Debussy, among others, are quoted and integrated into a musical collage. Although the musical gestures refer to other musical gestures outside the musical piece, they remain within the musical idiom. In that sense, they have a self-referential character, which an educated listener, that is, one able to situate a gesture in a particular historical and musical context, can understand.

The mechanism behind gesture in music seems to be that, through embodiment, sonic forms can be understood from the viewpoint of the listener's action-oriented ontology, and this ontology can be linked with a framework of other gestures and topics, both intra- and extra-musical. The reason we call musical patterns "gestures" has to do with the fact that they can be imitated through the human body. However, as gestures form an indispensable element in social interaction and social differentiation, it is likely that their imitation also implies the cultural acquisition of models for emulation. In that sense, the notion of gesture remains a highly fascinating object of study.

8 Conclusion

In this chapter, music, gesture, and the formation of meaning have been examined from the viewpoint of embodied music cognition and empirical musicology. It was argued that gestures form a central concept in music research because they express embodiment (the mirroring of action and perception), which is a central mechanism in the formation of musical meaning. The concept of gesture that emerges from this approach has the following characteristics:

- Multi-modal: when speaking about sonic gestures, or control gestures, we use the term "gesture" as a multi-modal term that includes both the confines of the audio modality (sound only) and the motor modality (movement only).
- Multi-level: gestures are multi-level in that they cover the deployment of movement in limited as well as more extended frames of space and time. These frames may have a hierarchical structure or a more complicated nested structure.
- Monistic: if we define mind and body as two substances (in the Cartesian way), then gestures can be said to have a character that bridges this Cartesian divide. The reason is that gestures can appear as automated motor sequences as well as representations, and, very often, mix these two aspects together in the sense that gesture have

an automated and a representational component. In other words, the action-oriented ontology of the human subject is based on body schemata and body images, and gestures fit with both of these because they appeal both to our conscious and our sub-conscious deployment of movement in space and time.

The characteristics mentioned above imply that the study of gestures cannot be reduced to merely objective measurements of sounds and body movements, nor to simply descriptions of personal experiences and interpretations thereof. Instead, a methodology is needed in which at least three different perspectives are combined: namely, the first-person, the second-person, and the third-person perspectives. The rationale behind this is that the concept of gesture is too complex to be understood from one single methodological perspective, even when considered purely from the viewpoint of an empirical approach (leaving hermeneutics aside). The third-person perspective focuses on measuring everything that moves, the first-person perspective emphasizes phenomenal self-observation (also related to experiences of flow, presence, and cause–effect), while the second-person perspective is particularly relevant for intentionality and social interaction (including the experiences of social bonding and empathy).

In this chapter, this three-fold distinction has been related to a layered (phenomenological) model of meaning formation, in which synaesthetic, kinaesthetic, and cenaesthetic transformations account for different processing levels that cover corporeal and mental activity. It was argued that the traditional narrative and phenomenological framework could be extended to include an empirical approach. This approach is based on refined technologies for measuring behavioural and neurophysiological components of human movement, and on techniques for probing the subjective experiences that are associated with the performance and the perception of gesture. The advantage of such an approach is that it may lead to useful applications in several domains where technologies are involved, including the cultural and creative sector.

My goal was not to give an exhaustive overview, but rather to show, by means of a few case studies carried out in my laboratory at Ghent University, how gesture and the formation of musical meaning formation can be studied from an approach that combines methods from the natural sciences with those of the human sciences. The power of this approach is that it allows the development of technologies that mediate between subjective experience and physical energy in both digital and electronic domains.

Note

1   The term *cenaesthesia* (also known as coenaesthesia) can be traced back to
the Greek words *koinos*, which means *common*, and *aisthesis*, which means
sensuous perception. The term refers to the sensation of existence, caused by
the functioning of the internal organs. In the older literature, this so-called
general sensibility is called sensus communis, somatognosis, or "Gemeinge-
fühl" (Fuchs, 1995). For example, in the Sixth Meditation of the "Méditations Métaphysiques" (1641/1979), Descartes uses the term *sensus communis*
to describe the mental sensing of the body parts. In more recent literature,
the term is similar to *the feeling of what happens*, that is, the perception
of the body scheme in a unitary body image (Damasio 1999). *Body image*
is thereby understood as a representational system, whereas *body schema*
addresses the motor capacities, abilities, and habits that enable movement
and the maintenance of posture (Gallagher and Cole 1995; Gallagher
2000).

References

Addessi, A. R. and Pachet, F. (2005). Young children confronting the Continuator:
an interactive reflective musical system. *Musicae Scientiae*, 10, 13–39.
Agnew, Z., Bhakoo, K., and Puri, B. (2007). The human mirror system: a motor
resonance theory of mind-reading. *Brain Research Reviews*, 54(2), 286–293.
Allanbrook, W. J. (1983). *Rhythmic Gesture in Mozart: Le Nozze di Figaro and
Don Giovanni*. Chicago: University of Chicago press.
Bargh, J. A. and Chartrand, T. L. (1999). The unbearable automaticity of being.
American Psychologist, 54(7), 462–479.
Berthoz, A. and Jorland, G. (eds.). (2004). *L'Empathie*. Paris: Jacob.
Bremmer, J. N. and Roodenburg, H. (1992). *A Cultural History of Gesture*.
Ithaca, N.Y.: Cornell University Press.
Broeckx, J. L. (1981). *Muziek, Ratio en Affect: Over de Wisselwerking van
Rationeel Denken en Affectief Beleven bij Voortbrengst en Ontvangst van
Muziek*. Antwerpen: Metropolis.
Camurri, A., Mazzarino, B., Ricchetti, M., Timmers, R., and Volpe, G. (2004a).
Multimodal analysis of expressive gesture in music and dance performances.
In A. Camurri and G. Volpe (eds.), *Gesture-Based Communication in Human-
Computer Interaction*, LNAI 2915. Berlin, Heidelberg: Springer, 20–39.
Camurri, A., Mazzarino, B., and Volpe, G. (2004b). Analysis of expressive
gesture: the EyesWeb expressive gesture processing library. In A. Camurri and
G. Volpe (eds.), *Gesture-Based Communication in Human-Computer
Interaction*, LNAI 2915. Berlin, Heidelberg: Springer, 469–470.
Camurri, A., Volpe, G., De Poli, G., and Leman, M. (2005). Communicating
expressiveness and affect in multimodal interactive systems. *IEEE
Multimedia*, 12(1), 43–53.
Clayton, M. R. L. (2007). Observing entrainment in music performance: video-
based observational analysis of Indian musicians' tanpura playing and beat
marking. *Musicae Scientiae*, 11(1), 27–59.
Coker, W. (1972). *Music and Meaning: A Theoretical Introduction to Musical
Aesthetics*. New York: Free Press.

Csikszentmihalyi, M. (1990). *Flow: The Psychology of Optimal Experience*. New York: Harper & Row.

Cumming, N. (2000). *The Sonic Self: Musical Subjectivity and Signification*. Bloomington: Indiana University Press.

Damasio, A. R. (1999). *The Feeling of What Happens: Body and Emotion in the Making of Consciousness*. San Diego: Harcourt.

Darwin, C. (1872). *The Expression of the Emotions in Man and Animals*. London: J. Murray.

De Bruyn, L., Leman, M., Moelants, D., and Demey, M. (2009). Does social interaction activate listeners? In S. Ystad, R. Kronland-Martinet, and K. Jensen (eds.), *Computer Music: Modeling and Retrieval*, LNCS 5493. Berlin, Heidelberg: Springer, 93–106.

Decety, J. and Jackson, P. L. (2004). The functional architecture of human empathy. *Behavioral and Cognitive Neuroscience Reviews*, 3(2), 71–100.

Descartes, R. and Robinet, A. (1641/1976). *Méditations Métaphysiques*. Paris: J. Vrin.

Desmet, F., Leman, M., Lesaffre, M., and De Bruyn, L. (2009). Statistical analysis of human body movement and group interactions in response to music. In A. Fink, B. Lausen, W. Seidel, and A. Ultsch (eds.), *Advances in Data Analysis, Data Handling and Business*. Berlin, Heidelberg: Springer, 399–408.

Elias, N. (1937/2000). *The Civilizing Process: Sociogenetic and Psychogenetic Investigations*. Oxford: Blackwell.

Friberg, A. and Sundberg, J. (1999). Does music performance allude to locomotion? A model of final ritardandi derived from measurements of stopping runners. *Journal of the Acoustical Society of America*, 105(3), 1469–1484.

Friberg, A., Sundberg, J., and Frydén, L. (2000). Music from motion: sound level envelopes of tones expressing human locomotion. *Journal of New Music Research*, 29(3), 199–210.

Fuchs, T. (1995). Coenaesthesia - History of general sensibility. *Zeitschrift Fur Klinische Psychologie Psychopathologie Und Psychotherapie*, 43(2), 103–112.

Gallagher, S. (2000). Philosophical conceptions of the self: implications for cognitive science. *Trends in Cognitive Sciences*, 4(1), 14–21.

Gallagher, S. and Cole, J. (1995). Body schema and body image in a deafferented subject. *Journal of Mind and Behavior, 16(4)*, 369–390.

Gallese, V. (2005). The intentional attunement hypothesis. The mirror neuron system and its role in interpersonal relations. In S. Wermter et al. (eds.), *Biomimetic Neural Learning for Intelligent Robots: Intelligent Systems, Cognitive Robotics, and Neuroscience*, LNCS 3575. Berlin, Heidelberg: Springer, 19–30.

Gallese, V. and Goldman, A. (1998). Mirror neurons and the simulation theory of mind-reading. *Trends in Cognitive Sciences*, 2(12), 493–501.

Gibet, S., Kamp, J. F., and Poirier, F. (2004). Gesture analysis: invariant laws in movement. In A. Camurri and G. Volpe (eds.), *Gesture-Based Communication in Human-Computer Interaction*, LNAI 2915. Berlin, Heidelberg: Springer, 1–9.

Grammer, K., Kruck, K. B., and Magnusson, M. S. (1998). The courtship dance: patterns of nonverbal synchronization in opposite-sex encounters. *Journal of Nonverbal Behavior*, 22(1), 3–29.

Hatten, R. S. (1994). *Musical Meaning in Beethoven: Markedness, Correlation, and Interpretation*. Bloomington: Indiana University Press.

Hatten, R. S. (2003). Thematic gestures, topics, and tropes. In E. Tarasti (Ed.), *Musical Semiotics Revisited*. Helsinki: Hakapaino, 80–91.

Iacoboni, M., Molnar-Szakacs, I., Gallese, V., Buccino, G., Mazziotta, J. C., and Rizzolatti, G. (2005). Grasping the intentions of others with one's own mirror neuron system. *Plos Biology, 3*(3), 529–535.

Jackson, P. L. and Decety, J. (2004). Motor cognition: a new paradigm to study self-other interactions. *Current Opinion in Neurobiology, 14*(2), 259–263.

Kaptelinin, V. and Nardi, B. A. (2006). *Acting with Technology: Activity Theory and Interaction Design*. Cambridge, MA: MIT Press.

Keller, P. (2008). Joint action in music performance. In F. Morganti, A. Carassa, and G. Riva (eds.), *Enacting Intersubjectivity: A Cognitive and Social Perspective on the Study of Interaction*. Amsterdam: IOS, 205–221.

Kilner, J. M., Paulignan, Y., and Blakemore, S. J. (2003). An interference effect of observed biological movement on action. *Current Biology, 13*(6), 522–525.

Knoblich, G. and Flach, R. (2003). Action identity: evidence from self-recognition, prediction, and coordination. *Consciousness and Cognition, 12*(4), 620–632.

Lakin, J. L., Jefferis, V. E., Cheng, C. M., and Chartrand, T. L. (2003). The chameleon effect as social glue: evidence for the evolutionary significance of nonconscious mimicry. *Journal of Nonverbal Behavior, 27*(3), 145–162.

Leman, M. (2008). *Embodied Music Cognition and Mediation Technology*. Cambridge, MA: MIT Press.

Leman, M., Desmet, F., Styns, F., Van Noorden, L., and Moelants, D. (2009). Sharing musical expression through embodied listening: a case study based on Chinese guqin music. *Music Perception, 26*(3), 263–278.

Li, H. and Leman, M. (2007). A gesture-based typology of sliding-tones in guqin music. *Journal of New Music Research, 36*(2), 61–82.

Lipps, T. (1903). *Ästhetik: Psychologie des Schönen und der Kunst*. Hamburg und Leipzig: L. Voss.

Lombard, M. and Ditton, T. (1997). At the heart of it all: the concept of presence. Journal of Computer-Mediated Communication, 3(2). (icmc.indiana.edu/vol3/issue2/Lombard.html)

McNeill, W. (1995). *Keeping Together in Time*. London: Harvard University Press.

Merleau-Ponty, M. (1945). *Phénoménologie de la Perception*. Paris: Gallimard.

Metzinger, T. (2003). *Being No One: The Self-model Theory of Subjectivity*. Cambridge, MA: MIT Press.

Monelle, R. (2000). *The Sense of Music: Semiotic Essays*. Princeton, NJ: Princeton University Press.

Nardi, B. A. (1996). *Context and Consciousness: Activity Theory and Human-Computer Interaction*. Cambridge, MA: MIT Press.

Niedenthal, P. M., Barsalou, L. W., Winkielman, P., Krauth-Gruber, S., and Ric, F. (2005). Embodiment in attitudes, social perception, and emotion. *Personality and Social Psychology Review, 9*(3), 184–211.

Pachet, F. (2003). The continuator: musical interaction with style. *Journal of New Music Research, 32*(3), 333–341.

Pachet, F. (2004). On the design of flow machines. In M. Tokoro and L. Steels (eds.), *A Learning Zone of One's Own, The Future of Learning*. Amsterdam: IOS Press.

Penttinen, H., Pakarinen, J., Valimaki, V., Laurson, M., Li, H., and Leman, M. (2006). Model-based sound synthesis of the guqin. *Journal of the Acoustical Society of America, 120*(6), 4052–4063.

Pratt, C. C. (1968). *The Meaning of Music: A Study in Psychological Aesthetics*. New York: Johnson Reprint Corp.

Puce, A. and Perrett, D. (2003). Electrophysiology and brain imaging of biological motion. *Philosophical Transactions of the Royal Society of London Series B-Biological Sciences, 358*(1431), 435–445.

Sebanz, N., Bekkering, H., and Knoblich, G. (2006). Joint action: bodies and minds moving together. *Trends in Cognitive Sciences, 10*(2), 70–76.

Tarasti, E. (ed.) (2003). *Musical Semiotics Revisited*. Helsinki: Hakapaino.

Truslit, A. (1938). *Gestaltung und Bewegung in der Musik*. Berlin-Lichterfelde: C.F. Vieweg.

Varela, F. J., Thompson, E., and Rosch, E. (1991). *The Embodied Mind: Cognitive Science and Human Experience*. Cambridge, MA: MIT Press.

Vines, B. W., Wanderley, M. M., Krumhansl, C. L., Nuzzo, R. L., and Levitin, D. J. (2003). Performance gestures of musicians: what structural and emotional information do they convey? In A. Camurri and G. Volpe (eds.), *Gesture-Based Communication in Human-Computer Interaction*, LNAI 2915. Berlin, Heidelberg: Springer, 468–478.

Wanderley, M. M. and Battier, M. (eds.) (2000). *Trends in Gestural Control of Music*. Paris: IRCAM.

Chapter 7

The Functional Role and Bio-kinetics of Basic and Expressive Gestures in Activation and Sonification

Leon van Noorden [1]

I Sound and Movement as Means for Communication

In this chapter we want to reflect upon the role sound and movement can have in a community of agents, such as fireflies, bees and dolphins, or even atoms, molecules, and people. The physical environment provides these agents with sound and light as means of communication. One cannot say that atoms and molecules are interested in communication; nevertheless, sound and light can make them move or vibrate in a coherent manner. Higher animals and people, as social agents, are interested in communication with their peers and will actively listen and look to them. Besides spoken and written language, music and movement constitute the main channels of communication. Music and movement have the advantage that they can support many-to-many communication, while spoken language supports only one-to-one or one-to-many communication.

In order to scrutinize the link between music and movement that, intuitively, we feel exists, we will walk along two paths: the functional or evolutionary path and the bio-kinetic path. First, the functional path will trace our knowledge of human evolution in order to answer the question why a relationship between music and movement may exist. We will distill the requirements for good gestures into *sonification*, i.e. the expression of the musician's movement into sound, and *activation*, the expression and enhancement of music through movement by a dancer. Second, the bio-kinetic path will analyze the relations between elementary gestures in music and dance and the kinetics of the human body. One concrete result found along this path is the resonance between our movements and our perception of the musical pulse at about 2 Hertz. We will investigate how we can employ basic and expressive gestures to analyze music and dance. In the second part of the chapter we will present a number of experiments and demonstrations to show how these ideas can be applied.

2 Functional Aspects of Music and Movement

First, it is necessary to develop an understanding of why our species would perform activities that involve both music and movement. Our main assumption is that music and dance are elements of social events. Individuals may have explored or exercised forms, methods, or tools on their own, but the reason that music and dance are universal phenomena among all human cultures is their importance in social events.

Bispham (2006), Hagen and Bryant (2003), Hagen and Hammerstein (in press), and Merker et al. (2009) have formulated relevant theories. We will follow Hagen and Bryant (2003) who offer a useful argument about the functionality of music and dance as group activity, which seems still relevant in our times. However, their theory is about the function of music and dance in an already rather advanced state of evolution; namely, a state in which music and dance have already progressed to a point where they can be identified as such. Before this, there must have been a state in which they could not be distinguished from a general social event.

2.1 Aspects of Social Events

An important aspect of a social event is the arousal of the agents. The most extreme cases are, respectively, the ones in which all of the agents are sleeping and ones in which they are all fighting one another. Unless there are special conditions, production of sound and movement are highly correlated, such that activation and sonification go hand in hand. An exceptional case might have been hunting or attacking enemies, in which case it is important to move quickly but silently.

Another important aspect of a social event is the degree to which the activities of the agents are synchronized. Proto-humans will have discovered very early on that many things become possible only if the movements are executed at the same moment in time. Heavy stones or trees can be transported over land only if all agents pull together at the same moment. Shouting together projects the sound much further than the cry of a single person (e.g. Merker et al. 2009). We will return to the way synchronization comes about in a later section.

2.2 The Evolutionary Function of Music and Dance

For Hagen and Bryant (2003) humans are a species of social agents who need to live in groups to survive. Groups can be in competition for territory and sexual relations. Humans are capable of working together in groups that are much larger than the close-knit family groups of our evolutionary cousins. In order not to have recurrent fighting between competing groups a signaling system is needed to give information about the quality and strength of the group, so that needless bloodshed can be prevented. Their hypothesis is that music and dance performances served this role during a long period of human evolution. They call this function "coalition quality signaling".

According to Hagen and Bryant, members of foreign groups can appreciate the significance of good performances. These performances demonstrate that the participants can perform a complex task. The performances also demonstrate that the participants were creative, given the range of various pieces and their continuous renewal, and that they had invested a lot of time and effort to make the performance perfect, i.e. well synchronized. Hagen and Bryant (2003, 31) present arguments and an experiment to show that good synchronization is recognized as a quality of a performance: "The coalition quality hypothesis (also) requires that learning and practicing music and dance be an important part of social life in traditional societies. Consistent with this, there is considerable ethnographic evidence that children are both motivated and encouraged to learn the musical repertoire of their group (. . .), perhaps even starting at birth".

The coalition signaling theory leads to a theory of the emotional expressiveness of music. Most emotions are temporal states of the human mind. The coalition signaling theory requires that music and dance performances need long periods of cooperation to signal group cohesion during a prolonged period. In order to have the right performance of the right emotional moment available the group needs to have a repertoire of emotionally well-determined pieces as we still do today. Emotional states of longer duration, which we may more accurately call attitudes, will naturally be reflected in all the elements in the repertoire of a group. This might be the most important reason for selecting a particular musical style as one's preferred music.

In addition to the benefits that come from signaling coalition quality to other groups, members who participate in the rehearsals and performances will also benefit themselves in a more direct way. They will feel happy and protected because they feel that they are part of a group. De Cremer and Van Vugt (1999) have shown that people that sing together trusted each other much more than the listeners to this singing in a subsequent prisoner's dilemma game.

The most vital point of the previous section is the importance of synchronization and variation. We will point out that there are at least two kinds of synchronization processes involved: entrainment and planning for movement to happen at the right moment.

3 Bio-Kinetics of Movement

3.1 Quasi-Static and Ballistic Movement of Individual Agents: Resonance

Movement of the body or body parts can be described with the laws of kinetics. This means that there is a relationship between the forces that act on the (part of the) body and the velocity and position as function of time. The forces that act on the body or its parts are gravity, reaction forces at the connection points of the extremities of the body (such as feet resting on the floor), linear and rotational inertial forces, and muscle forces.

Starting from an equilibrium situation, if the muscle forces are small the body will move slowly and stay more or less stable, i.e. the inertial and restoring forces will be in equilibrium. As soon as the muscles stop changing their position the body will stop moving. This we call quasi-static movement. If, however, the muscles exert a sudden impulse (jerk) the inertial forces will be more substantial and the resulting movement will only stop after all forces are in equilibrium again and the kinetic energy of the jerk has been absorbed by damping. This we call ballistic movement. We suppose that the body normally is in a more or less elastic equilibrium with its environment. This means that the restoring forces towards the equilibrium position increase gradually with the distance from the equilibrium point. Under these conditions, the body will have a characteristic pendulum movement around its point of equilibrium. It depends on the amount of damping whether this pendulum movement will die out quickly or not so quickly after a jerk or other disturbance. If the jerks are repeated with a frequency that is in agreement with the characteristic pendulum movement, its amplitude will reach a maximum. If the jerks come too quickly one after the other the body will not be able to follow the jerks any longer and the amplitude will tend to zero. This phenomenon of maximum amplitude at a certain frequency is called resonance: see Figure 7.1.

MacDougall and Moore (2005) placed an accelerometer in baseball hats worn by a number of participants and measured the movement signals during a whole day of normal activity. They discovered that, for all people, a strong spectral peak was present at 2 Hz. They argued that the main cause for the strong presence of this frequency is the frequency of our walking; namely, two steps per second or 120 steps per minute. This frequency does not systematically depend on age, height, weight, or body mass index of the people.

It should also be mentioned that this typical frequency is influenced by the magnitude of the gravity that keeps us on the ground. Without gravity we would not have our typical means of locomotion. Only walking on a

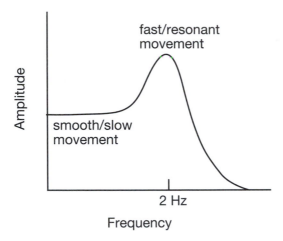

Figure 7.1 Resonant or ballistic movement versus smooth or quasi-static movement.

plane, or moving in a homogeneous medium, like water or air, could lead to optimization of locomotion frequencies in a narrow range.

3.2 Movement of Agents in Social Situations: Entrainment

Consider the movement patterns that can be observed in a crowd of agents. The agents can move around or move part of their bodies in different ways. They could on the one hand move (or not move at all) in an uncoordinated way, as if they had nothing to do with each other. On the other hand, they could move all together in the same way, as if they were one organism. Both of these situations would not lead to much information being transferred between agents. A more interesting situation is where some of the agents would move in one way and others would move in other ways.

Physicists have developed many models to analyze the behavior of collections of particles that can move in one way or another. So it is known that particles often vibrate at very precise frequencies—their resonance frequencies—and that vibrating particles make their neighbors vibrate at the same frequency with only a very little amount of energy exchange. As an example, we can take the two main ways in which light can be generated. One can heat up a wire with an electrical current, causing atoms in the wire to get hot and start to emit light. In this case, the atoms vibrate in a random and incoherent way. But, if one brings the atoms into an environment in which they can synchronize, they emit coherent light, as in a laser. This light is very pure: it consists of only one single frequency and propagates in the same direction.

The same can happen in groups of people: they can move in all directions in a disorganized manner, such as in a marketplace, or they can synchronize and walk in the same direction, such as in marching. Another example is applause. Normally clapping is incoherent, but in special occasions people fall into synchronous clapping (Néda et al. 2000). A characteristic common to all of these activities is that this synchronization happens only in a very narrow range of frequencies.

This type of synchronization, entrainment, is a rather physical process that is not under direct control of the agents involved. It happens for instance when two people walk alongside each other. They often become entrained without being aware of it just through visual and/or auditory contact (Zivotofsky and Hausdorff 2007). This is not the kind of synchronization that is meant by Hagen and Bryant (2003). The sequences of movements that lead to good performances, and thus have to be rehearsed, rely on advanced planning of movements. This planning is necessary so that the entrained synchronization is not disturbed. We will return to this idea below.

Dancing agents often share no physical characteristics and have as a consequence different "preferred" frequencies. Their mutual coupling can still bring about synchronization. In physics, this behavior can be modeled with dampened harmonic oscillators coupled in a network. To demonstrate this phenomenon we coupled twenty mass spring oscillators that differed in mass and spring constant in a range that would be as different as people are in a simulation. One of them has a starting position well outside the equilibrium position. After its release all oscillators start to vibrate, at first in an incoherent way, and after a while they come gradually into sync.

4 Temporal Aspects of Music

Most musical styles are characterized by temporal regularities, such as the regular occurrence of similar sounds. These regularities allow the listener to build up expectations and synchronize an overt or covert response to the music. It is said that he/she perceives the *pulse* of the music. The tempo of the pulse is important for the perceived tempo of the music. In our Western tradition composers have often used tempo terms to indicate how fast the music should be played. In musical dictionaries one can find the beats per minute (BPM) values for the tempo terms in the European classical music tradition. They go from Largo at 30 BPM, Allegretto at 120 BPM to Presto at 180 BPM.

Van Noorden and Moelants (1999) have shown that most pieces of music transmitted on radio stations, counted over many different stations and many different musical styles, have a pulse in the neighborhood of 120 BPM. However, the tempo of the pulse can vary quite substantially, and the pulse can also vary in clarity or even be absent all together. The pulse can be ambiguous so that people can disagree on the tempo of the pulse of a certain piece of music. The character of the pulse is an important aspect of a musical piece.

We can distinguish two broad classes of musical events on the basis of the clarity of the pulse: those in which most people just sit and listen to the musicians, and those where a large proportion of people participate in singing, instrument playing and/or dancing. The second is certainly characterized by the presence of a strong musical pulse.

5 Perception and Production

5.1 External Correlations

In the previous sections we discussed both external observations of agents with respect to their movements and objective aspects of the temporal characteristics of music. Table 7.1 is an overview of the tempi found in music, dance, locomotion and heartbeat, and breathing. It is easy to see that the range of tempi in all these cases is similar and that the 2 Hz is the neutral dividing line between slow and fast. MacDougall and Moore (2005) made the observation that the distribution of the movement frequency peaks is very close to the histogram of tempi found in musical pieces as determined by Van Noorden and Moelants (1999) (see

Table 7.1 Tempi in the different domains of human activity compared with some relevant measurements

musical tempi	dances	locomotion	body functions	domin. locomotion	histogram tempi	polyrh. tapping	BPM
prestissimo			max heart rate		x		220
	quick step	running			x	x	200
presto	jive		max breathing		x	x	180
		jogging		x	xx	xx	160
allegro	bossa nova			xxx	xxxx	xxxx	140
allegretto	west coast	march		xxxxx	xxxxx	xxxxx	120
moderato				xxx	xxxx	xxxx	100
andante	slow waltz	relaxed		x	xxx	xxx	80
adagio			min heart rate		xx	xx	60
					x	x	40
largo		funeral			x	x	30
			min breathing				20

Table 7.1). Bodily movement in response to music often has a periodic character. Obviously, the periodic movements in response to music are driven by structural properties of the music.

Now we have to turn to the hotspot of the interaction between music and movement: the perception and production processes that are internal to the agent.

5.2 Processes Inside the Agent

The coupling of sound and movement happens within the agent. Sound and movement enter the perception and production loop through the senses. Under the influence of memory and bodily dynamics, an output is generated that can take the form of sound or movement.

With present day techniques for visualizing the areas of the brain that are involved in perception and motor activities it becomes clear that these processes are strongly linked (e.g. Chen et al. 2006). It is therefore not strange that Van Noorden and Moelants (1999) and Moelants and Van Noorden (2005) have found that a number of phenomena of rhythm perception, such as subjective rhythmization, subjective grouping, the existence region of the musical pulse, and the strength of parts in polyrhythmic sequences, can be understood on the basis of a resonance with the perceptual system in the neighborhood of 2 Hz or 120 BPM, which can be identified with the bio-kinetic resonance discussed above.

How exactly these processes are linked, however, is still a question for debate. For example, Todd et al. (2007) argue that there is a direct link between the "preferred" frequency and details of the personal bio-kinetics. MacDougall and Moore (2005), however, explained the independence of the 2 Hz peak in the daily movement pattern by making the assumption that the tempo of our walking is perhaps determined by an internal control mechanism rather than directly by bodily mechanics. A recent study by Will and Berg (2007) on brain waves has shown that there is also a resonance of these waves at 2 Hz. This could support the suggestion of MacDougall and Moore, although it is not yet known what role brain waves have in the control of walking.

An important aspect of the potential of communication between agents is that they can copy movements and other expressions from each other. When a child sees another child hopping, he will "understand" that movement when he can also hop in the same way. In this context, one often mentions the "mirror neurons" as mechanisms that support this mimicking behavior (e.g. Rizzolatti and Craighero 2004). It is an interesting question whether mimicking behavior is more direct in the case of vision and movement than in the case of hearing and movement. We will return to this question in the section dealing with experiments.

The relative strength of the sensory input and the memory trace can vary substantially between different kinds of social events. In the case of performances, both musicians and dancers go through extensive rehearsals to store the piece in memory before performing it. In a live performance, however, they can adapt the execution of the memory-stored program to the live situation and to the timing of other performing agents. Moreover, in so-called improvisations memory is probably heavily involved, as many chunks of memory traces will be retrieved during the performance and sequenced according to the situation.

Only in very "primitive" situations will the society of agents fall back to very basic utterances of sound and movement in which memory does not play such an important role. One could think of riots or outcries of great happiness.

5.3 Basic Gestures

Dancing people make a series of movements in which the elements are in one way or the other aligned (synchronized) with elements of the sound stream. They synchronize, nearly as per definition, to the pulse of the music. The pulse of music can be considered as the awareness of the bio-kinetic resonance of our body. Van Noorden and Moelants (1999) used the term "effective resonance" as the apparent "addition" of the perceptual resonator to the input movement signal. These elements of movement sequences that are accessible for synchronization are elementary for basic gestures.

We introduce a corresponding refinement in the definition of gesture as given in Chapter 1 of this book. Their definition of gesture is defined as a movement of a certain duration and form which the subject (if he wants) can experience (and perhaps know) as a unity of action.

We distinguish basic gestures and expressive gestures. Basic gestures are quasi-static or ballistic gestures of moderate size without any expression of emotion or reference to a meaning outside the movement itself. Expressive gestures are basic gestures with the addition of expressiveness of intensity, emotions or references to external meanings of the movement. Basic gestures can be passive movements as a consequence of an external source.

There is a strong parallel between notes as notated in a score or MIDI file and basic gestures on the one hand, and between interpreted notes and expressive gestures on the other hand. The note as notated just tells the performer the starting time, the stopping time and the MIDI note number (and its velocity). The basic gesture is a little bit more difficult to notate: a starting time, stopping time, the starting location, the stopping location, and which limb is involved (and its velocity). Essentially, it is a neutral description without any interpretation.

Basic gestures are already applied extensively in the animation of avatars and robots.

5.4 Planning of Movement: Spatialization and Temporization

While the timing of the music-accompanying movements is basically aligned with the pulse of the music, the spatial layout of the movement is to a certain degree free. The music does not tell the dancer which spatial arrangement he has to make: see, for example, section 6.1 below.

In situations where the listener/dancer is free to choose the movements, he or she will start with movements of moderate size that cost little energy, and are adapted to the basic functions of the body. One of the simplest movements of the foot is a step in place. A simple movement of the arm might involve raising the lower part of the arm from a hanging position at one's side to more or less horizontal position as if to grab something.

Often the same gestures are repeated over and over again. As ballistic movements often return under the influence of the external force, it is an advantage to repeat the movement using the "natural" frequency of the limb. With very little energy, a substantial repetitive movement can be maintained. The tempo range of elementary gestures corresponds to the tempo range of bio-kinetic movements. Adjustments can be made to the stiffness of the coupling of the limb so that its resonance coincides with the tempo of the music. These kinds of movements with the arm are typical Becking curves (see Chapter 4). Another way to adapt to the tempo of the music is to choose a different form of a movement, such as the back-and-forth arm movements that accompany marching music and the more round forms that accompanied the music of the string quartet in the experiment discussed in section 6.3 below.

Another aspect of spatialization is the size of the gestures. The more the dancer gets involved and the louder the music becomes, the bigger the movements that will be made, as we also will see in section 6.3.

In contrast to the repetitive movements, concatenation of non-repetitive movements requires advanced planning due to space limitations or other functions that movement may have, such as steps that are not only gestures but also supportive of the body's weight. In formal dance performances, the sequence of movements is determined by the choreographer and has to be rehearsed. In more popular dances, the form of the movements is prescribed by the collection of moves that belong to a certain dance. It is essential to learn the right moment to place the weight of the whole body on one foot. If one places the weight on the foot at the wrong moment, an intended step cannot be executed.

This planning of dance movements can be compared with the planning of finger placements on a musical instrument. In order to obtain the correct temporal structure or even to consider the possibility of executing a phrase, determining the right fingering becomes an important part of rehearsal.

Although we said at the beginning of this section that music-accompanying movement is basically aligned with the pulse in the music, it can also be observed that the deviation from exact alignment (temporization) can be used by the dancers to give an extra accent or embellishment to the movement, just as the solo musician can get extra attention by deviating from the exact timing (Merker et al. 2009).

5.5 Expressive Gestures for Activation and Sonification

In order to be useful in a musical context, amplitude, timing, and form of basic gestures can be adapted to become expressive gestures.

Requirements for the expressiveness of gestures depend upon the purpose of the social event in which they are used. Social events that are aimed at one's own group require other expressive gestures than events aimed at other groups as in the case of coalition quality signaling. In the one case, one may want to prepare for risky actions. In the other case, one may want to express how self-controlled the group is by making perfect, well-timed, formal performances.

The most important quality of sonification is its effectiveness for reaching a certain well-defined activation level of the listeners. For the musicians this means that they should give clear signals for synchronization and a musical narrative that helps the dancers to perform a series of movements. They also have to produce the music in such a way that the collective emotion and attitude is provided to the dancers. The dancers should be able to detect the signal for synchronization in the music, follow the narrative in the music, and perform accordingly the sequence of movements and express the required emotions.

It is very difficult to express scientifically what are good gesture forms for certain activations. There are only some initial approaches to this question, such as:

- In studies about the character of pieces in different tempi, one often finds a correlation between the tempo and certain emotional aspects of the music. Very slow pieces have the tendency to represent music from sad occasions and fast pieces are usually perceived as more joyful.
- Manfred Clynes (Clynes 1978) suggests that each emotion has its specific temporal form (sentic form). In order to measure these shapes he developed the sentograph. People had to push a button to express the temporal form and spatialization of the emotions.
- Gustav Becking noticed that the rhythmical structure of Beethoven

and Mahler can be quite the same, but when worked out with conviction, it is recognized that Beethoven's beats stride and Mahler's
hover (Becking 1958). This is the expression of attitude, the expression of the composer's place in the world—his or her body language,
so to speak.

Among our experiments described hereafter we will return to an attempt
to measure the activation of people brought on by different pieces of
music by looking at their walking speed while listening to these pieces.

6 Experiments

In the following section experiments will be presented that have been
performed in our institute on the topic of music and movement during
recent years. These experiments have been performed in parallel with the
development of the ideas presented above. Although they were not directly intended as tests for these ideas, they happen to touch on a number
of points that have been raised earlier.

The first two experiments show that the spatialization of movements is
not self-evident. People need to have an example or convince themselves
that they are making the right form of movement.

The second group of three experiments goes deeper into the execution
of basic gestures. These experiments feature a demonstration of how
people move spontaneously to some typical musical pieces, an experiment
on walking to music, and an experiment on dancing the samba.

The final group of two experiments deals with social situations. The
first one seeks to find the capacity for synchronization in very young
children. The second one examines the influence of seeing each other on
synchronized hopping.

6.1 Writing Preparation Dance

In the past few years, a writing preparation method has reached a certain
degree of popularity in schools with the goal of obtaining "harmonious"
writing movements in children (*Schrijfdans* in Dutch). The method calls
for children to make large letter-like patterns in the air while music is
playing. A professor of education has investigated what examples should
be given to the children. The movements of children and student teachers
were registered with an extended joystick. The adult student school-
teachers were able to change their movements with the different
characters of the music, such as fluent or staccato. The children needed
explicit instruction on the form of the movement and on the expression of
the character of the movement (Brodelet 2006).

6.2 Arm Swinging to Guqin Music

Li and Leman (2007) asked subjects to make arm movements to solo pieces of Chinese *guqin* music (Chapter 6). The main conclusion for the present chapter is that it took several repetitions with increasingly more information given, such as inspection of the score, before the participants were happy with their movements. In fact, they had to develop their own movement strategy.

6.3 Arm and Foot Swinging to Music

Styns and Van Noorden (2006) used extended joysticks to record the arm and foot movements of 211 subjects. The experiment was carried out during a public exhibition in Ghent 2005. The audio stimuli consisted of a marching fragment (played at two different volumes), three metronome fragments, and a piece of baroque string music, all at 120 BPM.

A useful technique for the visualization of spatial and temporal characteristics of gestures is the so-called wave slicing technique. With this technique, it is easy to see whether a time signal is synchronized to another time signal. In this case, we look at the velocity of the movement of the subject and compare it with the beat period of the music. To this end, the signal of the movement velocities is broken up (sliced) in periods according to the duration of a multiple of the musical beat (in this case 120 BPM). These slices are then put vertically next to each other. Figures 7.2a and 7.2b show the visualization of the gestures of two subjects. In this visualization, periods of four musical beats were used as the slice length in order to capture both fast and slow gestures. The shading of the figure indicates the velocity. Lighter shading means higher velocity. If the light bands of higher velocity form horizontal bars then there is synchrony with the musical beat. From left to right one sees what happened during the succession of the musical excerpts and the metronomes. For instance, in Figure 7.2a one sees that the order of musical pieces was string music, louder march, and softer march, divided by short metronome fragments. It is clear that this subject moved with half the tempo during the string piece.

Another visualization of spatial characteristics can be obtained by looking at the effective position in space of the joystick. Figure 7.3 provides some examples of accumulated gestures, and the derived mean gestures. It seems that people use a limited set of gestures in response to the musical stimuli. Recurring movement shapes can be identified as raindrop-shaped movements, figure-eight-shaped movements, and banana-shaped movements, as shown in Figure 7.3. Moreover, these shapes have a similar form to Becking's curves, hence the idea to call this visualization of gestures "Becking curves."

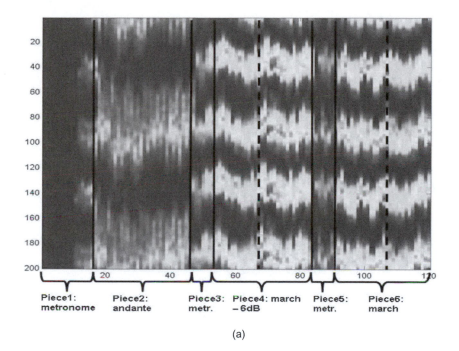

(a)

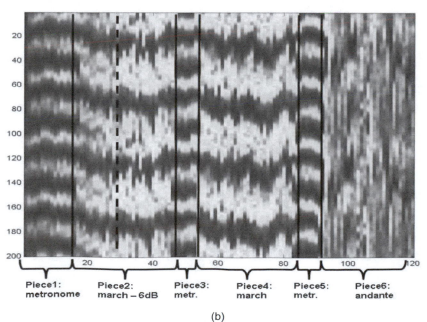

(b)

Figures 7.2a and 7.2b Wave slicing representation of the movement of the hand of two subjects. The vertical timescale is 4 beats at 120 BPM.

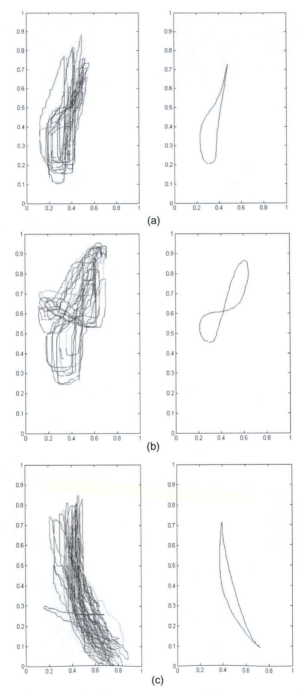

Figure 7.3 Three examples of gestures, represented as Becking curves.

The main conclusion of this demonstration was that the people found it very easy to make simple repetitive movements to the beat of the music. If they had to move both their hand and foot, the movements of the hand simplified. Some young adults could not maintain the synchrony because they wanted to make movements that were too complicated.

6.4 Walking to Music

In the context of the work of MacDougall and Moore (2005) discussed above, and the popularity of jogging to music, Styns et al. (2007) studied the effect of musical tempo on the activation of walking. Sixty-eight one-minute musical excerpts and twelve metronome excerpts distributed over a range of 50 BPM to 190 BPM were presented in random order. The subjects were asked to synchronize their steps with the musical beat. The experiment took place on an outdoor running track. The walking speed was measured with a GPS device and the step moments were measured by making sound recordings of the footsteps. The walking speed was taken as the activation measure.

The data of Figure 7.4 show that for all people the walking speed increases regularly until the tempo of about 114 BPM. At higher tempi the speed does not increase anymore and the spread of the walking speed becomes larger. From this figure it can be understood why military marches are standardized at tempi like 116 BPM (e.g. Germany, Brazil) and 120 BPM (e.g. USA). It is the highest tempo with which a group of people can walk over longer distances in a coherent way. The resonance expresses itself through the fact that step size is maximal around 120 BPM. At higher tempos there is not enough time to make large steps. Evidence was found that music has an activating effect, because the step sizes are significantly higher in response to music than in response to metronome sequences (see Figure 7.4b). In order to study the activation by different musical pieces of different musical styles in more detail another experiment was run with fifty-eight different pieces of the tempo 130 BPM.

In addition to walking, subjects also had to repeat the session with hand movements instead of walking and to answer a questionnaire about their subjective evaluation of the excerpts. The excerpts were also analyzed with respect to a number of audio descriptors. It was established that hand movements are more expressive than walking, in the sense that more significant correlations with the audio descriptors could be identified with the amounts of hand movement than with the distances walked. It was also found that the activation of the music could be negative. In that case subjects moved less with the music than with the neutral metronome. However, personal musical experience and preferences had a major impact (Styns 2009).

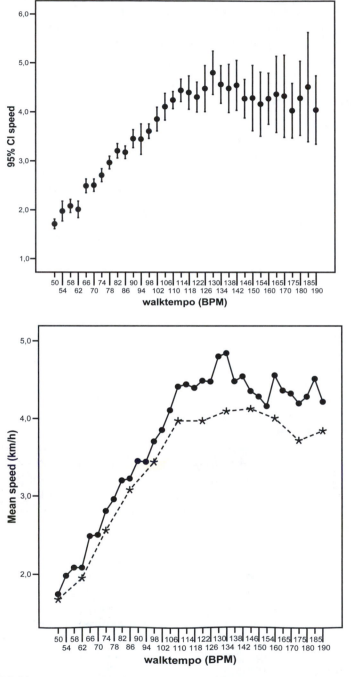

Figure 7.4 (a) Normalised walking speed—walking tempo relationship. (b) Difference between walking on music and walking on metronome stimuli.

6.5 Basic Gestures in Samba Dance

A close interaction between dance and music forms exists in samba music. Naveda and Leman (2008a; 2008b) developed a method in which they took this interaction as a starting point for the analysis of basic gestures. More particularly, in their method, musical meter is used as a lens to look at the basic gestures in dancing.

The method consists of two parts. In the first part, a metrical analysis is performed on the musical audio, which results in time durations for the period of the beat, as well as time durations for the subdivisions and multiples of the beat. In the second part, the dancing movements are analyzed. First, the dancing in response to music is recorded using a video analysis method, or better, an infrared camera system, which provides movement trajectories over time for each marked body part (e.g. head, shoulders, hands, knees, feet). These movement trajectories will typically display repetitive patterns, as the dance and the music are periodic. Second, these trajectories are analyzed using a signal decomposition technique called the periodicity transforms (Sethares and Staley 1999; Sethares 2007). This method needs information that guides the heuristics for finding these basic gestures in the data. Naveda and Leman (2008a) propose that the metrical grid provides the proper heuristics for the decomposition. The assumption is then that the temporal aspects of the basic gestures are related to the metrical levels in the music. The periodicity analysis then allows the extraction of the basic gestures in terms of their coherence with musical meter.

Figure 7.5 shows the result of such an analysis on the dancing choreography of a professional samba dancer. Different body parts of the dancer have been marked, such as the nose, right shoulder, left hand, right hand, right hip, left knee, right knee, left foot, right foot. The numbers below represent the metrical grid, divided into binary and ternary subdivision and multiples. Number 1 represents the beat, number 2 is the double of the beat, 0.33 is one-third of the beat and so on. For each body component, the movement trajectory is decomposed along the metrical units, and this decomposition then reveals the possible spatial characteristics of the basic gestures. The analysis reveals, for example, the hypothetical trajectory of the right hand at a metric level corresponding to two times the beat, three times the beat, and four times the beat, plus some additional smaller basic gestures at different other metric levels.

Using this method, it is possible to extract the basic gestures of the metrical levels and to display them as Becking curves. Figure 7.6 shows the Becking curves of basic hand and foot gestures of a male and female dancer. These curves have a length of two beats and they can be subdivided into smaller metrical units corresponding to the meter. Interestingly, by looking at the time stamps of these smaller units, it appears that

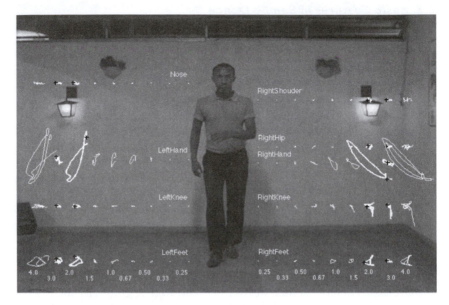

Figure 7.5 Samba dancer and analysis of basic periodic dance forms from the viewpoint of meter. Each row displays nine shapes (nine metric levels) that are decompositions of the trajectories of the body parts. These decompositions represent the repetitive dance movements that are performed along different periods of the musical meter.

basic gestures also relate to the subdivision of the meter. This suggests that dancing in response to music can embody major metrical levels of the music in different body parts through basic gestures. To validate the solutions found by this approach a sonification of the resultant basic gestures is produced. Experts can then evaluate the result of the analysis through a re-synthesis, which should again deliver basic samba rhythms (Naveda and Leman 2008b). So far, the results provide evidence for the hypothesis that the samba dancer embodies different metrical level of the music through different body parts, but further research is still needed to refine the methodology.

6.6 Tapping to Music by Children 3 to 11 Years Old

Studies about rhythm perception (Van Noorden and Moelants 1999), bodily movement (MacDougall and Moore 2005), and neural processes (Will and Berg 2007) have shown that a resonance at 2 Hz may link these domains. Is this frequency different at a younger age?

To make the task clear to very young children a cute avatar was designed that tapped on a drum in time with a musical selection (Figure 7.7). Five simple children's songs of about thirty seconds were presented

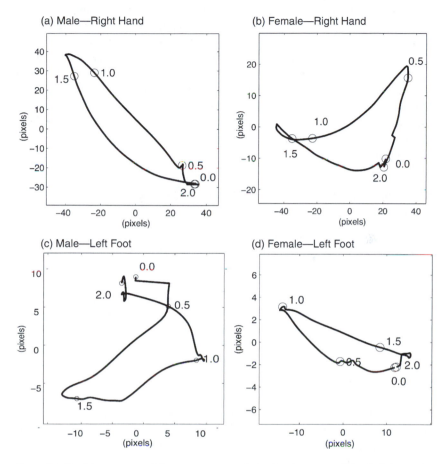

(a) Male—Right Hand

(b) Female—Right Hand

(c) Male—Left Foot

(d) Female—Left Foot

Figure 7.6 Becking curves of basic gestures of Samba dancers subdivided from the viewpoint of meter (< 2 beats). (a) male dancer, right hand, (b) female dancer, right hand, (c) male dancer, left foot, (d) female dancer, left foot.

in a sequence of increasing tempi of 80, 100, 120, 140 and 160 BPM through a loudspeaker at comfortable level. During the first fifteen seconds the avatar tapped together with the children, who continued until the end. The children performed the tasks in groups of four, with sticks on little toy drums with sensors. The signals were recorded separately. All children of a primary school with kindergarten participated (N = 220).

Preliminary results show that even some three-year old children are able to synchronize. However, with the tempi above 120 BPM, it becomes more difficult. Children beyond the age of six are able to synchronize well to all tempi. Factors that may contribute to the less precise results of the younger children may be their shorter attention span and a less precise motor control.

Children may have a faster walking rhythm, but the tempo to which they can synchronize is lower than that of adults. The limiting frequency seems to be 2 Hz. This supports the hypothesis that the 2 Hz resonance is related to the central locomotion control mechanism rather than directly to the mechanical properties of the body (see Styns et al. 2007). The fact that the capacity to synchronize is present so early in life supports the hypothesis of Hagen and Bryant (2003), that one of the main evolutionary functions of music is coalition signaling. Phillips-Silver and Trainor (2005) have shown that at seven months old, children already show signs of recognition of rhythmic patterns.

6.7 Moving to Music With and Without Seeing Other Dancers

In a situation where people can see each other they can probably synchronize their movements with each other better than in a purely auditory situation, in addition, they may move more (DeNora 2000).

De Bruyn et al. (2009) asked groups of four children and young adults to move along in synchrony with the beat of a number of musical excerpts. In one condition they could see each other, while in the other condition they could not. Figures 7.8 and 7.9 depict the two conditions. Movements of each participant were registered using Nintendo's *Wii Remote* in the dominant hand. The six musical excerpts varied in tempo, level of familiarity and rhythmical ambiguity.

The main results are that the mean synchronization is higher in the social condition for all songs. It is also obvious that the songs themselves have a great impact on the synchronization results. Participants scored significantly lower for the unfamiliar excerpts with rhythmical ambiguity. The others were pop songs with a very clear beat. Additionally, the participants move significantly more intensely in a group situation.

The data confirm that there is indeed an effect of social interaction. Movements measured in the social condition show a significantly higher intensity compared to the individual movements. The level of synchronization with the beat depends strongly on the complexity of and the familiarity with the music, but does not significantly change between conditions. Furthermore, it was established that participants within the groups synchronized their movements with each other, demonstrating the effect of social interaction and entrainment.

7 Discussion

Within the chosen framework of the combination of the social event, the coalition quality signaling theory (CQST) and the bio-kinetic

Figure 7.7 Avatar tapping.

Figure 7.8 Dancers not seeing each other.

Figure 7.9 Dancers seeing each other.

resonance theory (BKRT) it is possible to give a significant context to all the experiments that we set out to perform either in a rather intuitive fashion, or because they came out of a practical question.

It was confirmed that with simple repetitive movements it is easy to synchronize with repetitive music (experiments 6.3, 6.4, 6.5 and 6.6) as long as the spatial layout of the movement does not matter. However, if one asks which movements should be made with a certain piece of music, it needs either the example of an adult (experiment 1) or quite deliberate planning and checking of the rationality of the proposed solution (experiment 2 as an example of the coalition quality signaling theory).

The experiment involving samba dancing (experiment 6.5) has shown that samba dancers are able to perform complex movements that reflect simultaneously several layers in the musical structure in a way that is not obviously part of the skill-set of people of other cultures. This reflects the requirement of the coalition quality signaling theory that groups need to develop their own styles and innovations in order to show coalition strength.

The experiment with children (experiment 6.6) shows that children can already synchronize to a certain degree using simple movements at the age of three. This synchronization is so irregular that it is difficult to explain as a bio-kinetic resonance type of entrainment (Merkel et al. 2009). Irregularities in the motor control would be interfering too strongly. However, with some strong imagination one could suppose that the coalition quality signaling theory kind of planning synchronization is so important in our evolution that elements for it are already present at very young age.

The results of experiment 6.7 show that visible gestures are important in the activation of movement. Subjects in social situations who were able to view others moving displayed greater synchronization in their movements, and also made more movements, than the same subjects moving in isolation. Thus, visual isochronicity can support auditory-based isochronicity, as has been argued by Merker et al. (2009).

A weak point of the coalition quality signaling theory is that it is based on hypotheses about our evolution that are difficult to confirm. The authors suggest that this is only one of the possible uses of music and dance. This weakens the theory, as it cannot be judged how much the coalition quality signaling theory has determined evolution. We have already argued that music has certainly also a function towards the people of their own group, and in this case the necessary activation expressions could be quite different.

An important result obtained in this context is that we have been able to measure the gestural activation of listeners of different pieces of music and relate these to a number of descriptors of the audio signal. This opens the route to a deeper understanding of the expressive powers of music and movement.

8 Conclusions

The framework that we set out to develop in this chapter in order to understand the relationship between music and movement is based on two pillars: the bio-kinetic resonance of locomotion of the individual agent and the cooperative behavior of aggregations of these social agents to obtain goals unobtainable by individual agents. It is through resonance that agents can discover the potential for entrainment mediated by auditory and visual signals.

The special relation between music and movement allows them to activate each other without interference. They relate to each other in time but not in space. Music does not dictate the movement, nor does the movement dictate the music. In order to obtain a coherent work of art or just a coalition quality signal, planning and rehearsal are necessary.

The strong bonding that can exist between agents moving together to music can be exploited in both directions. It can be used to stimulate people to move and to help people to integrate more socially. Its potential deserves research in different directions, including development of new technology to enhance the experiences involved with keeping in time together.

It is arguable that the coalition quality signaling theory may have its weaknesses; nonetheless, it is clear that it is fully functional at present at the highest political levels. How else could we interpret such an event as the opening of the Olympic Games 2008 in Beijing?

Note

1   With contributions by Frederik Styns, Leen De Bruyn, Luiz Naveda, and Raven van Noorden.

References

Becking, G. (1958). *Der Musikalische Rhythmus als Erkenntnisquelle*. Stuttgart: Ichthys.

Bispham, J. (2006). Rhythm in music: what is it? Who has it? And why? *Music Perception*, 24(2), 125–134.

Brodelet, A. (2006). Empirisch Onderzoek naar de Spatio-temporele Relatie van Muziek en Beweging in Schrijfdans. MA thesis, Ghent University, Department of Musicology, Ghent.

Chen, J. L., Zatorre, R. J., and Penhune, V. B. (2006). Interactions between auditory and dorsal premotor cortex during synchronization to musical rhythms. *NeuroImage*, 32(4), 1771–1781.

Clynes, M. (1977). *Sentics, the Touch of Emotions*. New York: Doubleday Anchor.

De Bruyn, L., Leman, M., Moelants, D., and Demey, M. (2009). Does social interaction activate listeners? In S. Ystad, R. Kronland-Martinet, and

K. Jensen (eds.), *Computer Music: Modeling and Retrieval*, LNCS 5493. Berlin, Heidelberg: Springer, 93–106.

De Cremer, D. and Van Vugt, M. (1999). Social identification effects in social dilemmas: a transform of motives. *European Journal of Social Psychology*, 29(7), 871–93.

DeNora, T. (2000). *Music in Everyday Life*. Cambridge: Cambridge University Press.

Hagen, E. H. and Bryant, G.A. (2003). Music and dance as a coalition signaling system. *Human Nature*, 14(1), 21–51.

Hagen, E. H. and Hammerstein P (in press). Did Neanderthals and other early humans sing? Seeking the biological roots of music in the territorial advertisements of primates, lions, hyenas, and wolves. *Musicae Scientiae*.

Li, H. and Leman, M. (2007). A gesture-based typology of sliding-tones in guqin music. *Journal of New Music Research*, 36(2), 61–82.

MacDougall, H. and Moore, S. (2005). Marching to the beat of the same drummer: the spontaneous tempo of human locomotion. *Journal of Applied Physiology*, 99, 1164–1173.

Merker, B. H., Madison, G. S., and Eckerdal, P. (2009). On the role and origin of isochrony in human rhythmic entrainment. *Cortex*, 45(1), 4–17.

Moelants, D. and van Noorden, L. (2005). The influence of pitch interval on the perception of polyrhythms. *Music Perception*, 22(3), 425–440.

Naveda, L. and Leman, M. (2008a). Representation of Samba dance gestures, using a multi-modal analysis approach. In *Proceedings of the 5th International Conference on Enactive Interfaces (ENACTIVE'08)*. Pisa, Italy, 68–74.

Naveda, L. and Leman, M. (2008b). Sonification of Samba dance using periodic pattern analysis. In *Proceedings of the 4th International Conference on Digital Arts (Artech'08)*, Porto, Portugal, 6–26.

Néda, Z., Ravasz, E., Vicsek, T., Brechet, Y, and Barabasi, A. L. (2000). Physics of the rhythmic applause. *Physical Review*, E 61(6), 6987–6992.

Néda, Z., Ravasz, E, Brechet, Y, Vicsek, T., and Barabási, A. L. (2000). The sound of many hands clapping. *Nature*, 403, 849–850.

Phillips-Silver, J. and Trainor, L. J., (2005). Feeling the beat: movement influences infants' rhythm perception. *Science*, 308, 1430.

Rizzolatti, G., and Craighero, L. (2004). The mirror-neuron system. *Annual Review of Neuroscience*, 27, 169–92.

Sethares, W. A. and Staley, T. W. (1999). Periodicity transforms., *IEEE Transactions on Signal Processing*, 47(11), 2953–2964.

Sethares, W. A. (2007). *Rhythm and Transforms*. Berlin, Heidelberg: Springer.

Styns, F., and Van Noorden, L. (2006). Some basic observations on how people move on music and how they relate music to movement. In A. Gritten and E. King (eds.), *Proceedings of the Second International Conference on Music and Gesture*. Manchester: Northern College of Music.

Styns, F., Van Noorden, L., Moelants, D., and Leman, M. (2007). Walking on music. *Human Movement Science, 26(5)*, 769–785.

Styns, F. (2009). *Kenmerken van de Muzikale Basisbeweging in Stappen op Muziek. Een Empirisch Musicologisch Onderzoek naar de Grondslagen van de Relatie tussen Muziek en Beweging*. PhD thesis, Ghent University.

Todd, N. P. M., Cousins, R., and Lee, C. S. (2007). The contribution of anthropomorphic factors in individual differences in the perception of rhythm. *Empirical Musicology Review*, 2(1), 1–13.

Van Noorden, L. and Moelants, D. (1999). Resonance in the perception of musical pulse. *Journal of New Music Research*, 28(1), 43–66.

Will, U. and Berg, E. (2007). Brain wave synchronization and entrainment to periodic acoustic stimuli. *Neuroscience Letters*, 424(1), 55–60.

Zivotofsky, A. and Hausdorff, J. (2007). The sensory feedback mechanisms enabling couples to walk synchronously: an initial investigation. *Journal of NeuroEngineering and Rehabilitation*, 4(28), 1–27.

Part III

Gesture Generation and Control

Chapter 8

Gesture and Timbre

*Tor Halmrast, Knut Guettler, Rolf Bader,
and Rolf Inge Godøy*

1 Introduction

We can speak of music-related gestures at different timescales, from the more extended gestures that shape rhythmical, textural, or melodic patterns, to the micro-gestures that create minute inflections of pitch, dynamics, and other features in the course of a single tone. We often perceive a melodic phrase at the same time as we perceive both the various nuances of each tone within the phrase and the transitions between these tones. Such small-scale features at the level of tone-events are crucial for our experience of music, giving music both its expressive power and its characteristic sonic quality. In the present chapter we shall focus on the relationship between gestures and the small-scale features in music that are referred to as *timbre*.

It is generally agreed that "timbre" denotes the distinctive perceived sonic qualities of different musical instruments, human voices, or other sound sources, such as the quality which makes the tone of a violin sound different from that of a piano, a trumpet, or a female voice. The expression "tone color" (or the German word *Klangfarbe*) is sometimes used to denote such distinct sound qualities, but we prefer to use the word "timbre" to indicate that we are talking about more than just a stationary hue (or what we would call "stationary spectrum", see next section). One of the essential attributes of timbre is actually those elements that vary over time within any tone, meaning that although we may perceive a violin tone as being stable throughout its duration, it is the many fluctuations and the overall evolution of features over the course of its duration that contribute to its characteristic quality and to its rich and interesting sound.

Timbre is a multidimensional phenomenon involving several features, some of which run in parallel and some of which follow sequentially throughout the sound, and this makes it difficult to define exactly what timbre is. This may seem paradoxical given that we usually have no problem in identifying different sounds and the various details within these sounds. Our seemingly unproblematic perceptions of timbre are based on a complex interplay of different features over a certain stretch of time; furthermore, timbre is an emergent phenomenon dependent on both the physical features of instruments and the gestures that produce the sound. Essentially, timbral features are constrained by the physics of musical instruments; for example, a piccolo cannot be made to sound like a tuba, no matter how ingenious we may be. Yet within the constraints of each instrument (or the human voice), it is nonetheless possible to produce different timbres.

The aim of this chapter is to show how sound-producing gestures can be used to produce a variety of timbrally rich and expressive musical sounds. We shall first have a brief look at some elements of sound with timbral significance, and then review some examples of relationships between gesture and timbre, first in *sustained* instrumental sounds (produced by continuous effort) and then in *impulsive* instrumental sounds (produced by discontinuous effort). Finally, we shall consider some issues of *gestural control* in relation to electronic musical instruments; that is, in cases where we have no necessary physical relationship between sound-producing gestures and the resultant sounds, nor any constraints as to the repertoire of possible sound features.

2 Timbral Elements of Musical Sound

Musicians, sound engineers, or other people who work with sound, seem to have very detailed and nuanced concepts of timbral features. However, these concepts are often related to practical questions of sound production in a performance or recording context. Also, non-expert listeners are quite capable of discriminating various timbral features, both in musical contexts (e.g. Freed 1990; McAdams et al. 2004) and in more everyday contexts (Rocchesso and Fontana 2003). The widespread use of metaphors such as "grainy," "smooth," "rough," "bright," "dark," "brilliant," "dull," "hollow," etc. among both experts and novices is a testimony to the existence of more or less distinct concepts of timbral features in the minds of listeners. Such metaphors are quite useful in both practical musical communicative contexts, such as conductors' instructions at rehearsals or in recording sessions (Porcello 2004), and various research experiments (e.g. Schaeffer 1966; Kendall and Carterette 1993; Godøy 2006). In order to achieve a better understanding of how gestures can shape timbre, we need to review the workings of some acoustic elements. To assist readers unfamiliar with musical acoustics, this section gives a brief overview of some elements of sound, sound-production, and sound-perception, and summarizes how these various elements contribute to our sensations of timbre.

What is Sound?

A general, simplified definition might be: Sound is any vibrating stimulus that is transmitted to our brain. Traditionally, the definition of sound is limited to what we can perceive with our ears, meaning vibrations transmitted through air at rates between roughly 20 and 20,000 times per second.

The most common method of producing sound is that a person or a device moves some object and sets air vibrating. These movements of air particles are received by our outer ears, and in our inner ears are transformed to nerve impulses and transmitted to our brain. Sound transmitted by air consists of small, rapid changes in air pressure. Thus, if the weather changed very, very rapidly, the changes in air pressure would (theoretically) produce sound, and the weather forecast might appear as a musical score!

These changes in air pressure can be represented as a curve along a temporal axis, as what is commonly called a *waveform*. The top portion of Figure 8.1 shows the repeated patterns of vibration in the waveform

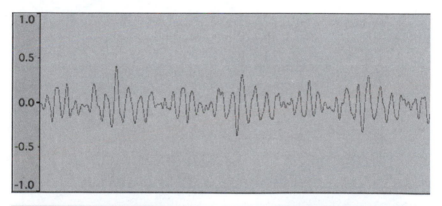

Figure 8.1 A fragment of the waveform of a piano tone (top), and a view of the waveform of the entire piano tone (bottom).

of a piano tone. The number of such repeated patterns per unit of time is the basis for the perceived *pitch* (or tone height) of the sound, and the vertical displacement, or the amplitude, of these patterns is the basis for our perceived *loudness* (or strength) of the sound. The bottom portion of Figure 8.1 shows the overall evolution of the whole piano tone. As we shall see, this overall evolution of the sound also contributes to our sensations of timbre, and it is in fact a combination of features at different timescales during the course of the sound that is the basis for our sensations of timbre.

A jagged waveform like that shown in the top part of Figure 8.1 can mathematically be regarded as a sum of several concurrent simpler regular waves, or *sine waves*, as shown in Figure 8.2. The number of

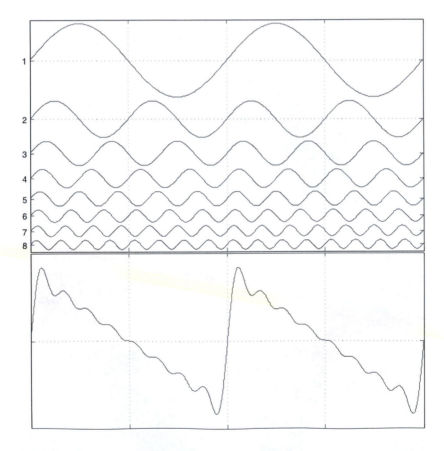

Figure 8.2 The top graph shows sine waves with different frequencies numbered from 1 to 8, while the bottom shows the sum of these, becoming more like a so-called *sawtooth wave*.

repeated cycles per seconds in these sine waves is referred to as the *frequency*, measured in Hz (after the German nineteenth century physicist Heinrich Rudolf Hertz), and the vertical displacement as the *amplitude*, measured either on an arbitrary scale (e.g. between 0 and 1 denoting, respectively, silence and maximum amplitude) or on a relative scale (e.g. in *decibels*, a logarithmic scale relative to the human threshold of hearing). We can build complex and musically more interesting sounds from simple sine waves in synthesizers and computers, and we can also use what is known as a *Fourier transform* to break down any sound into a collection of sine waves in order to view its constituent parts, or what is called its *spectrum*, see Figure 8.4.

The sine waves that make up a spectrum are usually referred to as *partials* (the terms *overtones* and *harmonics* are sometimes used to denote the components of the spectrum, but we shall use the term *partials* in this chapter), and it is the number, distribution, relative amplitude, and durations of these partials that determine the perceived timbral features of sound. If the frequencies of the partials are integer multiples of each other, i.e. in the proportions of 1:2:3:4:, etc. we speak of an *harmonic spectrum*, and the perceptual result of this will in most cases be sounds that have one more or less clear pitch, as is the case for many musical instruments. If the partials are not in integral proportions to each other, e.g. 1:2.9:5.7:9.6: etc. we speak of an *inharmonic spectrum*, typical of various bells and other percussion instruments. This often creates an ambiguous sensation of pitch. If we have a dense mass of partials of very short duration, or a spectrum that looks quite chaotic, we tend to perceive the sound as noise. In practice, we may have different spectral components in musical sound, e.g. in a piano tone we may have some inharmonic and noise components in addition to the predominant harmonic components. Furthermore, it is the relative strength of the partials, whether in harmonic or in inharmonic spectra, that shapes our notions of timbre. Thus, a sound with strong high frequency partials is usually perceived as "bright," and conversely, a sound with few or no high frequency partials is usually perceived as "dull."

The spectrum is the most important element of timbre and is the basis for our ability to distinguish sustained tones on different instruments, as well as different vowels in speech. This is probably why the term "tone color" is often used to denote timbre (Slawson 1985), but, as we shall see, the spectrum for most natural sounds is not stationary, and various fluctuations in the spectrum are very important for our sensations of timbre. The reason why these fluctuations occur is that the spectrum of any sound results from what are often quite complex physical interactions between performer and instrument (or vibrating object) and within the instrument itself. Therefore, we now need to review sound production in order to understand more about timbre.

Sound production

In order to produce airborne sound, one needs to move air. The most common ways of producing sound are by:

- Moving air directly (talking/singing/blowing instruments)
- Moving strings (plucking/striking/bowing)
- Moving or striking plates or membranes

Sound might also be produced by some mixture of the methods given above. Sound produced by walking (or dancing flamenco) makes impact noise, giving a short transient impulse and setting the floor (a membrane) moving and resonating. A superb example of using multiple methods of generating sound by movement is tap-dancing, where a skilled dancer uses both impact sound (middle and low frequencies), click sound (high frequencies), and the sound created by the friction of moving the shoe over the surface (broadband noise signals at the higher frequencies).

For the production of a sound, the object or instrument needs to produce a certain response when touched or blown. If this response comes with no time delay, we call it *resistance* (as when knocking on a stone). If some of the response comes with a time delay, we call it *reactance* (as when jumping on a trampoline). The combination of resistance and reactance is called *impedance*.

Most sounds produced naturally are actually not loud. In order to transport sound to the receiver, one needs some kind of *resonance*, (or what we might scientifically call *impedance matching*). The ancient Greeks described many of the facts of resonance, but the modern science of acoustics came much later, in the late 1800s, developing along with the growing knowledge of electronic circuits.

Resonance does not occur only in acoustics. We have examples of bridges falling down due to the resonance created by military marching or wind. Luckily, the resonance in the frequency region of music is not that dangerous (even if there is the example in the Bible of the walls of Jericho, which might be questioned scientifically).

The simplest way of describing resonance is through the example of a perfect string. Such a string, one that is tightly connected at both ends, cannot vibrate at the two endpoints. Therefore, the lowest mode of vibration is the one having a maximum at the middle, and no vibration at the ends. This gives a sine wave that has a wavelength of twice the length of the string. The string can, of course, also produce modes with two maxima, three maxima, etc. hence creating partials. As mentioned above, the relative strength of these different partials is the main factor in producing the timbre of each instrument, as it relates to the steady state of the sound, after the initial attack.

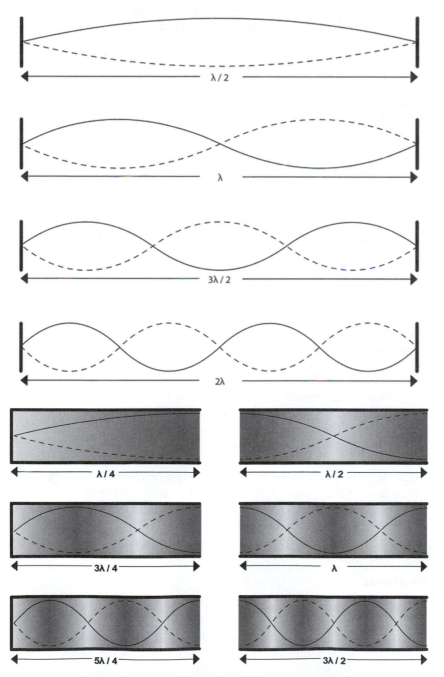

Figure 8.3 The vibration modes of a string (top) and in a tube (bottom). The Greek letter λ (lambda) is commonly used to indicate wavelength, i.e. the length of one cycle of vibration.

Tubes are used in wind instruments, including the organ. In this case, resonance is relative to the length of the tube, as longer tubes produce lower resonance frequencies. There are two types of tubes: those that are open at one end, and those that are open at both ends.

Additionally, the sound source may include various modifications of the spectrum, what in general is referred to as *filtering*. A well-known example of such filtering is the so-called equalizer found in various digital playback devices and software, allowing us to regulate the relative amplitude of different frequency regions, e.g. boosting the bass to obtain more "punch" in the sound or weakening high-frequency regions to make the sound more dull. However, as humans we carry with us a very sophisticated system for filtering. The human voice is a fantastic combination of sound production and filtering in that the glottis gives partials-rich "BZZ"-like sounds that are filtered by the throat and the mouth/lips/nose cavity. This filtering is much more elegant than any electronic filter yet made.

An analysis of a sound can be presented in three dimensions: time, frequency and intensity (sound level), by using a spectrogram, wherein the "darkness" represents amplitude. Figure 8.4 shows the results of two analyses of the same recording, a male speaking the words "see the sound in a spectrogram" in English. Here we see an interesting scientific fact: We cannot achieve good resolution both for frequency (pitch) and time (rhythm) at the same time. We have to choose which of them we should give priority.

An interesting phenomenon of timbre is found in what is called the *formants* of the human voice. Formants are peaks in the frequency spectra, independent of the pitch sung or spoken. This means that the vocal "e" has some timbral characteristics. To hear an easy example of formants, speak the following words: *"Heed," "Hid," "Head," "Had," "Hod," "Hawed," "Hood," "Who'd,"* and you will experience the change of the frequencies of the formants from high to low when changing the shape of your mouth. Formants are common also for some musical instruments, e.g. the oboe. The importance of formants is clearly understood when speech is frequency transposed by speeding up the playback of a recording.

Envelopes

A piano sound starts rather abruptly with the hammer hitting the string, and will decay slowly until it is no longer audible, and a violin sound may start softly and increase in loudness during its duration, depending on the action of the violinist. These changes in sound are often referred to as *envelopes*, meaning shapes that encompass the sound events from beginning to the end.

The start of a sound, what is often called the *attack segment* of

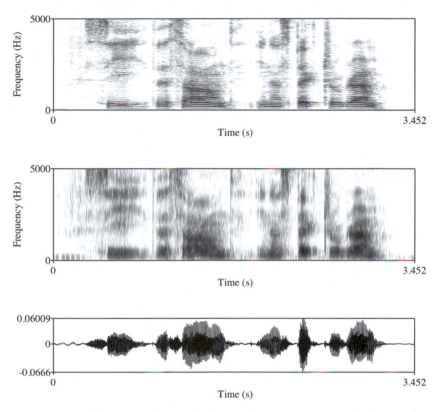

Figure 8.4 The upper part of the figure gives a good analysis of frequency and shows the partials of the vowels. The middle part of the figure gives a good analysis of time. Note that both analyses are taken from the same recording, and the lower part of the figure shows the waveform of this recording.

the envelope, is of particular importance for its timbre. Generally, if the attack is rapid, the sound will be perceived as "percussive" or as "plucked," and if it is slow, the sound will be perceived as "non-percussive" or "bowed like." Although the attack segments are at the beginning of the sound, these attack features are remembered and influence the rest of our perception of any sound event.

We can also speak of envelopes for other features, such as pitch and timbre, meaning that the pitch may vary in the course of the attack portion as well as throughout the sound, and that the spectrum also varies both in the attack portion and in the rest of the sound. These changes in the spectrum in the course of a sound are what make the sound interesting or "natural" to us, in contrast to some synthesized sounds that remain non-changing throughout their duration. It should however be noted that the term "spectral envelope" is also often used to denote the shape of the spectrum for a delimited portion of a sound, especially in the case of what could be called a quasi-stationary portion of a sound such as found in the distinct vowels of spoken language mentioned above. That musical sound contains several concurrent envelopes is the principal reason why timbre is such a complex phenomenon and why timbre in all its infinite variability and richness is so crucial for our experience of music.

Room Acoustics

Another factor that contributes to our perception of timbre is the acoustics of the room that the sound is produced in. Some of the sound may be absorbed by the walls, ceiling, floor, furniture, and various other objects in the room, as well as by the bodies of the audience and musicians, while other elements are reflected back and forth within the room. Differences in the materials of the room, as well as in its shape and size, will result in various modifications of the timbre we perceive. Every distinct reflection will entail that some frequencies arrive to the receiver "in phase," and some frequencies arrive "out of phase," meaning that they will cancel each other out, resulting, theoretically, in no sound for these frequencies. A distinct reflection will give a frequency response as can be seen in Figure 8.5. This is called a Comb Filter, and if more reflections are added in the same time interval, the frequency response will be smoothed. Such comb filter colorations are significant for timbral features (Halmrast 2000), and can to a certain extent also be varied by the instrumental displacement gestures that musicians make, e.g. clarinetists swaying their torso when playing.

Hearing

Our hearing is the most essential element when talking about timbre. The human ear is actually the best acoustic analyzer ever invented. The outer ear *(pinnae)* directs the sound to the ear channel (giving some "comb filter" reflections). Together with the time delay between the ears, and the shadowing effect of the head, this gives us information about the location of the sound source. When air vibrations reach the eardrum, the sound is transferred into mechanical vibration, vibration that in turn is passed on to the so-called *basilar membrane* inside the *cochlea* ("snail house") of the ear. In highly simplified terms, we could say that the basilar membrane separates the different frequency components of the sound and sends this information to various auditory-related parts of the brain where this information is processed for finding patterns in the sound, after which all this information is put

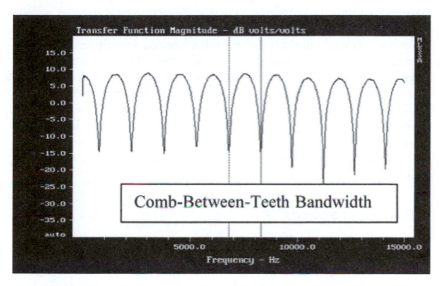

Figure 8.5 The frequency response of a comb filter. Notice the peaks in different frequency regions.

together and interpreted by the brain in order to make sense of what we hear.

With respect to timbre, there is no one-to-one relationship between the components of the acoustic signal and our perceptual image of the sound. For instance, on the one hand we may not hear some components in the sound due to so-called "masking," and, on the other hand, we may "hear" features that are not really in the sound because our auditory system creates these features from other information in the sound spectrum. Also, our sensations of loudness vary across different frequencies. This means that studying timbre centers on the attempt to establish *correlations* between the acoustic signal and our subjective sensations of sound features. One way of taking our hearing into account in studying timbre is the so-called *analysis-by-synthesis* strategy (Risset 1991), meaning that we can synthesize incrementally different variants of timbres (i.e. with control of the acoustic ingredients) and have listeners judge the various perceived features of the synthesized sounds.

The systematic study of timbre is a fast growing field, and increasingly sophisticated methods are being developed to capture the many transient features that are important for our experience of sound features, as well as methods for dealing with multidimensionality (see e.g. Kendall and Carterette 1993). One possible research strategy in light of the multidimensionality of timbre is to relate perceptually pertinent timbral features to gestural metaphors, as was suggested several decades ago by Pierre Schaeffer (Schaeffer 1966; Godøy 2006). In the following two sections, we will study in more detail both sustained sounds and impulsive sounds, following the taxonomy of Schaeffer. There is also a third category: that of *iterative* sounds. This includes sounds that are produced by rapid reiterated movement such as a tremolo, a drum roll, or in the stroking of a washboard. The idea behind the identification of these sound-producing categories is that they could form the basis for a taxonomy of timbre based on gestures, given that the gestures are biomechanically quite distinct, and produce acoustically quite distinct sounds.

3 Sustained Sounds

The sustained sounds of traditional Western musical instruments are typically those that are made by blowing, bowing, and singing, or in the case of the organ, by having an air flow coming from bellows. In playing the organ, the gestures of the performer regulate depression of the keys and pedals as well as pulling of the stops (and on some organs, the swell box), leaving little room for shaping the timbre. In the case of blown instruments, i.e. woodwind and brass, most of the timbral control is done by regulating the airflow, through breath and the shape of the mouth and lips, yet there is some room for controlling timbral features by moving the instrument and thus changing the reflections from the room. However, the most prominent means for gestural regulation on some blown instruments is through the use of various kinds of mutes. One well-known example of this is the so-called *wah-wah* mute, where the opening and closing of the mute acts as a time-varying filter. As for the human voice, the possibilities of timbral control seem almost unlimited (as can be heard in the vocal imitations of non-vocal sounds in so-called *beatboxing*), but in this case we are of course speaking of phonological gestures, i.e. small-scale movements of the vocal tract (Browman and Goldstein 1989). However, there can be no doubt that the performance of bowing gestures on string instruments present some of the most varied opportunities for timbral control, and we shall therefore discuss in more detail the relation of such bowing gestures to timbre.

Waveforms of Bowed String Sounds

During normal sound production (for example, in the case of the majority of tones produced in classical playing), a bowed string moves with a wave pattern referred to as *Helmholtz motion*, after the German acoustician Hermann von Helmholtz, who first reported it (Helmholtz 1862; see

Figure 8.6). Later, C. V. Raman and J. Schelleng contributed descriptions of the conditions necessary for maintaining this pattern, with respect to the three most important bowing parameters: the (normal) bowing *force*, the bowing *speed*, and the bow's *position* on the moving string (Raman 1920; Schelleng 1973). More recently, Guettler has shown how the Helmholtz pattern is generated, and illuminated the conditions for a quick transient, in which the bow's *acceleration* plays a crucial role (Guettler 2002). As we shall see later, stringent use of these four parameters can control a variety of tone characteristics.

Based on analyses performed by Raman, Schelleng constructed a diagram defining the set of conditions under which Helmholtz motion is maintained (known as the Helmholtz regime) with respect to the normal *bow force* (usually referred to as "bow pressure" by players) and *bowing position*, while keeping bow speed constant (see Figure 8.7). Increased relative force will give increased sharpening of the rotating corner, i.e. increased brilliance. Lowering the bow speed will move this diagram down in absolute force values, implying a sharpening of the Helmholtz corner.

The Guettler diagram is based on similar analysis for the tone onset, but here the operative word is *acceleration* (see Figure 8.8). In the bow-force/acceleration space a wedge will indicate the regime, in which the string's slipping on the bow hair will be regular and periodic from the first instant. Characteristic noises will be produced on either side of the wedge. Combining the information in the Schelleng and Guettler diagrams, the outlines of a "clean" attack can be visualized (see Figure 8.9, where the white area indicates clean stick-slip triggering).

Other parameters that affect timbre are (a) bow-hair tilt with respect to the string (Schoonderwaldt et al. 2003), which moderately sharpens the tone color when the bow is rolled some 30–50 degrees away from bridge; (b) left-hand finger-pad damping of the string's transverse waves, with soft and/or wide pads giving a duller sound; (c) direction of frictional pull, which gives a duller, less stable sound if the pull deviates from 90 degrees with respect to the string's orientation. This last condition occurs because a longitudinal force component will produce frequent small slips in the longitudinal direction and interfere with the Helmholtz triggering.

Some Bow-Stroke Examples

In *détaché* (from the French for separated and often referred to as "on the string") technique, the bow is moved forward and backwards, without any release of the bow "pressure," so that all tones are full sounding with individual clearly audible attacks (but usually unaccented). National anthems (e.g. "God Save the Queen") are typically played détaché. Most

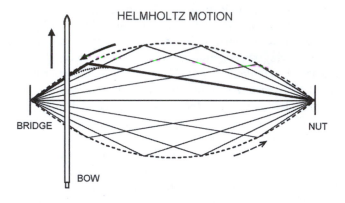

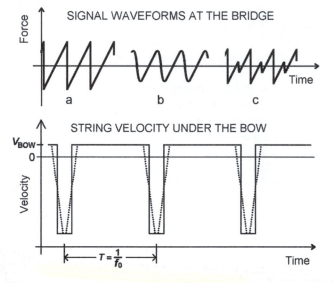

Figure 8.6 Bowed-string waveforms. In the Helmholtz motion regime, the string takes the shape of two straight lines joined in a rotating corner. Due to damping and string stiffness, this corner will be somewhat smeared out and rounded, causing the sound to become less brilliant (see fine dotted lines next to the bow in the upper panel, and compare waveforms *b* and *a* in the middle panel). The width of the rounded corner determines the spectral roll-off frequency. However, the corner is sharpened every time it passes the bow. If the string slips more than once per period, more corners occur, and the sound becomes "glassy" or "scratchy." (See waveform *c* in the middle panel.) The lower panel shows the string velocity under the bow during Helmholtz motion. During the stick period, the string follows the bow completely, while during the slip period the string rushes back on the bow hair with a relative velocity of $-V_{BOW}/\beta$, where β is the relative bowing position. In the case of a rounded string corner, the string's velocity is continuously varying during the slip (as shown by the dotted lines).

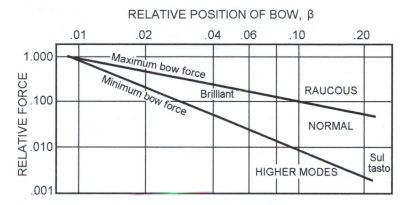

Figure 8.7 The Schelleng diagram. In this diagram a wedge outlines the Helmholtz-motion regime for a fixed bow speed. In logarithmic representation the minimum and maximum bow force can be drawn as two straight lines, their angles depending on the losses of resistance in the system. As the relative bow force is increased, the Helmholtz corner is sharpened and the tone color changing from *Sul tasto* to *Brilliant*.

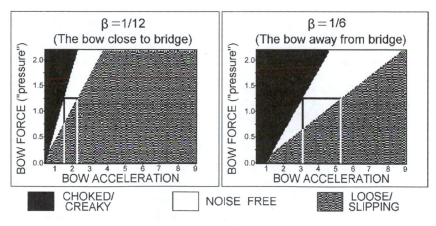

Figure 8.8 The Guettler diagram shows attack quality as a function of acceleration and bow force, with the bow starting from rest. The white wedge indicates attacks with regular, periodic slips, like those found in the Helmholtz regime. Too low or too high acceleration results in *choked/creaky* or *loose/slipping* tone onsets, respectively. Notice that the noise-free range diminishes as the bow is brought closer to the bridge. Rectangles are drawn to facilitate estimation of the "acceptable" acceleration range (in arbitrary units).

attacks would be found inside the white wedges of Figure 8.8. That is, the sound building quickly up, without noticeable noise.

When played *forte* or *mezzo forte* ("loud" or "moderately loud") the bow speed will typically follow the middle part of the white path in

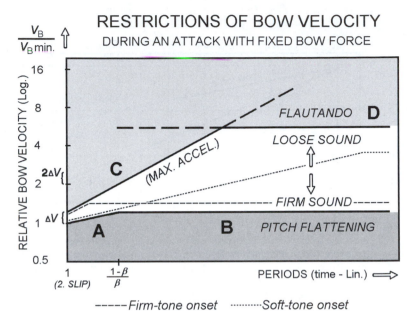

Figure 8.9 Anatomy of a clean attack with fixed bow force. During the first part of the tone onset the bow speed is restricted by lines A and C, indicating minimum and maximum acceleration respectively. After the expiration of the transient, the bow speed should be kept between lines B and D to maintain regular periodic stick-slip triggering. In a soft-color tone onset the bow speed should follow the slope of A until it approaches the line D (maximum speed—loose sound), while in a firm-tone onset the bow speed should follow maximum acceleration (C) until line B is just surpassed (i.e. minimum speed—firm sound).

Figure 8.9. For a *fortissimo* ("very loud") the bow force will be increased (most commonly the bow is also brought nearer to the bridge) while the bow speed will follow a path of maximum acceleration (C) until a speed near the minimum relative speed (B) for that particular bow force is obtained. Minimum relative speed provides the brightest sound, but the lowest physical power, and is fairly proportional to the applied bow force. Variations in timbre account for less than two decibels of the physical volume, but since the ear perceives sharper-sounding tones as louder, the player will normally utilize this perceptual effect to create the impression of a greater dynamic difference (Askenfelt 1986; Guettler 2003). The physical volume is approximately proportional to the bow speed for a given bowing position on the string.

Bringing the bow closer to the bridge has the three-fold effect of demanding greater bow force while maintaining, or even reducing, the bow speed. Both changes sharpen the tone color without losing string amplitude: in fact, the amplitude increases (see Figures 8.6 and 8.7). The price of this is a narrower range of acceptable accelerations during the attack (see Figure 8.8), making decent attacks more demanding. When bowed in the Helmholtz regime close to the bridge, the string's amplitude is nearly inversely proportional to the relative position, β. If not playing near the bridge in *forte* passages, one might quickly run out of bow when playing tones of a certain length.

In *martelé* (from the French for hammered) each bow stroke starts from the string with high bow force, causing the initial periods between slips to become slightly prolonged (with pitch flattened compared to the nominal frequency) and even sometimes irregular. The attacks would be found in the black areas of Figure 8.8. As long as this non-Helmholtzian triggering does not last more than some 20–30 milliseconds, the attack will appear as heavily accentuated with little noise or pitch distortion. The remaining part is often played *diminuendo* with (perceived) fading loudness and diminishing bow force so that the attack remains the most dominant part of the tone. The expression *martelé* is normally reserved for aggressive, short notes. A series of hard *martelé* attacks would often be performed as repeated *down bows* (i.e. bowed in the direction towards the *frog* or *heel* of the bow). For a successful martelé it is of utmost importance that the bow force be fully established *before* the first slip takes place in order to ensure high amplitudes from the very beginning. (Less skilled players have a tendency to increase the bow force during the first part of the transient, causing extra initial noise.) Good examples of *martelé* can be found in the aggressive repeated chords of the "Dances of the Young Girls" from Stravinsky's *The Rite of Spring*, and in the second variation of Paganini's *Moses Fantasy on the G-string*.

In *spiccato* (from the Italian *spiccare*, meaning clearly separated or cut off—often referred to as "off the string" or "bouncing"), the bow is thrown onto the string for each individual attack, with rapidly alternating bowing directions, as opposed to *ricochet* (from the French for "indirectly" or "rebounding"), where several successive tones are performed in one throw, and one bowing direction. Here it is essential for the bow to be rotating around a point near the frog, while the frog axis is translated in a straight line forward or backwards—without wobbling. Frog wobbling tends to dampen the rotational resonances of the bow stick (see Figure 8.10).

Studies of these bowing techniques have revealed that in a crisp *spiccato* the string is efficiently dampened by the bow between all strokes, while in *ricochet* the string is freely vibrating between strokes, and the bow is thus merely refreshing the already existing wave pattern (Guettler and Askenfelt 1998) (see Figure 8.11). Both types of strokes rely heavily on the bow quality to be successful.

In *spiccato* the trajectory of the bow is somewhat more complex than for

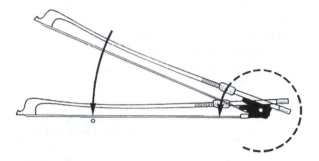

Figure 8.10 Ideal bow rotation during a ricochet attack. During this rotation, the frog is moved in a straight line forward or backwards. The bouncing rate increases with (a) the string's distance from frog, and (b) the firmness of the bow grip. It decreases with (a) the bow's distance from the bridge, and (b) the tilt of the bow hairs with respect to the string.

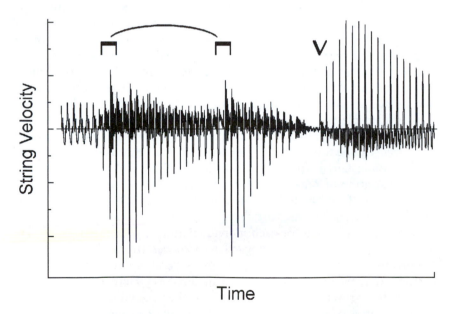

Figure 8.11 String velocity under the bow during two tones of *ricochet* (the two notes produced in the down-bow direction) followed by one of *spiccato* (here bowed in up-bow V direction). All attacks are "perfect," in the sense that all slips (seen as spikes in the figure) are regularly spaced. Notice also that the spiccato tone is preceded by an almost complete damping of string amplitudes, thus facilitating a quick and crisp build-up of the next tone (measurement from actual playing).

ricochet, where the frog is moving in one straight line and the tip bounces up and down, preferably at the desired rate. Figure 8.12 shows trajectories at different points of the bow stick during (a) a good, crisp *spiccato*, and (b) a scratchy, uneven *spiccato*. Figure 8.13 explains the effect of

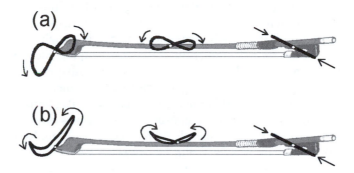

Figure 8.12 Trajectories of (a) "good" and (b) "bad" spiccato. The movement consists of a translational component (shown at the frog) and a rotational component of twice that frequency (their sum indicated at the tip and the middle of the stick).

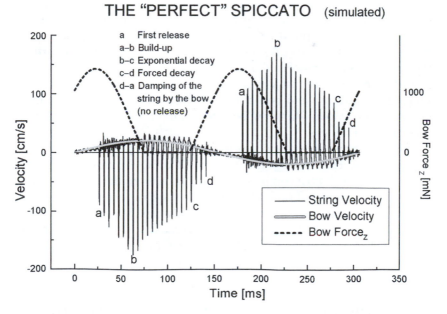

THE "PERFECT" SPICCATO (simulated)

a   First release
a–b Build-up
b–c Exponential decay
c–d Forced decay
d–a Damping of the
      string by the bow
      (no release)

String Velocity
Bow Velocity
Bow Force$_z$

Figure 8.13 The phases of a crisp spiccato. Notice that the bow, which is not in contact with the string between b and c, lands on the string (at c) while still moving in the "old" direction. This is contrary to the popular belief. Such a return facilitates a quick and quiet damping of the remaining string waves; a necessity for a rapid change in orientation of the rotating Helmholtz corner.

the "good" trajectory. In order to achieve a clear attack without excess slipping noise, two conditions must apply: (1) after the last tone the remaining string signal (waves) must be well damped to avoid interference with the new signal, which will produce slips in the reverse direction; (2) the first slip of each new tone must happen when the bow force ("pressure") is close to its maximum (see Figure 8.13). In both *ricochet* and *spiccato*, as well as in many other types of bow strokes, the player takes advantage of the bow's dynamics (elasticity, weight, rotational momentum, translational momentum, etc.) for shaping the tone. This implies that a good quality bow, when held with adequate flexibility, will do much of the work after the desired movement is initiated. Example of *ricochet* is found in the *Agitato* section of Paganini's Caprice no. 5 (where the original bowing consists of three notes down followed by one up), while the more frequently used *spiccato* is found, for example in the finale of Tchaikovsky's Violin Concerto. A very rapid *spiccato* is most easily performed with the bow's hair flat on the string.

Soft Attacks and Legato String Crossings

In soft attacks and legato string crossings the bow will gently approach the string from the air, producing extra slips for the first part of the tone (as indicated in the grey areas of Figure 8.8). In string crossings a slight overlap from the sound of the "old" string will easily mask the start of the new tone if the player is crossing the strings slowly. In a soft attack, the noise might be more audible, but usually perceived as "breathy" if played with care. Soft attacks can also be played within the noise-free range if acceleration and bow force are both increased simultaneously. On a violin or viola, tilting the bow hair (about 30–45°) is essential for these kinds of attacks.

These examples are some of the many possibilities for a string player's gestural control of timbre; common to all these examples is that the performer exerts both a continuous energy transfer to the instrument and a continuous control of timbral features. In the case of impulsive sounds where there is only discontinuous contact between the performer and the resonating object, we shall now see that the musician is faced with rather different challenges in the gestural control of timbre.

4 Impulsive Sounds

The basic principle of impulsive sounds is that there is a discontinuous transfer of energy from the performer to the instrument, typically such as in hitting by hand or with a mallet, or by plucking. This means that after the plucking or the impact of the hand or mallet on the instrument, there are only limited possibilities of shaping the timbre through modification of the resonance (or energy dissipation pattern) of the instrument. These possibilities include damping with the hand, changing the tension of the string or membrane, or even submerging the instrument in water (as can be done with, e.g. a gong, changing its timbre as well as its pitch). Nonetheless, instruments with impulsive sounds, such as percussion (including the piano) and plucked stringed instruments are capable of great timbral variety, as we shall discuss in the following section.

Gestures and the Timbre of Plucked Stringed Instruments

Obviously, there is a great variety both of playing techniques and of the resultant timbral features among guitars and other plucked instruments within different styles of music, including classical guitar, rock, pop, jazz, etc. Also, as discussed in several other chapters in this volume, when watching musicians perform, it may be difficult to draw the exact border between gestures that are strictly sound-producing and those that are more communicative and/or theatrical. Thus, different guitarists may variously make large whole arm/shoulder movements or smaller wrist/forearm movements to produce essentially similar sounds. When focusing on the details of performer-instrument interaction, we can see that various timbral features of the guitar sound depend, respectively, on the elements of the plucking device (finger, nail, plectrum or even hammer), plucking position on the string, and plucking mode and force (ranging from soft and barely audible to "slap-hand" type). One should notice that a major difference exists between the classical guitar (with a resonant body) and the electric guitar (with magnetic pickups) as far as gesture is concerned. While the magnetic pickups are sensitive only to metal strings crossing the magnetic flux lines in the *horizontal* plane, the body of the classical guitar is dependent on string movements in the *vertical* plane in order to resonate fully. This implies that while the plectrum of the electric guitar should be striking the strings horizontally, the finger plucking of the classical player should be more angled or even vertical. However, because the bridge of the classical guitar is much stiffer in the horizontal direction than in the vertical direction, and hence absorbs less energy from the string in that plane, the player can to some extent increase the sustain at the cost of volume by plucking horizontally. In practice, the classical string is in most cases rotating elliptically around its axis after having been released by the plucking finger, thus moving in both planes as a nice compromise.

Basically we have three possible ways of plucking a stringed instrument: (1) using a finger (with or without using the nail), (2) using a plectrum (made of plastic, or metal, perhaps attached to the finger(s) as is often used for banjos); and (3) striking the string, as with a dulcimer.

The plucking position changes the spectrum of the radiated sound.

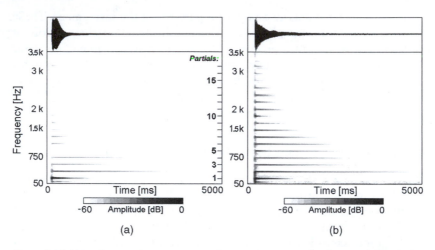

Figure 8.14 Waveform and spectrogram of two guitar tones, the first made by plucking at the middle of the string (a), and the second made by plucking near the bridge (b).

Figure 8.14 shows the frequency analysis of plucking at the middle of the string, and then near the bridge, of a classical guitar. With the tone on the right in Figure 8.14, made by picking close to the bridge, we see and hear a larger amount of higher partials which gives a more "metallic" sound.

Gestures and the Timbre of Percussion Instruments

There are many elements that affect the timbre of the sounds produced by percussion instruments: (1) the instrument body, (2) the stick or mallet, and the hand and arm, and (3) the body of the player. Interaction between these elements determines the gestures that are possible and, consequently, the sounds that can be produced.

The instrument body is a complex dynamic system. If we use a tom-tom as an example, we have a beat membrane, a back or resonance membrane, the air within them in the vessel, and the vessel itself. The membranes are responsible mainly for the lower frequencies and the punch of the sound while the vessel radiates the higher frequencies (Bader 2006). The interaction of the membranes is quite complicated. If the resonance membrane is not tuned to the precise pitch of the beat membrane, the resulting sound will have a pitch glide. The air enclosed in the tom-tom is a coupling mass between the membranes and the vessel. When playing a bass drum, this mass is often increased by inserting cushions that dampen the sound. Other drums, such as the tambourine, only have one membrane. In some xylophones and metallophones (such as in the Indonesian gamelan) the resonating body is coupled to a resonator, thus the Balinese *gender dasa* is coupled to a bamboo resonator that has the same frequencies as the fundamental frequencies of the bronze plates.

With respect to sound-producing gestures, performers quickly learn that different impact points on the instruments do not only sound different, but also have to be played differently. Physically, each point of strike on the percussion instrument body has a different *impedance* (cf. section 2 above). If impedance is high, the player needs considerable energy to drive the system. On the other side, if the impedance at a certain point is low, then the *admittance*, the willingness to react, will be high and the player needs only a little energy to drive the system. But the picture is a bit more complex, as each point has a different impedance for each frequency. Some points have a high impedance for higher frequencies and react very strongly to lower ones, some points are driven easily for higher frequencies and not so good for lower ones. In terms of gestures, this entails a different reaction of the body of the percussion instrument to the striking mallet or stick.

The nature of mallets and sticks are yet another factor to consider. A stick can be hard or soft, and it can have a larger or smaller striking area (Borg 1983). The shape of the impulse created by the stick determines the amplitude of the partials. If a stick is hard (wood or metal) and the striking area is small, its impulse is hard, similar to when a string is plucked near the bridge. If the stick is soft (made out of threads or silk or tissues) and its striking area is large, it generates fewer higher frequencies. Mallets for xylophones or vibraphones often have a wooden kernel with soft threads wrapped around it. If the player strikes softly, the soft region dominates and produces a sound with few partials. If the player uses more energy, the overall sound is stronger, and higher frequencies are more dominant. The instrument is reacting to the stick or mallet according to its impedance, giving a reactive force back.

While the softness of the mallet head pretty much determines the limiting frequency in the high end of the spectrum, the ratio between the dynamic mass of the mallet and that of the struck object determines the overall spectral slope below that frequency (Fletcher and Rossing 1998). When the dynamic mass of the mallet is much smaller than that of the instrument, the mallet is easily thrown back off the instrument, and the resultant spectral envelope is nearly flat. However, to obtain maximum sound the mallet's dynamic mass should approach the dynamic mass of the struck object, for example, in a marimba the stick's mass should be some 30 percent of the stave's mass. This, however, produces a spectral slope of about −6 dB per octave. A further increase of the mallet's mass would result in a shorter tone with an even steeper spectral slope. Notice that a tight mallet grip adds to the effective dynamic mass since in this case the mass of the player's arm gets coupled to the mallet.

The sound produced by percussion instruments is highly dependent on how one strikes the instrument. Figure 8.15 includes examples of contrasting sounds produced on a small gong by, respectively, a soft stroke, a hard stroke that makes the gong rotate (giving a phasing effect), and scratching the gong with the wooden part of the stick.

The gestures of the player depend upon the interaction of the stick-instrument system. For example, if a drummer strikes a tom-tom membrane, he will move his hand with the stick fixed between two fingers. When the stick hits the membrane, the membrane reacts. The drummer might try to dampen the return force of the stick by holding the hand-part of the stick more tightly, but mainly he is waiting for the stick to move freely back and then prepare for the next stroke. The basic idea behind his gesture is to let the physical system do the work, thus the drummer applies only a small amount of energy to the system at the start of each stroke.

We should also mention the case of *iterative* excitation, i.e. that of a drum roll or roll on a cymbal with hard or soft sticks. Such iterative gestures can create the effect of a sustained sound, for example, a crescendo roll with soft mallets on a cymbal will not only create a change in

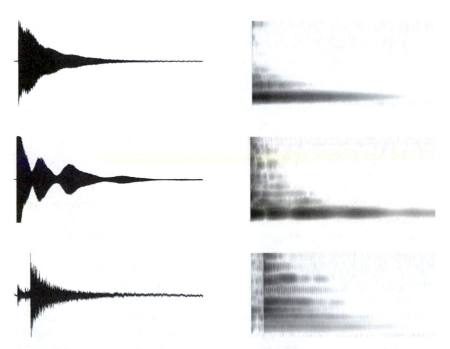

Figure 8.15 Top: the waveform and spectrogram (range 0–5000 Hz) of the sound of a gong struck softly. Middle: the sound of the same gong struck hard. Bottom: the sound of the same gong scratched with a stick.

dynamics but also a gradual change in timbre. With iterative gestures we have multiple excitations, meaning that the instrument is repeatedly set into motion before it has had time to decay to silence, producing a semblance of continuous sound. This technique is also used on the piano (typically in piano reductions of orchestral scores) to create the semblance of a crescendo (with change in both loudness and timbre of sustained tones).

The correspondences we have mentioned in this chapter between timbral features and the necessary sound-producing gestures are established through years and years of diligent practice. This process of mastering an instrument, involves what we could call an auditory-motor feedback loop (see for example Zatorre et al. 2007). However, we could also speak of a motor-haptic feedback loop here, in the sense that the musician senses the instrument through touch as well as through resistance or force feedback (Cadoz and Wanderley 2000). These auditory-motor and motor-haptic feedback loops are basic ingredients in gesture-timbre relationships. We shall now consider some issues that emerge in the gestural control of new electronic instruments where there are no pre-established feedback loops.

5 Control Gestures for Timbre with Electronic Musical Instruments

There are several elements that are common to all the examples of sound-producing gestures we have seen so far in this chapter, including:

- The transfer of energy from the human body of the performer to the instrument, cf. the aforementioned element of impedance.
- The role played by touch in the sound-producing and sound-modifying gestures of the performer, which affect the physics of the resonating objects either directly, through fingers, hands, lips, etc. or indirectly, through mallets, bows, plectrums, etc.
- The haptic feedback given by each instrument in addition to the auditory feedback.
- The limitations on each instrument as to its possible behaviors, meaning that there are certain sounds that cannot be made on a particular instrument, no matter how hard we try.

We could summarize these elements as a set of *constraints* at work in sound production, meaning that there are certain limits as to what can be done when playing on any kind of instrument. This would also hold true for any new musical instrument that we might construct, as long as we are talking about real physical objects that we play with our bodies. However, if we consider electronic instruments, these constraints no longer apply. The source of sound for electronic instruments will usually be some kind of loudspeaker, where the loudspeaker in turn is fed with a signal from an amplifier, a signal that originates in some kind of electronic circuitry. This electronic circuitry can of course be controlled by a gesture, e.g. by turning a knob that regulates the volume of the signal feed to the speaker. However, the turning of the knob is what we could call a control gesture: it does not by itself transfer energy from our body to any instrument of sound-production, nor can such a gesture modify any feature of the sound apart from its volume. Moreover, whatever haptic feedback we get from the dial is the same no matter how loud or soft the sound is.

In using computers to control the entire process of sound-production and playback, we may not even need to make gestures such as turning dials, thus dispensing with all the aforementioned constraints. However, this situation clearly presents us with some formidable challenges:

- Considering the rich set of timbral features made possible by traditional acoustic instruments through close bodily contact with the resonating objects, what substitutes can be found for such very intimate relationships between gestures and sound?
- Sound synthesis models and techniques typically require control input along dimensions (or parameters) that are rather abstract with regards to perceptually salient features. How, then, can control dimensions be organized and mapped so as to exert a more direct effect on the timbral features of sound in perceptually and aesthetically meaningful ways?
- When musicians are accustomed to getting physical feedback from their instruments in addition to the auditory feedback, what happens when this haptic feedback is no longer there?

These and similar questions have in the past couple of decades been given much attention, and are among the reasons for the growing interest in research on music-related gestures (Leman 2008). What is emerging now is an awareness of the need for developing control interfaces for timbral features of sound that are less abstract or disembodied and more in accordance with causal schemes as found in traditional instruments (see Miranda and Wanderley 2006 for an overview).

The topic of mapping control input to sound features has also received much attention (see, for example, Hunt et al. 2003 for an overview). A central motive of this research has been to forge links between gestures and timbral features, links that both make sense to the performer and allow for the desired level of detail control. Schematically, such links can be organized into *one-to-one, one-to-many, many-to-many*, and *many-to-one* types of mappings. In a one-to-one mapping, a gesture is used to control just one feature, such as a foot pedal used to control the overall volume of an instrument. A one-to-many mapping links one gesture to several features. A rather straightforward example is found in sampled piano instruments where the velocity, or speed, of the key-stroke on one key is mapped to different samples of piano tones. In this case low velocity is mapped to soft piano samples, and high velocity is mapped to loud piano samples, so that increased velocity results in the spectral changes typical of a real acoustic piano. As a similar example of one-to-many mapping on sustained sounds, consider the use of the so-called "aftertouch" on MIDI keyboards (i.e. continuous pressure on the key after the initial depression of the key). This pressure may control the overall amplitude and the harmonic content of the sound in parallel so that an increase in amplitude is coupled to an increase in the harmonic content of the sound (e.g. by regulating a filter to let through more high frequency components, thus making the sound more brilliant). In a many-to-many timbral control scheme, the point is to have alternative controls for several dimensions, by, for example, using the aftertouch to control both the filter and the overall amplitude, and using another controller, e.g. the so-called "modulation wheel" to likewise control both the filter and the overall amplitude. Finally, in a many-to-one timbral control scheme, the point is to let a number of different gestures control the same timbral dimension. For example the overall quantity of motion of many different gestures (captured by an accelerometer or a video camera) could regulate the overall high-frequency content of the sound.

Mappings may require much tinkering or adjustment to feel intuitive for a musician. They can also involve variable degrees of intelligent and/or context-sensitive modifications of control inputs which may enable the automation of more sophisticated mappings (Verfaille et al. 2006), and we shall probably see some significant advances in this field in the years to come. In tandem with this, we can expect some significant developments with respect to haptic feedback, based on the recognition of the multimodal (i.e. not only sound-based) nature of instrumental performance.

6 Conclusion

There can be no doubt that skilled musicians have a rich and nuanced repertoire of timbral expression, acquired through years and years of practice. The challenge for future research is to explore further the complex interactions between musicians' gestures and musical timbre and, with the use of increasingly sophisticated technology, to apply this knowledge to the development of better interfaces for electronic instruments.

References

Askenfelt, A. (1986). Measurements of the bowing parameters in violin playing. II: Bow–bridge distance, dynamic range, and limits of bow force. *Journal of the Acoustical Society of America*, 86, 503–516.

Bader, R. (2006). Finite-element calculation of a bass drum. *Journal of the Acoustical Society of America* 119(5), 3290–3290.

Borg, I. (1983). Entwicklung von akustischen Optimierungsverfahren für Stabspiele und Membraninstrumente. (Development of acoustical optimization methods for musical bars and membrane instruments.) PTB Report, Projekt 5267, Braunschweig 1983.

Browman, C. P. and Goldstein, L. (1989). Articulatory gestures as phonological units. *Phonology*, 6, 201–251.

Cadoz, C. and Wanderley, M. M. (2000). Gesture-Music. In M.M. Wanderley and M. Battier (eds.), *Trends in Gestural Control of Music[CD ROM]*. Paris: IRCAM, 71–93.

Fletcher, N. H, and Rossing, T. D. (1998). *The Physics of Musical Instruments*. Berlin, Heidelberg: Springer.

Freed, D. J. (1990). Auditory correlates of perceived mallet hardness for a set of recorded percussive sound events. *Journal of the Acoustical Society of America*, 87(1), 311–322.

Godøy, R. I. (2006). Gestural-sonorous objects: embodied extensions of Schaeffer's conceptual apparatus. *Organised Sound*, 11(2), 149–157.

Guettler, K. (2002). On the creation of the Helmholtz motion in the bowed string. *Acta Acustica united with Acustica*, 88, 970–985.

Guettler, K. (2003). A closer look at the string player's bowing gestures. *Journal of the Catgut Acoustical Society*, 4–7(II), 12–16.

Guettler, K. and Askenfelt, A. (1998). On the kinematics of spiccato and ricochet bowing. *Journal of the Catgut Acoustical Society*, 3–6 (II), 1–7.

Halmrast, T. (2000). Orchestral timbre, comb filter–coloration from reflections. *Journal of Sound and Vibration*, 352(1), 53–69.

Helmholtz, H. v. (1862). *On the Sensations of Tone*. New York: Dover (English translation 1954: Originally published as *Lehre von den Tonempfindungen* Braunschweig: Vieweg).

Hunt, A., Wanderley, M., and Paradis, M. (2003). The importance of parameter mapping in electronic instrument design. *Journal of New Music Research*, 32(4), 429–440.

Kendall, R. A. and Carterette, E. C. (1993). Identification and blend of timbres as a basis for orchestration. *Contemporary Music Review* 9 (Parts 1 and 2), 51–67.

Leman, M. (2008). *Embodied Music Cognition and Mediation Technology*. Cambridge, MA: MIT Press.

McAdams, S., Chaignec, A., and Roussaried, V. (2004). The psychomechanics of simulated sound sources: material properties of impacted bars. *Journal of the Acoustical Society of America*, 115 (3), 1306–1320.

Miranda, E. R. and Wanderley, M. M. (2006). *New Digital Musical Instruments: Control and Interaction Beyond the Keyboard*. Middleton, WI: A-R Editions, Inc.

Porcello, T. (2004). Speaking of sound: language and the professionalization of sound-recording engineers. *Social Studies of Science*, 34(5), 733–758.

Raman, C. V. (1920). On the mechanical theory of the vibrations of bowed strings and of musical instruments of the violin family, with experimental verifications of the results: Part II—Experiments with mechanically played violins. In *Proceedings of the Indian Association for the Cultivation of Science* (1920–1921), 19–36.

Risset, J.-C. (1991). Timbre analysis by synthesis: representations, imitations and variants for musical composition. In G. De Poli, A. Piccialli, and C. Roads (eds.), *Representations of Musical Signals*. Cambridge, MA: MIT Press, 7–43.

Rocchesso, D. and Fontana, F. (eds.) (2003). *The Sounding Object*. Firenze: Edizioni di Mondo Estremo.

Schaeffer, P. (1966). *Traité des Objets Musicaux*. Paris: Éditions du Seuil.

Schelleng, J. C. (1973). The bowed string and the player. *Journal of the Acoustical Society of America*, 53(1), 26–41.

Schoonderwaldt, E., Guettler, K., and A. Askenfelt, A. (2003). Effect of the bow hair width on the violin spectrum. In *Proceedings of the Stockholm Musical Acoustics Conference*. Stockholm, Sweden, 91–94.

Slawson, W., (1985). *Tone Colour*. Berkeley, Los Angeles, London: University of California Press.

Verfaille, V., Wanderley, M. M., and Depalle, P. (2006). Mapping strategies for gestural and adaptive control of digital audio effects. *Journal of New Music Research* 35(1), 71–93.

Zatorre, R. J., Chen, J. L., and Penhune, V. B. (2007). When the brain plays music: auditory–motor interactions in music perception and production. *Nature Reviews Neuroscience* 8, 547–558.

Chapter 9

Sensorimotor Control of Sound-producing Gestures

Sylvie Gibet

1 Introduction

In this chapter, we focus on sensorimotor models of sound-producing gestures. These models are studied from two different viewpoints: namely *theories of motor control* and *computational synthesis of avatars* that produce human gestures. The theories of motor control aim to understand gesture on the basis of its underlying biomechanics, whereas the computational synthesis aims to understand entire gestures on the basis of sensorimotor control models. The emphasis of this chapter is on hand–arm gestures, from simple control tasks such as pointing and reaching, to skilled tasks requiring complex coordination mechanisms such as in playing the piano.

The main interest in studying musical gesture from the viewpoint of biomechanics and sensorimotor control models is that it provides a dynamic understanding of the mechanisms responsible for sound-producing gestures, which can then be applied in different contexts such as computer animation, video games, interactive systems with embedded virtual agents, or humanoid robots. Furthermore, the dynamical approach may give an insight into the various parameters that are responsible for imbuing specific performances with the desired expressivity.

The chapter is organized as follows. In the first part, we present a general architecture for motor control. In the second part, we give an overview of the main theories of motor control and the ways in which they can be used for human–computer interaction and for musical gestures. In the third part, we present the main biomechanical concepts that are necessary for modeling human motion and controlling the motion of avatars. In the fourth part, we describe how sound-producing gestures of avatars can be simulated using sensorimotor control models.

2 General Architecture for Motor Control

2.1 Low Level Motor Control of Gesture

In playing a musical instrument, the musician establishes a more or less continuous interaction with the instrument. This interaction is based on action/reaction cycles, allowing the fine-tuning of the sound-producing gestures via feedback loops (see Chapter 8 in this volume).

The hypothesis that supports this causal approach relies on a theory of perception that states that the objects of our perception are linked to the gestural patterns that produce them. According to this hypothesis, organized sound, or music, contains gestural forms that are linked to its production. This approach entails that the manipulation of these forms might somehow preserve the expressive features of musical sound. Consequently, their manipulation can be based on control commands that may be simple and preferably close to the control commands of human intentions.

The playing of a musical instrument can thus be conceived as the coupling of two physical systems: namely, the sound-producing gesture and the musical instrument. The sound-producing gesture is then represented by a set of mechanical models that interact with the simulated instrument and produce sound (Gibet 1987; Gibet and Florens 1988), while the control of the gesture is represented by a sensorimotor control model (Gibet and Marteau 1991; 1994). The entire model can be simulated using a slowly evolving model through which both the structural characteristics of the gesture and its varying parameters can be manipulated. Handling gesture and instrument as similar physical models allows one to keep a coherent description of the physical link between both systems. This approach also enables the manipulation of higher-order actions that are closer to the production mechanisms of movement (Gibet 2002).

2.2 Higher Level Motor Control of Gesture

The issue of the control of movement raises the crucial problem of the complexity of human gestures, which includes the simultaneous control of numerous muscles, tendons, and articulations. One fundamental question is how the human central nervous system handles the connection from neural commands through muscle activation to movement kinematics (Bernstein 1967). In other words, what muscle parameters does the central nervous system control? Several candidate variables can be proposed such as force or torque, length, velocity, stiffness, viscosity, etc. The movement of a limb can be defined in terms of the contraction of individual muscles, but complex motor behaviors cannot be understood as a simple extrapolation of the properties of their elementary components. In that perspective, three main concepts underlying the production of gesture must be considered: namely, *motor equivalence*, *flexibility* and *prediction*.

One of the most convincing arguments that supports the idea of distributed control and non-specific muscle commands is related to motor equivalence, meaning that a movement pattern can be attained through the use of several different muscle combinations. For example, pianists can play a melodic fragment on the piano by either using large amplitude gestures (thus using all their arm joints and muscles), or they can play the same melodic fragment by reducing their gesture to the minimum amplitude. Similar observations have been made regarding speech, where it has been shown that intelligible speech can be produced when the proper vocal tract configurations are obstructed, requiring the use of different vocal tract configurations to achieve the desired phonation. Motor equivalence thus suggests that the mapping between the central nervous system command and the muscles command consists of several levels of control, with control variables distributed among a number of control structures, therefore allowing plasticity and flexibility in the organization of muscle synergies.

Flexibility refers to the capability of using the same planning strategies in the organization of muscle synergies (muscular groups having the same function), even if these synergies may differ. For example, if we consider an arm represented by a kinematic chain, composed of an assembly of segments and joints, the kinematic structure of this arm can be changed by adding a new segment to its extremity. This is the case when a drummer uses a stick during playing. With flexibility, the same goals can be achieved, using a stick or not, without having to learn the movement sequence twice. This property of the central nervous system also relates to the plasticity of the human brain, including the possibility of reconfiguring the brain areas in order to achieve various goals. This property of flexibility has been demonstrated for pointing hand-arm movements with a stick (Gibet, Lebourque, and Marteau 2001).

Beyond the cooperation capabilities of the motor control system, there is a necessity of prediction. Indeed, the brain has only a few milliseconds to react to a given situation and to select the appropriate sensors to achieve a movement. In considering skilled actions such as piano playing, it becomes difficult to ignore the role of anticipation in movement production and perception. As a matter of fact, the pianist playing from a score has to anticipate, so that he can perform the musical phrase while adjusting his hand-finger shapes in real time; otherwise he would be behind the tempo, or lose movement smoothness. Prediction capabilities are possible if internal representations or internal models of pre-learned gesture sequences are coded in the brain.

Flexibility and adaptability to new environmental changes require an organization that facilitates the distribution of activation signals over different muscle synergies and complex coordination and synchronization at different levels of control. Moreover, the need for reactivity suggests that motor control is based on automatisms acquired from former experience.

2.3 A Multi-Level Architecture for Motor Control of Musical Gestures

Given the above observations on low-level and high-level motor control, it is now clear that the motor control mechanisms which underlay musical gestures should be modeled by a multi-layered motor system, with each layer having its own operating mode and role in the overall system (Gibet 2002). Figure 9.1 gives an overview of a multi-level architecture for motor control. The hierarchical and adaptive nature of this system is inspired by the models proposed in the field of neuroscience (Paillard 1980).

The sensorimotor level is the lowest level. This accounts for forward continuous signals that enable the generation of movements in terms of

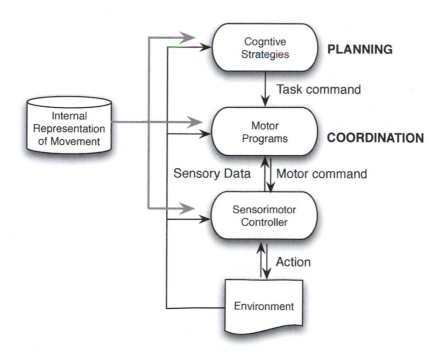

Figure 9.1 Multi-layer motor control system.

the control of particular muscles. At any moment in time, these forward continuous signals are linked with signals that come from sensory modules (auditory, visual, proprioceptive) so that the entire sensorimotor level is in fact based on a continuous action–reaction loop. The coordination level is the middle level. This accounts for more complex movements that involve sequences of movements and synchronization of actions. The planning level is the highest level. This accounts for the selection of strategies for motion control, typically using cognitive representations.

The layered approach draws upon action–reaction loops and upon the adaptation of the system both to the environment and to the task at all levels of control. In this approach, action is tightly linked with perception (see Chapter 5 in this volume). The control model implementation results in the cooperation of a forward and a feedback control mode. The forward control mode operates in *open loop* (not using sensory feedback during movement execution), while the feedback one operates in *closed loop* (using sensory feedback during movement execution). Each level must react to information coming from the environment, with varying reaction times according to the nature of information. Through this reactive and layered structure, motion control is a coherent system.

The sensory information is utilized by different fast control loops that focus on auditory, visual and proprioceptive aspects. Slower control loops focus on more complex perceptive information and memory of movements. These require information processing over longer time frames. Both the fast and slow control loops provide an effective way for sharing the task of data processing between the various layers of the system. In this setup, the response time of the entire system cannot exceed the response time of the slowest subsystem.

Moreover, each level of control exploits information that results from the nature of the task to be carried out and possibly from an internal representation of the movement acquired from former experiences. Such internal representations are indeed an effective way to limit the need for feedback loops, lessening the processing demands on the higher processing levels. Thus, during the acquisition of motor abilities, slow control in closed loop makes the learning of movement competence possible at first. Then, the competence having been acquired, the control exploits predictive sequences to correct, adapt, and improve the performances of the movement during execution. This slackening of the low level constraints consists in opening the control loops from the low level to the higher levels. It can be illustrated by considering the training schema for practicing a music instrument. The movements to be learned are initially carried out slowly, with continuous and multi-sensory guidance (in particular visual). Once the basic control schemes are acquired, continuous visual guidance is no longer required. Instead, visual clues at specific key-points for movement execution or proprioceptive clues for longer-term motion control are now sufficient. The learned patterns at lower levels thus liberate the processing load of the higher levels.

Action coordination, which is a central feature of musical gestures, refers to the capacity of the motor system to schedule actions in space and time, given a desired goal. This coordination can be carried out for a particular group of bones and muscle synergies, such as a hand–arm system that plays a musical instrument. In this case, the coordination rules follow specific laws that take into account biomechanical constraints, and that can be described and modeled by the dynamic equations that apply to a mechanical system. However, cognitive strategies can be used to check and direct the decision when several solutions are possible, and also when there is a perceptual ambiguity. For example, these cognitive strategies can play a role in the goal-directed guidance of certain complex movements according to internal representations of motion (mental images) and environmental representations during performance. At this control level, the mechanisms of prediction and the contribution of visual or motor mental imagery can be studied (Decety, Jeannerod, and Prablanc 1989). The multi-layer architecture presented above has been used as the background for modeling motion control in juggling gestures (Julliard and Gibet 1999).

3 Understanding Motor Control

The multi-layer architecture presented above provides a general outline for motion control of skilled gestures, where different sensory data are used to determine the next action to perform in a global action-perception loop. The sensorimotor level can be further refined using approaches that express motor control in terms of dynamics, kinematics, and sensorimotor feedback. Dynamics is the branch of classical mechanics concerned with the motion of bodies. Within dynamics, we may distinguish *kinematics* from *kinetics*. Kinematics deals with the space-time relationship of a given motion without considering the forces or torques that are the causes of the motion. Therefore, it only deals with the geometric aspect of motion. Kinetics is concerned with the motion of bodies under the action of given forces or torques. Sensorimotor feedback deals with the way in which sensing affects motor control. In what follows, we discuss different approaches for understanding motor control: namely, the *motor program* approach, the *biomechanical* approach, and the *non-linear dynamics* approach. These approaches are then analyzed in terms of *invariant laws* that characterize human movement. Finally, we present the concept of *internal model*, which explains the predictive capability in the control of gestures.

3.1 The Motor Program Approach

In the motor program approach, it is assumed that motor control is based on representations of movement, representations which are stored in memory in the form of plans or programs for movement execution (Keele 1968). Motor programs can be conceived as a set of muscle commands that are already structured before a movement sequence begins, and that allow the entire sequence to be carried out, even without the influence of any peripheral feedback. In short, motor programs are assumed to reflect pre-structured sets of motor commands at the highest cortical level, and they are used for the lowest level control of movement execution.

The motor program approach supports the hypothesis that there is no sensory feedback during the execution of that movement. Goal-based gestures such as moving the finger on a string are partly based on pre-programmed activity in that the corresponding motion is executed without visual or proprioceptive feedback.

In order to take into account a larger variety of movements, the concept of motor program has been extended to the concept of *generalized motor programs* (Schmidt et al. 1975; Schmidt 1975). These generalized motor programs are assumed to consist of stored patterns for movement controlled by generic rules that are associated with specific movement categories. These generic rules are based on former learning processes that account for efferent commands (the flow of information from the central nervous system to the periphery), sensory feedback, and environmental contexts.

Generalized motor programs can be modified or adapted during execution in response to changing environmental conditions, thanks to parameters that specify the particular context of execution. Invariant laws (see below) may describe the general kinematic properties that underlay generalized motor programs.

One important question for the motor program approach that has received a great deal of attention, is whether the motor control continuously operates in open loop or in closed loop (see above). Feedback control means that motor control uses perceptual information adaptively and continuously during performance to adjust and correct the movement. For example, when executing a glissando on a string, the finger may first make a movement that is pre-programmed, however, when touching the string, feedback information may be taken into account (see Chapter 6 in this volume). Typically, sensory feedback may reduce instabilities of the gesture and guarantee more accuracy in the execution of the gesture (see also Chapter 8 in this volume).

However, this feedback is time constrained and, depending on the amount of time available for corrections in operations, it is likely that gestures may be controlled by visual, proprioceptive, or additional tactile and kinesthetic feedback. In the case of grasping movements, for example, the central nervous system would typically need 300 ms between the observation of an error in the movement and its correction. When a hand moves at about 50 cm per second, a distance of 15 cm will be traveled before the trajectory can be modified. Therefore, it can be deduced that the continuous visual guidance of fast movements is often not possible. In general, movements of which the duration does not exceed 200 ms cannot be visually guided and therefore, they must be under the control of a centralized program. However, under certain conditions, very fast corrections of movement can be based on proprioceptive feedback, where reaction times are estimated to be in the order of 120–130 ms. Additionally, tactile sensing, which gives information about the nature of the skin contact, may be processed even more rapidly (reaction times in the order of less than 100 ms). This is also the case for processing tensions developed within the muscles. This latter type of information makes it possible for movements to be corrected during the execution of the musical gestures that control sound production.

The above observations imply that rapid gestures require an open loop type of control. The global gesture will be established in advance, and executed without using the sensory feedback. This is the case in piano playing, where the finger movements are extremely rapid, leaving no time for visual or other sensory feedback. However, actions that require precision, like the execution of a specific attack on the piano in slow passages, may need a closed loop type of control. The gestures are then based on the sensing of force feedback.

3.2 The Biomechanical Approach

The biomechanical approach focusses on the idea that limb dynamics and biomechanical properties themselves may significantly contribute to motion control. The approach entails that the control processes responsible for the formation of movement trajectories are not explicitly programmed, but are emerging properties of the dynamics of the system itself. Often, this biomechanical approach is combined with the motor program approach. For example, according to the so-called *equilibrium point hypothesis* (Feldman 1966), movements arise from shifts in the equilibrium position of the muscles. A motor program would then specify a succession of discrete targets (equilibrium points), while between two targets, motion would be generated according to the inherent dynamics of the mechanical system.

Several equilibrium point models have been proposed. Balance can result in the mutual canceling out of the forces of stretching and relaxation being exerted on the pairs of agonist–antagonist muscles. Alternatively, to account for the properties inherent in the muscular-skeleton system, mechanical models composed of a set of masses and springs have been elaborated. The successful achievement of a final equilibrium position, regardless of starting position and of any rapid disturbances carried out during the execution of movements, has justified this point of view. Equilibrium point models have been applied to discrete multi-point tasks, and to movement trajectories between two points (Bizzi et al. 1992), while numerous other studies have been carried out on cyclic or rhythmic movements, such as movements for locomotion (Brown 1914; Stein 1995).

3.3 The Non-Linear Dynamics Approach

In addition to the above approaches that focus on motor programs and biomechanical constraints, other theories have been developed around the concept of dynamic systems (Kelso and Schöner 1988; Kugler and Turvey 1986; Kay et al. 1991; Haken and Wunderlin 1990; Kelso et al. 1992). The non-linear dynamics approach is based on the idea that movements may result from the dynamic interaction between elements of a neuromuscular system involved in movement execution. This can be modeled by a set of oscillators that are coupled with each other. The approach is typically applied to the modeling of rhythmic or oscillatory movements, but it can also cover learned movements, such as drawing movements, or automated movements.

Rhythmic movements indeed often display some characteristics of self-organized systems. They can be considered as generated by a system whose energy quickly decreases, because of the existence of dissipative forces (friction forces in particular). However, their movements can be maintained by adding energy from neuromuscular interactions. This flow of energy is accompanied by a work amount that ensures the dynamic stability of the system. In that configuration, the dissipative forces are compensated by the sustaining ones. Such a system presents stable states, which operate like attractors of the behavior. This can be modeled by non-linear oscillators with stable limiting cycles (Kay et al. 1991). The oscillators represent the use of the muscles in a behavioral situation. Non-linear dynamic models of musical gestures have been successfully applied to force-feedback manipulated movements (Gibet 1987; Gibet and Florens 1988).

3.4 Invariant Laws in Movement

Apart from the above approaches that put motor control at work in terms of kinematics, dynamics, and sensorimotor feedback, it is also of interest to look at the invariant features of motor performance. Here, the hypothesis is that these invariants are the result of some general laws that underlie the organization of motor control. These laws can be described in terms of a relationship between several kinematic variables, whose values are based on measurements of the movement. The invariants are valid for a large variety of gestures, including goal-directed gestures such as simple or multiple pointing gestures, and also repetitive cyclic gestures in two or three dimensions. As musical gestures can be broken down into more elementary movements, the invariant laws may be verified on these elementary movement chunks.

Without trying to give an exhaustive view of these laws (Gibet, Kamp and Poirer 2004), we review some of the more typical invariants of movement trajectories. They include the invariance of the velocity profile, Fitts's law, the two-thirds power law, and some other laws, related to minimum jerk and minimum variance.

Invariance in Velocity Profiles

Multi-point movements produce *velocity profiles* whose global shape is approximately bell-shaped. This shape displays an asymmetry depending on the speed of the movement. As the speed increases the curve becomes more symmetrical until the direction of the asymmetry is reversed (Zelaznik et al. 1986; Bullock and Grossberg 1988). This velocity profile is illustrated in Figure 9.2 for pointing gestures of different speeds and distances to the target.

The Isochrony Principle and Fitts's Law

The *isochrony principle* (Freeman 1914) expresses the invariance of the execution duration of a movement in relation to its amplitude. There seems to be a spontaneous tendency to increase the velocity of the motion according to the distance to be traveled, when no constraint on the mean velocity is imposed. Following this idea, Fitts defines a relationship between the time duration, the distance to the target, and the accuracy of the target, for rapid movements between two points in a plane (Woodworth 1899; Fitts 1954). Several studies use this law to analyze the

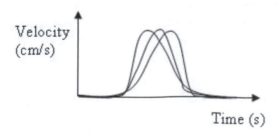

Figure 9.2 Velocity profiles varying with speed conditions.

processes related to motor performances, while others use it to evaluate the credibility and the adaptability of machine interaction devices, where the law allows the comparison of various devices independently of the experimental conditions (Radix et al. 1999). The law can also be extended to other classes of motion, such as multi-scaled pointing gestures (Guiard et al. 1999), communicative gestures (Lebourque and Gibet 2000), or accurate ballistic gestures (Gibet, Kamp and Poirer 2004).

The Two-Thirds Power Law

For handwriting and drawing movements there is a relationship between the kinematics of elliptical motion and the geometrical properties of the trajectory, which is known as the *two-thirds power law* (Viviani and Terzuolo 1980; 1982; Viviani and Flash 1995). This law establishes a relationship between the tangential velocity and the curvature of the movement (using a two-thirds power factor). It has been suggested as a fundamental principle that the movement trajectory of the effector end-point (such as the finger of a hand) be constrained, in particular when performing rhythmic movements. Using the two-thirds power law, complex movements can thus be broken down into elementary motor action units. The law is obeyed for planar drawing patterns consisting of ellipses, three-dimensional movements of the hand-arm system (Lebourque and Gibet 2000), and cyclic patterns produced by the stick during drumming gestures (Gibet and Bouënard 2006).

Other Invariant Laws

Other invariant features of movement can be modeled with the *minimum jerk* model. For point-to-point movements, this model ensures that among all possible solutions for generating a trajectory, the motor control system chooses the one that maximizes the smoothness of the movement. This solution can be obtained from the minimization of a global cost function that is expressed in terms of the derivative of the acceleration (Wann and Nimmo-Smith 1991). Obviously, the model for minimum jerk assumes that the movement can be determined by a parametric equation, describing the state of the system at every moment. Basically, the model avoids overly large variations in movement acceleration (Hogan 1984; 1985; Flash 1987). Applied to dynamic systems, the minimum jerk model can be modified so that a minimum torque is reached for point-to-point movement trajectories. The minimum torque-change can be viewed as a measurement of energy and smoothness (Uno et al. 1989).

More recently, the *minimum variance* theory of motor planning has been proposed for both eye and arm movements (Harris and Wolpert

1998; Wolpert et al. 2001). In this theory, it is assumed that noise is part of the neural signals, thus causing trajectories to deviate from the desired path. These deviations accumulate over the duration of a movement, leading to variability in the end-point position (Körding and Wolpert 2006). According to this theory, variability of signals in human sensori-motor systems can be assumed to be the expression of noise variability, but that smooth movements reduce this variability.

Internal Models

Apart from the invariance in movements, there is another important concept that should be taken into account in motor control modeling: namely, the concept of internal model. This is defined as an internally coded model that simulates the actual behavior of the motor system (Kawato et al. 1990; Jordan et al. 1994). These internal models can be used to predict the output sensory signals (Miallet and Wolpert 1996) in order to adapt movements to new environmental conditions or for planning purposes.

In modeling musical gestures, one of the main problems concerns the determination of the proper movement trajectories on the basis of a given set of constraints. For instance, if we consider the movement of the fingers of a pianist playing melodic phrases, then different successions of fingers are possible but these successions are determined by the kinematic morphology (dynamics and shape) of the hand and the fingers, the musical context in which they are executed (past and future notes), the expressive qualities of the instrumental gesture, and last but not least, the dynamic characteristics such as pressure and inertia. In that context, the invariant laws may provide useful clues for explaining the organization of the movements.

4 Synthesis of Gesture in Avatars

After having introduced a general architecture for motor control, and surveyed the different approaches to modeling motor control, we now turn to a discussion of the ways in which an entire gesture can be handled. We thereby focus on the synthesis of realistic gestures in avatars. The synthesis of realistic human-like gestures is indeed one of the greatest challenges in computer graphics, because of the high sensitivity of human visual perception to natural posture and biological motion. However, controlling the motion of avatars necessitates dealing with the complexity of the human body, which is composed of 206 bones, more than 200 joints, as well as soft tissues. To achieve a realistic synthesis, a layered approach to the representation of human characters is generally adopted, in which skeletons support one or more layers, typically muscle, fatty tissue, skin, and clothing layers. In what follows, we distinguish between the modeling of avatars, including anatomy, biomechanics and musculo-skeletar models, and the modeling of motion control to make them move.

4.1 Modeling the Avatar

Modeling Anatomy

By modeling anatomy, we mainly mean the skeleton muscles, that is, the so-called voluntary muscles (unlike smooth muscles or cardiac muscles which are involuntary muscles). There are approximately 650 skeletal muscles in the human body, and they are all controlled through the nervous system. Skeletal muscles are typically composed of a contractile part and two extremities, called tendons, which are the insertions of the muscle on the bone. Anatomists also consider two types of contractions, which they call isometric contraction and isotonic contraction. With the isometric contraction (same length), the muscle contracts and its form changes but not its length. Therefore, there is no motion involved. With the isotonic contraction (same tonicity), the form and the length of the muscle change simultaneously, and that induces a motion of the bones. Generally both contractions are involved in human movement, but in computer animation only the isotonic one is considered.

Biomechanics

Skeletal muscles are anchored to bones by means of tendons. By applying forces to bones and joints, skeleton movement is effected. The strength of the skeletal muscle is directly proportional to its length and cross-sectional area. The strength of a joint, however, is determined by a number of biomechanical principles, including the distance between muscles, the pivot points, and the muscles' size.

Muscles are normally arranged in opposition to each other, so that as one group of muscles contracts, another group relaxes or lengthens. Antagonism in the transmission of nerve impulses to the muscles means that it is impossible to stimulate the contraction of two antagonistic muscles at the same time. During ballistic motions, such as throwing a ball, the antagonist muscles act to slow down the agonist muscles throughout the contraction, particularly at the end of the movement. In the example of throwing a ball, the chest and front of the shoulder contract to pull the arm forward, while the muscles in the back and rear of the shoulder also contract to slow down the motion in order to avoid injury. Part of a training process in throwing a ball would consist in learning to relax the antagonist muscles in order to increase the force output of the chest and anterior shoulder.

At present there does not exist a precise model of muscles that takes into account the attachment of muscles to articulations, although approximate models can be found in the literature. In these latter models, muscle/tendon systems are represented by a mechanical model that is typically composed of three elements, namely one spring for the tendon, in tandem with two parallel springs representing the muscle (Hill 1938; Winters and Stark 1987) (Figure 9.3). Each muscle is thus composed of an active part consisting of an elastic element in tandem with a contractile element, and a parallel passive part containing an elastic element (see also Zajac and Winters 1990).

Skeletons are usually represented by hierarchical structures (trees or graphs) composed of a set of rigid segments linked by mechanical joints. The relative position and orientation of these joints determine the position of the different segments. Within this tree structure, articulated chains characterizing the upper limbs, the legs, or the spinal column may be identified. For any one specific articulated chain, it is possible to calculate the location of the end-point of the chain by iteratively computing the changing coordinates from one joint to another.

Modeling the Musculo-Skeletar System

In the human body, each group of muscle cells is associated with motor neurons and, collectively, these neurons and muscle cells are called motor units. If more strength is needed in order to carry out a certain task, then motor neurons recruit more motor units, and they increase the frequency at which neurons fire (and thus are activated). When modeling a biological muscular skeleton system, it is necessary to take into account this neuronal activity as well as the biomechanical constraints of the human body. However, this is extremely difficult, and therefore, more simple

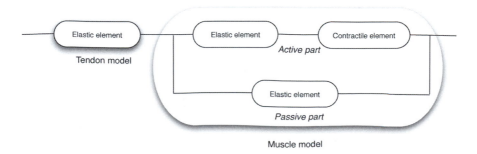

Figure 9.3 Tendon-muscle scheme adapted after Hill (1938).

models of movement control are generally proposed. One possibility is to model functional blocks that express the different stages of transformation from the neuronal signals to the motor commands of the musculo-skeletar apparatus.

Figure 9.4 shows a schema for such a biomechanical human model. The biological motor system produces neural signals of muscular activation, which are transformed into motor commands applied to a set of agonist–antagonist muscles attached to the skeleton. These commands are distributed into equivalent efforts (torques, forces) applied to the joints, according to the dynamics model of the limb skeleton. The dynamics model computes the next state values according to the current state values of the system. The skeletar kinematics block diagram transforms the state signal into the sensory information, which can be represented by the perceived position of the limb.

Motion Control and Inverse Problems

When animating avatars, it is necessary to design specific controllers for the skeletar kinematics (taking into account cinematic trajectories) or for the skeletar dynamics (taking into account effort). As both of these skeletar systems are redundant ones, dynamics and kinematics transformations can be represented by many-to-one mappings. In other words, multiple inputs can produce the same output. Therefore, control may be based on so-called *inverse transformation*.

Two inverse problems are generally considered: namely the *inverse kinematics* problem and the *inverse dynamics* problem.

The inverse kinematics problem (IK) consists in determining the joint angles (state) of a multiple-joint arm given the desired end-arm position (sensory information). Because of the redundancy of the arm, even when the time course of the hand position is specified, the joint angles cannot uniquely be determined. For example, an arm with seven degrees of freedom engaged in moving a finger along a desired path in a three dimensional space can achieve this task using different sequences of arm postures (Figure 9.6a).

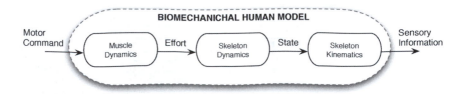

Figure 9.4 Scheme of a biomechanical human model.

The inverse dynamics problem can consist in determining agonist and antagonist muscle tensions when the state of the system (joint angles) is given (Figure 9.5, ID1). Even when the time course of the joint angles is specified, there are indeed an infinite number of tension waveforms of the muscles that make the arm move (Figure 9.6b). Another formulation of the inverse dynamics problem is to find the equivalent effort that is applied to the joints of the skeletar dynamics, given a specific state of this system (Figure 9.5, ID2).

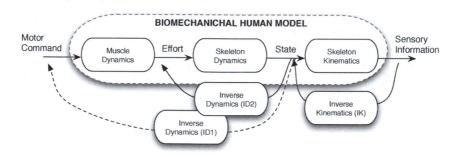

Figure 9.5 Inversion of a biomechanical human model.

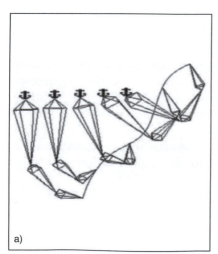

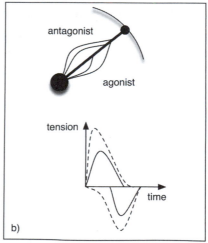

Figure 9.6 Representations of inverse problems in biomechanics. (a) Inverse kinematics as the calculation of angular joint coordinates from the arm endpoint positions. The figure shows the endpoint positions of a skeleton arm on a continuous curve. The angles refer to wrist, elbow, and shoulder of this skeleton arm. (b) Inverse dynamics as the calculation of tension on a pair of agonist and antagonist muscles. The upper figure represents the muscles on opposite sides of a limb, the lower figure shows the tension of these opposite muscles as a function of time.

5 Synthesis of Sound-Producing Gestures

In this section, we present models for the synthesis of sound-producing gestures. The credibility of the produced movements is a crucial element in making avatars that move or perform in a realistic, life-like manner. Furthermore, taking into account all the available sensory data that accompany the movement can help improve real-world motion performance. This is the case, for example, in music performance, where sensorimotor modeling provides a better understanding of how neuromuscular fatigue may be reduced and strain injuries avoided. Understanding sensorimotor control may also facilitate performance training for musicians, by allowing them to adapt their technique to their specific biomechanical capacities. Given the close link between perception and action, virtual reality simulation can promote a better understanding of the perception phenomena that are at work in visual and musical arts. Finally, understanding the essence of movement is important for characterizing the nature of expressive gestures, such as dance gestures or the physical gestures of producing music.

The two main approaches for the synthesis of sound-producing gestures, and realistic gestures in general, are *data-driven animations* and *model-driven animations*.

5.1 Data-Driven Synthesis of Gesture

Motion capture systems provide recordings of various gestures of real performers and allow for the subsequent development of data-driven synthesis of gestures. The gestures are most of the time represented by the position and orientation of markers located on the performer. Based on that information, the skeleton can be reconstructed at each sampling time.

The general framework for animating avatars that use motion capture data is shown in Figure 9.7. The controller can be reduced to simple

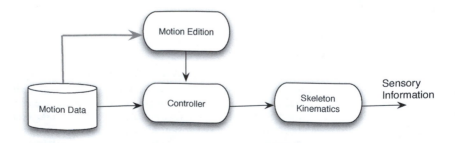

Figure 9.7 Schema of a data-driven approach to the synthesis of gestures.

forward mechanisms, such as reading motion captured data, or inter-polation techniques between key-postures. In this case, the control necessitates no inversion, since all the data postures are available in the motion database. However, the controller may also be linked to a motion editing module whose role is to transform the time series data, using signal processing or statistics techniques.

The main advantage of the data-based approach is that it makes possible the generation of highly realistic gestures, with relatively low computational costs. However, the main drawback is a lack of flexibility. Indeed, it remains difficult to modify the recorded motions while keeping the realism of the gesture. Taking into account the great variety of human gesture, it is illusory to think it possible to generate human movements for a very large set of gestures that would work in varying contexts and with various expressive styles. Furthermore, the adaptation of existing motions to avatars with different morphologies is not trivial.

Two main factors can be identified as features that further determine the biological plausibility of synthesized human gesture: namely, the occupation of the surrounding space, and the fluidity of motion. Some studies aim to improve the naturalness of the reconstructed motion and compare different rendering techniques. Other studies aim to reduce the number of sensors/markers to a minimum and to recover the performer motion by applying pertinent constraints to the avatar posture (Peinado et al. 2004), and by using inverse kinematics methods (see above) (Boulic et al. 2006). In the domain of music-related gestures, several studies use motion capture but most of these studies have focused on analysis rather than synthesis (Wanderley 2002; Dahl 2000; 2005; Camurri et al. 2004; see also Chapters 3, 6, and 10 in this volume).

5.2 Model-Driven Synthesis of Gesture

Within the model-based methods for controlling an avatar, we focus in this section on the sensorimotor approach that was first presented in (Gibet and Marteau 1994; Gibet, Marteau, and Julliard 2002), and exploited for computer animation purpose in (Lebourque and Gibet 1999; 2000; Gibet and Marteau 2003). This approach assumes that there exists a relationship between the sensory information and the motor command, taking into account the task to be performed (Figure 9.8). The sensory information, observed from specific sensors, includes visual information (visual perception of the gesture and the environment), proprioceptive information (state of the biomechanical system), and auditory information. The motor command determines the state of the system at each time, and is calculated from either an inverse kinematics or an inverse dynamics process, or both of them, depending on the nature of the avatar model (kinematics or dynamics). In this model, the task is

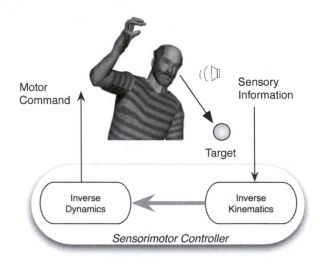

Figure 9.8 Schema of a sensorimotor approach to the synthesis of gesture.

represented in a space which is homogeneous to the observation space and which includes sensory information (for example a target or a sequence of targets in the visual space).

For animators, the inverse problems are of great importance because it is indeed far simpler to express gesture in terms of spatial end-point trajectories than in terms of joint angles or torques. However, the avatar is made up of multi-articulated components; therefore there are an infinite number of solutions to these inverse problems (see above). Moreover, these avatars contain both passive and active elements: the passive elements can be characterized by mechanical parameters such as inertia, stiffness and viscosity, while the active elements are responsible for the activation of the muscles. For such systems, there is no general method to design a controller that can handle the various parameters of the system. A possible approach is therefore based on the definition of inverse processes with specific constraints, which identify the best solutions from the range of potential solutions. By way of illustration, we briefly present below some studies that have brought interesting insights on the problem.

In particular, inverse kinematics has been solved by introducing specific constraints, such as kinematic or kinetic constraints (Boulic et al. 1996), or by establishing priorities between constraints (Boulic et al. 2006). Other approaches assume that sensorimotor properties are fulfilled. Thus Soechting (1989) presents empirical studies, which can be used for controlling a human arm. His model (Soechting and Flanders 1989a; 1989b) has been reused by (Koga and Latombe 1994) for motion planning. A sensorimotor inverse kinematics model for arm trajectory formation, using invariant laws in motion, has also been proposed by (Gibet and Marteau 1990; 1994). This approach is based on a gradient descent method associated with relevant biological functions directly integrated into the sensory motor loop (Bullock and Grossberg 1988). Inverse kinematics may also be solved by learning human postures (Grochow et al. 2004), or local mappings between the state variables and the sensory information (Gibet, Lebourque, and Marteau 2001; Gibet and Marteau 2003).

An architecture for the synthesis of sound-producing gestures (Figure 9.9) has also been proposed. It is composed of both the animation of an avatar and the simulation of a physical model instrument (Bouënard et al. 2008a). From a functional point of view, the architecture is divided into three main parts. The first part deals with the motion capture database. Time series extracted from captured motion are first processed, and then used to drive the sensorimotor controller. The second part is the sensorimotor controller itself, which is composed of a learned inverse kinematics module, and an inverse dynamics based on classical actuators (Marteau and Gibet 2007). The whole sensorimotor controller drives the dynamics human model through the specification of forces and torques applied on specific joints. The third part is the instrument simulation, which is dedicated to the simulation of vibrating objects. Both the avatar and the instrument are displayed in real time, thanks to a 3D rendering engine.

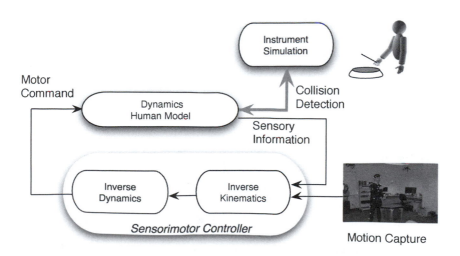

Figure 9.9 Architecture for the synthesis of sound-producing gestures.

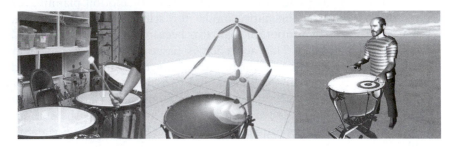

Figure 9.10 Synthesis of timpani playing gestures, based on motion capture data and a dynamical model of an avatar. (a) Capturing the movement of a real performer, (b) analysis of the gestures in the light of biomechanical invariant laws, (c) re-synthesis of these gestures using a dynamical model of an avatar.

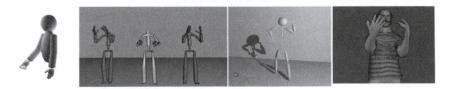

Figure 9.11 Illustrations of different rendering techniques for avatar animation.

Different simulations were attempted for timpani gestures (Figure 9.10) captured on real performers (Bouënard et al. 2008a). In these simulations, our aim was to analyze the gestures in the light of biomechanical invariant laws (Bouënard et al. 2008b), and to re-synthesize these gestures using a dynamic model of an avatar. In order to validate the approach, perception tests are carried out for various experimental conditions. This is done by changing some simulation parameters and visualization techniques (Figure 9.11).

6 Conclusion

This chapter has introduced the main concepts and methods related to the modeling of human gestures, from the viewpoint of biomechanical sensorimotor control, with special attention to the computational modeling of sound-producing gestures. From this discussion, the following points can be highlighted: First, gestures, whether they are simple everyday gestures or skilled sound-producing gestures, are characterized by specific properties of motor equivalence, flexibility, and anticipation. Second, human motion can be considered from the viewpoint of a multi-layered architecture. Motor control problems thereby appear as problems that the nervous system and the biomechanical system must solve. Third, some invariants exist in the kinematics and the dynamics of human movement. Fourth, when modeling realistic gestures, it is worth taking into account the biomechanical properties of the human body, and considering the sensorimotor control mechanisms underlying the motor control system in the light of these biomechanical properties. Fifth, virtual reality, and in particular the synthesis of gesture in avatars in a three-dimensional scene, offers a potentially rich environment for the study of movement analysis and synthesis.

Human gesture is a very complex phenomenon. In modeling the motor control of sound-producing systems, it is necessary to understand thoroughly the underlying sensorimotor mechanisms that characterize gesture performances. This level of understanding assumes that the several scientific communities involved in the study of gesture exchange ideas on the different paradigmatic models. Therefore, multidisciplinary projects, bringing together biomechanics, cognitive science, computer science, and music (performers or/and composers), should be strengthened in the near future, for the benefit of all these fields of research.

References

Bernstein, N. A. (1967). *The Coordination and Regulation of Movements*. London: Pergamon Press.

Bizzi, E. N., Hogan, N., Mussa-Ivaldi, F. A., and Giszter, S. (1992). Does the nervous system use equilibrium point control to guide single and multiple joint movements? *Behavioral and Brain Sciences*, 15(4), 603–613.

Bouënard, A., Gibet, S., and Wanderley, M. M. (2008a). Enhancing the visualization of percussion gestures by virtual character animation. In *Proceedings of the International Conference on New Interfaces for Musical Expression (NIME'08)*. Genova, Italy, 38–43.

Bouënard, A., Wanderley, M. M., and Gibet, S. (2008b). Analysis of percussion grip for physically based character animation. In *Proceedings of the 5th International Conference on Enactive Interfaces (ENACTIVE'08)*. Pisa, Italy, 22–27.

Boulic, R., Mas, R., and Thalmann, D. (1996). A robust approach for the control of the center of mass with inverse kinetics. *Computers and Graphics*, 20(5), 693–701.

Boulic, R., Peinado, M., and Le Callenec, B. (2006). Challenge in exploiting prioritized inverse kinematics for motion capture and postural control. In S. Gibet, N. Courty, and J.-F. Kamp (eds.), *Gesture in Human-Computer Interaction and Simulation*, LNAI 3881. Berlin, Heidelberg: Springer, 176–187.

Brown, T. G. (1914). On the nature of the fundamental activity of the nervous centers; together with an analysis of rhythmic activity in progression, and a theory of the evolution of function in the nervous system. *Journal of Physiology*, 48, 18–46.

Bullock, D. and Grossberg, S. (1988). Neural dynamics of planned-arm movements: emergent invariants and speed accuracy properties during trajectory formation. In S. Grossberg (ed.), *Neural Networks and Natural Intelligence*. New York: MIT Press, 553 – 622.

Camurri, A., Mazzarino, B., and Volpe, G. (2004). Analysis of expressive gesture: the EyesWeb expressive gesture processing library. In A. Camurri and G. Volpe (eds.), *Gesture-Based Communication in Human-Computer Interaction*, LNAI 2915. Berlin, Heidelberg: Springer, 469–470.

Dahl, S. (2000). The playing of an accent: preliminary observations from temporal and kinematic analysis of percussionists. *Journal of New Music Research*, 29(3), 225–234.

Dahl, S. (2005). *On the Beat: Human Movement and Timing in the Production and Perception of Music*. PhD thesis, KTH Royal Institute of Technology, Stockholm.

Decety, J., Jeannerod, M., and Prablanc, C. (1989). The timing of mentally represented actions. *Behavioral Brain Research*, 34(1–2), 35–42.

Feldman, A. G. (1966). Once more on the equilibrium point hypothesis (lambda model) for motor control. *Journal of Motor Behavior*, 18(1), 17–54.

Fitts, P. M. (1954). The information capacity of the human motor system in controlling the amplitude of movement. *Journal of Experimental Psychology*, 47(6), 381–391.

Flash, T. (1987). The control of hand equilibrium trajectories in multi-joint arm movements. *Biological Cybernetics*, 57(4–5), 257–274.

Freeman, F. N. (1914). Experimental analysis of the writing movement. *Psychological Review (MonographsSupplement)*, 17, 1–46.

Gibet, S. (1987). *Codage, Représentation et Traitement du Geste Instrumental. Application à la Synthèse de Sons Musicaux par Simulation des Mécanismes Instrumentaux*. PhD thesis, Institut National Polytechnique de Grenoble.

Gibet, S. (2002). *Modèles d'Analyse-Synthèse du Mouvement*. Habilitation to Direct Research, University of Bretagne Sud.

Gibet, S. and Bouënard, A. 2006. Simulation of dynamical gesture interacting with drums. In K. Ng (ed.), *Proceedings of the COST287-ConGAS 2nd International Symposium on Gesture Interfaces for Multimedia Systems*. Leeds, UK.

Gibet, S. and Florens, J. L. (1988). Instrumental gesture modeling by identification with time-varying mechanical models. In *Proceedings of International Computer Music Conference (ICMC'88)*. Cologne, Germany, 28–40.

Gibet, S., Kamp, J.-F., and Poirier, F. (2004). Gesture analysis: invariant laws in movement. In A. Camurri and G. Volpe (eds.), *Gesture-Based Communication in Human-Computer Interaction*, LNAI 2915. Berlin, Heidelberg: Springer, 1–9.

Gibet, S., Lebourque, T., and Marteau, P.-F. (2001). High level specification and animation of communicative gestures. *Journal of Visual Languages and Computing*, 12(6), 657–687.

Gibet, S. and Marteau, P.-F. (1990). Gestural control of sound synthesis. In *Proceedings International Computer Music Conference (ICMC'90)*. Glasgow, UK, 387–391.

Gibet, S. and Marteau, P.-F. (1994). A self-organized model for the control, planning and learning of nonlinear multi-dimensional systems using a sensory feedback . *Applied Intelligence*, 4(4), 337–349.

Gibet, S. and Marteau, P.-F. (2003). Expressive gesture animation based on non parametric learning of sensory-motor models. In *Proceedings of the 16th International Conference on Computer Animation and Social Agents (CASA'03)*. New Brunswick, NJ, 79–85.

Gibet, S., Marteau, P.-F., and Julliard, F. (2002). Models with biological relevance to control anthropomorphic limbs: a survey. In I. Wachsmuth and T. Sowa (eds.), *Gesture and Sign Language in Human-Computer Interaction*, LNAI 2298, 105–119.

Grochow, K., Martin, S. L., Hertzmann, A., and Popovic, Z. (2004). Style-based inverse kinematics. *ACM Transactions on Graphics*, 23(3), 522–531.

Guiard, Y., Beaudoin-Lafon, M., and Mottet, D. (1999). Navigation as multiscale pointing: extending Fitts' model to very high precision tasks. In *Proceedings of the SIGCHI Conference on Human factors in Computing Systems: the CHI is the Limit*. Pittsburgh, PA, 450–457.

Haken, H. and Wunderlin, A. (1990). Synergetics and its paradigm of self-organization in biological systems. In H.T.A. Whiting, O.G. Meijer, and P.C.W. van Wieringen (eds.), *The Natural-physical Approach to Movement Control*. Amsterdam: VU University Press, 1–36.

Harris, C. M. and Wolpert, D. M. (1998). Signal-dependent noise determines motor planning. *Nature*, 394, 780–784.

Hill, A. V. (1938). The heat of shortening and the dynamic constants of muscle. *Proceedings of the Royal Society of London*, B126, 135–195.

Hogan, N. (1984). An organizing principle for a class of voluntary movements. *Journal of Neuroscience*, 4(11), 2745–2754.

Hogan, N. (1985). The mechanics of multi-joint posture and movement control. *Biological Cybernetics*, 52(5), 315–331.

Jordan, M., Flash, T., and Arnon, Y. (1994). A model of the learning of arm trajectories from spatial deviations. *Journal of Cognitive Neuroscience, 6(4), 359–376*.

Julliard, F. and Gibet, S. (1999). REACTIVA: Motion synthesis based on a reactive representation. In A. Braffort, R. Gherbi, S. Gibet, J. Richardson, and D. Teil (eds.), *Gesture-Based Communication in Human-Computer Interaction*, LNAI 1739. Berlin, Heidelberg: Springer, 265–268.

Kawato, M., Maeda, Y., Uno, Y., and Suzuki, R. (1990). Trajectory formation of arm movement by cascade neural network model based on minimum torque criterion. *Biological Cybernetics*, 62(4), 275–288.

Kay, B. A., Saltzman, E. L., and Kelso, J. A. (1991). Steady-state and perturbed rhythmical movements: a dynamical analysis. *Journal of Experimental Psychology: Human Perception and Performance*, 17(1), 183–198.

Keele, S. W. (1968). Movement control in skilled motor performance. *Psychological Bulletin*, 70(61), 387–403.

Kelso, J. A. S., and Schöner, G. (1988). Self-organization on coordinative movement patterns. *Human Movement Science*, 7(1), 27–46.

Kelso, J. A. S., Ding, M., and Schöner, G. (1992). Dynamic pattern formation: a primer. In J. E. Mittenthal and A. B. Baskin (eds.), *Principles of Organization in Organisms. SFI Studies in the Sciences of Complexity, Proc. Vol. XIII*. Reading MA: Addison-Wesley, 397–439.

Koga, Y. and Latombe, J.-C. (1994). On multi-arm manipulation planning. In

Proceedings of the IEEE International Conference on Robotics and Automation, San Diego, CA, 945–952.

Körding, K. P. and Wolpert, D. M. (2006). Bayesian decision theory in sensorimotor control. *TRENDS in Cognitive Sciences*, 10(7), 319–326.

Kugler, P. N. and Turvey, M. T. (1986). *Information, Natural Law, and the Self-Assembly of Rhythmic Movement*. New York: Lawrence Erlbaum.

Lebourque, T. and Gibet, S. (1999). High level specification and control of communication gestures: the GESSYCA system. In *Proceedings of the Computer Animation*. Washington, DC: IEEE Computer Society, 24.

Lebourque, T. and Gibet, S. (2000). A complete system for the specification and the generation of sign language gestures. In A. Braffort, R. Gherbi, S. Gibet, J. Richardson, and D. Teil (eds.), *Gesture-Based Communication in Human-Computer Interaction*, LNAI 1739. Berlin, Heidelberg: Springer, 227–238.

Marteau, P.-F. and Gibet, S. (2007). Learning for the control of dynamical motion systems. In *Proceedings of the Seventh International Conference on Intelligent Systems Design and Applications (ISDA'07)*. Rio de Janeiro, Brazil, 454–459.

Miall, R. C. and Wolpert, D. M. (1996). Forward models for physiological motor control. *Neural Networks*, 9(8), 1265–1279.

Paillard, J. (1980). The multichanneling of visual cues and the organization of a visually guided response. In G. E. Stelmach and J. Requin (eds.), *Tutorials in Motor Behavior*. Amsterdam: North-Holland, 259–279.

Peinado, M., Herbelin, B., Wanderley, M. M., Le Callennec, B., Boulic, R., and Thalmann, D. (2004). Towards configurable motion capture with prioritized inverse kinematics. In *Proceedings of the Third International Workshop on Virtual Rehabilitation (IWVR'04)*. Lausanne, Switzerland.

Radix, C. L., Robinson, P., and Nurse, P. (1999). Extension of Fitts law to modeling motion performance in man-machine interfaces. *IEEE Transactions on Systems, Man and Cybernetics Part A: Systems and Humans*, 29(2), 205–209.

Schmidt, R. A. (1982). The motor program. In J.A.S. Kelso (ed.), *Human Motor Behavior: An Introduction*. Hillsdale NJ: Erlbaum, 187–218.

Schmidt, R. A., Zelaznik, H. N., Hawkins, B., Franck, J. S., and Quinn, J. T. (1975). Motor-output variability: a theory for the accuracy of rapid acts. *Psychological Review*, 86(5), 415–451.

Soechting, J. F. (1989) Elements of coordinated arm movements in three-dimensional space. In S. A. Wallace (ed.), *Perspectives on the Coordination of Movement*. Elsevier, Amsterdam, 47–83.

Soechting, J. F., and Flanders, M. (1989a). Sensorimotor representations for pointing to targets in three-dimensional space. *Journal of Neurophysiology*, 62, 582–594.

Soechting, J. F., and Flanders, M. (1989b). Errors in pointing are due to approximations in sensorimotor transformations. *Journal of Neurophysiology*, 62, 595–608.

Stein, P. S. G. (1995). A multiple-level approach to motor pattern generation. In W. R. Ferrell and U. Proske (eds.), *Neural Control of Movement*. New York: Plenum Press, 159–165.

Uno, Y., Kawato, M. and Suzuki, R. (1989). Formation and control of optimal trajectory in human multi-joint arm movement. *Biological Cybernetics*, 61(2), 89–101.

Viviani, P. and Flash, T. (1995). Minimum-jerk, two-thirds power law, and isochrony: converging approaches to movement planning. *Journal of Experimental Psychology: Human Perception and Performance,* 21(1), 32–53.

Viviani, P. and Terzuolo, C. A. (1980). Space-time invariance in learned motor skills. In G. E. Stelmach and J. Requin (eds), *Tutorials in Motor Behavior.* Amsterdam: North-Holland, 525–533.

Viviani, P. and Terzuolo, C. A. (1982). Trajectory determines movement dynamics. *Neuroscience,* 7(2), 431–437.

Wanderley, M. M. (2002). Quantitative analysis of non-obvious performer gestures. In I. Wachsmuth and T. Sowa (eds.), *Gesture and Sign Language in Human-Computer Interaction,* LNAI 2298, Berlin, Heidelberg: Springer, 241–253.

Wann, J. P. and Nimmo-Smith, I. (1991). The control of pen pressure in handwriting: a subtle point. *Human Movement Science,* 10(2–3), 223–246.

Winters, J. M. and Stark, L. (1987). Muscle models: what is gained and what is lost by varying model complexity. *Biological Cybernetics,* 55(6), 403–420.

Wolpert, D. M., Ghahramani, Z., and Flanagan, J. R. (2001). Perspectives and problems in motor learning. *TRENDS in Cognitive Sciences,* 5(11), 487–494.

Woodworth, R. S. (1899). The accuracy of voluntary movement. *Psychological Review,* 3, 1–119.

Zajac, F. E. and Winters, J. M. (1990). Modeling musculoskeletal movement systems: joint and body segmental dynamics, musculoskeletal actuation, and neuromuscular control. In J. M. Winters and S. L. Y. Woo (eds.), *Multiple Muscle Systems.* Berlin, Heidelberg: Springer, 121–147.

Zelaznik, H. N., Schmidt, R. A., and Gielen, S. C. (1986). Kinematic properties of rapid aimed hand movements. *Journal of Motor Behavior,* 18(4), 353–372.

Chapter 10

Visual Gesture Recognition
From Motion Tracking to Expressive Gesture

Antonio Camurri and Thomas B. Moeslund

1 Introduction

Human beings seem to have little or no problem with perceiving and understanding the expression of gestures of musical performers and dancers on a scene. Even when we are not able to see all details of the performers' movements and/or bodies, for example due to poor lighting, occlusion, or distance, we usually quickly sense the expressive character of these movements, i.e. whether the movements are slow, fast, calm, agitated, and from those gestures, we can often easily infer whether the person moving is happy, sad, tired, or elated. In looking at gestures, we also perceive parts of the body that may be momentarily occluded because of an unfavourable viewing angle, i.e. we will in most cases correctly assume that a person continues to move the whole body even though we actually only see some parts of the body moving.

Our abilities to sense quite accurately both the actual movements and their expressive and emotive features become even more remarkable when we try to replicate these abilities with machines. What's easy for us may be very difficult or even impossible for machine-based systems of vision. Yet developing technologies for machine-based vision and gesture recognition has attracted considerable effort, because such artificial systems of vision and gesture recognition may have many applications in human–computer interaction (HCI), in various everyday tasks, and in multimedia, but also because such machine-based systems can tell us more about our own human capabilities of vision and gesture recognition. In our context of music-related gestures, this research on machine-based vision and gesture recognition is then a central topic that we shall focus on in this chapter.

The chapter gives an introduction of how cameras can be used as sensors to capture human gestures and how different methods overcome the inherent difficulties associated with the recognition process. Following this, ongoing research into expressive gestures is presented. In this perspective, a particular focus is on dance and music performances as first-class conveyors of expressive and emotional content.

2 Processes Required for Visual Gesture Recognition

The process of extracting gestures using images, illustrated in Figure 10.1, is similar to using other sensor technologies. First a sensor, in this case a camera, measures some signal. Then this signal is processed and a number of features are extracted. These features can be seen as a compact representation of the input signal. Based on the features the gesture present in the input signal, if any, is recognised and converted into a symbol. When a system is running it outputs a string of symbols which can then be used to control music production or something completely different.

When the sensor is a camera then the feature extraction process is called computer vision (also referred to as image processing or image analysis) and the gesture recognition process is called pattern recognition. However, not all systems contain a gesture recogniser. There are situations where the extracted features are used directly as control signals. For example, a user moves sideways in front of a camera and the feature extracting process captures this movement and uses it directly to control the volume of a sound system. The term "gesture" will in the remainder of this chapter be interpreted as covering (1) body gestures, where the entire human body is involved, (2) arm gestures, performed by one or both arms, and hand gestures, performed by either the fingers or the hand(s).

Before computers became widespread in society, not much research was done in the field of visual gesture recognition, or more generally the field of capturing the motion of living creatures. Early work in this area was mostly within the research field of the natural sciences, basically with a view to gaining a better understanding of the physical and biological environment. One of the first studies was done by Muybridge (Muybridge 1887; 1957). He used a series of connected cameras to capture a "movie" (sequence of images) in order to prove that a horse has a flight phase where all its limbs are in the air at the same time. He also did a number of similar experiments on humans in order to gain knowledge regarding walking styles, etc. More quantitative motion data were obtained in the following years by attaching markers to the subject whose motion is to be captured (Ladin 1995; Braune and Fischer 1987). The idea is to capture

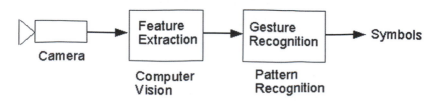

Figure 10.1 The different processes required for visual gesture recognition.

the subject from multiple cameras at the same time. Afterwards the markers can be identified in all images and three-dimensional data can be obtained using a technique called triangulation. The principle behind triangulation is illustrated in Figure 10.2. The lines L1 and L2 are three-dimensional lines spanned by the marker's projection into the images and the optical centre of each camera. If we know the relative position between the two cameras then we have two three-dimensional lines in space and their intersection allows us to calculate the position of the marker with respect to the cameras.

Markers can take many different shapes and sizes, and they can be constructed of different materials. The most common approach is to use spherical objects (to avoid directional dependencies) painted with some highly reflective paint. Systems where these markers are used are often constructed in such a way that the image is very dark except for the markers, which are very bright. Such images are therefore often referred to as moving light displays (MLD) or point light displays (PLD).

This more than 100-year-old concept of using markers and triangulation is still being used today in motion capture technology (MoCap). Over the last ten to twenty years, commercial MoCap studios have been established and these studies have contributed to relevant research in health science, sports, and entertainment. For example in sports, MoCap has been used to capture the motion of each limb of an athlete during a high jump. Afterwards the MoCap data are mapped to a three-dimensional model, meaning that the jump can be observed from all possible directions. This can be a great improvement compared to simply recording the jump on video. For both application areas the MoCap data can also be used to analyze the kinematics and kinetics of the movement. In many of the big Hollywood movies, MoCap data is used together with computer graphics to generate virtual actors and other special effects. For example, in the *Jurassic Park* movies, many of the movements of the dinosaurs were based on MoCap data from elephants. In the *Lord of the Rings* movies,

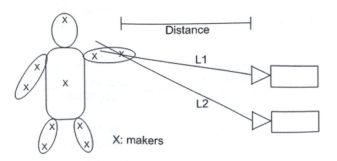

Figure 10.2 Basic Schema of Triangulation, using two cameras.

the movements of an actor (Andy Serkis) were MoCaped and used to control the Gollum creature. In recent years, MoCap techniques have been used in music research, to better understand the movements of musicians while playing (e.g. Baader et al. 2005; Loehr and Palmer 2007).

However, in some application areas it is not desirable (or possible) to use markers, such as in visual surveillance and in human computer interaction. For example, in surveillance, it will mostly be abnormal and/or hostile actions that a system is looking for, while in human computer interaction applications, the system may look for particular gestures that are defined beforehand and that are operative in a controlled environment. Music production based on visual gesture recognition can be considered as a special case of human computer interaction.

3 Feature Extraction

The purpose of feature extraction is then to convert an image of a human gesture into a symbolic representation of that gesture. The symbols are derived from features, where each feature characterises some aspect of the gesture, such as its motion or its shape. Feature extraction is a general requirement in any computer vision system. Many of the pattern recognition methods that are applied to visual gesture recognition are very general, and therefore, they can be applied to the recognition of gestures using any sensor technology. However, in this section, the focus will be on so-called non-invasive approaches, and less on marker-based systems. Moreover, we only focus on relatively simple (or low-level) features that can be extracted directly from the image. For example, the overall movement of a human body can be represented as the movement of the centre-of-mass of this body. As explained below, the movement of the whole body is thereby reduced to the movement of a single point. In contrast, high-level features, such as the extraction of joint angles from body movement, would require more complicated processing (Moeslund et al. 2006b). Features describing expressive qualities of movement and gesture, faced in section 5 of the chapter, can be considered high-level features as well.

The focus here is on low-level features because they are relatively fast and easy to calculate, and at the same time often sufficient for defining a rich set of gestures for control. Many different low-level features exist and they can be grouped in different ways. We here group them with respect to the type of information in the image they are based on. These groups are: silhouette-based features, appearance-based features, and motion-based features. Low-level features are also inspired by studies on visual perception, and are studied to build computational models inspired by perception. Certain theories (e.g. Marr 1982) thereby refer to the role of shape and dynamic cues in visual perception.

3.1 Silhouette-Based Features

The idea behind silhouette-based features is illustrated in Figure 10.3. The first step is to extract the silhouette of the human from the input image and the second step is to calculate some features from the silhouette, here illustrated as the position of the head, hands, centre-of-mass, and feet.

The silhouette can be extracted in a number of different ways and the technique that is most often used is the one illustrated in Figure 10.4. It is based on the assumption that the background (everything besides the human) is static. This is a realistic assumption for indoor environments with only little sunlight, but for outdoor scenes or more complicated indoor scenes different methods are applied (Moeslund and Granum,

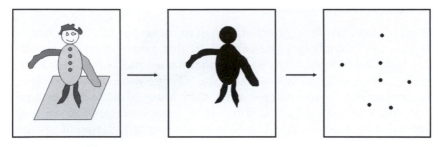

Figure 10.3 The principle of silhouette-based feature extraction.

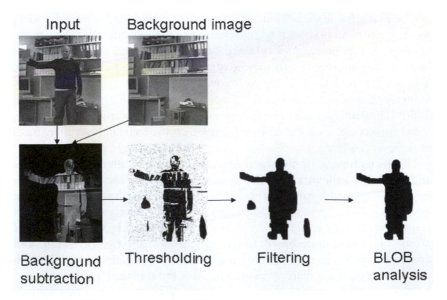

Figure 10.4 Background subtraction.

2001; Moeslund et al. 2006b). Given that the background is static, we can simply subtract an incoming image from the background image and obtain the foreground. Each pixel of the resulting image is then compared to a threshold value and a binary image is obtained where pixels different from the background are black and pixel similar to the background are white. Overall, this process is denoted "background subtraction."

Due to an imperfect camera sensor, small fluctuations in the lighting, and the human wearing clothing similar to the background, there will always be some errors in the silhouette. These errors are called "noise." It appears both in the resulting silhouette image in the form of missing pixels inside the silhouette and silhouette-pixels outside the actual silhouette (see Figure 10.4). In general, the noise will have a negative influence on the quality of the features that are going to be extracted. Therefore, it is necessary to remove noise (if possible), using some kind of filtering.

Small isolate silhouette-pixels outside the actual silhouette can often be removed using a simple median filter, which replaces a pixel's value by the median of the pixels in the neighbourhood (Gonzalez and Woods 2002). The holes inside the silhouette can often be removed using a morphologic closing operation. The basic idea is first to dilate the silhouette to the point where all holes are filled and then erode the resulting silhouette back to its original size. Since the filtering is done automatically, there is no guaranty that all noise pixels are removed and especially the silhouette-pixels outside the actual silhouette can cause problems for the subsequent calculation of the features. To solve this problem, a connected component analysis can be performed. This process finds all pixels that are connected and group them into one entity called a binary large object or BLOB. After this process, the image is transformed into a number of BLOBs. The size, shape, and position of the BLOBs are used to find the BLOB representing the human gesture and all other BLOBs are deleted.

Having extracted the silhouette, it is now possible to calculate the features. The most straightforward feature is called the centre-of-mass, and it is represented by two numbers. The first number states the average horizontal position of the human silhouette in the image and is calculated simply by summing all the horizontal coordinates of the silhouette-pixels and dividing by the total number of silhouette-pixels. The second number is calculated in the same manner, using the vertical coordinates of the silhouette-pixels. Even though the centre-of-mass feature is very simple, it can be very powerful, due to the fact that this feature can be calculated rather robustly and very fast. A slightly more complicated version is to divide the silhouette into a number of regions, as shown in Figure 10.5, and then to calculate the centre-of-mass in each region. This can actually allow for a crude approximation of the whereabouts of the user's limbs.

Another straightforward feature is the bounding box of the silhouette,

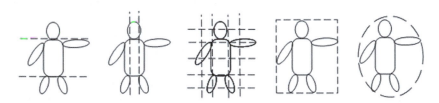

Figure 10.5 The first three figures on the left show different ways of dividing the silhouette into regions. The two figures on the right show a bounding box and a bounding ellipse representation of the silhouette.

as shown in Figure 10.5. A bounding box is the smallest rectangle enclosing the silhouette. By observing the changes of its width and height over time, certain actions can be recognized. The EyesWeb open software platform (www.eyesweb.org) contains a module that segments the bounding box into smaller sub-boxes, corresponding roughly, in some postures, to parts of the body. Another module divides the bounding box into four sub-bounding boxes using the coordinates of the centre of mass, and this process continues recursively in each sub-bounding box. Another module identifies parts of the silhouette that move together as a sub-part (roughly, a sort of implementation of the "common fate" rule of Gestalt perception), which can then be further analyzed in its shape and dynamics. Another module finds the smallest circle or ellipse that contains the silhouette and then uses the circle/ellipse parameters as features for further processing. Bounding shapes can also be applied to smaller regions, as was the case for the centre-of-mass features. For the bounding shapes and the centre-of-mass features, a better result is obtained if the smaller regions actually correspond to body parts. For example, in Störring et al. (2004), hand gestures are recognised by finding the centre of the hand using a distance image (see Figure 10.9), and using this information to separate the hand from the arm.

3.2 Appearance-Based Features

If a system can extract the position of the head and the hands in a silhouette-image, then this may be sufficient for the recognition of a number of gestures. However, in some situations it is not possible to extract these position features, due to the setup (for example non-static background), clothing conditions, or real-time requirements. Therefore, as an alternative, appearance-based methods can be applied. They are based on the idea that the user has a different colour compared to the background. At one extreme, the background has only one colour, for example, green, which the user is not wearing. By detecting all non-green pixels, the silhouette of the user can be found. This principle is called Chroma-keying and is being used intensively, for example in TV weather forecasts. At the other extreme, the system finds the hands and face of the user by first searching for skin-colour pixel in the image and then grouping them. Somewhere in between these extremes, special coloured markers can be placed on the user and these colours can be found by searching for a particular type of colour-pixel. Using skin-colours or markers can sometimes be combined with the silhouette approach, by only searching for the special coloured pixels among the silhouette-pixels.

Introduction to Colours

A colour-pixel is represented in a camera by an amount of red (R), an amount of green (G), and an amount of blue (B). This is called the RGB-representation. Say we have eight bits to represent each colour, then we can make 256 different shades of each colour. Combining the three colours provides $256^3 = 16.777.216$ different colours. The colour-value of one pixel is usually written as RGB[123,45,76]. In this terminology a maximum red pixel is RGB[255,0,0], a completely white is RGB[255,255,255], and a completely black pixel is RGB[0,0,0]. Using this terminology a colour can be represented as a point in a three-dimensional cube spanned by the three colours, as shown in Figure 10.6. If we travel along a line passing through a point and the origin, RGB[0,0,0], then all points along this line will have the same colour but different intensities. This means that if we search for a certain colour, say skin-colour, and the level of the light is lowered, then the colour will remain the same, corresponding to travelling towards RGB[0,0,0] along a "skin-coloured" line in space. Due to this fact we are interested in an alternative colour representation where the colour and intensity are separated. Such a representation is called Hue-Saturation-Intensity (HSI)

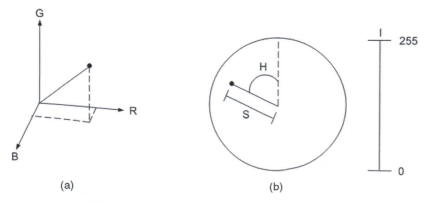

Figure 10.6 The RGB representation (a); the HSI representation (b).

(Gonzalez and Woods 2002) and therefore this is often used when extracting features for gesture recognition. The HSI representation is illustrated in Figure 10.6. Hue is the colour and is measured as an angle, the saturation is the purity of the colour measured as the distance from the centre, and the intensity is measured as the level of the incoming light (independent of colour). So, when analyzing a colour-pixel, only the Hue and Saturation values need to be considered. In practice, too dark or too white pixels are ignored independent of their Hue and Saturation values. This is due to the inherent uncertainties in pixel values close to the maximum and minimum values of a camera.

Detecting Colour-pixels

When looking at the actual pixels of an object, it is obvious that no object consists of just one colour, that is, one point in the RGB or HSI space. In order to detect pixels belonging to a certain object, the system needs to *learn* the values of the pixels belonging to an object, as shown in Figure 10.7. The detection of object pixels is carried out by comparing an incoming pixel value to the learned pixel values. For example, say that we have *learned* that an object has Hue values [50,80], then all incoming pixels having a value within this interval will be classified as belonging to the object and those outside are part of the background. A number of different pattern recognition methods exist for this purpose (Duda et al. 2000). The simplest method is a box-classifier. Here the minimum and maximum Hue and Saturation values found during training are used to define a box in Hue-Saturation space. If a pixel is inside the box it is an object-pixel, otherwise not (see Figure 10.7). However, the training data can also be modelled by a multivariate Gaussian distribution and the use of statistical pattern recognition methods, such as a Bayesian classifier (Duda et al. 2000).

Following this segmentation approach, it should be possible to identify regions where only pixels belonging to one single object are present. After dealing with the noise in the output image (using the same methods as described above) further features can then be extracted. These can be as complicated as those described for the silhouette, but usually just the centre-of-mass is applied.

The idea of skin detection is appealing, but it may turn out to be very difficult in real systems (see Figure 10.7). Therefore markers are often applied in appearance-based systems for gesture recognition. Typical markers are special coloured-clothing, gloves, ribbons, and circular objects attached to the clothing.

Saturation

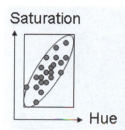

Hue

Figure 10.7 The figure on the left shows the distribution of the trainings data. The box illustrates the decision boundaries of a box classifier, whereas the ellipse illustrates the decision boundaries of a Bayesian classifier. The middle and right figures show the application, with input image and classified skin-pixels, respectively (adapted from Petersen and Skalski 2006).

3.3 Motion-based Features

Motion-based features are based on the same assumption as the silhouette-based features are, namely that the background is static. Motion-based features are generally less dependent on the assumption of a static background, and more discriminative features can be extracted from silhouettes. Two different approaches can be applied, namely, image subtraction and motion displacement.

Image Subtraction

The procedure for extracting motion-based features using image subtraction is similar to the one shown in Figure 10.4. The only difference is that the background is not learned and subtracted from the incoming images. Instead, the incoming image is subtracted from the previous image, and hence features can only be extracted when the user is moving in the scene. This is reasonable. since a gesture often requires some kind of movement. Figure 10.8 illustrates the result of subtracting two images from each other. Clearly the silhouette of the user is not obtainable from this data. However, features such as the level of motion can very easily be calculated by counting the number of black pixels in Figure 10.8d. Furthermore, the location of the motion in the image can also be easily calculated. Based on these simple features a great number of successful applications of human computer interaction have been developed, such as controlling the lights and sounds in installations. By dividing the image into regions, as shown in Figure 10.5, and counting the number of pixels for each region, quite advanced interfaces can be developed.

Extracting the above features requires very little processing effort and it seldom fails, hence its success. However, the derivation of more advanced

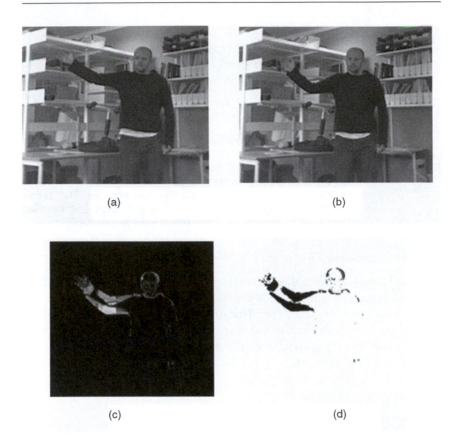

(a)   (b)

(c)   (d)

Figure 10.8 (a) Input image at time *t*. (b) Input image at time *t* + 1. (c) Difference image. (d) Thresholded difference image.

features is more complicated. For example, if the position of the user is known, then the activity feature can be calculated with respect to, for example, the left and high arms/legs of the human subject, and "up and down" will also have relative meanings. One approach to position estimation is based on the combination of skin detection and silhouette processing, as described above. Another approach is to use a texture-based model to detect and track the face. The Viola–Jones approach is currently the foundation for such methods (Viola and Jones 2004).

A number of other low-level static as well as dynamic features are available in the literature and are supported in interactive systems. For example, the EyesWeb open platform includes a number of software modules and related examples (as program patches) that implement a number of feature extraction techniques, including the ones described in this section.

4 Gesture Recognition

The features that are extracted from an image or a stream of images can be further processed into symbols or parameters that serve as control signals for interactive music and multimedia systems. The general process of mapping features into symbols or parameters is called *pattern recognition* (Duda et al. 2000), but when focused on human movement, the pattern becomes a gesture and the approach is called *gesture recognition* (Buxton 2003; Moeslund 2003; Park and Aggarwal 2004; Moeslund et al. 2006b).

In gesture-based sound control, simple features and simple recognition methods are often applied, as more complicated features and methods can be too computational demanding for real-time processing. However, simple features and recognition methods often produce inaccurate results, but this may be compensated by the fact that visual gesture-based sound control is often used in new interfaces where inaccurate results might actually be a quality of the system. This is especially the case in artistic contexts.

Another characteristic of the commonly used recognition methods in gesture-based sound control is that these methods often operate on static data, that is, on gesture recognition in one single image, as opposed to gesture recognition based on a number of consecutive images. We denote these two types of recognition as *static* and *dynamic* gesture recognition.

4.1 Static Gesture Recognition

The centre-of-mass can be used as a control parameter for the volume and pitch of a sound, and in a more advanced version, this can be combined with a number of regions in the image (see Figure 10.5), so that the extracted features from each region control one or more parameters of the sound system. However, strictly speaking, such systems do not contain a gesture recognition part. In fact, a genuine gesture recognition system should map the features into one or more symbols, for example, either on or off. For example, the image can be divided into a number of regions and the amount of motion in each region can be calculated and compared to a threshold value. If the amount of motion is above the threshold it is concluded that some activity is present in this particular region and then it can be used to control an event in the sound system. Such events can be further parameterised using the actual values of one or more features. This is for example the type of movement recognition used in interactive systems like VNS (Very Nervous System) (http://homepage.mac.com/davidrokeby/vns.html), Isadora (http://www.troikatronix.com/isadora.html), and Eyecon (http://eyecon.palindrome.de/).

Störring et al. (2004) provides an example of a system that recognises gestures based on a number of regions. First, the centre of the hand is found and this is then used to define a number of concentric circles, as shown in Figure 10.9. For each of the circles the number of BLOBs is found and used to count the number of fingers. The approach allows the recognition of five different gestures.

While the methods described above can be characterised as ad hoc methods, other methods are based on statistics. These follow the notion of creating a model of each gesture to be recognised and then compare the features from the incoming image with all models, and the model most similar to the input is the recognised gesture. For example, if five features

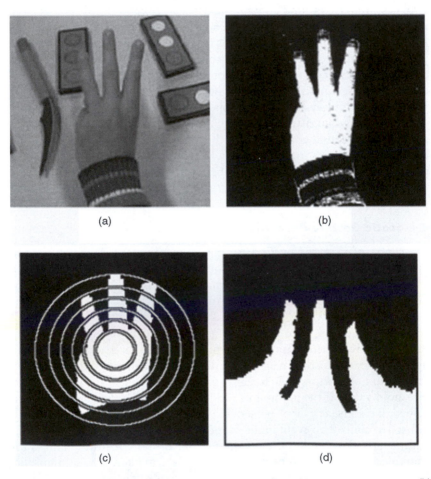

(a)

(b)

(c)

(d)

Figure 10.9 Gesture recognition by counting the number of fingers. (a) Input image. (b) Colour-segmented image using skin-colour. (c) Six concentric circles centred at the centre-of-mass. Note that the silhouette has been filtered to remove noise. (d) The actual implementation where the silhouette is polar-transformed based on the centre-of-mass. This transforms the search circles into search lines, which are easier to handle (Störring et al, 2004).

represent a gesture, then this gesture can be represented as a point in a five-dimensional space. Each incoming image is a new point in this five-dimensional space and recognition is then a matter of calculating the distance between the new point and the points that represent the possible (to be recognized) gestures.

Obviously, there will always be some diversity in how different users perform a gesture. Furthermore, image noise will also result in some diversity of the features representing the gesture. The consequence is that a model cannot actually be represented simply by one point, but must be represented by a number of points in the five-dimensional space. A number of training images containing the gesture can be analyzed in order to capture this diversity. This approach can be handled by the so-called k-nearest neighbour method. It operates by finding a number (k) of nearest training points and investigates which gesture they come from. The most frequent gesture among the k points defines the gesture.

Bayes's rule operates in a different manner. It (often) assumes that the training points for one gesture are normally distributed. If this is the case, then the training data for one gesture can be modelled by an ellipsoid whose axes are defined by the variance and covariance of the different features (Duda et al. 2000). The distance from the input point to each gesture is then measured in variances. Bayes's rule furthermore allows the use of the *a priori* likelihood of each gesture. That is, if one gesture is far more likely to be observed in the image than another gesture, then this gesture will have a higher likelihood of being selected. If the gestures are equally likely, then Bayes's rule becomes the Mahalanobis distance (Duda et al. 2000).

When doing recognition of static gestures one must always consider two issues, namely, noise and the Midas Touch problem. Many systems will contain noise resulting in uncertainties in the feature extraction. Having an uncertain input to the gesture recogniser will often result in an uncertain output. Therefore, a static gesture is often recognised only after being present for a number of consecutive images or by filtering the output, for example, using a median filter or a mean filter.

A different problem with a related solution is the Midas Touch problem. The phrase "Midas Touch" comes from an old Greek myth where everything king Midas touched turned into gold. At first this was wonderful, but in the end he hated it because he couldn't touch anything without spoiling it. A similar situation is present in gesture recognition. For example, when is a user simply moving his hand and when is he doing a gesture? Normally a gesture recogniser is set to classify each incoming image as containing one of the possible gestures, which results in many false positives when the user is not (intentionally) doing a gesture. The solution is often to include some temporal filtering as mentioned above. While this can remove some of the false positives, it also slows down the entire interaction since a user is required to hold the same gesture for some time, for example one second.

4.2 Dynamic Gesture Recognition

Dynamic gesture recognition is based on methods that use some filtering over subsequent images. A gesture can then be defined as a transition from one configuration to another. Moeslund and Nørgaard (2006a) estimate the configuration of the thumb in each image where the index finger is outstretched (pointing gesture). If the thumb is found to be close to the hand in an image followed by a situation where it is far from the hand in the next image, then a "click" gesture is recognised. Even though these recognisers apply temporal information they will typically not be named dynamic gesture recognisers, but rather recognisers based on static gestures followed by some filtering.

Genuine dynamic gesture recognizers process a sequence of static gestures as a trajectory through the feature space. This is schematically illustrated in Figure 10.10a, which also illustrates some of the inherent difficulties associated with recognition of dynamic gestures. Firstly, a start and stop point are required, since the feature extractor produces one long sequence of features. This has to be divided into sub-sequences each representing an individual gesture. No standard solution to this problem exists and therefore many systems either use some ad hoc solution or the system is only tested on sequences where the start and stop time is given.

The second inherent problem concerns the fact that different users might spend more time, or less time, in performing a gesture, compared to

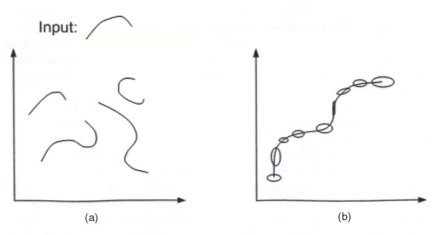

Figure 10.10 (a) 2D representation of four dynamic gestures together with an input. (b) A dynamic gesture (trajectory) represented as a number of states (the ellipses).

the model gesture. This will make the trajectory longer or shorter and make recognition more difficult. If it is just a matter of the speed then the trajectory can be rescaled to have the same duration as the models, but if it is more complicated, then this rescaling will not be sufficient. A way around this problem is to apply Dynamic Time Warp (Myers and Rabiner 1981) which to some degree handles this problem.

Another approach is to split the trajectory into smaller pieces that can be recognised independently and put together afterwards to recognise a gesture. This approach has been used in Fihl et al. (2006), where different arm gestures are being recognised. A gesture trajectory is segmented (Figure 10.10b) and each of the segments is being recognised as part of a gesture, or gesture state. In this approach, the sequence is then compared to all the models using the Edit Distance principle (Levenshtein 1965), a principle that is also used for automatic spell checking. Alternatively, Hidden Markov Models (HMMs) can be used (Rabiner 1989). A HMM is a statistical approach where each gesture is represented by a sequence of states linked by transition probabilities, that is, the likelihood of a state in the current image given another state in the previous image. The HMMs take the input sequence and compute which gesture model is most likely to have produced the input. However, the HMM approach requires a massive amount of training compared to the Edit Distance approach. Nevertheless, HMM is the most commonly applied approach.

5 Expressive Gesture and Gesture Analysis for Music and Dance

Given the above overview of feature extraction and gesture recognition methods, we shall now discus some examples of how these methods can be applied to non-verbal mechanisms of expressive and emotional communication in music and in dance.

Several definitions of gesture exist in the literature (see Chapter 2). In artistic contexts in particular, gestures are often intended to *express*, rather than to *denote*. That is, they don't point to something in the environment, but the information they contain and convey is related to the affective and emotional domain. Expressive gestures carry what Cowie et al. (2001) call "implicit messages," and what Hashimoto (1997) calls KANSEI. They are responsible for the communication of a kind of information (what we call expressive content) that is different and in most cases independent, even if often superimposed on, a possible denotative meaning. The content, expressed in terms of corporeal articulations, may be used to display a mental state, feelings, moods, affects, and emotional intentions.

In that sense, a gesture can be performed in several ways, by stressing different qualities of the gesture. Using this information, it is possible to recognize a person from the way he/she walks, but it is also possible to get information about the emotional state of a person by looking at his/her gait, for example, if he/she is angry, sad, or happy. In the case of gait analysis, we can therefore distinguish among several objectives and layers of analysis. First, a level that aims at describing the physical features of the movement in order to classify it (e.g. Liu et al. 2002). Second, a level that aims at extracting the expressive content of the gait, for example, in terms of information about the emotional state that the walker communicates through his/her way of walking. From this point of view, walking is an expressive gesture, conveying a specific expressive content. Even if no denotative meaning is associated with it, it still communicates information about the emotional state of the walker. In fact, in this perspective, the walking action fully satisfies the conditions stated in the definition of gesture by Kurtenbach and Hulteen (1990), namely, that walking is "a movement of the body that contains information."

Some studies aim at analysing the expressive intentions conveyed in everyday gestures. For example, Pollick et al. (2001) investigated the expressive content of gestures like knocking or drinking. However, we face a more general concept of expressive gesture that includes not only everyday gestures but also specific musical and visual (e.g. computer-animated) related gestures. Our concept of expressive gesture is somewhat broader than Kurtenbach and Hulteen's, since it considers cases where, with the aid of technology, communication of expressive content takes place even without an explicit movement of the body, or, at least, the movement of the body is only indirectly involved in the communication process. This can happen, for example, when, in visual media, the expressive content is conveyed through a continuum of possible ways ranging from realistic to abstract images and effects, such as cinematography, cartoons, virtual environments with computer animated characters and avatars, expressive control of lights in a theatre context (e.g. related to actor's physical gestures).

Consider, for example, a theatre performance where the director asks actors, dancers, and musicians to communicate by means of expressive gestures in dance and music. Technology can then be used to extend these gestures, for example, to map motion or music features onto particular configurations of lights, onto movements of virtual characters, or onto automatically generated computer music and live electronics. In this way, "extended" expressive gestures can be created that while still have the purpose of communicating expressive content, although the resulting content is only partially related to explicit body movements. In a way, such "extended expressive gestures" can be considered the result of a juxtaposition of several dance, music, and visual gestures. In addition, it also includes the artistic point of view of the director who created it. Consequently, the expressive gesture of the piece is perceived as a multimodal gesture by human spectators.

Approaches to high-level expressive gesture analysis are usually based on the extraction of a set of features that can provide quantitative information on different qualities of the expressiveness of the gesture. These features related to fluency, impulsiveness, energy, contraction, and so on. They are grounded on studies from different disciplines, such as computer vision, biomechanics, experimental psychology, research on multisensory perception, and theories from arts and humanities, such as Rudolf Laban's theory of effort and Pierre Schaeffer's approach to sound morphology. A collection of features based on these sources has been developed, although most of these are extracted from full-body movement that is captured by video cameras (e.g. see Camurri et al. 2000; 2005; 2008; Castellano et al 2008).

Consider the example of a high-level feature called "fluidity" in a human subject that is moving in a free space, starting from the signal of one video camera. This analysis will typically start from low-level feature analysis as described above. We will thereby assume that the human subject wears appropriate clothes (that is, not including large freely moving tissues hiding body parts, and of an appropriate colour that can be distinguished from the fixed background), that lighting is appropriate (fixed or slowly changing), and so on. In general, however, these constraints are not so restrictive as in usual MoCap setups, and they can be relaxed, depending on concrete artistic contexts. For example, in the setup of an Opera by Luciano Berio, called *Cronaca del Luogo* (performed at the opening of the Salzburg Festival of 1999), we enforced the video tracking with special IR diodes on the helmet and on the costume of the actor/singer. This allowed a less constrained environment like the effective stage where the performance occurred.

In the analysis of "fluidity," the first task to perform is to analyze and validate what we intend to extract with this cue, using all the different viewpoints, from biomechanics to humanistic and artistic theories (including music, theories from choreography), to psychology. For example, we can consider an analogy with the concept of "legato/staccato" in music, or with the concept of "flow" in Rudolf Laban's theory of effort (Laban and Lawrence 1947). The approach may start from the extracted silhouette of the human subject, and a segmentation of this silhouette in sub-parts (BLOBs) according to dynamic and static (shape) features as described above, in order to detect phrases and single gestures (e.g. based on the shape of a feature called Quantity of Movement).

In the extraction of the "fluidity" feature, one may then consider the trajectories of the centres-of-mass of each BLOB of the silhouette in each single gesture, and analyze to what extent they have a "staccato/legato" characteristic in the "gesture phrase." The length and the density of gesture phrases in a given time unit thereby defines how much of the movement is segmented. This may be another cue for extracting the "fluidity" feature, namely, to define fluidity in terms of the amount of segments (few segments is more fluidity). The staccato/legato character can be obtained by adopting a feature extraction method that is analogous to the analysis of inter-onset interval in the music signal. A "fluid" gesture then shows a tendency to be "legato" in all the trajectories of the centres-of-mass of each blob of the silhouette.

The testing of these high-level features for expressiveness should be done by comparing the results of the automated annotation, for example, of "fluidity," with a manual annotation of the same cue performed by a set of subjects, using techniques from experimental psychology (Camurri et al. 2003). The fluidity module of the Expressive Gesture Library in the EyesWeb XMI open software platform has the above-mentioned aspects, as well as some other aspects (so it is more complex).

At the InfoMus Lab in Genova, research on expressive gesture recognition is focused on the development of interactive multimedia systems that enable novel interaction paradigms and allow a deeper engagement of the users by explicitly observing and processing their expressive gestures. This is now extended to social interactions, and emotional communication. In social interaction, we focus on aspects of synchronization, entrainment, and empathy, using relations between expressive cues. In emotional communication, we focus on (1) expressive gestures as a way to communicate a particular emotion to the audience (cognitive emotion), and (2) expressive gestures as a way to emotionally engage the audience in felt emotions, causing "strong emotional response." Recently, each of these emotional communication perspectives has been studied in experiments that aim to understand which features of an expressive gesture are responsible for the communication of the expressive content, and how the dynamics of these features correlates with a specific expressive content. The aim of these experiments was (1) to find out which auditory and visual features are mostly involved in conveying the performer's expressive intentions and (2) to test the developed model by comparing their performances with spectators' ratings of the same musical performances. For the analysis of expressive gesture in experiments of this kind, a unifying conceptual framework was adopted.

Camurri et al. (2003) studied the communication of four basic emotions, namely anger, fear, grief, and joy by comparing a dance gesture recognition system with spectators' appreciations. The research hypotheses are grounded on the role of the Laban's effort dimensions in dance gesture, as described in Laban's theory of effort (Laban and Lawrence 1947; Laban 1963), namely:

1. that the time dimension is specified in terms of the overall duration of time and tempo changes, which can be elaborated as the underlying structure of rhythm and flow of the movement;

2. that the space dimension is related to Laban's notion of personal space, that is, the extent in which limbs are contracted or expanded in relation to the body centre;

3. that the flow dimension is specified in terms of an analysis of shapes of speed and energy curves, and features that relate to the frequency and rhythm of motion and pause phases;

4. that the weight dimension is specified in terms of the amount of tension and dynamics in movement, for example, the vertical component of acceleration. In this study, these features were associated in different combinations to each emotion category.

Timmers et al. (2006), studied the communication of emotional intensity through visual and auditory performance gesture and the effect of it on spectators' emotional engagement. The research hypotheses combine Laban's theory of effort with hypotheses stemming from performance research (Palmer 1997; Timmers 2002) and research on the intensity of emotion and tension in music and dance (Krumhansl 1996; Krumhansl and Schenk 1997), namely, that (1) emotional intensity is reflected in the degree of openness (release) or contraction (tension) of the torso of the performer, (2) that emotional intensity is communicated by the main expressive means for a pianist: tempo and dynamics, and (3) that intensity increases and decreases with energy level (speed of movements, loudness, tempo). Intensity is related to the performer's phrasing. It increases towards the end of the phrase and decreases at the phrase boundary with the introduction of new material.

The extraction of features that characterize aspects of expressive gestures may rely on computer vision techniques like those described in the first part of the chapter. However, in measuring expressiveness, we are not interested in *what* kind of gesture is performed, but in *how* the gesture is performed. For that aim, the features that provides descriptions of the expressive character of the gesture need further specification in view of specific theories of perception and movement, depending on the application one has in mind. So, it may happen that very different gestures are similar in terms of their expressive character. Nonetheless, many techniques described in the first part of the chapter can be very useful to start the analysis of expressiveness.

For example, the auditory and visual features that were most involved in conveying the performer's expressive intentions were assumed to be key-velocity, inter-onset interval, movement velocity, and the openness or contraction of the performer's posture. In addition, a relationship between phrasing and emotional tension-release was expected. However, in some cases, the analyses of the performance data suggested an opposite relationship between emotional intensity and the performer's posture. For example, it was found that the pianist leaned forward for softer passages and backward for intensive passages. In addition it suggested a differentiation in expressive means with tempo on one side and key-velocity and movement velocity on the other side.

When relating the performers' data to the listeners' data, this differentiation in expressive means was confirmed. Tempo communicates phrase boundaries, while dynamics is highly predictive for the intensity of felt emotion. Emotional engagement correlated strongly with key-velocity, which means that emotional engagement tended to increase with increase of dynamics and decrease at points of softer dynamics. This does not mean that soft passages were without emotional tension, but they were points of relative emotional relaxation. Hardly any evidence was found for movement features that could influence listeners' ratings. The sound seemed the primary focus of the participants and vision seemed subsidiary. The local phrase-boundaries indicated by tempo did not lead to release of emotional intensity. The modulation of dynamics over a larger time-span communicates the overall form of the piece and, at that level, intensity did increase and decrease within phrases.

A Unifying Layered Conceptual Framework

The above examples show that gestures cover both the auditory and visual modality, and for that reason, gestures are said to have a multimodal characteristic. Indeed, gestures in music performance not only relate to the expressive and functional gestures of a performer, but also to the expressive gestures that are present in the produced sound. When we define gestures as structural units that have internal consistency and are distinguished in time and quality from neighbouring units, it is possible to analyse gestures in both modalities. In order to deal with this multimodal perspective, we adopt the unifying conceptual framework of Camurri et al. (2005). It is based on a layered approach that ranges from low-level physical measures (such as position, speed, acceleration of body parts for dance gestures, sampled audio signals or MIDI control messages for music gesture) to descriptors of overall gesture features (such as motion fluency, directness, impulsiveness for dance gestures, analysis of melodic and harmonic qualities of a music phrase for music-related gestures). This layered approach is sketched in Figure 10.11, where each layer is depicted with its inputs, its outputs, and the kind of processing it is responsible for.

The conceptual framework can also be applied for the synthesis of expressive gesture, for example for the generation and control of the movement of avatars, virtual characters, or robots in mixed reality scenarios, as well as for the synthesis and interpretation of music. Examples of synthesis of expressive movement and expressive audio content are documented in the literature, such as the EMOTE system (Chi et al.

High-level expressive information: (Experiment 1) emotions classification (e.g. anger, fear, grief, joy); (Experiment 2) prediction of spectators' engagement.

Layer 4: Concepts and Structures – modeling, classification, prediction; e.g., based on machine learning techniques.

Motion segmentation and gesture representation: e.g., gesture segments, musical phrases, and trajectories representing gestures in semantic spaces.

Layer 3: Mid-level Features and Maps – Techniques for motion and gesture segmentation (e.g., in pause and motion phases), segmentation of the musical signal in phrases, and representations in feature spaces (e.g., energy-articulation spaces, Laban's Effort spaces).

Motion and audio descriptors: e.g., quantity of motion in movement, loudness in audio, amount of contraction/expansion, spectral width and melodic contour, fluency, impulsiveness, and roughness.

Layer 2: Low-level features – Computer vision techniques, statistical measures, and audio signal processing techniques.

Movement detection, trajectories (e.g., body silhouette, trajectories of body parts, trajectories of subjects considered as points moving in their general space – e.g. a dancer on stage), and features from MIDI and audio signals (spectral and temporal low-level features)

Layer 1: Physical Signals – Low-level analysis of video and audio signals, from signal conditioning and techniques for audio and video pre-processing and filtering, to background subtraction, motion detection, and motion tracking (e.g., color blob tracking, optical flow based feature tracking).

Data from several kinds of sensors: e.g., images from video cameras, sampled audio, MIDI messages, accelerometers data, physiological data, etc.

Figure 10.11 Conceptual framework (adopted from Camurri et al. 2005).

2000) for generating the movement of avatars and virtual characters based on high level motion qualities, and the systems for synthesis of expressive music performances developed at KTH (Friberg et al. 2000) and the DEI-CSC group at the University of Padova (Canazza et al. 2000).

Finally, it should be noticed that in the perspective of developing novel interactive multimedia systems for artistic applications, such a framework should be considered in the context of a broader mixed reality scenario in which avatars, who behave both as observers and as agents, perform the four layers of processing in the analysis of observed expressive gestures and in the synthesis of expressive gestures to communicate (directly or remotely) with other real and virtual subjects.

6 Conclusion

The first part of this chapter focused on the basic methods for feature extraction and gesture recognition, using video analysis. The second part of this chapter focused on expressive gestures, and an extension of the basic methods towards higher-level approaches to music and dance performances.

Obviously, the video camera is just one of many different devices that are currently available for sensing human body movement and expressive gestures. However, as opposed to many other sensors, the video camera offers a non-invasive solution that makes it very attractive as a tool for sensing, especially in artistic contexts.

The basic principles of visual gesture recognition apply to all kinds of sensors, and the division between feature extraction and gesture recognition applies to all of them. Whereas the feature extractor stage may differ in its details from sensor to sensor, the gesture recognition part is rather similar for most other sensors. Many of methods that were introduced in this chapter can be directly experienced by the reader by using the Eyes Web XMI open platform (freely available from www.eyesweb.org). The platform provides software modules that implement the methods for low-level feature extraction, as well as the higher-level feature extraction that is related to expressive characteristics of the gesture.

To summarise, we can say that the modelling of expressive gesture is receiving growing importance from both research and industry communities, even if we can consider it in its infancy. The main outputs of our research are the definition of a unified multimodal conceptual framework for expressive gesture processing, the experimental results obtained from the two described experiments, and a collection of software modules for cue extraction and processing. The conceptual framework proved to be useful and effective in two different scenarios, well represented by the two experiments.

The dance experiment can be considered as a first step and a starting point toward understanding the mechanisms of expressive gesture communication, not only limited to dance. A collection of cues that have some influence in such a communication process has been individuated, measured, and studied. A first attempt of automatic classification of motion phases has been carried out and some results have been obtained (e.g. an average rate of correct classification not particularly high, but well above chance level). Expressive cues like *impulsiveness* and *fluency* should be further worked out. Moreover, perceptual experiments would be needed to empirically validate the extracted expressive cues.

The music experiment can be considered as a first step towards the understanding of the multimodal relationship between movement and sound parameters of a performance, their expressive forms and functions, and their communicative function for spectators. A next step should involve a larger variety of performances and a larger collection of calculated cues, and cues should be fitted to the responses of individual spectators in order to get a deeper as well as broader understanding.

References

Baader, A. P., Kazennikov, O., and Wiesendanger, M. (2005). Coordination of bowing and fingering in violin playing. *Cognitive Brain Research*, 23(2–3), 436–443.

Braune, C. and Fischer, O. (1987). *The Human Gait*. Berlin, Heidelberg: Springer.

Buxton, H. (2003). Learning and understanding dynamic scene activity: a review. *Image and Vision Computing*, 21(1), 125–136.

Camurri A., Hashimoto S., Ricchetti, M., Trocca, R., Suzuki K., and Volpe G. (2000). EyesWeb. Toward gesture and affect recognition in interactive dance and music systems. *Computer Music Journal*, 24(1), 57–69.

Camurri, A., Lagerlöf, I., and Volpe, G. (2003). Recognizing emotion from dance movement: comparison of spectator recognition and automated techniques. *International Journal of Human–Computer Studies*, 59(1–2), 213–225.

Camurri, A., De Poli, G., Leman, M., and Volpe, G. (2005). Communicating expressiveness and affect in multimodal interactive systems, *IEEE Multimedia*, 12(1), 43–53.

Camurri, A., Canepa, C., Coletta, P., Mazzarino, B., and Volpe, G. (2008). Mappe per affetti erranti: a multimodal system for social active listening and expressive performance. In *Proceedings of the International Conference on New Interfaces for Musical Expression (NIME'08)*. Genoa, Italy.

Canazza, S. De Poli, G., Drioli, C., Rodà, A., and Vidolin, A. (2000). Audio morphing different expressive intentions for multimedia systems. *IEEE Multimedia*, 7(3), 79–83.

Castellano, G., Mortillaro, M., Camurri, A., Volpe, G., and Scherer, K. (2008). Automated analysis of body movement in emotionally expressive piano performance. *Music Perception*, 26(2), 103–119.

Chi, D., Costa, M., Zhao, L., and Badler N. (2000). The EMOTE model for effort and shape. In *Proceedings of the 27th Annual Conference on Computer*

Graphics and Interactive Techniques (SIGGRAPH '00). New York: ACM Press/Addison-Wesley, 173–182.

Cowie, R., Douglas-Cowie, E., Tsapatsoulis, N., Votsis, G., Kollias, S., Fellenz, W., and Taylor, J. (2001). Emotion recognition in human–computer interaction, *IEEE Signal Processing*, 18(1), 32–80.

Duda, R. O., Hart, P. E., and Stork, D. G. (2000). *Pattern Classification*. New York: Wiley Interscience.

Fihl, P., Holte, M. B., Moeslund, T. B., and Reng, L. (2006). Action recognition using motion primitives and probabilistic edit distance. In F. Perales and R. Fisher (eds.), *Articulated Motion and Deformable Objects*, LNCS 4069. Berlin, Heidelberg: Springer, 375–384.

Friberg, A., Colombo, V., Frydén, L., and Sundberg, J. (2000). Generating musical performances with Director Musices. *Computer Music Journal*, 24(3), 23–29.

Gonzalez, R. C. and Woods, R. E. (2002). *Digital Image Processing*. Upper Saddle River, NJ: Prentice Hall.

Hashimoto S. (1997). KANSEI as the third target of information processing and related topics in Japan. In A. Camurri (ed.), *Proceedings of the International Workshop on KANSEI: The technology of emotion*. Genova: AIMI (Italian Computer Music Association) and DIST-University of Genova, 101–104.

Krumhansl, C. L. (1996). A perceptual analysis of Mozart's piano sonata K.282: Segmentation, tension and musical ideas. *Music Perception*, 13(3), 401–432.

Krumhansl, C. L. and Schenk, D. (1997). Can dance reflect the structural and expressive qualities of music? A perceptual experiment on Balanchine's choreography of Mozart's Divertimento No. 15. *Musicae Scientiae*, 1(1), 63–85.

Kurtenbach, G. and Hulteen, E. A. (1990). The art of human–computer interface design. In B. Laurel (ed.), *Gestures in Human–Computer Communication*. Reading, PA: Addison Wesley, 309–317.

Laban, R. v. (1963). *Modern Educational Dance*. London: Macdonald and Evans.

Laban, R. v. and Lawrence, F.C. (1947). *Effort*. London: Macdonald and Evans.

Ladin, Z. (1995). Three-dimensional analysis of human movement. In P. Stokes, I. Allard and J.-P. Blanchi (eds.), *Three-Dimensional Analysis of Human Movement*. Champaign, IL: Human Kinetics.

Levenshtein, V. I. (1965). Binary codes capable of correcting deletions, insertions and reversals. *Doklady Akademii Nauk SSSR*, 163(4), 845–848.

Liu Y., Collins, R. T., and Tsin, Y. (2002). Gait sequence analysis using frieze patterns. In A. Heyden, G. Sparr, M. Nielsen, and P. Johansen (eds.), *Computer Vision – ECCV 2002*. Berlin, Heidelberg: Springer, 733–736.

Loehr, J. D. and Palmer, C. (2007). Cognitive and biomechanical influences in pianists' finger tapping. *Experimental Brain Research*, 178(4), 518–528.

Marr, D. (1982). *Vision: A Computational Investigation into the Human Representation and Processing of Visual Information*. San Francisco: W. H. Freeman.

Moeslund, T. B. (2003). *Computer Vision-Based Motion Capture of Human Body Language*. PhD thesis, Lab of Computer Vision and Media Technology, Aalborg University, Denmark.

Moeslund, T. B. and Granum, E. (2001). A survey of computer vision-based human motion capture. *Journal of Computer Vision and Image Understanding*, 81(3), 231–268.

Moeslund, T. B. and Nørgaard, L. (2006a). Recognition of deictic gestures for wearable computing. In S. Gibet, N. Courty, and J.-F. Kamp (eds.), *Gesture in Human Computer Interaction and Simulation*, LNAI 3881. Berlin, Heidelberg: Springer, 112–123.

Moeslund, T. B., Hilton, A., and Kruger, V. (2006b). A survey of advances in vision-based human motion capture and analysis. *Journal of Computer Vision and Image Understanding*, 104 (2), 90–126.

Muybridge, E. (1887/1957). *Animal Locomotion*. Reprinted in L.S. Brown (ed.), *Animal in Motion*. New York: Dover.

Myers, C. S. and Rabiner, L. R. (1981). A comparative study of several dynamic time-warping algorithms for connected word recognition. *The Bell System Technical Journal*, 60(7), 1389–1409.

Palmer, C. (1997). Music performance. *Annual Review of Psychology*, 48, 115–138.

Park, S. and Aggarwal, J. K. (2004). Semantic-level understanding of human actions and interactions using event hierarchy. In *Proceedings of the IEEE Conference on Computer Vision and Pattern Recognition – Workshop on Articulated and Non-rigid Motion*. Washington DC, U.S.A., 12–12.

Petersen, J. S. and Skalski, L. D. (2006). *Face Detection in Image Sequences*. MA thesis, Laboratory of Computer Vision and Media Technology, Aalborg University, Denmark.

Pollick, F. E., Paterson, H., Bruderlin A., and Sanford, A.J. (2001). Perceiving affect from arm movement. *Cognition*, 82 (2), B51–B61.

Rabiner, L. R. (1989). A tutorial on Hidden Markov Models and selected applications in speech recognition. *Proceedings of the IEEE*, 77 (2), 257–286.

Störring, M., Moeslund, T. B., Liu, Y., and Granum, E. (2004). Computer vision-based gesture recognition for an augmented reality interface. In *Proceedings of the 4th IASTED International Conference on Visualization, Imaging, and Image Processing*. Marbella, Spain, 766–771.

Timmers, R. (2002). *Freedom and Constraints in Timing and Ornamentation: Investigations of Music Performance*. PhD thesis, Maastricht: Shaker Publishing.

Timmers, R., Camurri, A., Marolt, M., and Volpe, G. (2006). Listeners' emotional engagement with performances of a Scriabin Étude: an explorative case study. *Psychology of Music*, 34(4), 481–510.

Viola, P. A. and Jones, M. J. (2004). Robust real-time face detection. *International Journal of Computer Vision*, 57(2), 137–154.

Chapter 11

Conductors' Gestures and Their Mapping to Sound Synthesis

Gunnar Johannsen and Teresa Marrin Nakra

1 Introduction

Conductors use movement, gesture, and facial expressions to motivate a group of musicians to perform with expertise and expression. Conductors are the only musicians who do not normally make sound while performing. The techniques of conducting have evolved slowly over many hundreds of years, from the ancient musical hand-sign-language of chironomy[1] to the modern gestures that have been established and documented for Western classical music. Conducting is not only a gestural art form; it is also the specialized currency of a group of highly skilled musicians who are respected for their abilities in musicianship, inner hearing, memorization, motivation, and personnel management. With a rich history and lore, conducting is an interesting area to study and to transform with digital technologies.

It is our goal to provide the reader with answers to questions such as the following: What exactly is conducting? How do conducting gestures relate to cognitive processes and to emotions? How can these gestures convey musical meaning to a group of musicians? How can conducting gestures be measured and interpreted? What are the state-of-the-art methodologies and technologies for investigating conductors' gestures and for mapping them to sound?

This chapter aims to present various ways in which musicians, scientists, and technologists have worked to describe, analyze, and synthesize conducting. First of all, the characteristics of conducting are outlined in section 2. The following two main sections deal with the use of computers, sensors, and synthesis methods—in section 3, for the analysis and acquisition of conductors' gestures and, in section 4, for the mapping of gestures to sound synthesis.

2 Characteristics of Conducting

2.1 What Exactly is Conducting? Why is it Important?

Conducting is defined as leading and coordinating a group of musicians (instrumentalists and/or singers) in a musical performance or rehearsal. Expert conducting requires intense coordination between the body and the mind, and demands superior musicianship (Green and Gibson 2004). Conducting also requires quick mental reflexes, strong inner hearing, and clear facial expressions, although the technique is primarily defined for the hands and arms. This technique is based on a precise system of gestures that has evolved its symbolic meanings over approximately 300 years, and has been well documented in pedagogical texts. Beyond pure technique, however, there is also a common understanding that successful conductors "inhabit" and "breathe" the music in a natural way, and are able to freely communicate their intentions together with their feelings and expressions. As the Australian conductor Simone Young states, "three-quarters of being a conductor is what's going on in your head, and the rest of communication, through your hands, through your face, through words, though really more through gesture and expression. And it's what's going on in the conductor's head that's much more interesting, because a conductor's mind has to work on lots and lots of different levels . . ." (Ford 2003).

The role of the conductor (as a professional position) evolved during the nineteenth century. This can be attributed to the increasing complexity of orchestration, the growing size of orchestras, and expanding attention to musical elements such as timbre, texture, balance, and dynamics. It was during this time that the conventions of conducting were first formalized. Hector Berlioz' essay, "Le Chef d'Orchestre: Théorie de son art," was the first attempt to describe the special functions of the conductor (Berlioz 1855). This essay appeared in the second edition of his *Grand Traité d'Instrumentation et d'Orchestration Modernes* (Berlioz 1844). A later German version was extended and revised by Richard Strauss (Berlioz and Strauss 1986). A new English translation of Berlioz' *Traité* with commentary was published recently (Berlioz and Macdonald 2002).

It was also during the nineteenth century that the use of a baton became the prevailing norm, gradually decreasing in size from its initial, staff-like ancestor. The baton in its reduced modern scale and with its importance for directly leading the whole orchestra was first introduced by Louis Spohr of Kassel, Germany in 1820 (Bowen 2003). To this day, many notable conductors continue to prefer to use their hands rather than any baton.

The twentieth century has seen the gradual development of a system of formal rules and techniques from what were at first stylistic conventions.

These rules have been taught to advanced music students in conservatories and training programs since the 1920s (e.g. Boult (1968) and Scherchen (1990), who first published their textbooks on conducting in 1920 and 1929, respectively). The existence of this system of formal rules is further witnessed by the establishment of international competitions during the last fifty years, which evaluate students based on shared criteria for clarity, expressiveness, and technique. Despite this, there are many examples of famous professional conductors who have developed individual and iconoclastic styles, far removed from the standard techniques, as has been noted by Green and Gibson (2004).

Contemporary conducting techniques consist of rules for moving a baton with the right hand and giving expressive indications with the left hand. The right hand uses "beat-patterns" to indicate pulse, meter, tempo, rubato, subdivisions, and articulations. The left hand is used to indicate cues, dynamics, emphasis, accents, and pauses. Each of the basic rules has many possible variations, which reflect personal style, regional convention, or the preference of one's teacher.

Two important aspects of conducting will be outlined in the two following subsections. The supervisory, real-time, and cognitive aspects of conducting are dealt with in section 2.2. Thereafter, aspects of gestural transformations, clarity, and expressiveness are introduced in section 2.3.

2.2 Conducting as Supervisory Control

The concept of "supervisory control" helps to explain the processes of real-time interaction and communication between conductor and orchestra musicians. This concept, originally developed in human-centred systems engineering, may generally be considered as guidance by humans of cooperative systems—either human or computerized technical systems (Johannsen 2002). It can be applied to every conductor–orchestra relationship. As defined by Sheridan and Johannsen, "the human supervisor performs upper level goal-oriented functions such as planning system activity, directing intelligent subsystems, monitoring system behaviour, adjusting parameters on-line when appropriate, and intervening in emergency or for normal redirecting or repair" (Sheridan and Johannsen 1976). The individual orchestral musicians with their respective instruments are regarded as the intelligent subsystems. They are organised in subgroups including strings, woodwinds, brass, and percussion.

The goals prescribed as the inputs to the overall system of the conducted orchestra are contained in the score of the musical composition. The conductor as supervisor conveys his or her mental image of the complete musical work in real-time to the subgroups and to each individual musician of the orchestra by means of gestural expressiveness. This hierarchical organization is also supported by the leaders of the subgroups and by the concertmaster, who are human-interactive mediators between the other orchestra musicians and the conductor. The gestural and expressive control inputs of the supervisor, i.e. the conductor, are directed towards the part leaders and the concertmaster as well as the subgroups and all individual musicians. Their teamplay can further be regarded as the cooperation of partly autonomous agents under the leadership of the supervisor. The musicians coordinate their activity by means of agent–agent communication, i.e. by listening to each other, and through motions or gestures.

Excellent conductors tend to be more strict and persuasive during rehearsals (i.e. more supervisory control), whereas they allow more freedom during final concert performances (i.e. more agent–agent communication). Sometimes, the conductor may even be superfluous as supervisor. For example, a smaller ensemble may opt not to use a conductor. Also, professional orchestras, who will never play below a certain level of quality, may just ignore a conductor if they feel his or her quality does not meet their standard.

In supervisory control, the three levels of sensorimotor, gestural, and cognitive control are strongly related to each other. Musicians interacting with their instruments are in a situation of highly trained automated sensorimotor behaviour. Gestural control is additionally involved in playing musical instruments (Wanderley and Depalle 2004), as means for expressiveness. In conducting, sensorimotor behaviour is also the psychophysiological basis for gestural control. Various control processes are usually overlaid for the purpose of conscious understanding, planning, and navigation, and they possess both controlling and evaluative power. This varies with the different modes of supervisory control and agent–agent communication with the orchestra musicians in rehearsal and concert situations.

The mental image of the musical work in the conductor's mind determines the gestures and their expressiveness in supervisory control. The mental image of the musical work is based on the composer's score. Therefore, the conductor has to perform a thorough musical analysis of the score in all its aspects, possibly supporting this with related material such as work descriptions. This intimate study of the musical score is in some ways the reverse of the composing process, and has to be completed well before any first rehearsals. In studying the score, the conductor builds up an elaborate mental image of the musical work for later retrieval during rehearsals and concert performances.

The form and detailed structure of the work is of utmost importance, as a kind of framework for the various mental images that the conductor acquires as his or her model of the musical work. This framework comprises the basic structure, its parts and themes, their variations and transformations, as well as all of the relations among these. Thereby, different time horizons are considered in parallel, from very near (e.g. the next effective subdivision or event in the next bar) to very far (e.g. the next or even the last movement of the work). Further, the mental images include tempo and meter, dynamics, orchestration, rhythmic and melodic textures, harmonic progressions, tonal/atonal relations, the role of dissonances and clusters, etc., all down to detailed possibilities and difficulties that may occur for single instrumentalists. These mental images are later fine-tuned and modified where necessary, during and between rehearsals.

2.3 Gestural Transformations, Clarity and Expressiveness

The conductor's job is then to transform the mental image of the musical work into gestures. These gestural transformations have to be both clear and expressive in order to show the music without using words. Also, the gestural transformations have to be practised well before any rehearsal, particularly those parts which are assumed to be difficult for all or some musicians. The full repertoire of transformations from basic to complex and supporting gestures cannot be explained here, as it is too rich in all its facets. However, some important aspects are described below.

Special gestural patterns have evolved for all meters (2/2, 3/4, 4/4, 5/4, 6/8, etc.). Such gestural patterns have to be conducted for each bar of the musical work. Regardless of the meter, all different gestural patterns start with a vertical downbeat on the first time unit of each bar (see Figures 11.1–11.2), with point (a) as the start of the downbeat (shown in Figure 11.1, top left). This provides musicians with a clear indication of every time instant "1" for all bars. At the beginning of the work or when the tempo changes, the conductor has to display the tempo and the meter one time unit (i.e. one count or one beat) in advance. This preparatory stroke before an event is important in order for the musicians to grasp the tempo from the travelling time of the hand and/or the tip of the baton between two successive beats. Also, this beat indication one time unit ahead allows the musicians to prepare their sound generation, e.g. breathing with wind instruments and bow movements with strings (see also the "predictive" accents, one beat preceding the intended ones, in Figure 11.8). Such beat indications are particularly necessary and important as upbeats at the beginnings of the musical work, of its movements, and its phrases, or with specific events.

Figure 11.1 shows gestural patterns of conducting for 4/4 time. The basic gestural schema with expressive-legato is indicated in the top left part of Figure 11.1. Other basic gestural patterns exist for 3/4, 6/8, etc. The top of the vertical line (a) in Figure 11.1 (top left) is generally the starting point in the continuous conducting pattern in cases without an upbeat. This point (a) is also the starting point for all other patterns. With an upbeat, point (b) in Figure 11.1 (top left) is the starting point. The dots

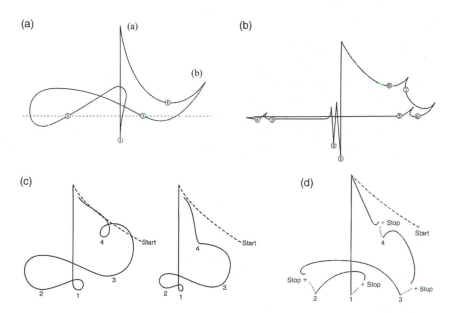

Figure 11.1 Gestural schemas of 4-beat conducting patterns for 4/4 time. (a) Basic schema, expressive-legato. (b) Schema subdivided into eight (Rudolf 1995, pp. 22 and 113). (c) Curved ictus in legato. (d) Staccato gesture (Green and Gibson 2004). Reprinted with permission from Pearson Education, Upper Saddle River, N.J.

and numbers 1–4 in Figure 11.1 (top left; and bottom left and right) represent the exact time instances of the four beats. In order to be clearly perceivable, they should be conducted with a certain small flick (called ictus) and rebound of the wrist, normally of the right hand. All four of these flicks are to be performed on a horizontal plane of a virtual table about one handbreadth below the conductor's elbows, on the level of the waist. Thereby, the vertical downbeat rebounds somewhat below this virtual horizontal plane. The gestural pattern is not executed in a strictly vertical plane but more away from the conductor's body as if to embrace a big ball, and this in order to convey lively gestures in a more voluminous space.

Different subdivisions between two successive beats slightly change the character and length of the movement between the two beats. Even additional smaller flicks for particular subdivisions are feasible (see for example Figure 11.1, top right). The usefulness of such subdivisions is clear from Figure 11.9 in section 3.2. There, the transition from the basic gestural schema of the four-beat conducting pattern for 4/4 time (Figure 11.1, top left) to its related gestural schema subdivided into eight (Figure 11.1, top right) is indicated with the right bicep's EMG (electromyographic) signal of the beat patterns. This example from Tchaikovsky's *Symphony no. 6* demonstrates the changes from beats given every quarter to beats given every eighth for the purpose of specifying the dynamics of a crescendo.

Smooth continuous movements between the flicks of the gestural beat patterns indicate legato (see Figure 11.1). The full staccato is conducted expressively by motions with a stop on each count and with a characteristic bouncing on the downbeat. The differences between expressive gestures for legato and staccato are shown in Figure 11.1 (bottom left and right). Thus, the right hand does not only demonstrate the meter and the timing of the music but also certain expressive features. The latter can also be amplified with the left hand.

Smaller, more neutral and intermittent movements with stronger flicks for accented beats, emphasize a more precise rhythmic microstructure. Special preparatory gestures are needed for certain rhythmic features. As an example, syncopation is indicated by a stop in the baton one entire count before the gesture of syncopation, which is a turning-a-key-like gesture on the next count, after which the musicians will respond as requested in the score (see Figure 11.2, upper parts).

Tempo changes from slow to fast are indicated by placing the last ictus of the slow tempo low in space with a stop, followed by the preparatory gesture in the new tempo (see Figure 11.2, lower parts).

Different parallel timescales in the music (thinking: one beat ahead, now, past, one phrase ahead, one movement ahead) correspond to the different time horizons with their respective mental images, as mentioned above. These timescales influence the conducting patterns and may be reflected in the facial expression of the conductor. Further factors influencing the conducting patterns are the musical content and the musicians' anticipated needs for support. These influences lead to modifications of the described basic patterns—sometimes more strict, sometimes more soft—to the point where the musicians may even be allowed to play by themselves for a while. Such strategies are more flexible with professional instrumentalists.

Max Rudolf once summed up the experience of conducting simply, yet deeply, as: "the relation between gesture and response" (Rudolf 1995a). The advantage that his perspective provides is that it formalizes conducting into a symbolic gestural language, and defines the mapping of specific gestures to musical information. He also demonstrates how expressive parameters are added by varying and embellishing the rigid framework of a beat structure. Conducting, from his perspective, is a highly developed symbolic language for music. This explains the importance of Rudolf's work for electronic conducting devices, as described in section 4.

Expressive parameters are important ingredients of artistic conducting gestures. They are communicated through appropriate variations in the

(a) GoS on Four:

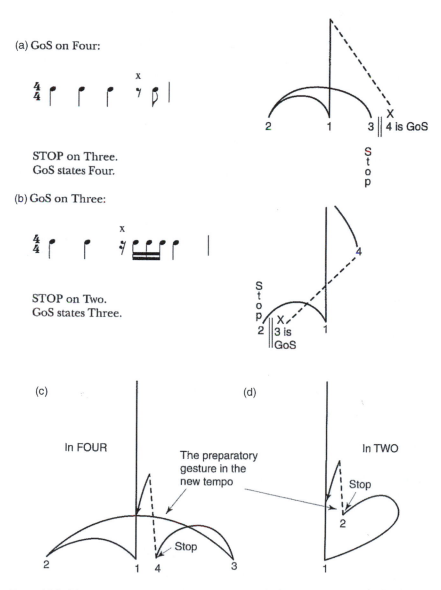

STOP on Three.
GoS states Four.

(b) GoS on Three:

STOP on Two.
GoS states Three.

(c)   (d)

Figure 11.2 (a) and (b) The gesture of syncopation (GoS). (c) and (d) Change of tempo (Green and Gibson 2004). Reprinted with permission from Pearson Education, Upper Saddle River, N.J.

beat patterns of the right hand, and are supported by indications of the left hand. Expressiveness in the performing arts should, amongst other things, communicate emotions. However, the methods by which emotions are transformed and conveyed through gestural expressions are not well understood. This remains an active area of current research. The complex relationship between music and emotion is discussed in a review of the relevant literature by Juslin and Sloboda (2001).

All performers—conductors as well as players and opera singers—need to affect and influence the audience in a contagious way. Emotions, which should ultimately be perceived and experienced by the audience in a concert performance, have first to be imagined and analyzed by the conductor as those emotions that have been intended by the composer. They then have to be transformed into expressive gestures. As a result, all gestural movements should convey the emotional content of the musical work. However, if the performers only experience the emotions themselves, and fail to accomplish their transformations into expressive gestures, then they cannot communicate the emotions and thus lose the opportunity to affect their audiences. Even in such extreme cases as the famous opening downbeats by the conductor Wilhelm Furtwängler, which started with a short, intensive trembling high in the air, gestures can only create their extreme emotional effects when performed with well-controlled expressiveness.

Having presented some basic principles of conducting, we shall now review methods for the acquisition of conductors' gestures and the use of these gestures in sound synthesis.

3 Analysis and Acquisition of Conductors' Gestures

The study of capturing, representing, and evaluating the gestures of conductors is a new field that is growing in importance (Nakra 2001; 2002), and numerous technologies now exist to track the movements of hands and batons. Some technologies and examples of systems for tracking or accompanying conductors' gestures are dealt with in section 3.1. This is followed, in section 3.2, by a concise overview of the Digital Baton and the Conductor's Jacket.

3.1 Some Technologies and Examples of Systems

The first documented device that mechanized the conducting baton was invented in Brussels during the 1830s. This electromechanical device was very similar to a piano key: when pressed, it would close an electrical circuit that turned on a light. This system was used to communicate the conductor's tempo to an offstage chorus, and Hector Berlioz mentions the use of this device in his treatise on conducting (Berlioz 1855). It is interesting to note that, since that time, the only other known methods for conducting an offstage chorus have made use of either secondary conductors or video monitors—the latter being the method that has been in use at professional opera houses for many years now.

Since that pioneering effort, there have been many other attempts to automate or augment the process of conducting. Some of these projects have been driven by the availability of new technologies; others have been created in order to perform specific new compositions, to add multimedia triggers to live performances, or to record the gestures of established conductors (Grüll 2005; Lee et al. 2006a; 2006b).

We shall now review some of the technologies used for capturing conductors' gestures, beginning with some commonly used sensors that can transform human movement to streams of data to be used in various conducting systems:

- *Accelerometers* sense acceleration along one axis; three can be attached together at ninety-degree angles to create a three-dimensional acceleration profile.
- *Gyroscopes* detect changes in orientation, and can be used to measure roll, pitch and yaw. These measurements can be used to analyze rotations in the hands and arms, or combined with accelerometers to correct problems of drift.
- *Pressure sensors* can be used to measure a conductor's grip on a baton; these often come in the form of small and flexible Force Sensitive Resistors (FSRs).
- *Infrared (IR) sensors* can be used to detect position changes of a baton, hands, or arms. Several commercially available systems exist, in either active or passive mode. In active mode, an Infrared LED emits signals at a fixed frequency band (measured in nanometers). The position of the LED is simultaneously measured by a Position Sensitive Diode (PSD) array in a camera-like device nearby. In passive mode, the conductor wears reflective markers on his/her clothing, and fixed infrared frequencies are beamed at that person. The incident IR signals bounce off the markers, and are measured by a nearby PSD.
- *Electric Field Proximity sensors* make use of the physical properties of the human body to create electric potentials and displacement currents within electrical fields. Examples of these sensors include the Theremin (see Chapter 8, this volume) and numerous interfaces built by Joseph Paradiso and others at the MIT Media Laboratory (Paradiso 1997; Gershenfeld and Paradiso 1997).
- *Electromagnetic sensor arrays* are active sensors that sense their position and orientation with respect to a reference electromagnetic transmitter. These systems have become quite important in computer animation and movie production studios for capturing and rendering natural human movement.

In addition to commercially available sensor systems, several individual inventors and musicians have built their own sensor systems into conducting interfaces. The following subsections describe examples of such systems invented for tracking or accompanying conductors' gestures.

The Radio Baton

The Radio Baton system (Boulanger and Mathews 1997) consists of two or more radio-transmitting batons, each of which transmit a distinct frequency, and which are tracked in three dimensions above a flat, sensitive plane (see Figure 11.3).

The Radio Baton uses a coordinate system of radio receivers to determine its position. The array of receivers sends its position values to a control computer, which then sends commands for performing the score to the Conduct program, which runs on an Intel 80C186 processor on an external circuit board. The control computer can either be a Macintosh

Figure 11.3 Max Mathews performing on the Radio Baton. Reprinted with permission from cSounds.com

or a PC, running either "BAT," "RADIO-MAC," or the "Max" programming environment. For measuring force in combination with the beat detection, a velocity algorithm determines the "hardness" of the stroke by measuring the velocity of the stick as it crosses a trigger plane a fixed distance above the surface of the table (Mathews 1989; 1990). Double triggering is avoided by an additional threshold (a short distance above the trigger threshold). Two successive beats have to be separated by lifting the baton or stick just high enough to reset this mechanism. This means a little extra effort for the user, but also reduces a significant source of error within the system.

The Radio Baton and its sibling, the Radio Drum (Boie et al. 1989), have both had works written for and performed on them. Numerous composers and performers have used the Radio Drum over the years, but the Radio Baton has not enjoyed as widespread a success. According to one professional conductor, this is because the Radio Baton's sensing mechanism requires that the baton remain above a small table-like surface to generate every beat; this is not natural in traditional conducting, and is impractical in communicating to assembled musicians.

The MIDI Baton

Developed in 1990 by David Keane, Gino Smecca, and Kevin Wood at Queen's University in Canada, the "MIDI Baton" was a hand-held electronic conducting system (Keane et al. 1990). It consisted of a brass tube that contained a simple handmade accelerometer, connected to a belt pack unit with an AM transmitter and two switches ("stop/continue" and "reset"). The belt-pack transmitted three channels of information (data from the accelerometer and switches) to the AM receiver. A microprocessor decoded the beat and switch information, translated it into a MIDI-like code, and sent that code to command sequencing software on a computer. The system was operated by holding the baton and making beat-like gestures in the air; the beats were used to control the tempo of a MIDI score. The MIDI Baton system offered a somewhat limited degree of freedom to the conductor.

The Conductor–Computer Music Communication System

Researchers at Waseda University in Tokyo asserted that, for performance with human musicians, a computer-based system would have to be intelligent, flexible, adaptive, and inclusive of numerous sensory inputs (Morita et al. 1991). A MIDI-based electronic orchestra was created that responded to the gestures of a human conductor. The system tracked conducting gestures for both right and left hands.

Morita et al. (1991) observed that human performers use two different layers of information when performing a piece: "basic" and "musical performance expression (Mpx)." "Basic" information is conveyed through the static symbols on a musical score, whereas "Mpx" information is subjective and dynamic, conveyed by conductors and remembered by musicians.

An elaborate and comprehensive interactive system based on this framework is detailed in Figure 11.4. Right-handed motions of an infrared light on the baton are tracked by a CCD video camera, while an electronic Data Glove (made by VPL Research) senses the position-coordinates of the fingers' measured left-hand gestures.

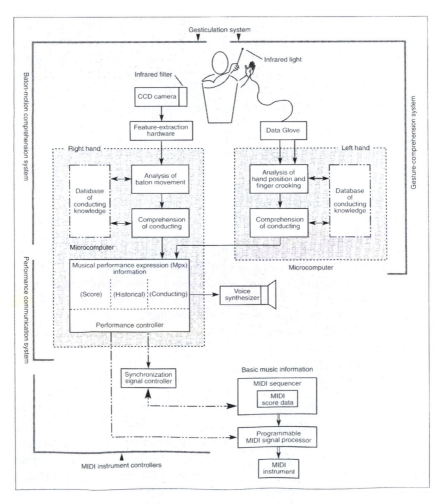

Figure 11.4 Schematic diagram of Morita, Hashimoto and Ohteru's system (Morita et al. 1991, p. 47). Reprinted with permission from IEEE.

The strength of the two-handed conducting system lies in its software for gesture recognition and analysis of musical response. The authors acknowledge that, since conducting is not necessarily clear or standardized among individuals, they therefore made use of a common set of rules that they claimed to be a general grammar of conducting. Using that set of rules as a basis, they generated a set of software processes for recognizing the gestures of conducting—and succeeded in performing Tchaikovsky's first *Piano Concerto* along with a live pianist and conductor.

3D Acceleration Sensing

Sawada et al. (1995) proposed a system for sensing conducting gestures with a three-dimensional accelerometer (an inertial sensor which detects changes in velocity in *x*, *y*, and *z*). The proposed device was intended to measure the force of gesticulation of the hand, rather than positions or trajectories of the feature points using position sensors or image processing techniques (as had been done in Morita et al. 1991). This decision was justified by arguing that the most significant emotional information conveyed by human gestures seems to come from the forces that are created by and applied to the body. The design of a five-part software system is detailed; this system extracts kinetic parameters, analyzes gestures, controls a musical performance in MIDI, makes use of an associative neural network to modify the sounds, and changes timbres in the different musical voices for emotional effect. Some different versions of the system were built and demonstrated: a performance control system, a sound generation system, and a conducting system.

Conducting Gesture Recognition

Paul Kolesnik developed a system that attempts to improve upon standard tempo and amplitude tracking methods (Kolesnik 2004; Kolesnik and Wanderley 2004). Kolesnik's system uses Hidden Markov Models (HMMs) implemented in the MAX/MSP software environment to track conducting gestures, and uses those tools to recognize expressive and indicative gestures of real conductors. The system is able to track both right-hand beat and amplitude indicative gestures, as well as left-hand expressive gestures. Source data for training the HMMs were provided by a doctoral conducting student in the School of Music at McGill University, who wore a coloured glove.

Kolesnik used two USB cameras to track three-dimensional features of the conductor's hand movements. The video streams from the cameras were sent to the EyesWeb software (see Chapter 10) to acquire and process the images using blob colour tracking techniques. The EyesWeb software computed the positional coordinates of the coloured glove and passed those parameters via a network to the gesture analysis software in MAX/MSP.

The gesture analysis software computed the beat amplitude and beat transition points based on the lowest and highest points of the gestures, and passed that information to an audio stretching algorithm (Borchers et al. 2002). In parallel, a video of the McGill Symphony Orchestra was similarly time-stretched using the Jitter environment in MAX/MSP. The resulting system allowed conductors to make realistic conducting gestures and witness the audio and video recordings of a real orchestra react to their movements in real-time.

Watch and Learn

Andrew Wilson and Aaron Bobick built an online adaptive real-time algorithm for learning gesture models (Wilson and Bobick 2000). In this system, Hidden Markov Models (HMMs) were used to represent the spatial and temporal structure in the gestures. However, the time-consuming training stage of HMMs was avoided by having the algorithm adapt in real-time to incoming data by users of the system. This design allowed the system to be used by a wide range of users without constraining what they were allowed to do.

The system, called "Watch and Learn," was set up to allow the general public to stand in a space and move their hands in the air to conduct a symphonic MIDI score. The system used two video cameras and a training algorithm that followed the extremes of an oscillating pattern of movement from a few seconds of video. The extremes were automatically labelled "upbeat" and "downbeat," and allowed the system to lock onto the oscillating frequency. The frequency directly controlled the tempo of the output sequence, with some smoothing to account for a range of errors in the various processing stages.

One great advantage of Wilson's method was that it did not use prior knowledge about hands or even attempt to track them; it just located an oscillating pattern in the frame and locked onto it in real-time. This means that the gestures do not have to be fixed in any particular direction, as is the case with many other gesture recognition systems.

3.2 The Digital Baton *and the* Conductor's Jacket

In 1995 and 1996, a team of researchers at MIT (including Teresa Marrin Nakra and Joseph Paradiso) designed and built a "Digital Baton" sensor interface to conduct a MIDI-based music system in Tod Machover's *Brain Opera* production. The baton was a hand-held gestural interface that was designed to be wielded like a traditional conducting baton by practiced performers. It featured a ten-ounce molded polyurethane handle that held a thin plexiglass tube and infrared LED at the tip. The baton incorporated eleven sensory degrees of freedom: three degrees of position, three orthogonal degrees of acceleration, and five points of pressure. The many sensors were robust and durable, particularly the pulse-modulated infrared position tracking system that worked under a variety of stage lighting conditions. The Digital Baton was used to trigger and shape multiple layers of sound in performances of the *Brain Opera*. By early 1997, however, the research team concluded that the Digital Baton was a problematic interface for performing music, due to its large size, heavy handle, constrained mappings, free-flapping wire, and lack of intuitive mappings for how to convert sensor signals to sounds.

In an attempt to address various problems encountered with the Digital Baton, the "Conductor's Jacket" project began with several investigations into sensors and data acquisition methods, and the first effort evaluated the usefulness of electromyography (EMG) sensors for measuring conducting gestures. Data were collected from several different muscle groups performing a variety of conducting gestures, and some interesting results emerged:

- All the major muscle groups of the upper right arm registered clear peaks for beat gestures. This suggested that electromyography sensors would be able to indicate beat information if placed in correct locations on the right arm.
- The amplitude envelope of each peak seemed to reflect the force profile of the muscle in the execution of the gesture. This indicated that it would be possible to record the strength or emphasis of arm gestures.
- There were noticeable differences between different muscle groups; the biceps tended to give clear spikes at the moment of the beat, whereas the triceps and lateral deltoid (shoulder) muscles provided a smoother rise and decay with secondary modes on either side of the beat. This suggested that a variety of muscles should be measured simultaneously in order to understand the components and details within complicated conducting gestures.

The pilot study indicated that electromyography sensors might yield promising results with conductors. Other similar trials were done with sensors for respiration, heart rate, galvanic skin response, temperature, and position.

System Design

The wearable designs for the Conductor's Jacket ranged in style from white oxford cloth shirts to red spandex; in all, four different versions were designed, and eight jackets were constructed and worn. Each subject in the study was fitted and interviewed to ensure that they would be comfortable with the style and size of the outfit. Regardless of the appearance and fit, however, all of the jackets incorporated three functional aspects: channelled conduits through which the sensor leads could be drawn, looped strain reliefs for keeping the sensors in place, and elastics for holding the sensors immobile on the skin surface. Each design also took into account issues of cleaning the sensors and the cloth. In some cases, the channels were constructed with zippers so that the sensors could be easily taken out, but in other cases the sensors could not be removed and the jackets had to be cleaned using spray-on, evaporating cleaners.

Into each jacket were sewn physiological sensors for measuring muscle tension, breathing, heart rate, skin conductance, and temperature. The simplest version of the jacket had eight sensors and sampling rates of 330 Hz; the most elaborate version incorporated sixteen sensors, two computers, and timed acquisition at 4 kHz per channel. The basic equipment in each jacket included the following sensors:

- 4 electromyography (EMG) sensors with differential measurement and 1000x amplification from Delsys, Inc.
- 1 respiration sensor from Thought Technology, Inc.
- 1 heart rate monitor from Polar, Inc.
- 1 galvanic skin response sensor (GSR) from Thought Technology, Inc.
- 1 temperature sensor from Thought Technology, Inc.

In addition, one of the professional subjects wore an eight-sensor UltraTrack magnetic position-sensing device. Figure 11.5 demonstrates the placement of the different sensors in the Conductor's Jacket; different subjects had slightly different arrangements, but all resembled this image.

Design Criteria

The most important factor in the design of the Conductor's Jacket system was that the device should not constrain, encumber, or cause discomfort to a conductor during rehearsals and performances. Other important considerations included the need for noise reduction, minimal motion artefacts, safety to the wearer, and relatively high data sampling rates. The number and placement of sensors was also critical, particularly in the choice of muscle groups.

The decision was made to gather data in a real musical context, as opposed to a laboratory situation, in order to generate useful and significant results. Because of this choice, the demands of the musical rehearsal

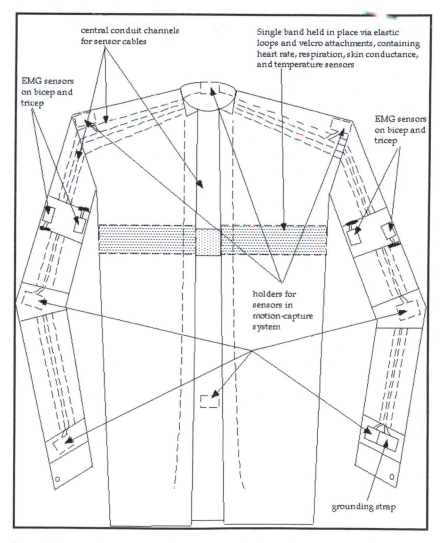

Figure 11.5 Integration of physiological sensors into wearable form of the Conductor's Jacket (Nakra 2000, p. 62). Courtesy of MIT.

or concert had to be respected and the conductor's agenda was more important than the experiment. The researchers could not change or disrupt the general plan for the rehearsal. The outfit would have to be light, easy to put on and take off, simple to plug in, allow for free movement of the upper body, and be robust enough to withstand the lively, energetic movements of an animated subject. To ensure that the conductor could move around freely, the jacket had to be mobile. This latter requirement was achieved in two ways: with the use of a long (30-foot) cable, and with a connector that could be removed quickly. Wireless data transmission was investigated and a four-channel prototype was built, but it was ultimately determined that the wire was more reliable.

Another design criterion was the number and placement of the sensors, so as to capture enough degrees of freedom to detect the quality and complexity of the subjects' motions. For the EMG sensor placement, the following muscle groups were chosen: trapezius (shoulder), biceps (upper arm), extensor (forearm), and opponens pollicis (hand). The triceps muscle was not used, since it opposes the motion of the biceps and therefore yields a signal that is almost equivalent to the biceps signal.

Captured Conducting Gestures

A total of six conductors agreed to participate in the project, including three professionals (P1, P2, P3) and three students (S1, S2, S3). The professional subjects conducted orchestras during their sessions, while the students conducted a single pianist as part of their Advanced Conducting class at the Boston Conservatory. In all cases, physiological data was collected while they were actively rehearsing or performing, along with a videotape of the session. The videotape was used afterwards to help identify important events and record the gestures so as to pick out significant features in the data streams.

One first result was the very clear separation between conductors' use of their right and left arms. Since EMG is a measure of muscle tension and not necessarily movement, the EMG signal elucidates when the arm becomes engaged and actively generates signals. The EMG signals often supported the idea that the left hand is used to provide supplementary information and expression. P1's EMG signals demonstrate very clearly how he uses his left hand for extra emphasis. As an example, subject P1 used his left hand to indicate a drastic reduction in loudness at the very end of a movement. As shown in Figure 11.6, the right hand gave all the beats leading up to the ending, but at the last moment the left hand was raised (as the right hand was withdrawn) to indicate a quick volume change and a quiet ending. Thus, the right hand does not indicate the final beat. This drastic change in the use of the hands seems purposeful; the video shows that the subject looked directly at the wind section during this moment, as if he wanted to indicate a very different character for the final woodwind chords.

One of the most important functions of a conductor is to cue musicians to begin playing, particularly if they have waited silently for a long time. At measure 32 of the Dance movement in Prokofiev's *Romeo and Juliet* suite, many of the woodwind section are to play after many measures of

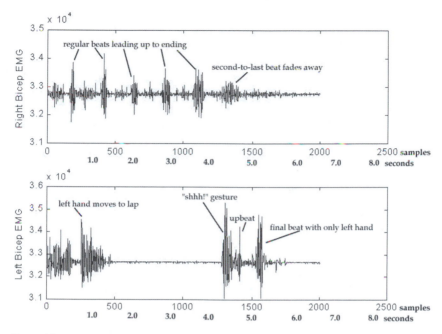

Figure 11.6 Use of the left hand to indicate drastic change in volume (Nakra 2000, p. 78). Courtesy of MIT.

silence. Leading up to this event, P1 used his left hand normally, and then, two measures before the wind entrance, stopped using it completely (a flatlining effect). Then, just in time for the cue, he gave a big pickup and downbeat with the left arm. In repetitions of the same passage, the same action is repeated. This is demonstrated in Figure 11.7, from P1's left bicep's EMG signal.

The "predictive" anticipatory phenomenon, whereby the conductor indicates specific events on the beats directly preceding the intended ones, has not previously been shown by any quantitative methods. Figure 11.8 shows a segment of the score to Prokofiev's dance movement (from *Romeo and Juliet*) with the accents highlighted and aligned with the accents given by subject P1. As indicated, the preparatory accents are given one beat ahead of the intended beat. The dark lines show how the EMG signals line up with the beats in the score, while the light lines show the relationship between the conducted accent and the accent where it is to be played. The first short accent in the soft arrival section around sample 1100 indicates an anticipation of the new, softer dynamic level marked piano.

Rate encoding is the modulation of the frequency of repetitive events in order to imply amplitude changes. It is analogous to frequency

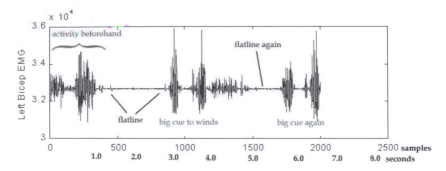

Figure 11.7 The characteristic flatline in the left biceps before a major event (Nakra 2000, p. 80). Courtesy of MIT.

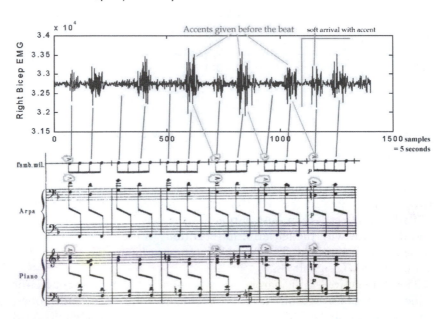

Figure 11.8 "Predictive" accents and their relation to the score (Nakra 2000, p. 86). Courtesy of MIT.

modulation, but instead of reflecting the frequency of a sinusoid, it is the frequency of a specified event. Conductors sometimes use rate encoding (often by subdividing the beat pattern) to specify intensity or dynamic changes. The example in Figure 11.9 corresponds with measures 5–8 after rehearsal cue A in the score to Tchaikovsky's *Symphony no. 6*. Subject P1's EMG0 signal shows the left biceps signal and the EMG2 signal reflects the right biceps. P1 starts the crescendo by increasing the amplitude of EMG tension with his right arm, adds the left arm,

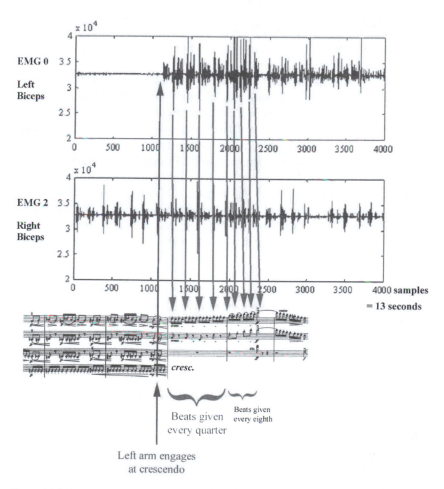

Figure 11.9 Rate Encoding in P1's beat signals compared with the score (Nakra 2000, p. 98). Courtesy of MIT.

and finally doubles the frequency of his beats for the last bar, leading strongly to the fortissimo. By subdividing the beat, he increases the rate of his movements, and thereby indicates a sharp increase in intensity.

This project demonstrates that the moment of a beat, which is not always obvious from the videotape, is immediately obvious from the right bicep's EMG signal. The amount of emphasis in the beat, which is not always proportional to its velocity, is nonetheless clear in the muscle tension signal. The findings of this study suggest that the tensing of a muscle and the resultant effects on force and momentum of an arm are visually perceivable. Thus, orchestra musicians are able to perceive and respond to physiological changes of the conductor. However, these aspects are very difficult to quantify or express in language, because they involve complex changes that happen continuously over very small time intervals. The physiological sensors are able to capture this information and express it as a signal.

Of the six different types of signals that were collected from conductor subjects (EMG, respiration, galvanic skin response (GSR), temperature, heart rate, position), it appeared that the most significant results came from the volitional signals. That is, the signals that are under the purposeful control (and of which the subject is naturally aware) tend to be the ones with the greatest information content. Physiological signals that are not volitional, such as GSR, temperature, and heart rate, did not consistently correlate with the music. The respiration signals have an extremely interesting and complex relationship to the music, but remain challenging to understand. The features in the EMG signals are much more meaningful, and therefore we believe in the near future real-time systems may be able to make the greatest use of EMG sensors.

The Jacket continues to be developed in related ways, as an interface for both research and musical performances. A 2006 research collaboration with the Boston Symphony Orchestra and McGill University (Daniel Levitin and Stephen McAdams) featured updated versions of the Conductor's Jacket; the results of that research are still being processed.

4 Mapping of Gestures to Sound Synthesis

The advent of powerful computers and software now offers many possibilities for using gestures to control sound synthesis, and various systems for this will be the focus in the present section. These systems can be classified as systems for live performances (section 4.1), for home entertainment (section 4.2), for interactive public installations (section 4.3), and for training conductors (section 4.4).

4.1 Systems for Live Performances

Several commercial digital orchestra systems have been developed for live performances. These systems may supplement, or even partially replace, live musicians. We shall here discuss one such system: the *Sinfonia* of Realtime Music Solutions, a New York-based commercial venture of Fred Bianchi and David Smith. Originally entitled the *Virtual Orchestra*, the integrated system simulates a live orchestra using a custom application together with outboard sample playback devices. During the past ten years, the *Sinfonia* system has been quite successful, and Bianchi and Smith now count among their clients Music Theatre International (which rents music to independent productions), Cirque du Soleil, several national Broadway tours, and London West End productions produced by Cameron Macintosh.

The *Sinfonia* system makes use of a musician-operator, who sits at a complex computer–musical instrument in the pit that reacts to the gestures of the conductor to guide, flexibly, the tempo and other parameters of the performance in mimicry of the playing of a traditional musician (Smith et al. 2000). The system makes use of multiple instrument layers as well as multiple audio channels, and therefore has enough flexibility to adapt to the many unexpected events that can occur with a live stage production.

Not surprisingly, Realtime Music Solutions has also generated considerable controversy. After the 1995 production of *Hansel and Gretel* at the Kentucky Opera House, music critic Charles Parsons of *Opera News* had this to say about it: "The continuing development of this technology has ominous implications for opera and all music. The digitization process (Bianchi & Smith) is another case of the dehumanization of society and the deterioration of education." (Parsons 1996)

In 2003, the New York Musicians' Union held a strike that shut down Broadway for four days to protest the planned use of the *Sinfonia* in theatre productions. The New York Musicians' Union has continued to fight aggressively against the use of virtual orchestra technology in theatre productions and has enlisted support from unions all over the United States. According to Bianchi, the way *Sinfonia* has developed has been entirely directed by the needs of the music industry. Serious composers and academics have sometimes disparaged this method, but Bianchi feels strongly that the result of his method yields better and more practical results. The *Sinfonia* has been optimized over many years to solve real-world problems; it does not fit the typical computer music model of an idiosyncratic system built for one composer or one piece. Rather, it is a general-purpose system that can be used by many different producers of many different types of music.

4.2 Systems for Home Entertainment

Several conducting systems have been developed with the aim of providing an interactive experience for would-be conductors to try in the comfort of their own homes. The motivating idea for these developers is to create a product that people will use informally and find satisfying either as a solitary experience or together with friends and family. While a large demand for these products has not yet been demonstrated, some researchers feel nonetheless that this is a promising area for potential commercial applications.

Satoshi Usa worked on a system for automatic conductor recognition at Yamaha and Kogakuin University for approximately three years,

1996–1999. His system had two components: (1) advanced feature recognition techniques that detected nuances (i.e. staccato vs. tenuto) of real orchestra conductors' movements, and (2) multi-modal interactive feedback with accelerometers, eye-tracking and breath sensors.

Usa's hardware consisted of a small hand-held device containing two electrostatic accelerometers (detecting vertical and horizontal accelerations of the right hand), and a virtual reality helmet with eye tracking and breath sensors. Usa and Mochida (1998) described the system in five stages:

1. The data were sampled at a minimum rate of 100 Hz, band-pass filtered using a 12th-order moving average, and the DC component removed.
2. A Hidden Markov Model (HMM) was used to recognize beats: a five-state HMM with thirty-two labels describing different possible gestures. The system was trained with 100 samples using the Baum-Welch algorithm.
3. A Fuzzy Logic system decided if incoming beats were correct as recognized: if a beat arrived too soon after the previous beat, then it was discarded. This removed problematic double-triggers.
4. A Score Follower determined where the system was in relation to the score and with respect to the meter on beats 1, 2, 3, or 4.
5. A final stage synthesized the previous stages together and played a MIDI-based orchestral score with appropriate tempo and dynamics.

Other features of the system included a preparatory beat at the beginning of every piece, a variable output delay based on the tempo, different following modes (loosely or tightly coupled to the beats), proportional dynamics (loudness of notes determined by the absolute magnitude of the acceleration), and appropriate differentiations between staccato and legato gestures.

The assumptions about conducting techniques came from the rule-based system proposed by Max Rudolf in *The Grammar of Conducting* (Rudolf 1995b). Usa's results were extremely strong; his beat recognition rates were 98.95–99.74 percent accurate. Much of the success can be attributed to the multi-staged HMM process that allowed each successive stage to error-correct on its predecessors. Usa also incorporated pulse, eye tracking (gaze point, blinking), GSR, and respiration sensing into extensions of this system.

A few years afterwards, Usa added a MIDI control program to produce the nuances in real time; recently, Yamaha built a tapping ensemble system for music classrooms using aspects of Usa's system. As of 2006, this adapted system is in use at Yamaha's R&D studio in Tokyo, undergoing marketing tests.

In reflecting on his work (personal communication via email and questionnaire), Usa wrote that his HMM system contributed improved performance of the recognition tasks. In retrospect, he commented that the multi-modal eye and breath sensors never left the experimental stage. Looking forward, he recommended that if conducting systems are to be developed into consumer products, they will need: improved performance of gesture recognition algorithms, a wide range of musical expression features for individuals, improved sound quality, and batons that are wireless, small, lightweight, and robust, and have long battery life. Usa also wrote that while consumer products that feature conducting do exist (such as video games and PC applications), they are not sensitive enough to respond accurately to users' gestures with a compelling range of musical expression and feeling. He argued that these systems "aren't musical instruments but toys". He speculated that the launch of the Nintendo *Wii* system might stimulate a profitable market for conducting systems, and encourage larger companies to consider developing new products in this area.

4.3 Systems for Interactive Public Installations

Personal Orchestra, You're the Conductor, and iSymphony

Jan Borchers has been working on interactive conducting exhibits for the public. His first exhibit, WorldBeat, debuted at the Ars Electronica Center in Linz, Austria in 1996; it featured a custom MIDI application written in MAX with two Buchla Lightning infrared batons and several different interactive musical activities. He and his research group have since developed several successful conducting exhibits at public venues and published several influential papers (Borchers et al. 2004; Lee and Borchers 2005; Lee et al. 2005; 2006a).

Borchers's "Personal Orchestra" exhibit opened in 2000 at the Haus der Musik in Vienna (Borchers et al. 2002). It featured video footage of the Vienna Philharmonic that was pre-time-stretched to various tempos and cross-faded to reflect the speed of the user's beat. This was somewhat flexible and sensitive to the conducting gestures of the user; the gestures were measured by means of one Buchla lightning baton. A prominent feature of this exhibit was the fact that the orchestra would stand up and insult the user if he or she conducted too quickly or irregularly. If instead the user conducted "well," the orchestra would applaud.

In 2003, Teresa Marrin Nakra and Immersion Music collaborated with Borchers to develop the "You're the Conductor" system at the Boston Children's Museum (Lee et al. 2004). This exhibit featured video footage of the Boston Pops Orchestra performing John Philip Sousa's *Stars and*

Stripes Forever. As users approach the exhibit, they see a looping video of the Boston Pops Orchestra tuning up. They then step up to the custom music stand and pick up a wired conducting baton. When they raise the baton, the musicians raise their instruments. When they move the baton, the orchestra begins to play. As they move the baton, they are in direct control of the tempo of the music. If they stop, the music stops. If they resume moving, the music will pick up where it left off. If the user abandons the exhibit, the system waits for thirty seconds before reverting the tuning loop.

The Boston Pops Orchestra recorded the *Stars and Stripes Forever* at a fixed tempo and dynamic level. The dynamic time-stretching algorithm, written by Eric Lee, used a modified phase vocoding technique to slow down and speed up the audio in real-time without noticeable noise artefacts. Nakra and Immersion Music contributed a custom infrared baton system and gesture-tracking software; the gesture processing software, running on a separate computer, analyzes the speed and relative size of the gestures and determines the tempo and loudness of the output. After a successful year in Boston, the "You're the Conductor" system toured children's museums around the United States for two years. Subsequently, in 2007, it returned to the Boston Children's Museum as a semi-permanent exhibit in their new building.

In 2005, Borchers and his research group at RWTH in Aachen developed the "iSymphony" system and installed it in the Betty Brinn Museum in Milwaukee, Wisconsin (Lee et al. 2006b). This project leveraged student research to improve upon the earlier exhibits and design a more robust and adaptive system. The iSymphony features adaptive gesture recognition of three different gesture types: four-beat neutral-legato, up-down, and random. The system determines which gesture style the user is using and then follows the indicated tempo. A recording of a Milwaukee student orchestra was used, and one Buchla Lightning device was strengthened and modified to ensure that it would not be damaged by the public.

The DIVA System

Tapio Takala and several contributors and students have built a system called DIVA (Digital Interactive Virtual Acoustics),[2] with the goal of creating an interactive virtual orchestra experience in which a participant can conduct a band of animated musicians with a baton, and hear their sound as it reverberates in a virtual hall (Hiipakka et al. 1997; Savioja 1999; Savioja et al. 1999; Huopaniemi 1999; Ilmonen and Takala 1999; Lokki et al. 1998; 2002; Ilmonen 2006). The screen graphics of the DIVA system are demonstrated in Figure 11.10.

The system can play any MIDI-encoded score, with tight synchroniza-

Figure 11.10 Four virtual musicians in the DIVA system (snapshot of the SIGGRAPH '97 demonstration; from DIVA 2003). Reprinted with permission from Helsinki University of Technology.

tion of sound and motion. The researchers are interested in accurate detection of conducting gestures, not only *on* the beats but also *between* them. For example, a tenuto or fermata can be generated by slowing the movement of the baton. The system relies primarily on baton movements, with a few additional gestures with the left hand, and no other input than the hands. The artificial musicians use correct grips on their instruments, and the acoustics are simulated with a variety of options.

Based on discussions with professional conductors, the researchers determined that the baton should be the main source of information, thus less attention was given to the left hand or other bodily gestures. They also determined that systems that invite interaction from the general public require simplified controls.

The hardware setup for DIVA consists of a magnetic motion tracker on a baton, accelerometers, computers, a visual display, and a sound system (Ilmonen and Jalkanen 2000). The software platform is a virtual environment with four available musicians playing flute, guitar, bass, and drums (see Figure 11.10). The user can select different 3D acoustic spaces, such as a small studio, concert hall, or metro station. The instruments are appropriately synthesized, and then the different reverberant models are applied to make the sounds seem more realistic and appropriate to the 3D virtual space. Figure 11.11 demonstrates the system architcture.

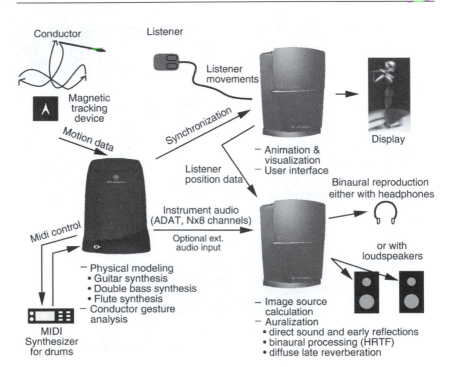

Figure 11.11 Architecture of the DIVA system (Savioja 1999; Savioja et al. 1999). Reprinted with permission from Helsinki University of Technology.

DIVA makes use of an artificial neural network (ANN) to convert the baton motion (read in as a sequence of 2D baton positions) to musical timing information (Ilmonen and Takala 1999). It outputs signals that indicate the relative timing between musical beats or within a given duration (such as a bar). Some anticipation (on the order of 200 milliseconds) is required to overcome the processing delays, and in order to signal to the virtual musicians to prepare to play. The artificial neural network (ANN) has been trained by motion data that was collected from professional conductors conducting beat patterns along to a metronome. The musical output is generated in MIDI notes that are played with flexible timing that has been determined based upon the outputs of the ANN. Additional filters are also used to avoid problematic playback (such as abrupt tempo changes) due to noisy sensor data.

In addition to tracking baton movements, DIVA has also implemented left hand controls, such as the dynamics indication of up = louder and down = softer. The animated musicians react to these indications with appropriate movements.

4.4 Systems for Training Conductors

The Arizona State University (ASU) initiated a project called the Digital Conducting Laboratory (DCL), where students of conducting and conducting pedagogy were able to enhance their skills with the assistance of new technology. Utilizing a Digital Conducting Feedback System designed by Teresa Marrin Nakra and Immersion Music, the laboratory simulated the basic ensemble/conductor interactions with an interactive program that reacted to students' tempo, articulation, and dynamics (loudness) cues. In addition to immediate, aural feedback, the system allowed conductors to review their performances via sound files, video playback, and analysis of muscle-tension profile.

The system featured a set of etudes that progressed the student through a review of basic conducting gestures. Compiled and arranged by the laboratory's founder and director, ASU Professor Gary W. Hill, the etudes were principally derived from familiar orchestral music, freeing the user to focus primarily on his or her gestures and the auditory result.

Several formal studies utilizing the Digital Conducting Feedback System of the DCL have taken place (Kraus et al. 2004; Kun 2004). Analysis of results revealed that the Digital Conducting Feedback System treatment was significantly more effective than simple practice in improving fundamental conducting gestures that initiate sound, illustrate sustained sound, demonstrate certain articulations, and stop sound.

5 Conclusions and Future Perspectives

The main sections of this chapter have provided a basic, up-to-date overview of the nature of conducting, of the analysis and acquisition of conducting gestures, and of the mapping of these gestures to sound synthesis. It has been shown that various new technological means for gesture acquisition and for gesture-sound mapping lead to valuable additional insights into the highly developed art of conducting. In addition, these technological advances have already demonstrated a strong potential for new interactive computer music applications and sound installations.

In his book *The Computer Music Tutorial*, Curtis Roads writes in the chapter on musical input devices: "The original remote controller for music is the conductor's baton" (Roads 1996). This straightforward definition implies that conducting gestures are control inputs, cognitively located between the processes of gesture creation and gesture perception. In many ways, this relates to all the tools and systems for gesture acquisition and gesture-sound mapping that were discussed in sections 3 and 4 of this chapter. However, state-of-the-art in research and technology is still far away from capturing the whole nature of conducting, as outlined in section 2.

Both the process of gesture creation on the conductor's side, and the process of gesture perception on the side of the musicians (or of the automated musical instruments and sound synthesizers), include a larger number of cognitive and expressive aspects. In order for a synthetic conducting system to be effective, it will be necessary to model not only the activity (the gestural outcome), but also the neurocognitive thought processes. Also, professional conductors perform a much richer repertoire of gestures (see Rudolf 1995b), than the basic gestures that have been considered so far in research and in today's technological tools and systems. More degrees of freedom of the conducting hand for more sophisticated realistic conducting patterns have to be captured in the future.

Finally, the communication mechanism between a conductor and a group of musicians goes beyond the main transfer process of gestural communication. Other aspects of conductors' communication that require more research include eye contact, facial expression, and speech (only in rehearsals, but always concise and specific), as well as numerous aspects of behavioural psychology and social interaction.

Eye contact and facial expression are the most important of these additional communication aspects. Max Rudolf (1995b) discusses this in *The Grammar of Conducting* in respect to cueing: "Most of the time, the best way of cueing in your players is to look at them. Turn your eyes toward the players one count in advance in moderate tempo, and about two counts in fast tempo. Using your eyes is best for two reasons: First, you should not use more motion than you need in conducting; second, the expression of your eyes and your general facial expression can tell the players more about your intentions than fancy hand waving." Taking a holistic approach and including eye movements, facial expressions, posture, and whole-body movements as well, we have very many challenges ahead in our endeavours to better understand the complex and many-faceted art of musical conducting.

Notes

1 Chironomy is an ancient art of using hand signals to direct vocal music performances. It was applied in early Egyptian performances, was widespread in the ancient world (including Greek, Gregorian, and Jewish chant), and continued into medieval times. The hand gestures represent musical values and indicate melodic lines and ornaments.
2 www.tml.tkk.fi/Research/DIVA/ (accessed October 2008).

References

Berlioz, H. (1844). *Grand Traité d'Instrumentation et d'Orchestration Modernes*. Paris: Schonenberger.

Berlioz, H. (1855). Le chef d'orchestre: théorie de son art. In *Grand Traité d'Instrumentation et d'Orchestration Modernes* (English translation: Treatise on Instrumentation and Orchestration. London: Novello and Co, 1856).

Berlioz, H. and Macdonald, H. (eds.) (2002). *Berlioz's Orchestration Treatise: A Translation and Commentary*. Cambridge: Cambridge University Press.

Berlioz, H. and Strauss, R. (1986). *Instrumentationslehre* (in German, reprinted from 1905). Frankfurt am Main, Leipzig: Edition Peters. (English version: *Treatise on Instrumentation*. New York: Dover Publications, 1991.)

Boie, R., Mathews, M.V., and Schloss, A. (1989). The radio drum as a synthesizer controller. In *Proceedings of the 1989 International Computer Music Conference (ICMC'89)*, Columbus, Ohio, 42–45.

Borchers, J., Lee, E., Samminger, W., and Mühlhäuser, M. (2004). Personal orchestra: a real-time audio/video system for interactive conducting. *Multimedia Systems*, 9(5), 458–465.

Borchers, J., Samminger, W., and Mühlhäuser, M. (2002). Engineering a realistic real-time conducting system for the audio/video rendering of a real orchestra. In *Proceedings of the 4th IEEE International Symposium Multimedia Software Engineering (MSE '02)*. Newport Beach, CA, 352–362.

Boulanger, R. and Mathews, M.V. (1997). The 1997 Mathews' radio baton and improvisation modes. In *Proceedings of the 1997 International Computer Music Conference (ICMC'97)*. Thessaloniki, 395–398.

Boult, A. (1968). *A Handbook on the Technique of Conducting*. London: Paterson's Publications (first published 1920).

Bowen, J.A. (2003). The rise of conducting. In J.A. Bowen (ed.), *The Cambridge Companion to Conducting*. Cambridge: Cambridge University Press, 93–113.

Cole, R. and Schwartz, E. (2008). *Virginia Tech Multimedia Music Dictionary*. Virginia Polytechnic Institute and State University, Department of Music and New Media Center. www.music.vt.edu/musicdictionary/ (accessed October 2008).

Ford, A. (2003). Simone Young discusses the business of conducting. *The Music Show*. Sydney: ABC Radio National (15.11.2003). www.abc.net.au/rn/musicshow/stories/2003/1012022.htm (accessed October 2008).

Gershenfeld, N. and Paradiso, J.A. (1997). Musical applications of electric field sensing. *Computer Music Journal*, 21(2), 69–89.

Green, E.A.H. and Gibson, M. (2004). *The Modern Conductor* (7th edition). Upper Saddle River, NJ: Pearson Prentice Hall.

Grüll, I. (2005). *conga: A Conducting Gesture Analysis Framework*. Diploma thesis, University of Ulm.

Hiipakka, J., Hänninen, R., Ilmonen, T., Napari, H., Lokki, T., Savioja, L., Huopaniemi, J., Karjalainen, M., Tolonen, T., Välimäki, V., Välimäki, S., and Takala, T. (1997). Virtual orchestra performance. In *Visual Proceedings of SIGGRAPH '97*. Los Angeles, CA:ACM, SIGGRAPH, 81.

Huopaniemi, J. (1999). *Virtual Acoustics and 3-D Sound in Multimedia Signal Processing*. PhD thesis, Helsinki University of Technology, Espoo, Finland.

Ilmonen, T. (2006). *Tools and Experiments in Multimodal Interaction*. PhD thesis, Helsinki University of Technology, Espoo, Finland.

Ilmonen T. and Jalkanen, J. (2000). Accelerometer-based motion tracking for orchestra conductor following. In *Proceedings of the Eurographics Workshop on Virtual Environments*. Amsterdam.

Ilmonen, T. and Takala, T. (1999). Conductor following with artificial neural networks. In *Proceedings of the International Computer Music Conference (ICMC'99)*. Beijing, 367–370.

Johannsen, G. (2002). Human supervision and control in engineering and music – Foundations and transdisciplinary views. *Journal of New Music Research*, 31(3), 179–190.

Juslin, P.N. and Sloboda, J.A. (eds.) (2001). *Music and Emotion. Theory and Research*. Oxford: Oxford University Press.

Keane, D., Smecca, G., and Wood, K. (1990). The MIDI Baton II. In *Proceedings of the 1990 International Computer Music Conference (ICMC'90)*. Glasgow, UK, 151–154.

Kolesnik, P. (2004). *Conducting Gesture Recognition, Analysis and Performance System*. M.S. thesis, Montreal: McGill University.

Kolesnik, P. and Wanderley, M. M. (2004). Recognition, analysis and perform-ance with expressive conducting gestures. In *Proceedings of the 2004 International Computer Music Conference (ICMC'04)*, Miami, Florida.

Kraus, B.N., Gonzalez, G.M., Hill, G.W., and Humphreys, J.T. (2004). Inter-active computer feedback on the development of fundamental conducting skills. *Journal of Band Research*, 39 (Spring), 35–44.

Kun, J.V. (2004). *A Real-Time Responsive/Interactive System for Musical Conducting Using Motion Capture Technology*. PhD thesis, Arizona State University.

Lee, E. and Borchers, J. (2005). The role of time in engineering computer music systems. In *Proceedings of the International Conference New Interfaces for Musical Expression (NIME '05)*. Vancouver, 204–207.

Lee, E., Karrer, T., and Borchers, J. (2006a). Toward a framework for interactive systems to conduct digital audio and video streams. *Computer Music Journal*, 30 (1), 21–36.

Lee, E., Kiel, H., Dedenbach, S., Grüll, I., Karrer, T., Wolf, M., and Borchers, J. (2006b). iSymphony: an adaptive interactive orchestral conducting system for digital audio and video streams. In *Extended Abstracts on Human Factors in Computing Systems (CHI '06)*. Montreal: ACM, 259–262.

Lee, E., Nakra, T. Marrin, and Borchers, J. (2004). You're the conductor: a real-istic interactive conducting system for children. In *Proceedings of the International Conference New Interfaces for Musical Expression (NIME '04)*. Hamamatsu, 68–73.

Lee, E., Wolf, M., and Borchers, J. (2005). Improving orchestral conducting sys-tems in public spaces: examining the temporal characteristics and conceptual models of conducting gestures. In *Proceedings of the SIGCHI Conference Human Factors in Computing Systems*. Portland, Oregon: ACM, 731–740.

Lokki, T., Hiipakka, J., Hänninen, R., Ilmonen, T., Savioja, L., and Takala, T. (1998). Real-time audiovisual rendering and contemporary audiovisual art. *Organised Sound*, 3(3), 219–233.

Lokki, T., Savioja, L., Väänänen, R., Huopaniemi, J., and Takala, T. (2002). Creating interactive virtual auditory environments. *IEEE Computer Graphics and Applications*, 22(4), 49–57.

Mathews, M.V. (1989). The conductor program and mechanical baton. In M.V. Mathews and J.R. Pierce (eds.), *Current Directions in Computer Music Research*. Cambridge, MA: MIT Press, 263–281.

Mathews, M.V. (1990). *Three Dimensional Baton and Gesture Sensor*. U.S. Patent No. 4,980,519.

Morita, H., Hashimoto, S., and Ohteru, S. (1991). A computer music system that follows a human conductor. *IEEE Computer Magazine*, 24(7), 44–53.

Nakra, T. Marrin (2000). *Inside the Conductor's Jacket: Analysis, Interpretation and Musical Synthesis of Expressive Gesture*. PhD thesis, Department of Media Arts and Sciences, Cambridge, MA: MIT. immersionmusic.org/ HTMLThesis/Dissertation.htm (accessed October 2008).

Nakra, T. Marrin (2001). Translating conductor's gestures to sound. In G. Johannsen, O. Werner and P. Zerweck (eds.), *Human Supervision and Control in Engineering and Music*. Kassel: Systems Engineering and Human-Machine Systems, University of Kassel, 139–144. www.engineeringandmusic.de/ individu/ nakrmarr/Nakra-Paper.html (accessed October 2008).

Nakra, T. Marrin (2002). Synthesizing expressive music through the language of conducting. *Journal of New Music Research*, 31(1), 11–26.

Paradiso, J. A. (1997). Electronic music – New ways to play. *IEEE Spectrum*, 34(12), 18–30.

Parsons, C.H. (1996). The money pit: how did Kentucky Opera solve its rising-cost dilemma? By substituting a synthesized orchestra for real musicians. *Opera News*, 60(12). New York, NY: The Metropolitan Opera (The Met Opera Guild). www.metoperafamily.org/operanews/_archive/3296/ KentuckyOp.3296.html (accessed May 2009). See also Opera News Online of The Metropolitan Opera: www.metoperafamily.org/operanews/

Roads, C. (1996). *The Computer Music Tutorial*. Cambridge, MA: MIT Press.

Rudolf, M. (1995a). Max Rudolf Dies. *Newsletter of the Conductor' Guild*, 1–7.

Rudolf, M. (1995b). *The Grammar of Conducting: A Comprehensive Guide to Baton Technique and Interpretation*. Belmont, CA: Schirmer-Wadsworth, a part of Cengage Learning, Inc. (first published 1950).

Savioja, L. (1999). *Modeling Techniques for Virtual Acoustics*. PhD thesis, Helsinki University of Technology, Espoo, Finland.

Savioja, L., Huopaniemi, J., Lokki, T., and Väänänen, R. (1999). Creating interactive virtual acoustic environments. *Journal of the Audio Engineering Society*, 47(9), 675–705.

Sawada, H., Ohkura, S., and Hashimoto, S. (1995). Gesture analysis using 3D acceleration sensor for music control. In *Proceedings of the International Computer Music Conference (ICMC'95)*, 257–260.

Scherchen, H. (1990). *Handbook of Conducting*. Oxford: Oxford University Press. (English translation: Lehrbuch des Dirigierens, in German, 1972, Mainz: Schott, first published 1929.)

Sheridan, T.B. and Johannsen, G. (eds.) (1976). *Monitoring Behavior and Supervisory Control*. New York: Plenum Press.

Smith, D.B., Umezaki, K., Bianchi, F.W., and Campbell, R.H. (2000). New control technologies for virtual orchestra playback (abstract). *The Journal of the Acoustical Society of America*, 108(5), 2537.

Usa, S. and Mochida, Y. (1998). A conducting recognition system on the model of musicians process. *Journal of Acoustical Society of Japan*, 19(4), 275–287.

Wanderley, M. M. and Depalle, P. (2004). Gestural control of sound synthesis. *Proceedings of the IEEE*, 92(4), 632–644.

Wilson, A. D. and Bobick, A. F. (2000). Realtime online adaptive gesture recognition. In *Proceedings of the International Conference Pattern Recognition (ICPR '00)*. Barcelona, 270–275.

Contributors

Rolf Bader, Institute of Musicology, University of Hamburg, Neue Rabenstr. 13, D-20354 Hamburg, Germany

Frédéric Bevilacqua, IRCAM, 1, Place Igor Stravinsky, 75004 Paris, France

Roberto Bresin, TMH - Department of Speech, Music and Hearing, KTH - Royal Institute of Technology, Drottning Kristinas v. 31, SE - 100 44 Stockholm, Sweden

Antonio Camurri, DIST - Università di Genova, Viale Causa, 13, 16145, Genova, Italy

Martin Clayton, The Music Department, The Open University, Walton Hall, Milton Keynes MK7 6AA, United Kingdom

Sofia Dahl, Aalborg University Copenhagen, Department of Media Technology, Section for Medialogy, Lautrupvang 15, DK-2750 Ballerup, Denmark

Sylvie Gibet, VALORIA, Université de Bretagne-Sud - Campus de Tohannic, 56000 Vannes, France

Rolf Inge Godøy, Department of Musicology, University of Oslo, P.B. 1017 Blindern, N - 0315 Oslo, Norway

Knut Guettler, Norwegian Academy of Music, P.O. Box 5190 Majorstua, N-0302 Oslo, Norway

Tor Halmrast, Department of Musicology, University of Oslo, P.B. 1017 Blindern, N - 0315 Oslo, Norway

Alexander Refusm Jensenius, Department of Musicology, University of Oslo, P.B. 1017 Blindern, N - 0315 Oslo, Norway

Gunnar Johannsen, University of Kassel, Moenchebergstrasse n. 19, D - 34109 Kassel, Germany

Laura Leante, The Music Department, The Open University, Walton Hall, Milton Keynes MK7 6AA, United Kingdom

Marc Leman, IPEM, Department of Musicology, Ghent University, Blandijnberg 2, B - 9000 Ghent, Belgium

Thomas Moeslund, Laboratory of Computer Vision and Media Technology, Aalborg University, Niels Jernes Vej 14 (3–109), DK-9220 Aalborg East, Denmark

Teresa Marrin Nakra, Department of Music, The College of New Jersey, P.O. Box 7718, Ewing, NJ 08628, USA

Isabella Poggi, Dipartimento di Linguistica, Università di Roma Tre, Via Castro Pretorio 20, 00185 Rome, Italy

Nicolas Rasamimanana, IRCAM, 1, Place Igor Stravinsky, 75004 Paris, France

Albrecht Schneider, Institute of Musicology, University of Hamburg, Neue Rabenstr. 13, D-20354 Hamburg, Germany

Leon van Noorden, IPEM, Department of Musicology, Ghent University, Blandijnberg 2, B - 9000 Ghent, Belgium

Marcelo Wanderley, Faculty of Music, McGill University, Strathcona Music Building, Room E203, 555 Sherbrooke Street West, Montreal, Quebec H3A 1E3, Canada

Index